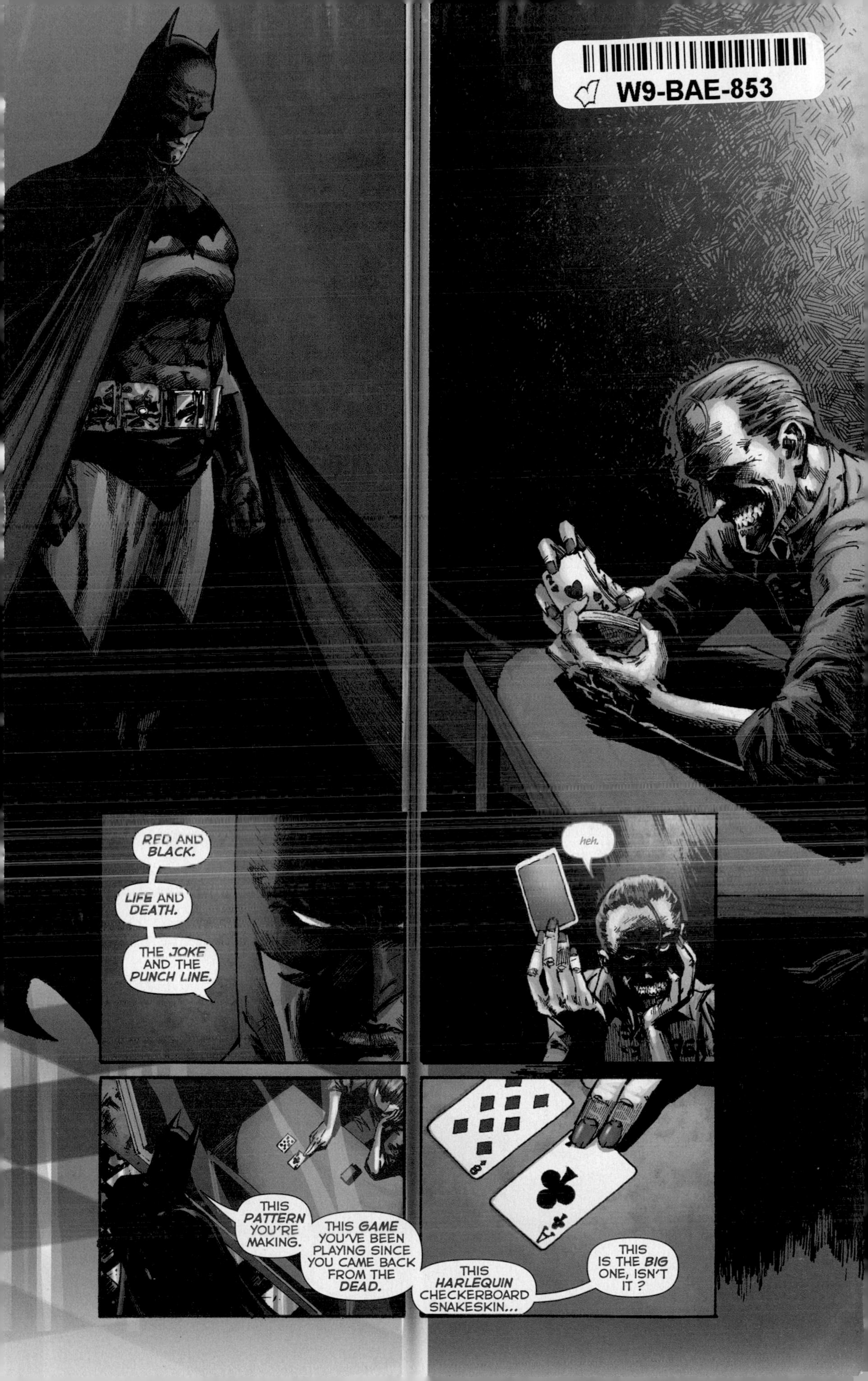

RED AND BLACK.
LIFE AND DEATH.
THE JOKE AND THE PUNCH LINE.
heh.
THIS PATTERN YOU'RE MAKING.
THIS GAME YOU'VE BEEN PLAYING SINCE YOU CAME BACK FROM THE DEAD.
THIS HARLEQUIN CHECKERBOARD SNAKESKIN...
THIS IS THE BIG ONE, ISN'T IT?

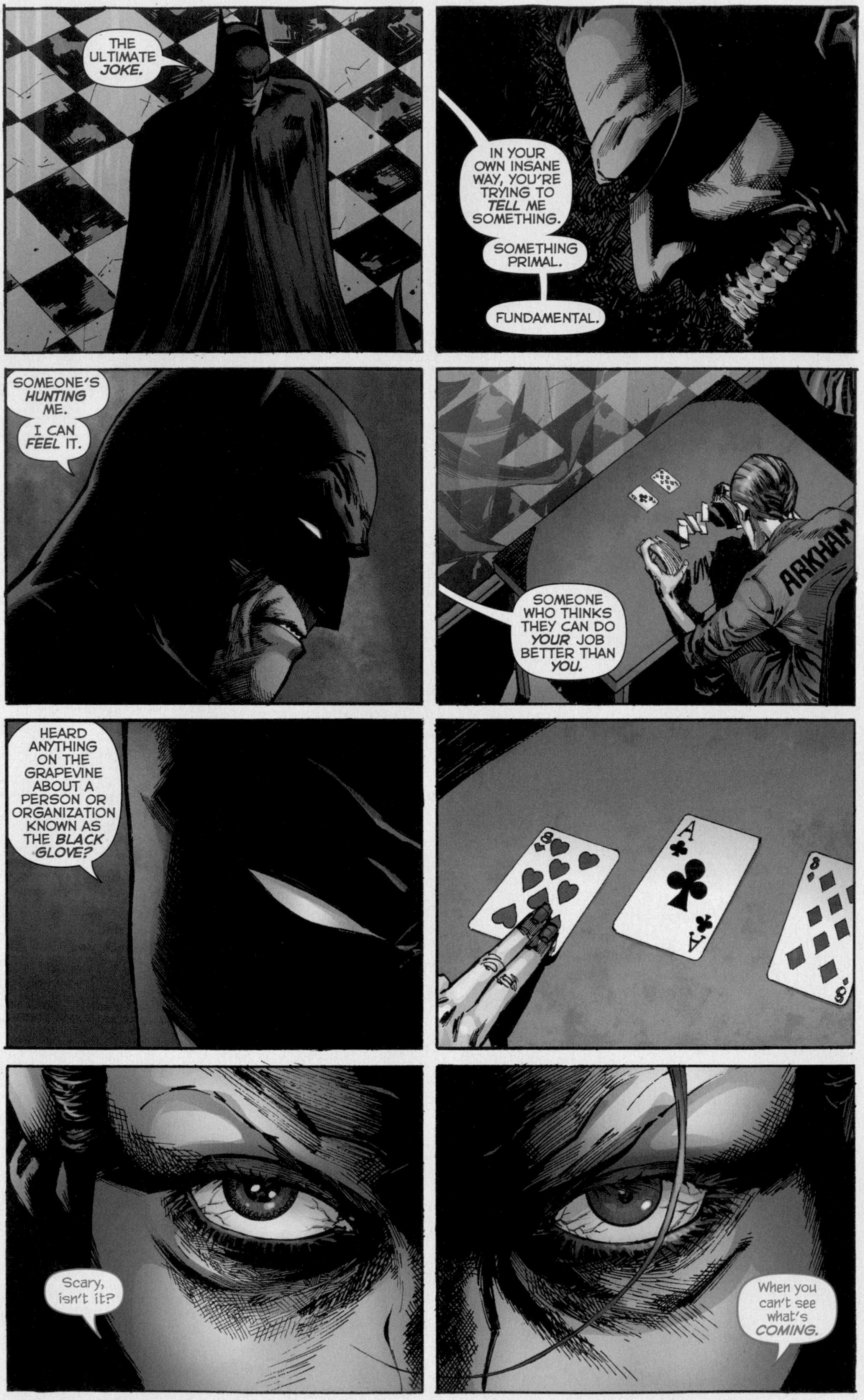

THE ULTIMATE JOKE.
IN YOUR OWN INSANE WAY, YOU'RE TRYING TO TELL ME SOMETHING.
SOMETHING PRIMAL.
FUNDAMENTAL.
SOMEONE'S HUNTING ME.
I CAN FEEL IT.
SOMEONE WHO THINKS THEY CAN DO YOUR JOB BETTER THAN YOU.
ARKHAM
HEARD ANYTHING ON THE GRAPEVINE ABOUT A PERSON OR ORGANIZATION KNOWN AS THE BLACK GLOVE?
Scary, isn't it?
When you can't see what's COMING.

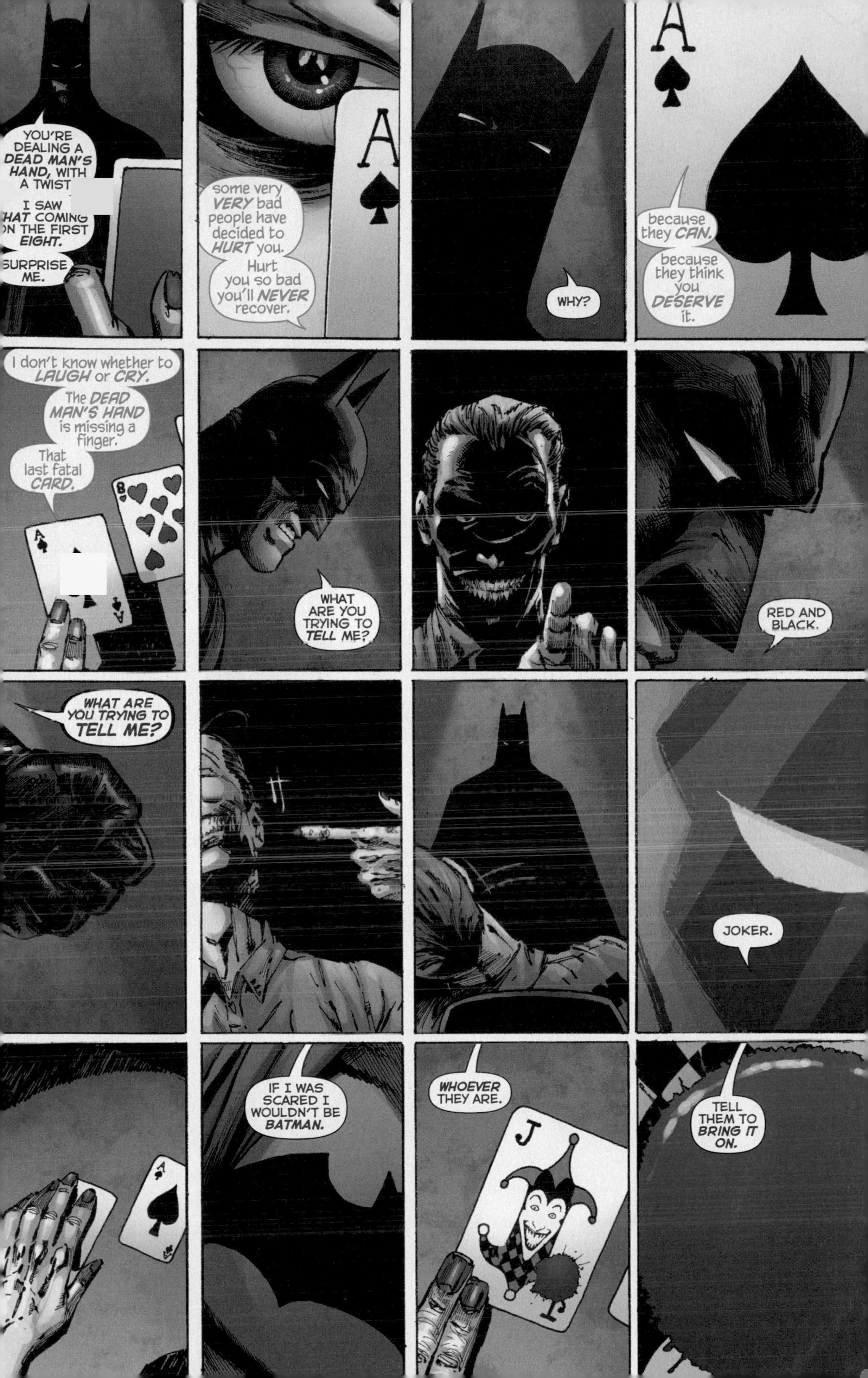

YOU'RE DEALING A DEAD MAN'S HAND, WITH A TWIST
I SAW
HAT COMING
N THE FIRST EIGHT.
SURPRISE ME.
some very VERY bad people have decided to HURT you.
Hurt you so bad you'll NEVER recover.
WHY?
because they CAN.
because they think you DESERVE it.
I don't know whether to LAUGH or CRY.
The DEAD MAN'S HAND is missing a finger.
That last fatal CARD.
WHAT ARE YOU TRYING TO TELL ME?
RED AND BLACK.
WHAT ARE YOU TRYING TO TELL ME?
JOKER.
IF I WAS SCARED I WOULDN'T BE BATMAN.
WHOEVER THEY ARE.
TELL THEM TO BRING IT ON.

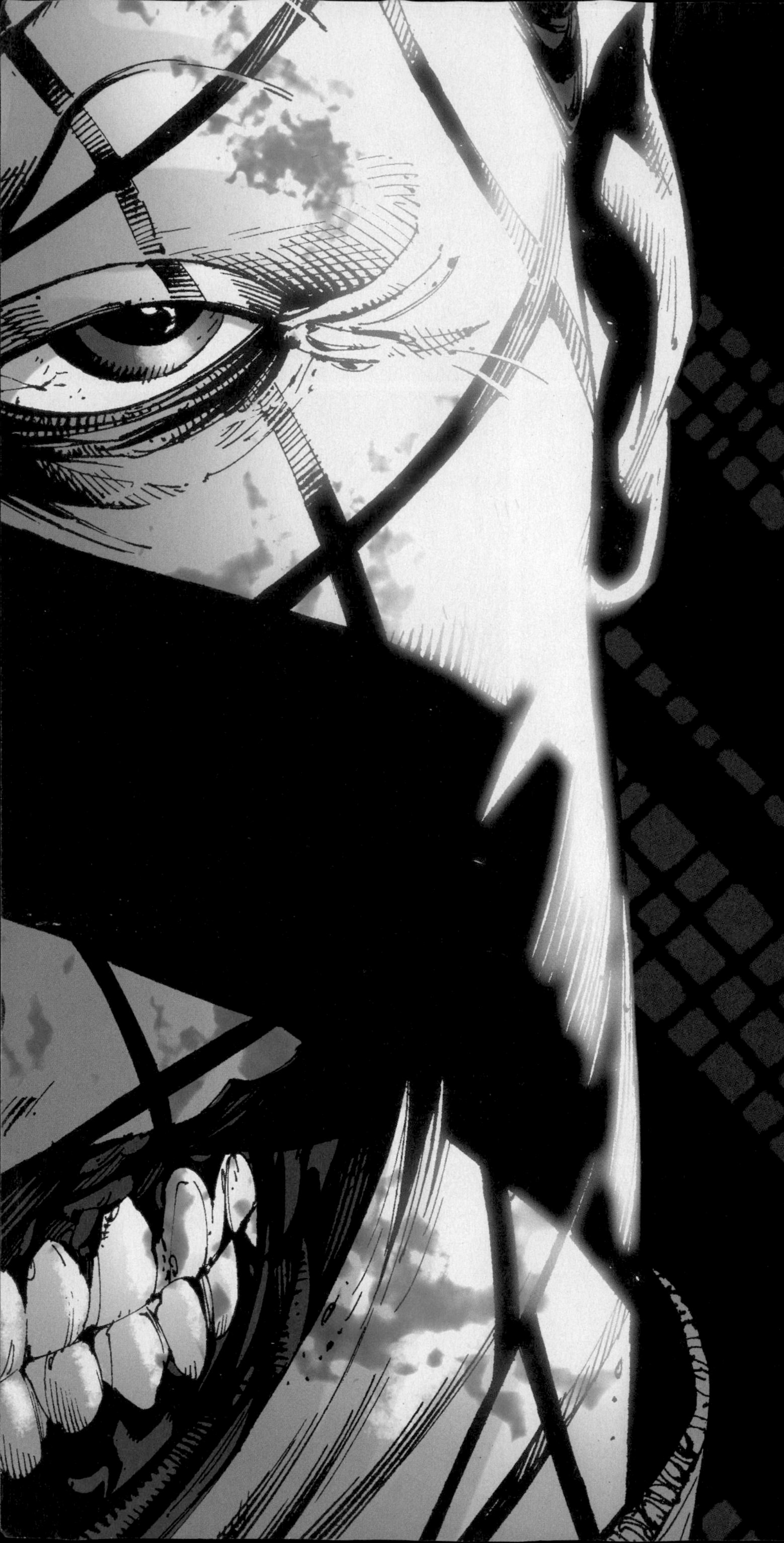

R.I.P.

BATMAN

written by
Grant Morrison

art by
Tony S. Daniel
Sandu Florea
Lee Garbett
Trevor Scott

colored by
Guy Major
Alex Sinclair

lettered by
Randy Gentile
Jared K. Fletcher
Nick J. Napolitano

painted cover art by
ALEX ROSS

variant cover art by
TONY S. DANIEL

Batman created by
BOB KANE

Mike Marts
Editor-Original Series
Jeanine Schaefer
Associate Editor-Original Series
Bob Harras
Assistant Editor-Original Series
Group Editor-Collected Editions
Robbin Brosterman
Design Director-Books
Scott Nybakken
Editor

DC Comics
Diane Nelson
President
Dan DiDio and Jim Lee
Co-Publishers
Geoff Johns
Chief Creative Officer
Patrick Caldon
EVP-Finance and Administration
John Rood
EVP-Sales, Marketing and
Business Development
Amy Genkins
SVP-Business and Legal Affairs
Steve Rotterdam
SVP-Sales and Marketing
John Cunningham
VP-Marketing
Terri Cunningham
VP-Managing Editor
Alison Gill
VP-Manufacturing
David Hyde
VP-Publicity
Sue Pohja
VP-Book Trade Sales
Alysse Soll
VP-Advertising and Custom Publishing
Bob Wayne
VP-Sales
Mark Chiarello
Art Director

Cover art by Alex Ross
Publication design by Robbie Biederman

BATMAN R.I.P.
Published by DC Comics.
Cover and compilation Copyright © 2010
DC Comics. All Rights Reserved. Originally
published as BATMAN 676-683 and
DC UNIVERSE 0 Copyright © 2008
DC Comics. All Rights Reserved.
All characters, their distinctive likenesses
and related elements featured in
this publication are trademarks of
DC Comics. The stories, characters and
incidents featured in this publication are
entirely fictional. DC Comics does not read
or accept unsolicited submissions of
ideas, stories or artwork.
DC Comics
1700 Broadway,
New York, NY 10019
A Warner Bros. Entertainment Company.
Printed by World Color Press, Inc.
Dubuque, IA, USA 5/5/10. First Printing.
ISBN: 978-1-4012-2576-6

Table of Contents

Prologue
1
from
DC UNIVERSE #0
art by Tony S. Daniel
colors by Alex Sinclair
letters by Nick J. Napolitano

Batman R.I.P.

Part One:
Midnight in the
House of Hurt
9
from
BATMAN #676
pencils by Tony S. Daniel
inks by Sandu Florea
colors by Guy Major
letters by Randy Gentile
variant cover color by
Guy Major

Part Two:
Batman in the
Underworld
33
from
BATMAN #677
pencils by Tony S. Daniel
inks by Sandu Florea
colors by Guy Major
letters by Jared K. Fletcher
variant cover color by
Guy Major

Part Three:
Zur En Arrh
57
from
BATMAN #678
pencils by Tony S. Daniel
inks by Sandu Florea
colors by Guy Major
letters by Randy Gentile
variant cover color by
Dave McCaig

Part Four:
Miracle on Crime Alley
81
from
BATMAN #679
pencils by Tony S. Daniel
inks by Sandu Florea
colors by Guy Major
letters by Randy Gentile
variant cover color by
Guy Major

Part Five:
The Thin White
Duke of Death
105
from
BATMAN #680
pencils by Tony S. Daniel
inks by Sandu Florea
colors by Guy Major
letters by Randy Gentile
variant cover color by
Guy Major

Part Six:
Hearts in Darkness
131
from
BATMAN #681
pencils by Tony S. Daniel
inks by Sandu Florea
colors by Guy Major
letters by Jared K. Fletcher
variant cover color by
Guy Major

Last Rites

The Butler Did It
165
from
BATMAN #682
pencils by Lee Garbett
inks by Trevor Scott
colors by Guy Major
letters by Jared K. Fletcher
variant cover color by
Guy Major

The Butler Did It Again
191
from
BATMAN #683
pencils by Lee Garbett
inks by Trevor Scott
colors by Guy Major
letters by Jared K. Fletcher
variant cover color by
Guy Major

sketchbook by
Tony S. Daniel and
Grant Morrison
217

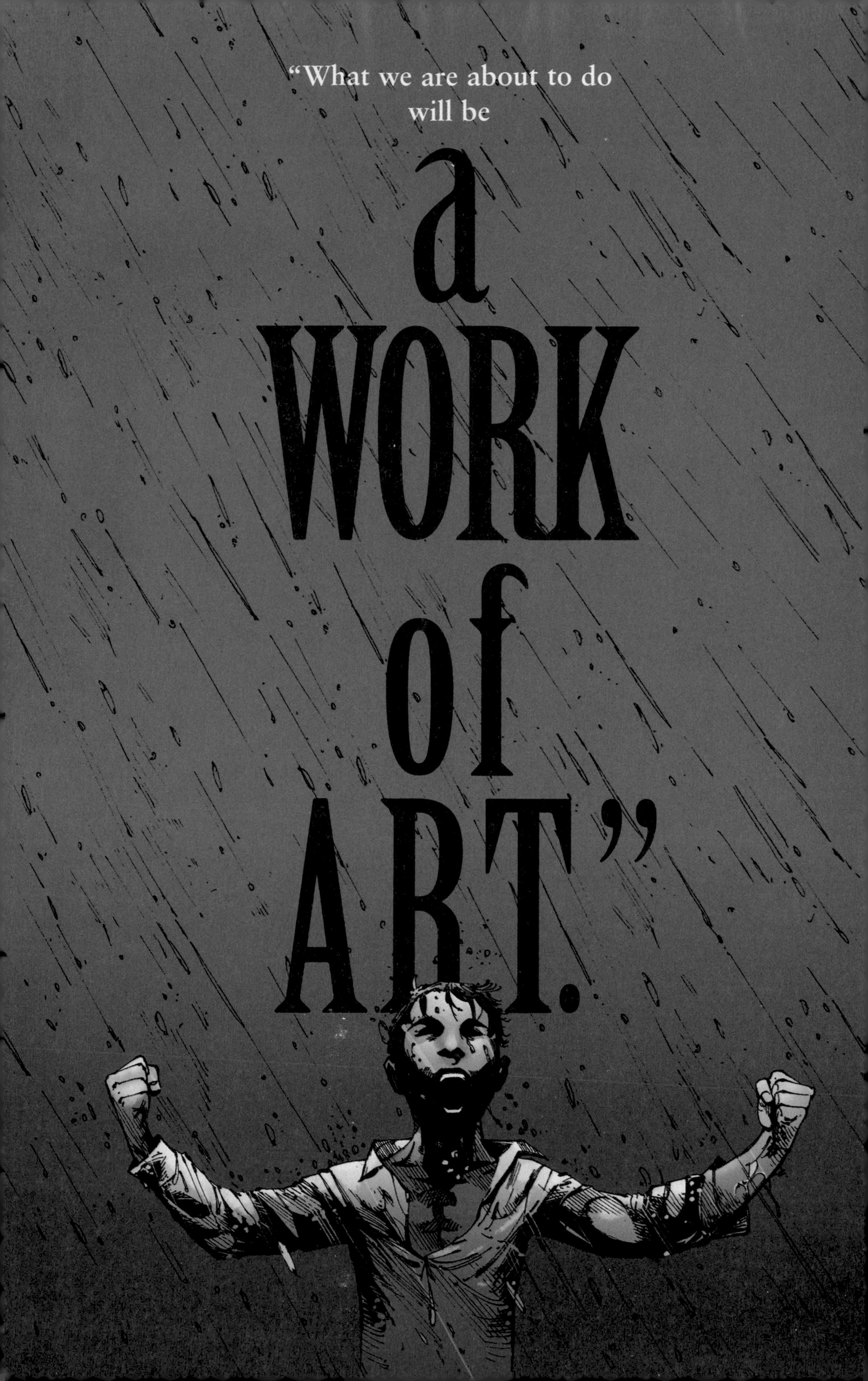
"What we are about to do
will be
a
WORK
of
ART."

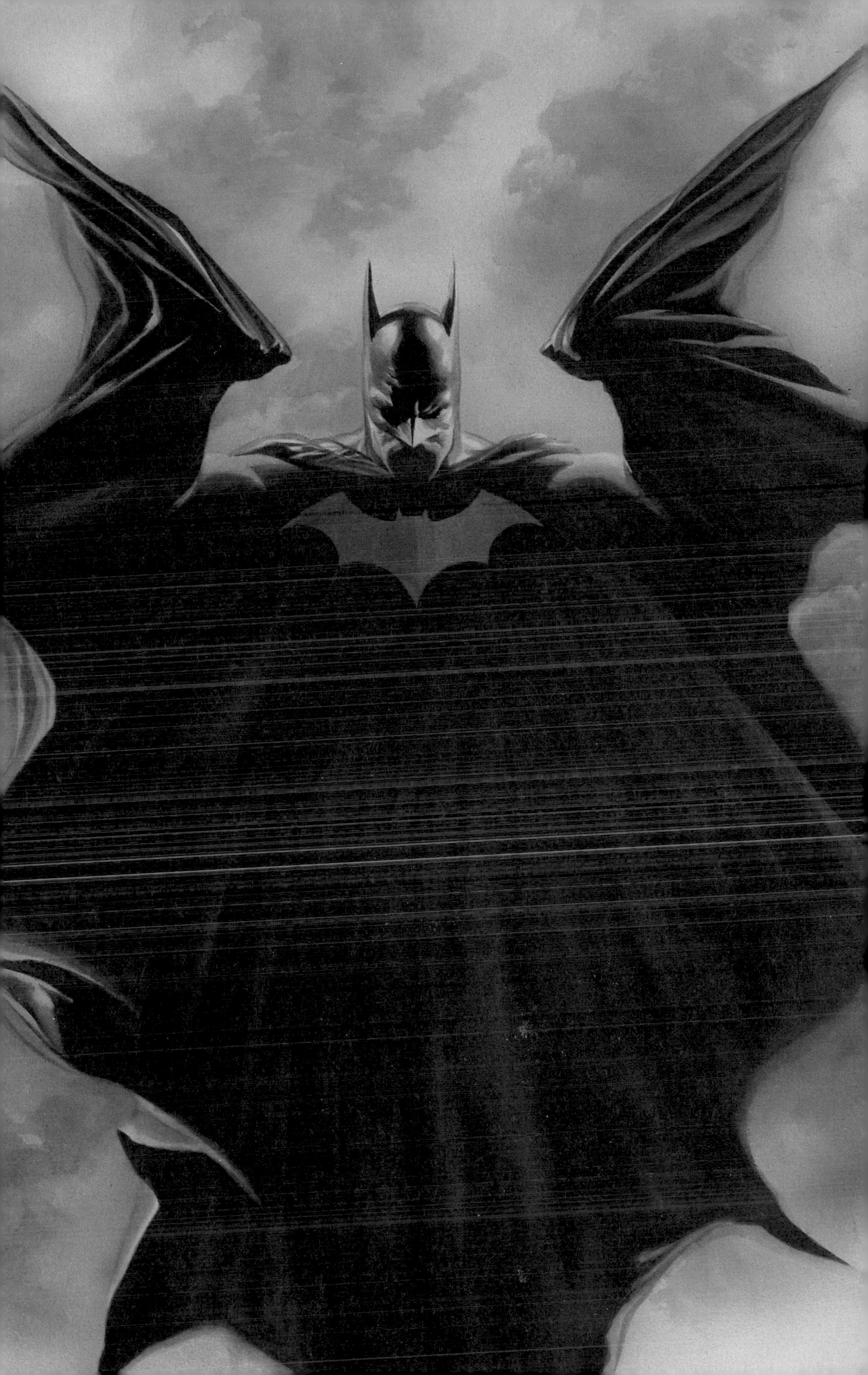

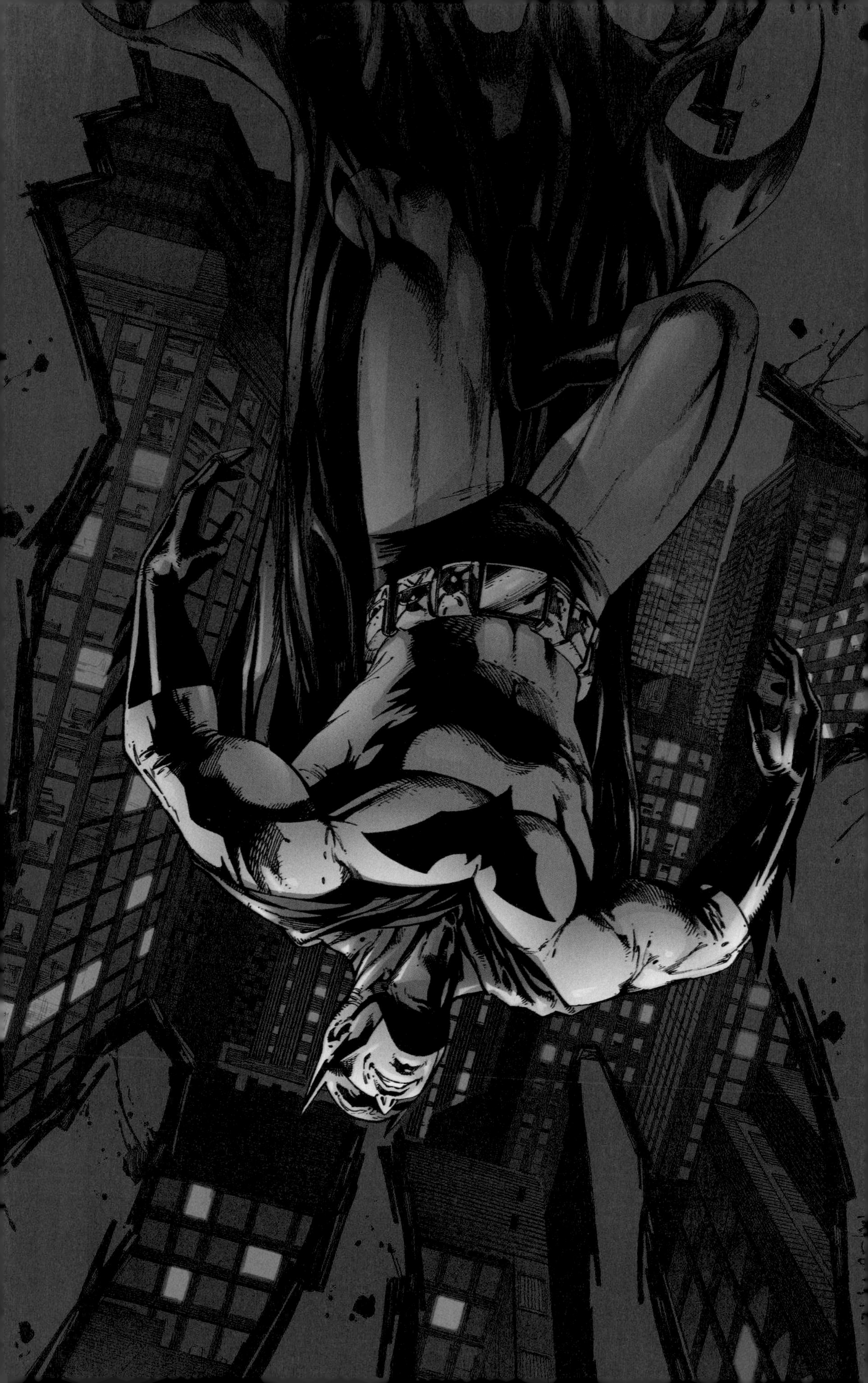

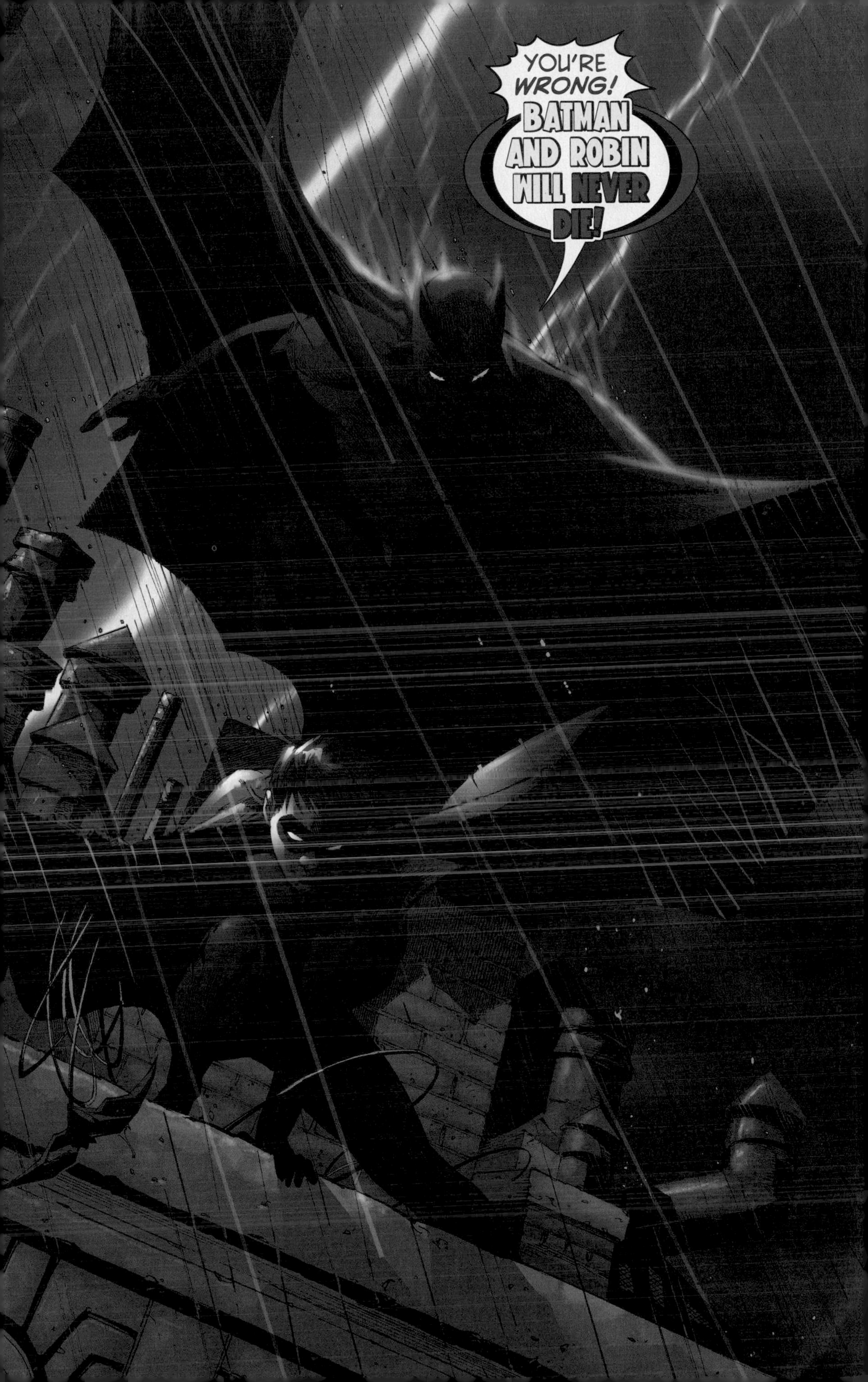
YOU'RE WRONG! BATMAN AND ROBIN WILL NEVER DIE!

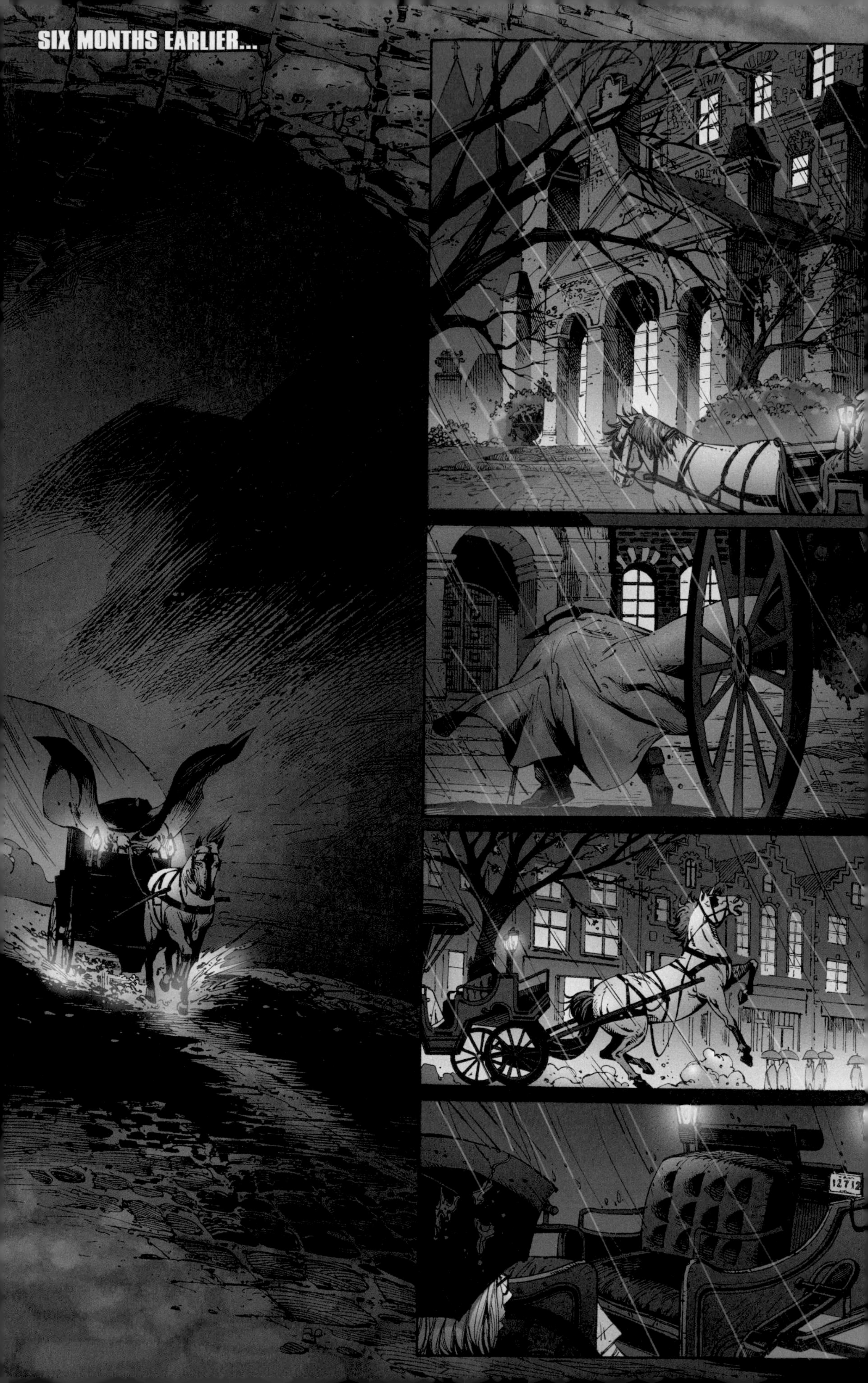
SIX MONTHS EARLIER...
12712

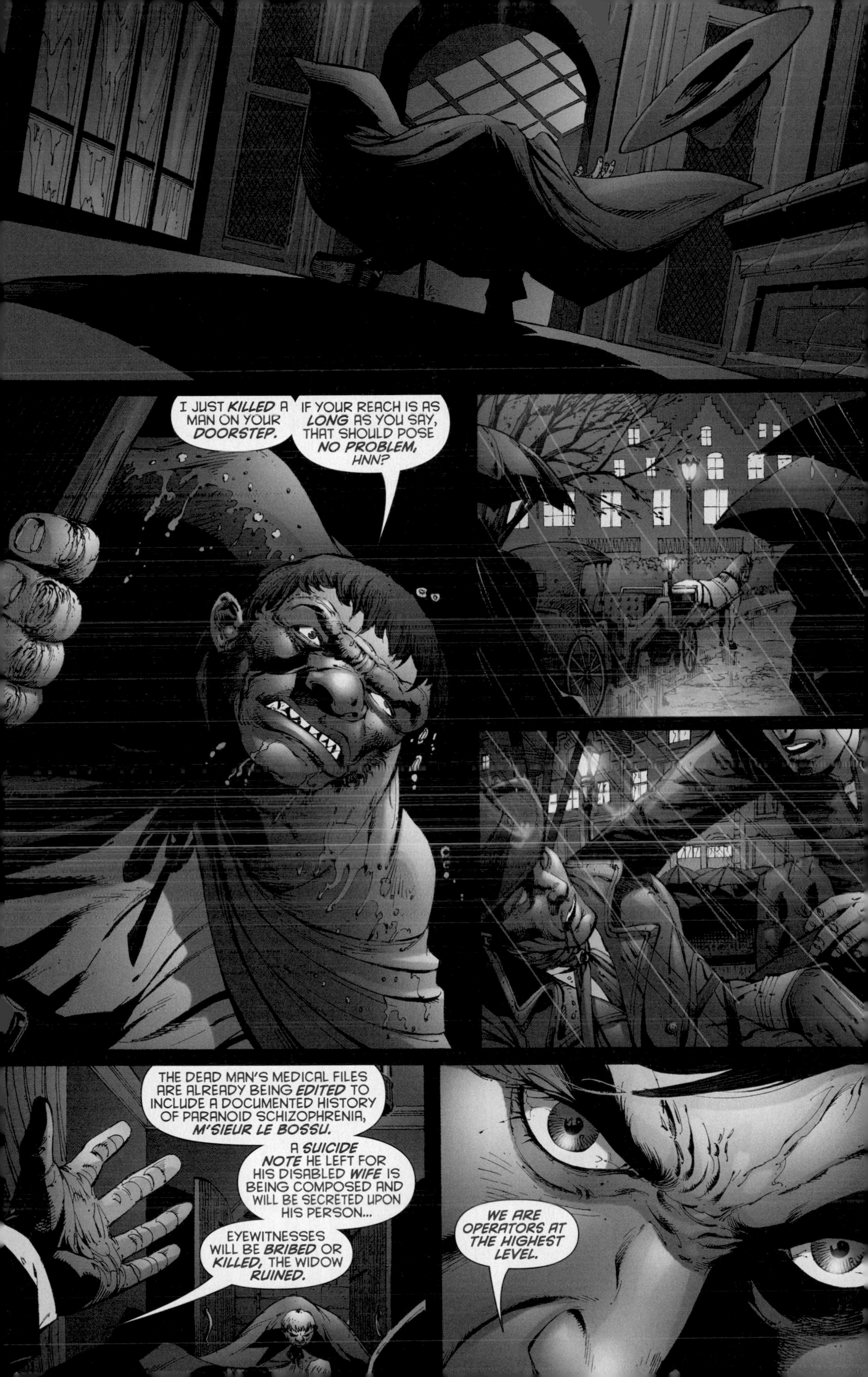
I JUST KILLED A MAN ON YOUR DOORSTEP.
IF YOUR REACH IS AS LONG AS YOU SAY, THAT SHOULD POSE NO PROBLEM, HNN?
THE DEAD MAN'S MEDICAL FILES ARE ALREADY BEING EDITED TO INCLUDE A DOCUMENTED HISTORY OF PARANOID SCHIZOPHRENIA, M'SIEUR LE BOSSU.
A SUICIDE NOTE HE LEFT FOR HIS DISABLED WIFE IS BEING COMPOSED AND WILL BE SECRETED UPON HIS PERSON...
EYEWITNESSES WILL BE BRIBED OR KILLED, THE WIDOW RUINED.
WE ARE OPERATORS AT THE HIGHEST LEVEL.

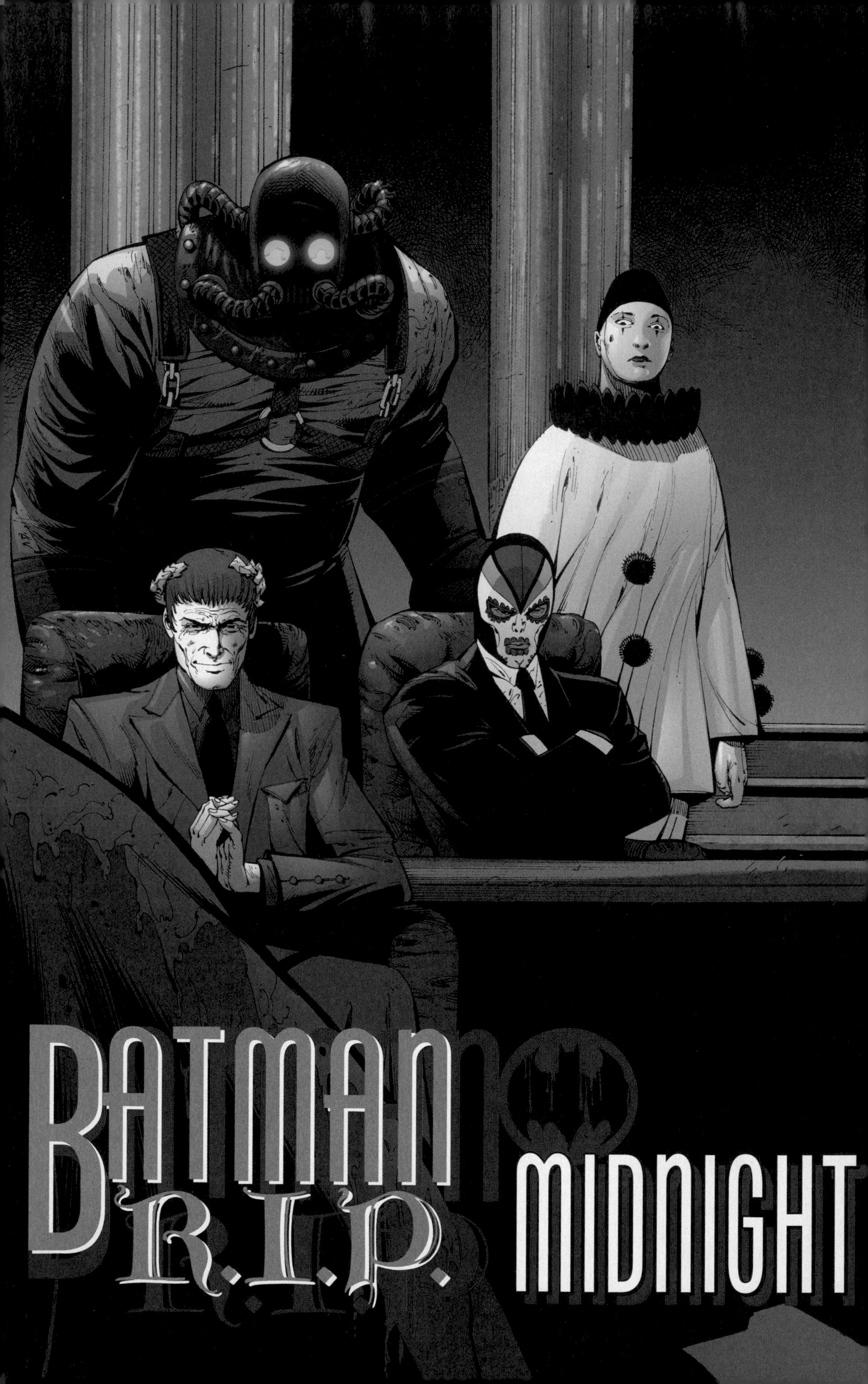
BATMAN
R.I.P.
MIDNIGHT

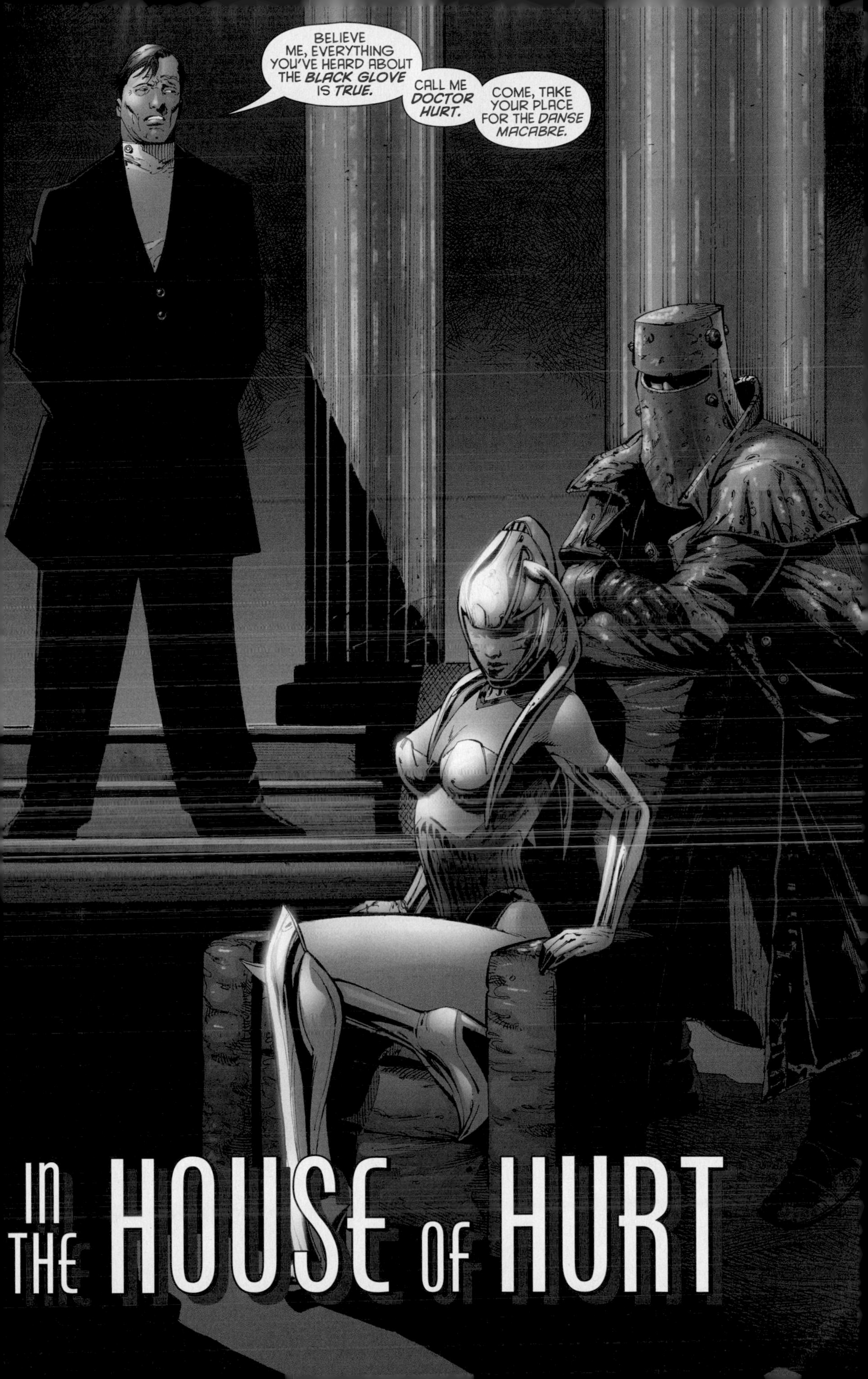
BELIEVE ME, EVERYTHING YOU'VE HEARD ABOUT THE *BLACK GLOVE* IS *TRUE.*
CALL ME *DOCTOR HURT.*
COME, TAKE YOUR PLACE FOR THE *DANSE MACABRE.*
IN THE HOUSE OF HURT

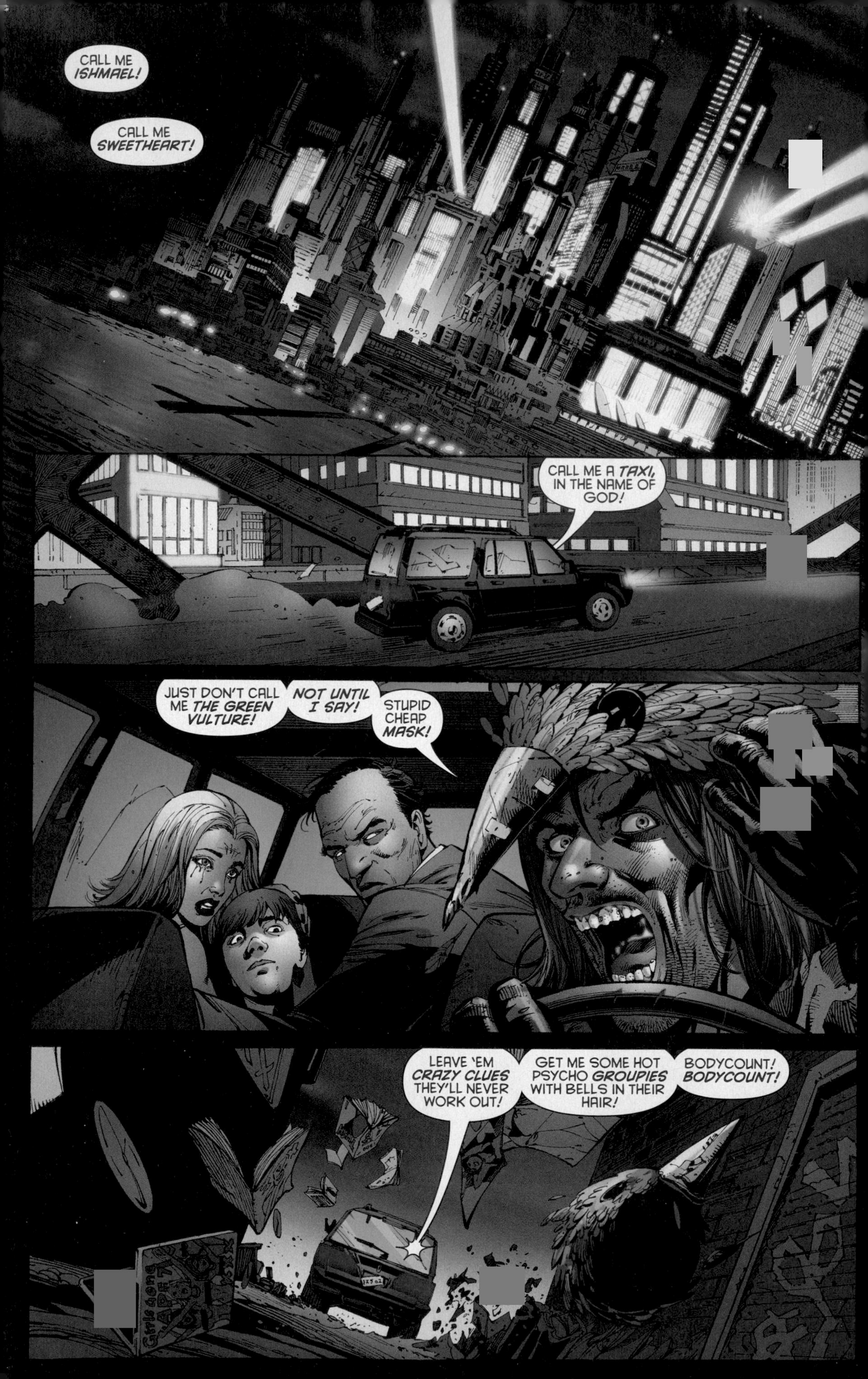
CALL ME *ISHMAEL!*
CALL ME *SWEETHEART!*
CALL ME A *TAXI,* IN THE NAME OF GOD!
JUST DON'T CALL ME *THE GREEN VULTURE!*
NOT UNTIL I SAY!
STUPID CHEAP *MASK!*
LEAVE 'EM *CRAZY CLUES* THEY'LL NEVER WORK OUT!
GET ME SOME HOT PSYCHO *GROUPIES* WITH BELLS IN THEIR HAIR!
BODYCOUNT! BODYCOUNT!

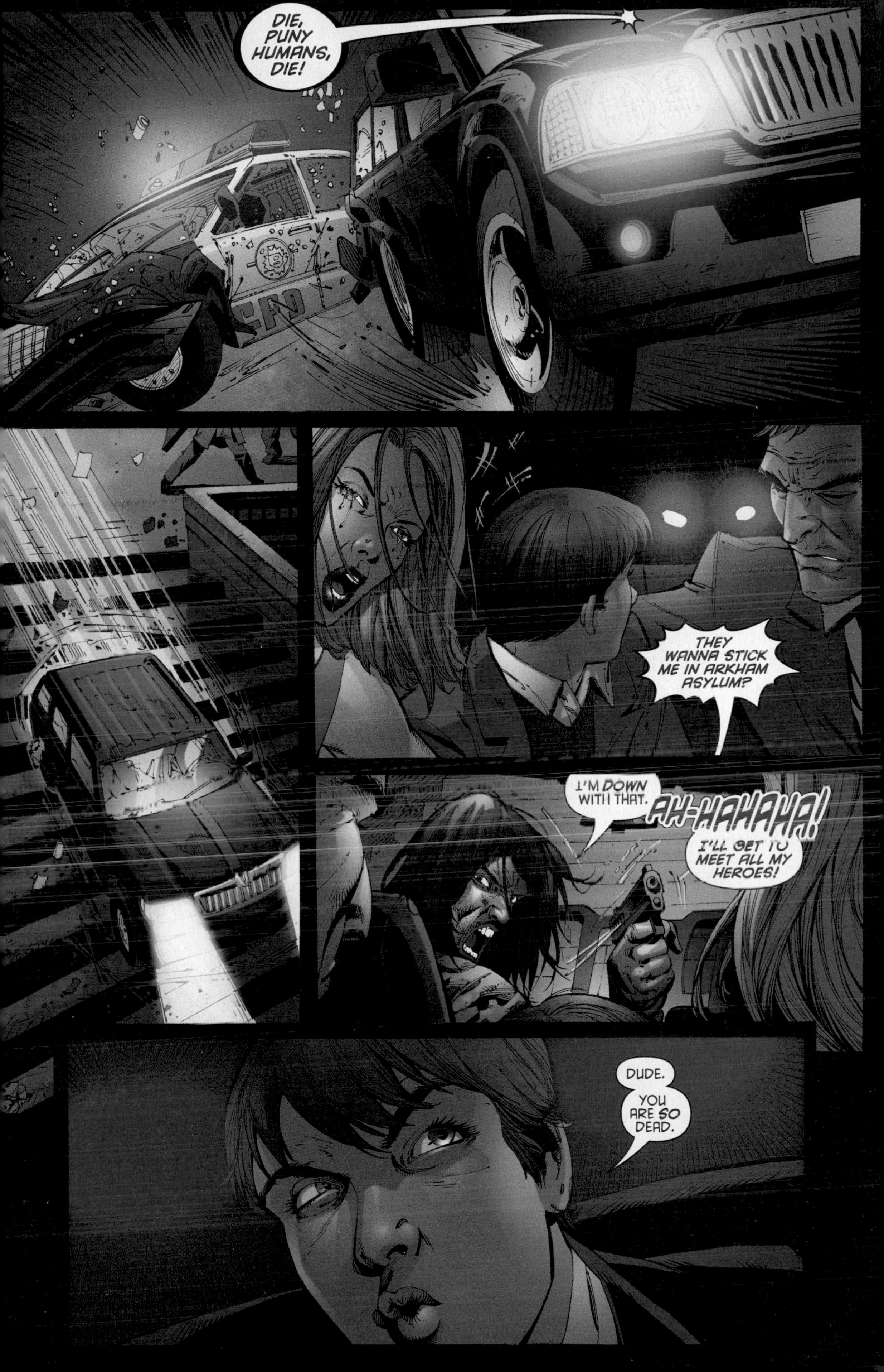
DIE, PUNY HUMANS, DIE!
THEY WANNA STICK ME IN ARKHAM ASYLUM?
I'M DOWN WITH THAT.
AH-HAHAHA!
I'LL GET TO MEET ALL MY HEROES!
DUDE.
YOU ARE SO DEAD.

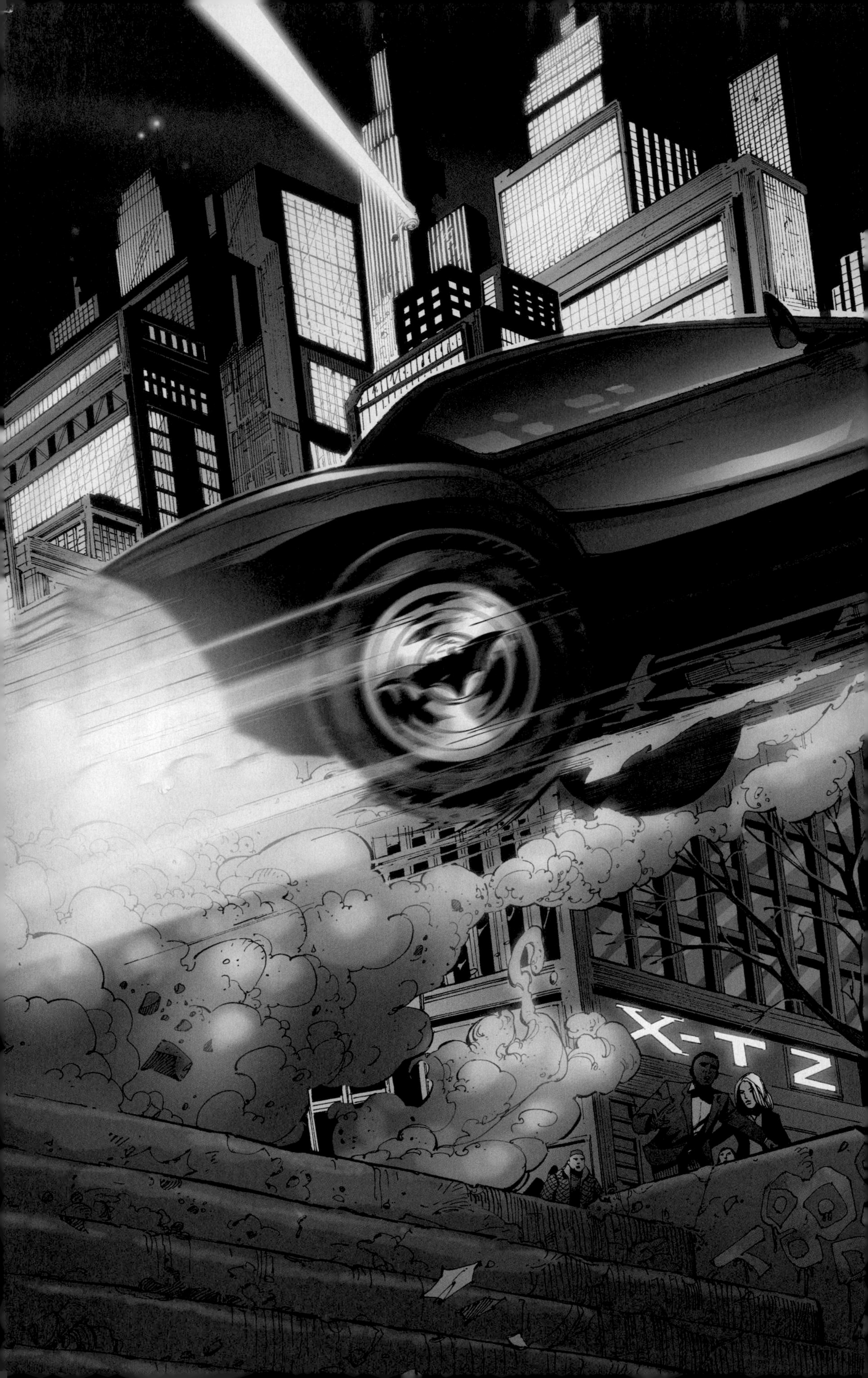
X-T Z

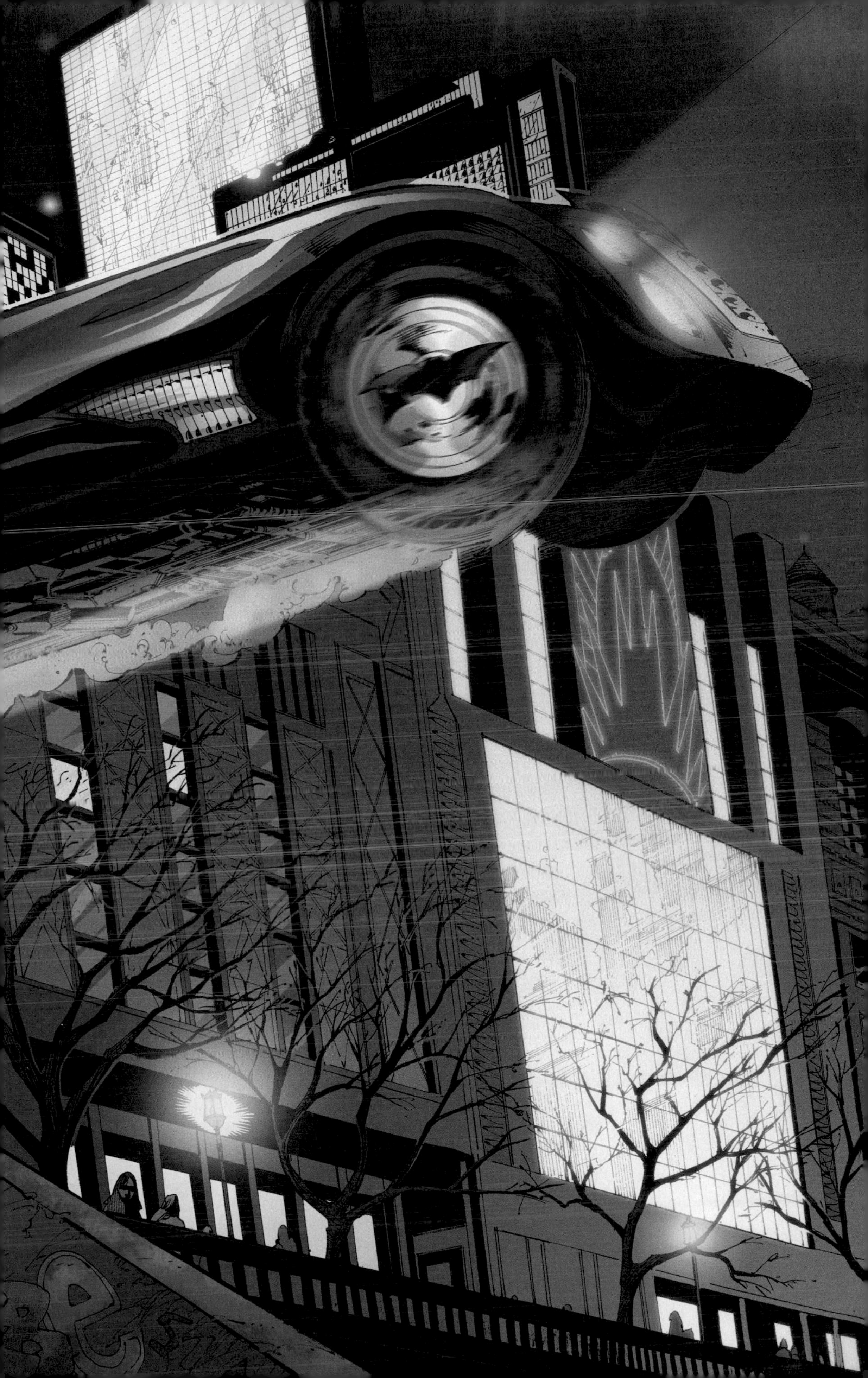

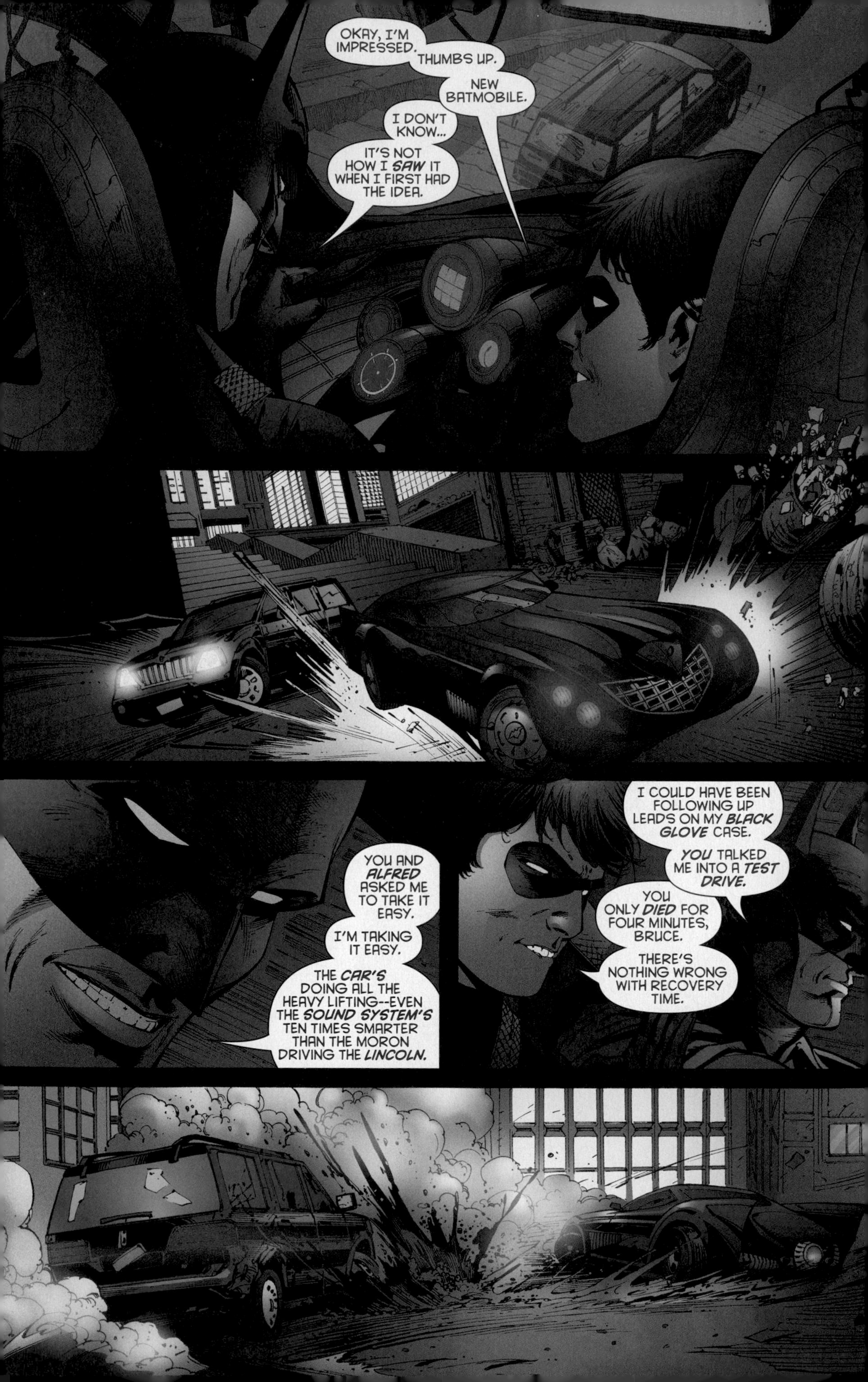
OKAY, I'M IMPRESSED. THUMBS UP.
NEW BATMOBILE.
I DON'T KNOW...
IT'S NOT HOW I SAW IT WHEN I FIRST HAD THE IDEA.
YOU AND ALFRED ASKED ME TO TAKE IT EASY.
I'M TAKING IT EASY.
THE CAR'S DOING ALL THE HEAVY LIFTING--EVEN THE SOUND SYSTEM'S TEN TIMES SMARTER THAN THE MORON DRIVING THE LINCOLN.
I COULD HAVE BEEN FOLLOWING UP LEADS ON MY BLACK GLOVE CASE.
YOU TALKED ME INTO A TEST DRIVE.
YOU ONLY DIED FOR FOUR MINUTES, BRUCE.
THERE'S NOTHING WRONG WITH RECOVERY TIME.

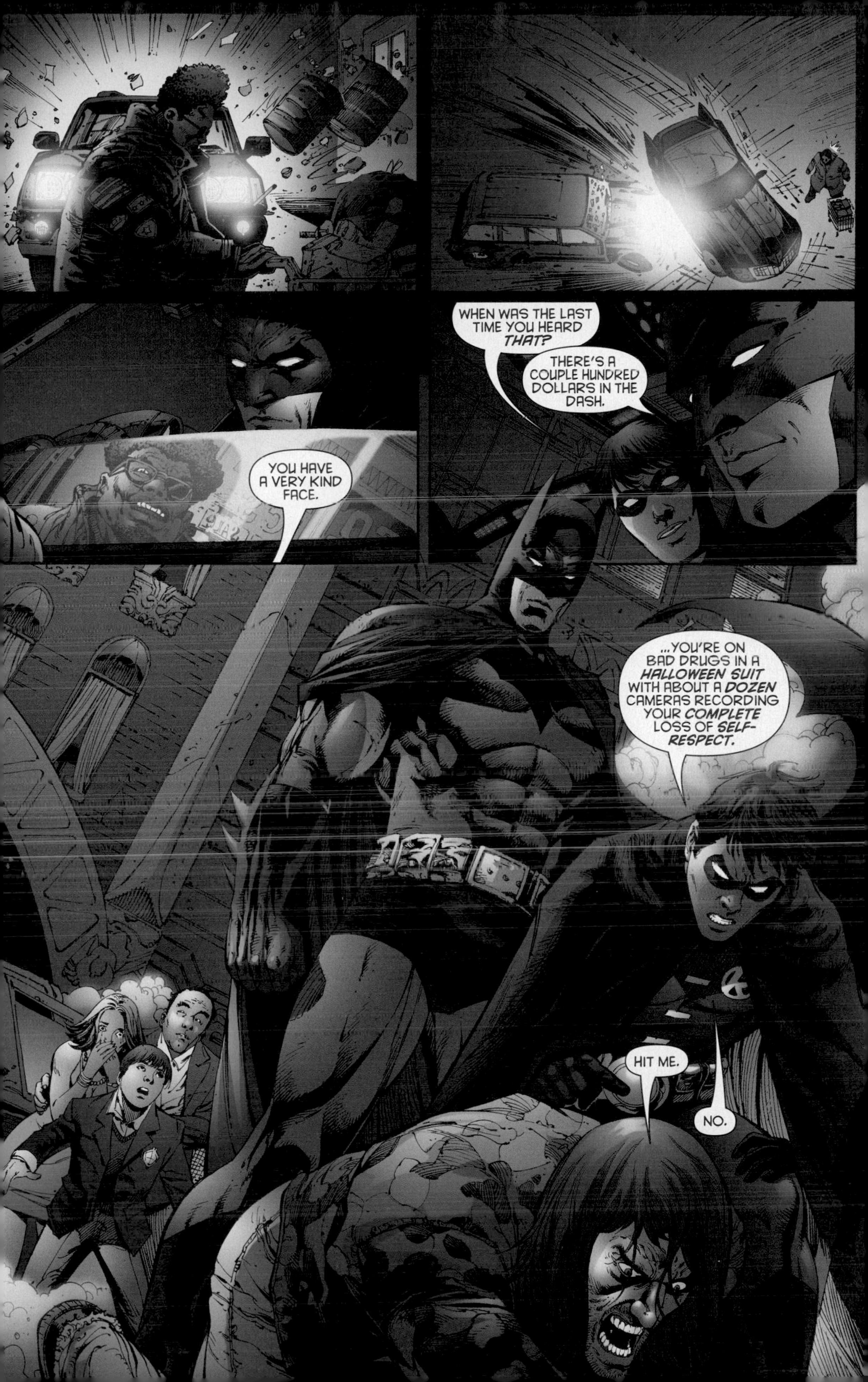
WHEN WAS THE LAST TIME YOU HEARD *THAT?*
THERE'S A COUPLE HUNDRED DOLLARS IN THE DASH.
YOU HAVE A VERY KIND FACE.
...YOU'RE ON BAD DRUGS IN A *HALLOWEEN SUIT* WITH ABOUT A *DOZEN* CAMERAS RECORDING YOUR *COMPLETE* LOSS OF *SELF-RESPECT.*
HIT ME.
NO.

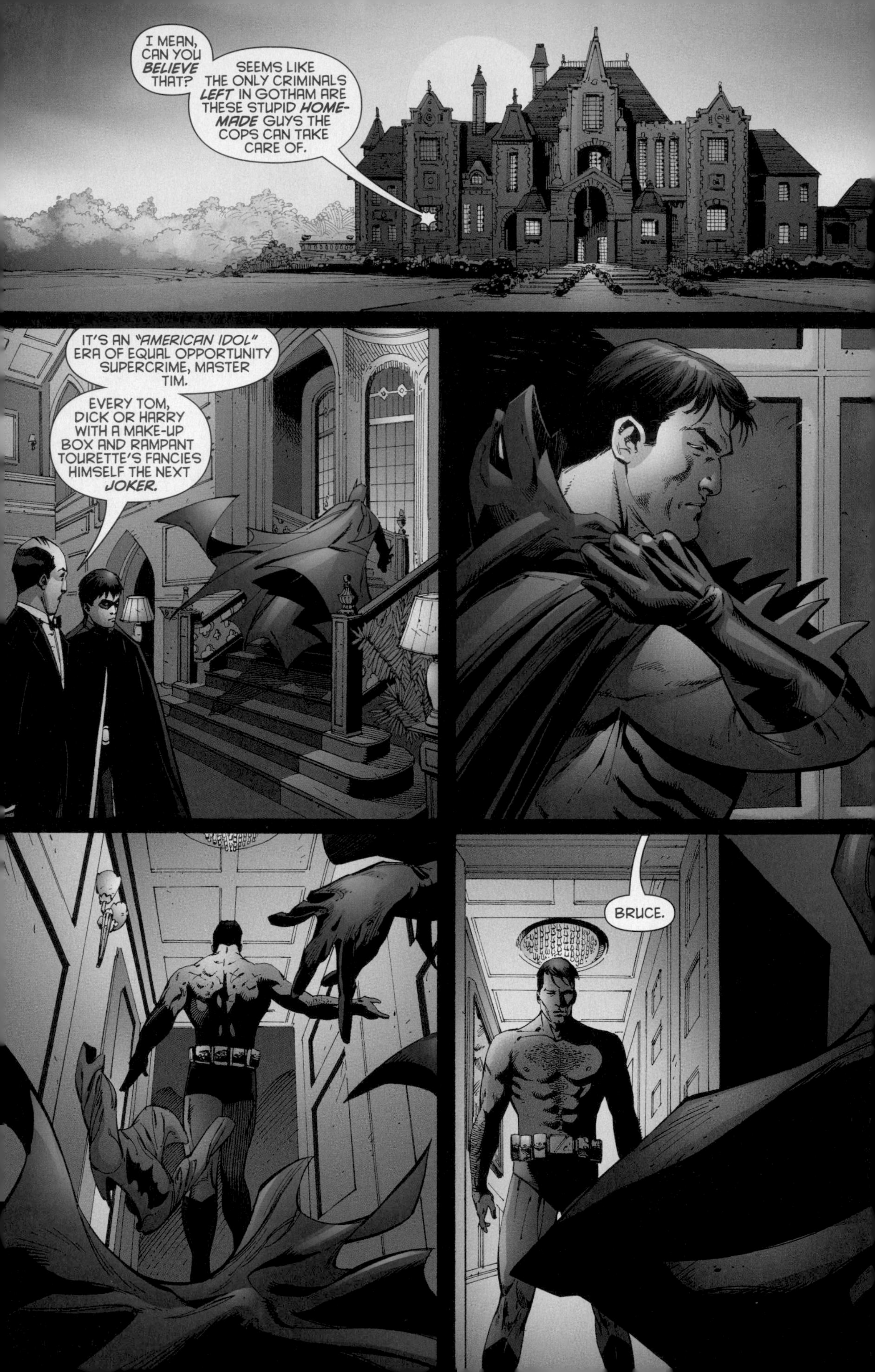
I MEAN, CAN YOU *BELIEVE* THAT?
SEEMS LIKE THE ONLY CRIMINALS *LEFT* IN GOTHAM ARE THESE STUPID *HOME-MADE* GUYS THE COPS CAN TAKE CARE OF.
IT'S AN *"AMERICAN IDOL"* ERA OF EQUAL OPPORTUNITY SUPERCRIME, MASTER TIM.
EVERY TOM, DICK OR HARRY WITH A MAKE-UP BOX AND RAMPANT TOURETTE'S FANCIES HIMSELF THE NEXT *JOKER.*
BRUCE.

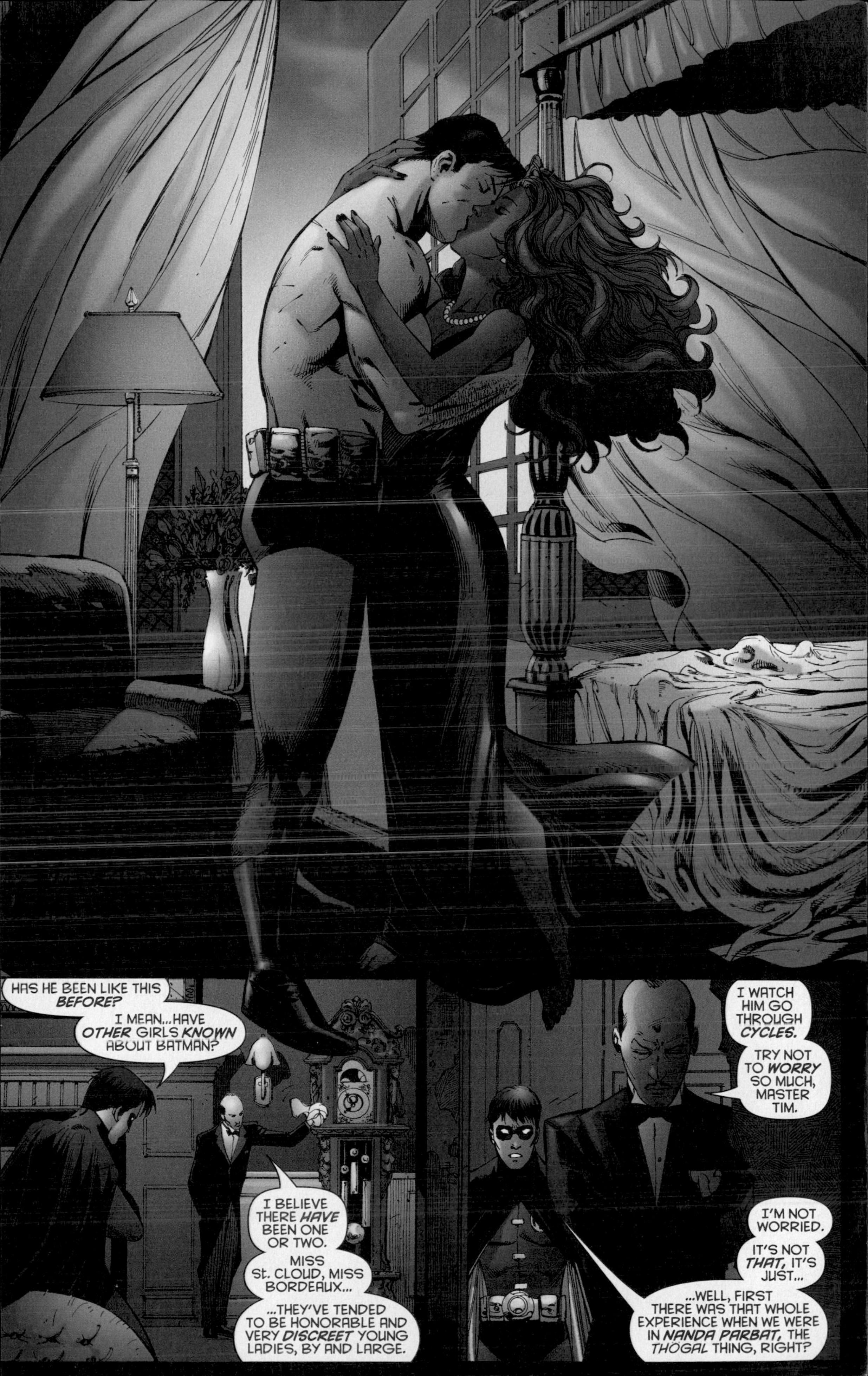
HAS HE BEEN LIKE THIS BEFORE?
I MEAN...HAVE OTHER GIRLS KNOWN ABOUT BATMAN?
I BELIEVE THERE HAVE BEEN ONE OR TWO.
MISS St. CLOUD, MISS BORDEAUX...
...THEY'VE TENDED TO BE HONORABLE AND VERY DISCREET YOUNG LADIES, BY AND LARGE.
I WATCH HIM GO THROUGH CYCLES.
TRY NOT TO WORRY SO MUCH, MASTER TIM.
I'M NOT WORRIED.
IT'S NOT THAT, IT'S JUST...
...WELL, FIRST THERE WAS THAT WHOLE EXPERIENCE WHEN WE WERE IN NANDA PARBAT, THE THÖGAL THING, RIGHT?

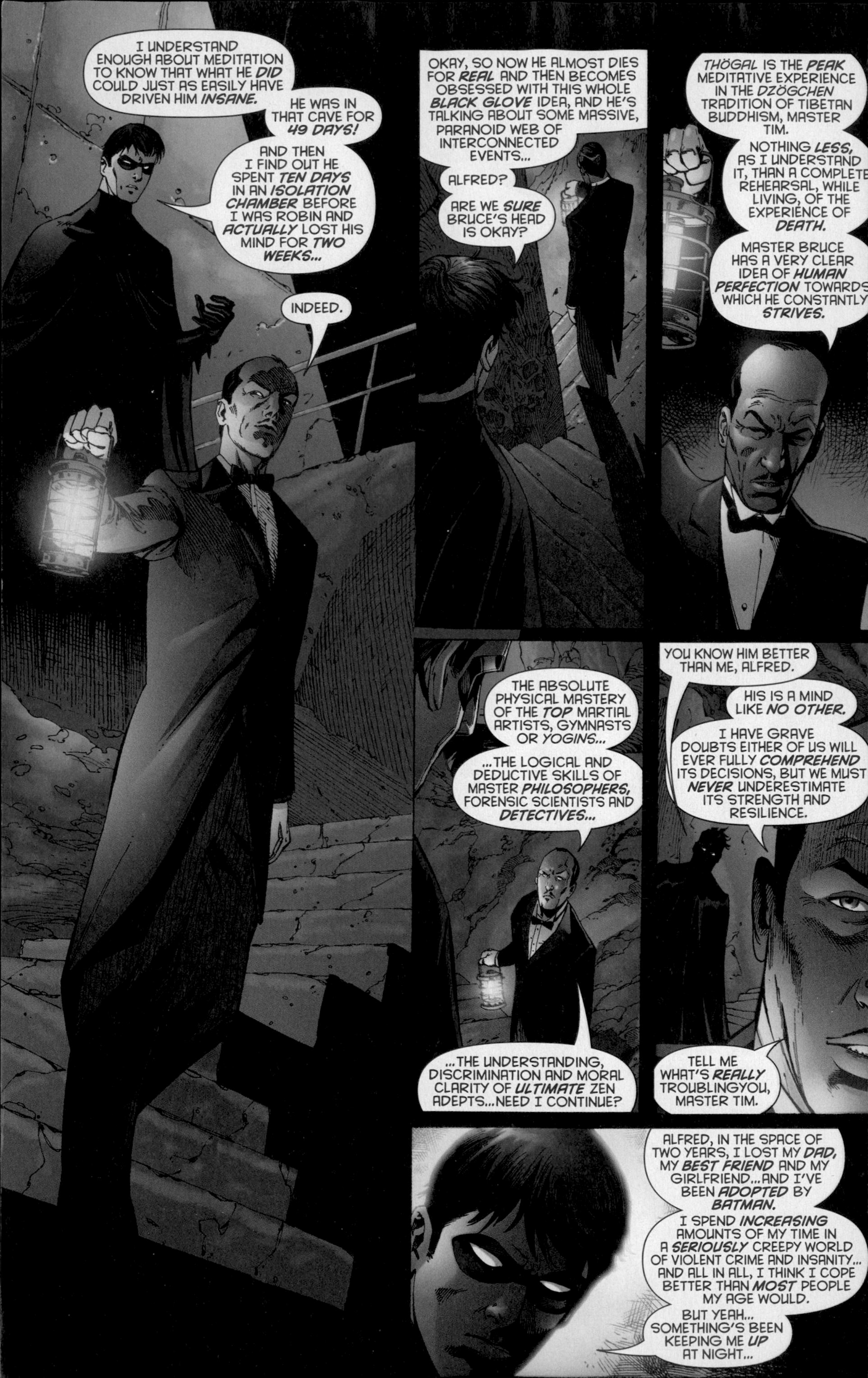
I UNDERSTAND ENOUGH ABOUT MEDITATION TO KNOW THAT WHAT HE DID COULD JUST AS EASILY HAVE DRIVEN HIM INSANE.
HE WAS IN THAT CAVE FOR 49 DAYS!
AND THEN I FIND OUT HE SPENT TEN DAYS IN AN ISOLATION CHAMBER BEFORE I WAS ROBIN AND ACTUALLY LOST HIS MIND FOR TWO WEEKS...
INDEED.
OKAY, SO NOW HE ALMOST DIES FOR REAL AND THEN BECOMES OBSESSED WITH THIS WHOLE BLACK GLOVE IDEA, AND HE'S TALKING ABOUT SOME MASSIVE, PARANOID WEB OF INTERCONNECTED EVENTS...
ALFRED?
ARE WE SURE BRUCE'S HEAD IS OKAY?
THÖGAL IS THE PEAK MEDITATIVE EXPERIENCE IN THE DZÖGCHEN TRADITION OF TIBETAN BUDDHISM, MASTER TIM.
NOTHING LESS, AS I UNDERSTAND IT, THAN A COMPLETE REHEARSAL, WHILE LIVING, OF THE EXPERIENCE OF DEATH.
MASTER BRUCE HAS A VERY CLEAR IDEA OF HUMAN PERFECTION TOWARDS WHICH HE CONSTANTLY STRIVES.
THE ABSOLUTE PHYSICAL MASTERY OF THE TOP MARTIAL ARTISTS, GYMNASTS OR YOGINS...
...THE LOGICAL AND DEDUCTIVE SKILLS OF MASTER PHILOSOPHERS, FORENSIC SCIENTISTS AND DETECTIVES...
...THE UNDERSTANDING, DISCRIMINATION AND MORAL CLARITY OF ULTIMATE ZEN ADEPTS...NEED I CONTINUE?
YOU KNOW HIM BETTER THAN ME, ALFRED.
HIS IS A MIND LIKE NO OTHER.
I HAVE GRAVE DOUBTS EITHER OF US WILL EVER FULLY COMPREHEND ITS DECISIONS, BUT WE MUST NEVER UNDERESTIMATE ITS STRENGTH AND RESILIENCE.
TELL ME WHAT'S REALLY TROUBLINGYOU, MASTER TIM.
ALFRED, IN THE SPACE OF TWO YEARS, I LOST MY DAD, MY BEST FRIEND AND MY GIRLFRIEND...AND I'VE BEEN ADOPTED BY BATMAN.
I SPEND INCREASING AMOUNTS OF MY TIME IN A SERIOUSLY CREEPY WORLD OF VIOLENT CRIME AND INSANITY... AND ALL IN ALL, I THINK I COPE BETTER THAN MOST PEOPLE MY AGE WOULD.
BUT YEAH... SOMETHING'S BEEN KEEPING ME UP AT NIGHT...

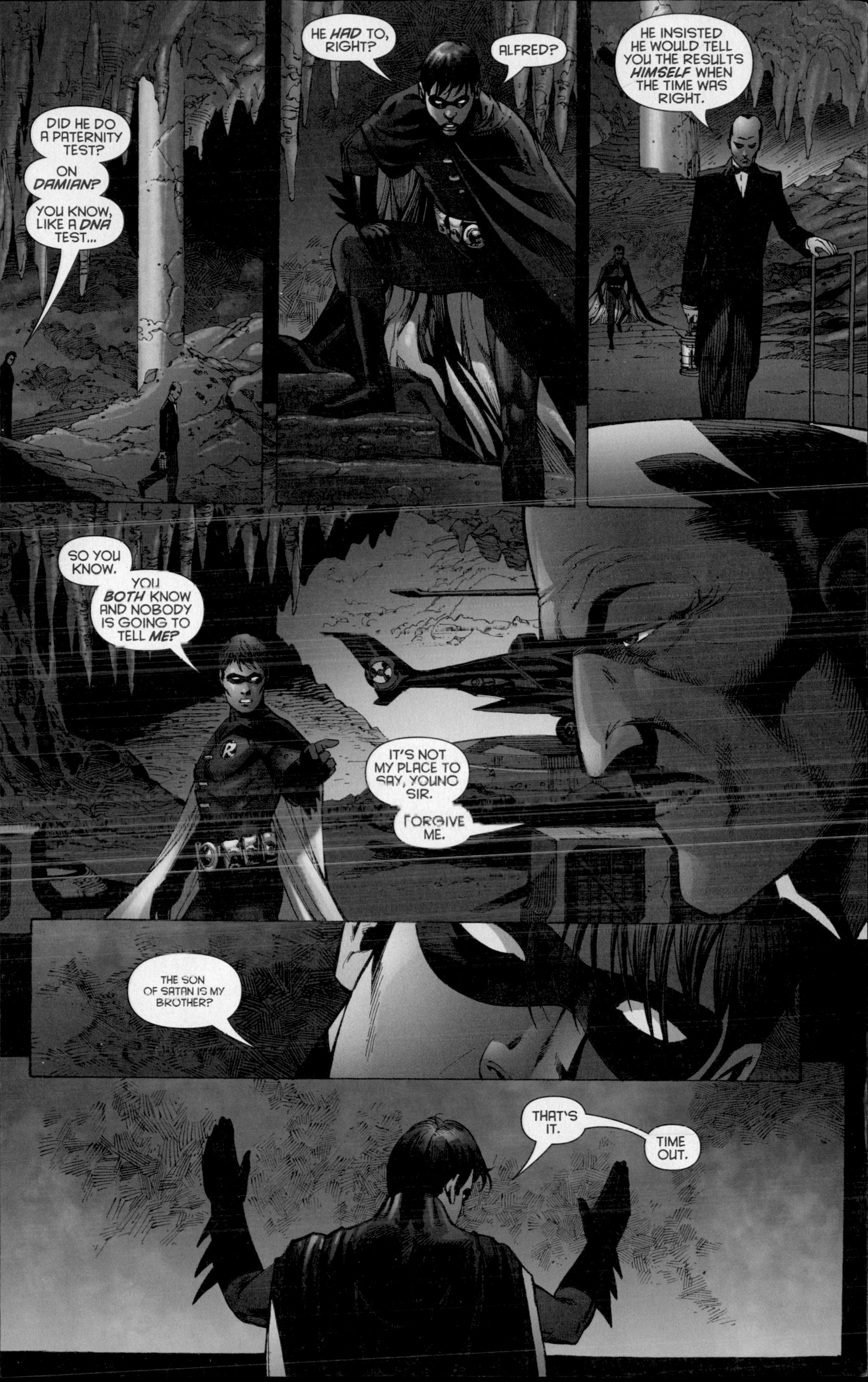
DID HE DO A PATERNITY TEST?
ON DAMIAN?
YOU KNOW, LIKE A DNA TEST...
HE HAD TO, RIGHT?
ALFRED?
HE INSISTED HE WOULD TELL YOU THE RESULTS HIMSELF WHEN THE TIME WAS RIGHT.
SO YOU KNOW.
YOU BOTH KNOW AND NOBODY IS GOING TO TELL ME?
IT'S NOT MY PLACE TO SAY, YOUNG SIR.
FORGIVE ME.
THE SON OF SATAN IS MY BROTHER?
THAT'S IT.
TIME OUT.

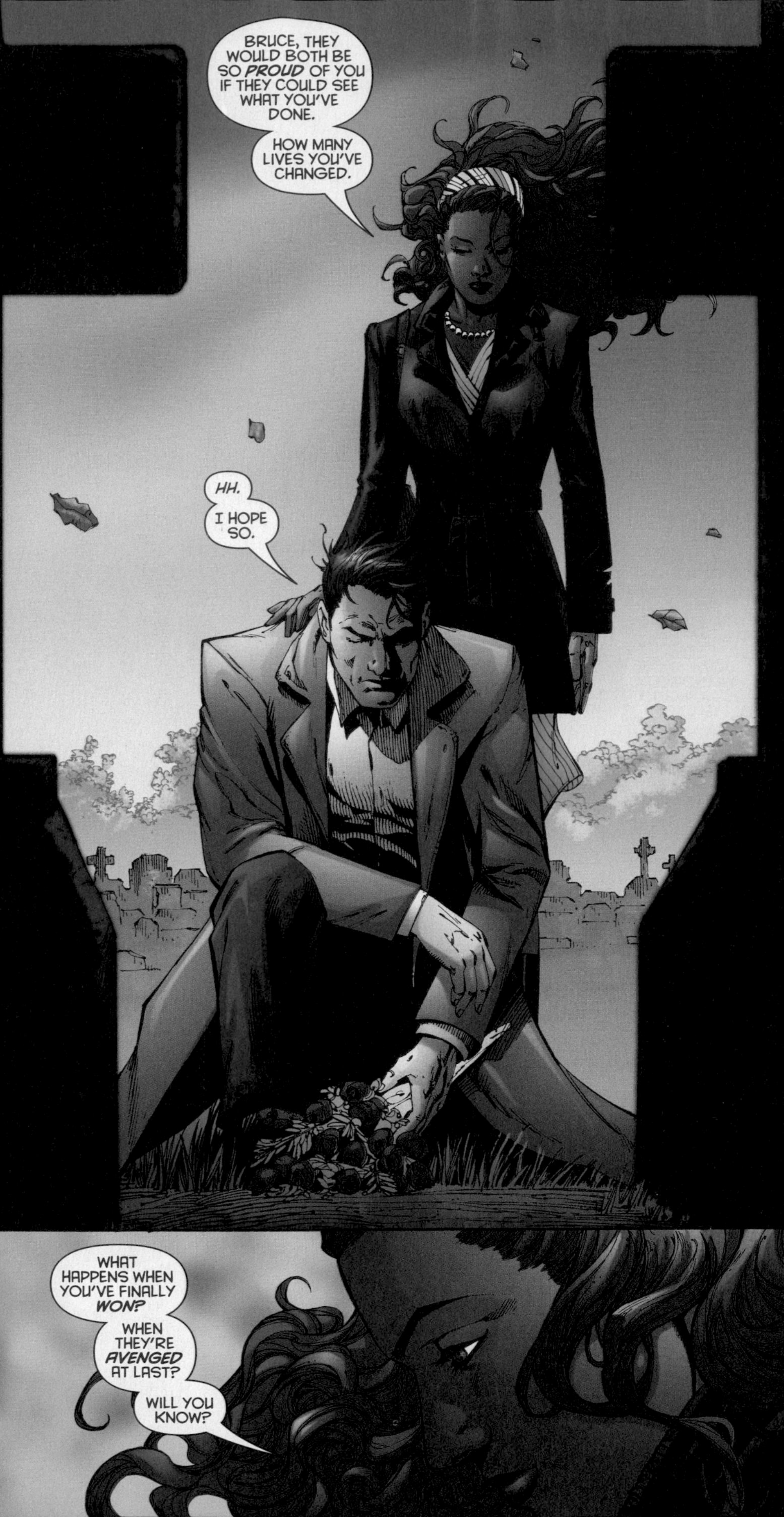
BRUCE, THEY WOULD BOTH BE SO PROUD OF YOU IF THEY COULD SEE WHAT YOU'VE DONE.
HOW MANY LIVES YOU'VE CHANGED.
HH.
I HOPE SO.
WHAT HAPPENS WHEN YOU'VE FINALLY WON?
WHEN THEY'RE AVENGED AT LAST?
WILL YOU KNOW?

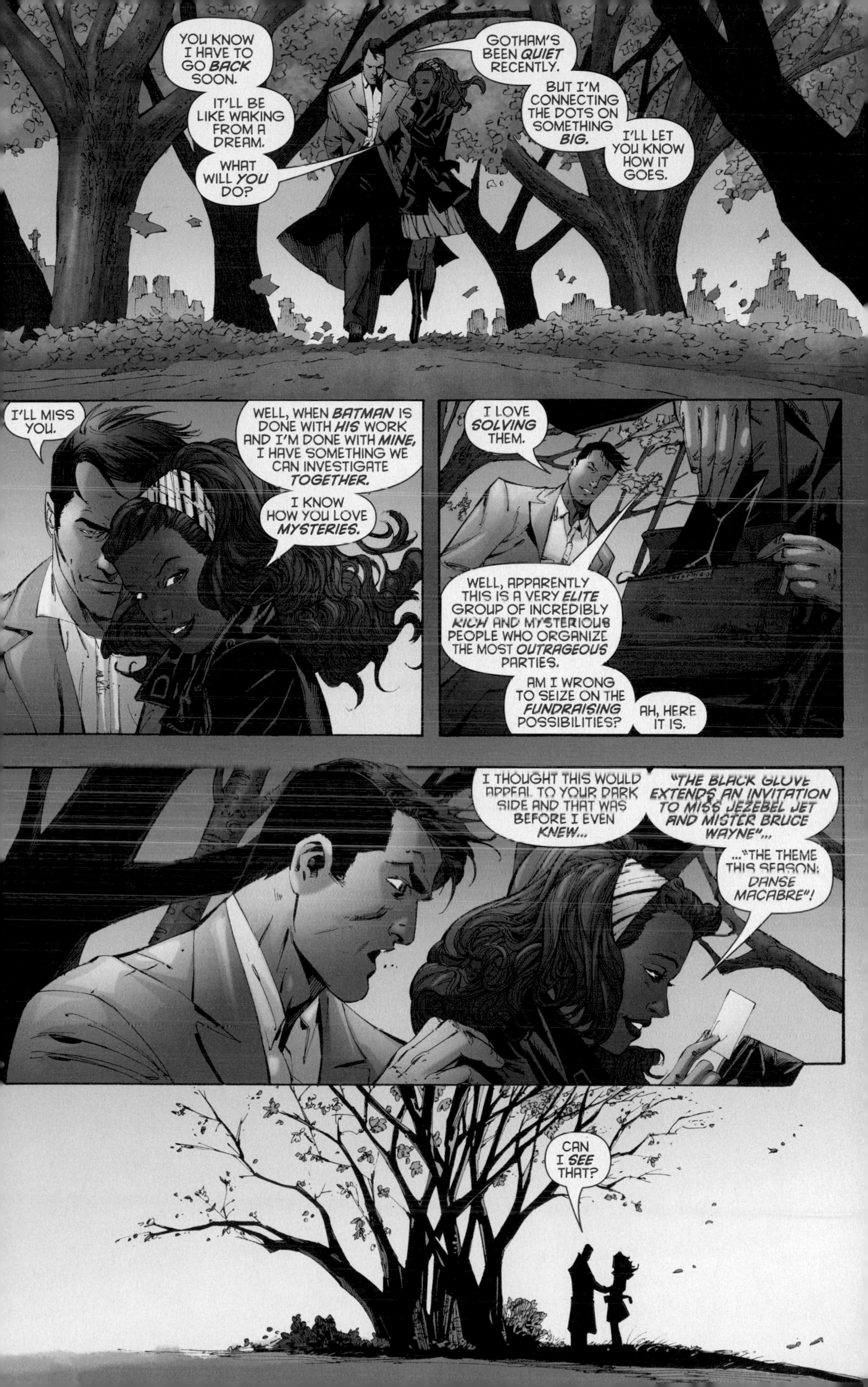
YOU KNOW I HAVE TO GO BACK SOON.
IT'LL BE LIKE WAKING FROM A DREAM.
WHAT WILL YOU DO?
GOTHAM'S BEEN QUIET RECENTLY.
BUT I'M CONNECTING THE DOTS ON SOMETHING BIG.
I'LL LET YOU KNOW HOW IT GOES.
I'LL MISS YOU.
WELL, WHEN BATMAN IS DONE WITH HIS WORK AND I'M DONE WITH MINE, I HAVE SOMETHING WE CAN INVESTIGATE TOGETHER.
I KNOW HOW YOU LOVE MYSTERIES.
I LOVE SOLVING THEM.
WELL, APPARENTLY THIS IS A VERY ELITE GROUP OF INCREDIBLY RICH AND MYSTERIOUS PEOPLE WHO ORGANIZE THE MOST OUTRAGEOUS PARTIES.
AM I WRONG TO SEIZE ON THE FUNDRAISING POSSIBILITIES?
AH, HERE IT IS.
I THOUGHT THIS WOULD APPEAL TO YOUR DARK SIDE AND THAT WAS BEFORE I EVEN KNEW...
"THE BLACK GLOVE EXTENDS AN INVITATION TO MISS JEZEBEL JET AND MISTER BRUCE WAYNE"...
..."THE THEME THIS SEASON: DANSE MACABRE"!
CAN I SEE THAT?

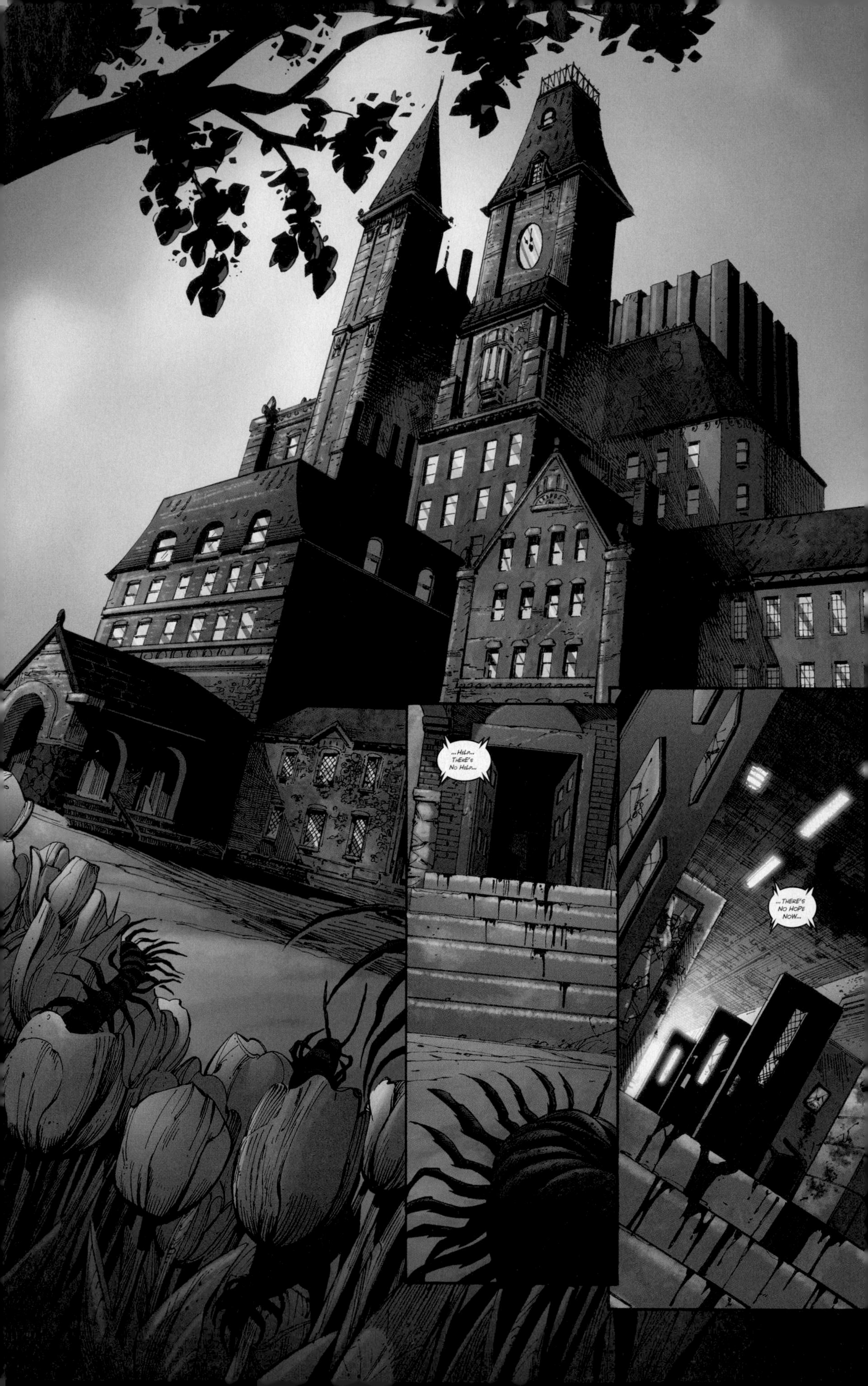
...HELP... THERE'S NO HELP...
...THERE'S NO HOPE NOW...

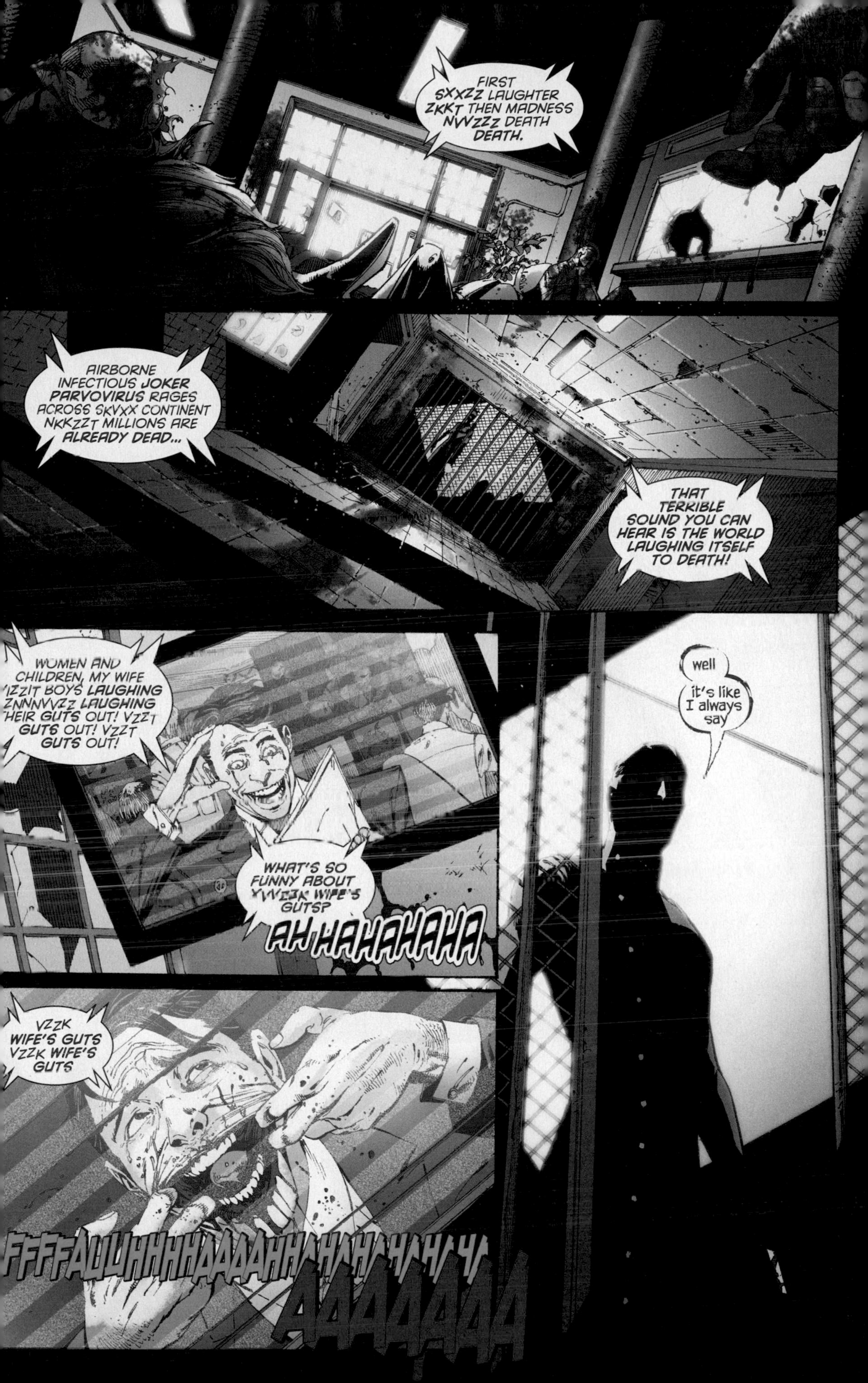
FIRST SXXZZ LAUGHTER ZKKT THEN MADNESS NVVZZZ DEATH DEATH.
AIRBORNE INFECTIOUS JOKER PARVOVIRUS RAGES ACROSS SKVXX CONTINENT NKKZZT MILLIONS ARE ALREADY DEAD...
THAT TERRIBLE SOUND YOU CAN HEAR IS THE WORLD LAUGHING ITSELF TO DEATH!
WOMEN AND CHILDREN, MY WIFE VZZIT BOYS LAUGHING ZNNNVVZZ LAUGHING THEIR GUTS OUT! VZZT GUTS OUT! VZZT GUTS OUT!
WHAT'S SO FUNNY ABOUT XVVZZK WIFE'S GUTS?
AH HAHAHAHAHA
well
it's like I always say
VZZK WIFE'S GUTS VZZK WIFE'S GUTS
FFFFAUUHHHHAAAAHHAHAHAHAHA
AAAAAA

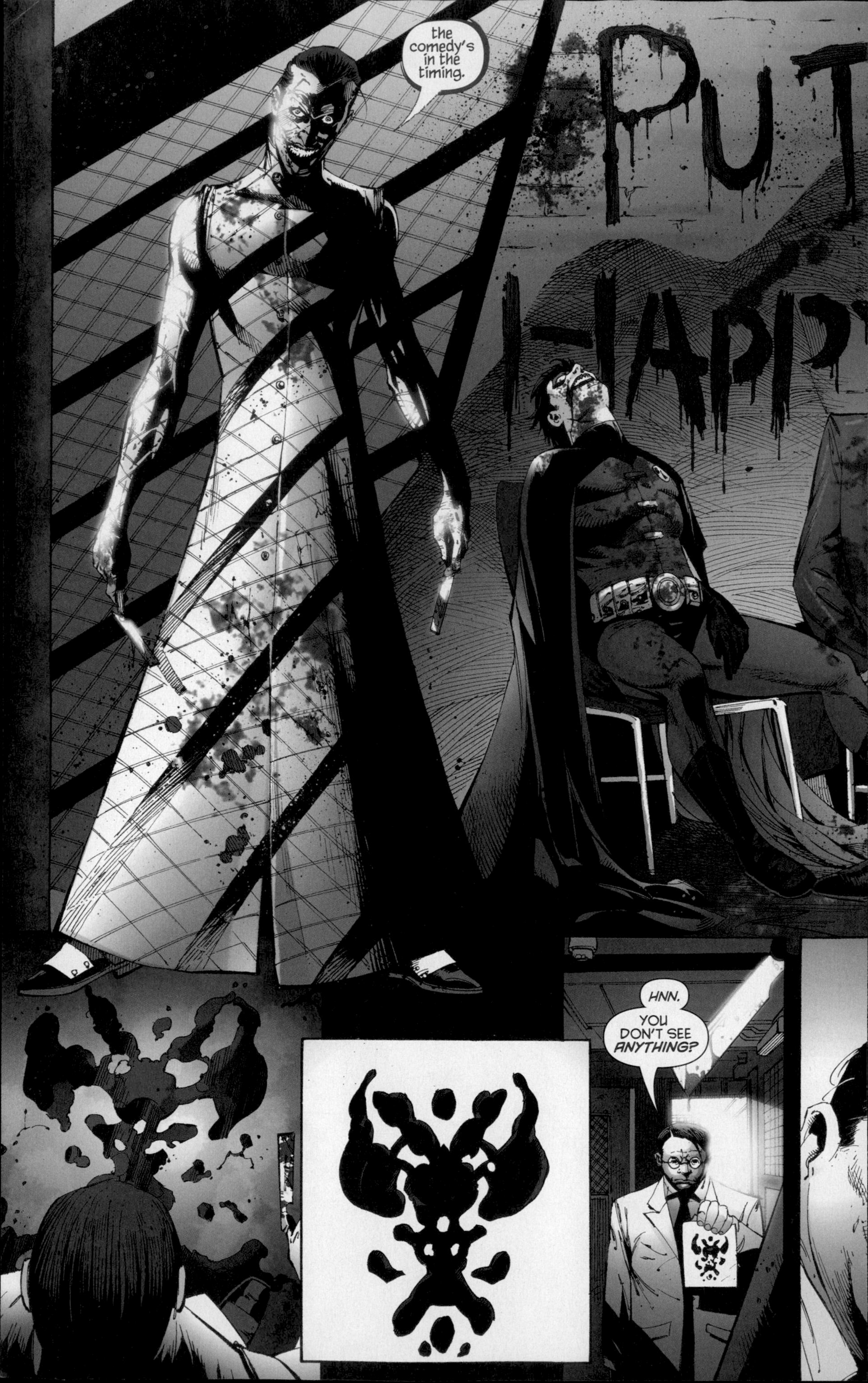
the comedy's in the timing.
PUT
HAPP
HNN.
YOU DON'T SEE ANYTHING?

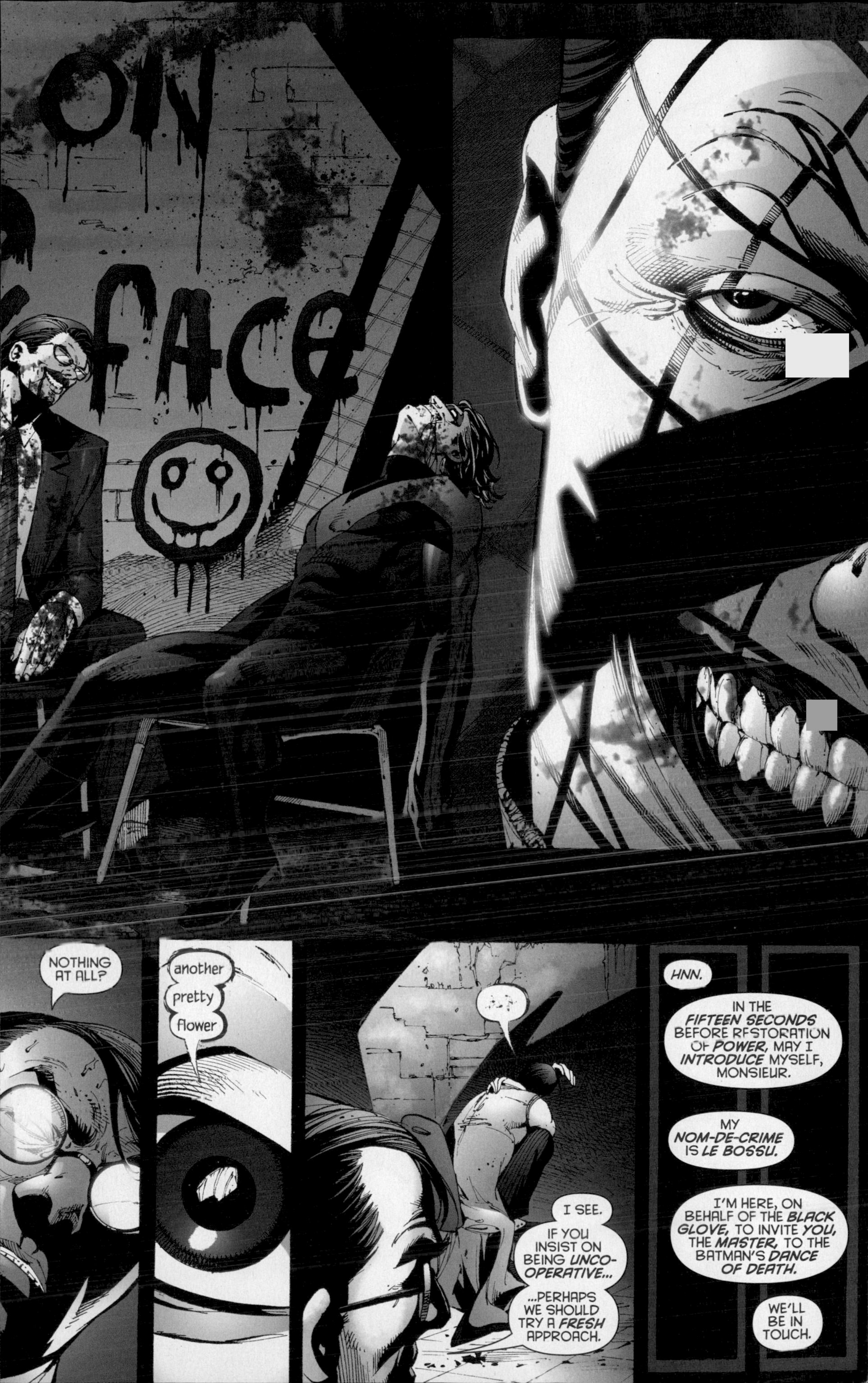
ON
FACE
NOTHING AT ALL?
another pretty flower
I SEE.
IF YOU INSIST ON BEING UNCO-OPERATIVE...
...PERHAPS WE SHOULD TRY A FRESH APPROACH.
HNN.
IN THE FIFTEEN SECONDS BEFORE RESTORATION OF POWER, MAY I INTRODUCE MYSELF, MONSIEUR.
MY NOM-DE-CRIME IS LE BOSSU.
I'M HERE, ON BEHALF OF THE BLACK GLOVE, TO INVITE YOU, THE MASTER, TO THE BATMAN'S DANCE OF DEATH.
WE'LL BE IN TOUCH.

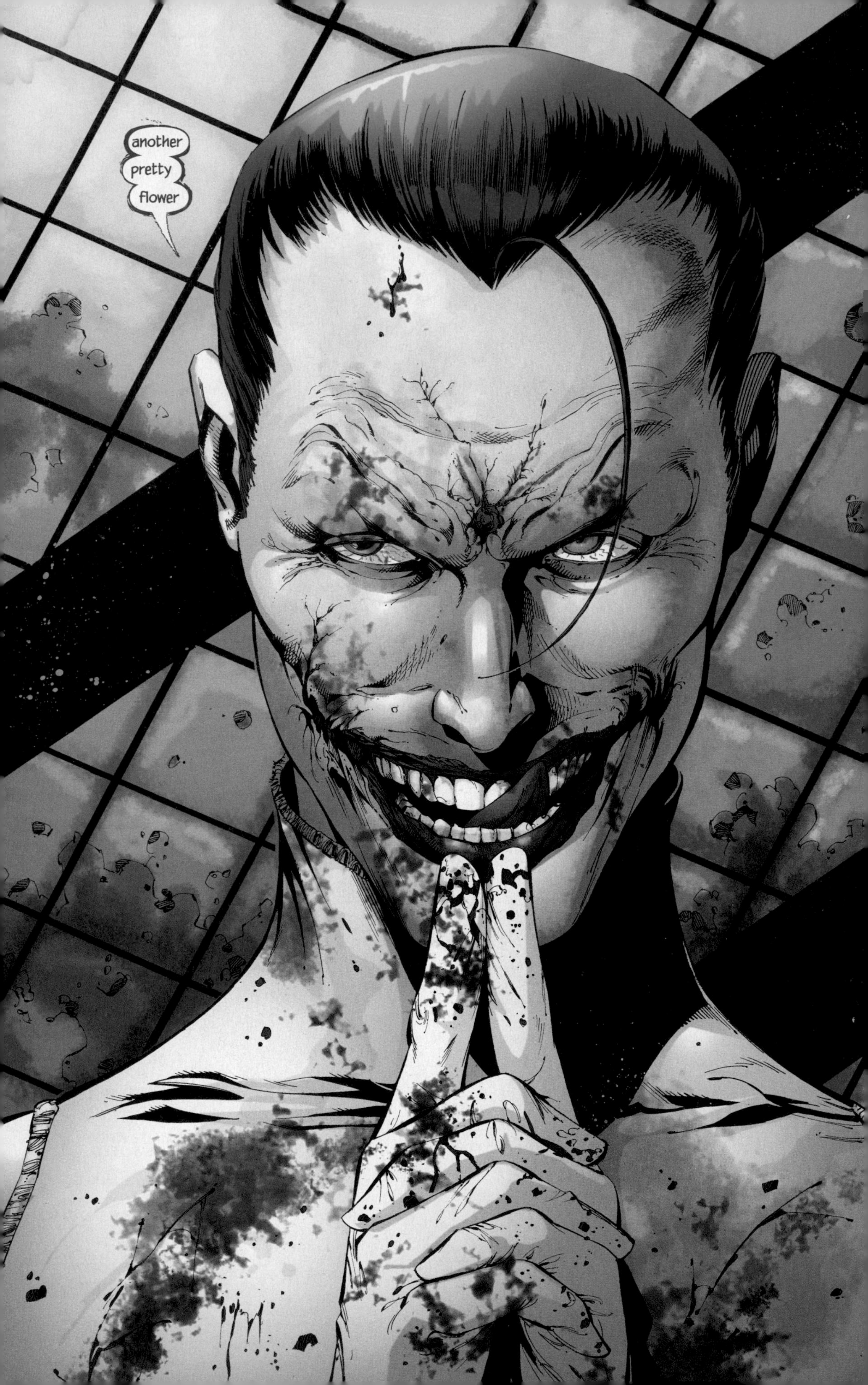
another pretty flower

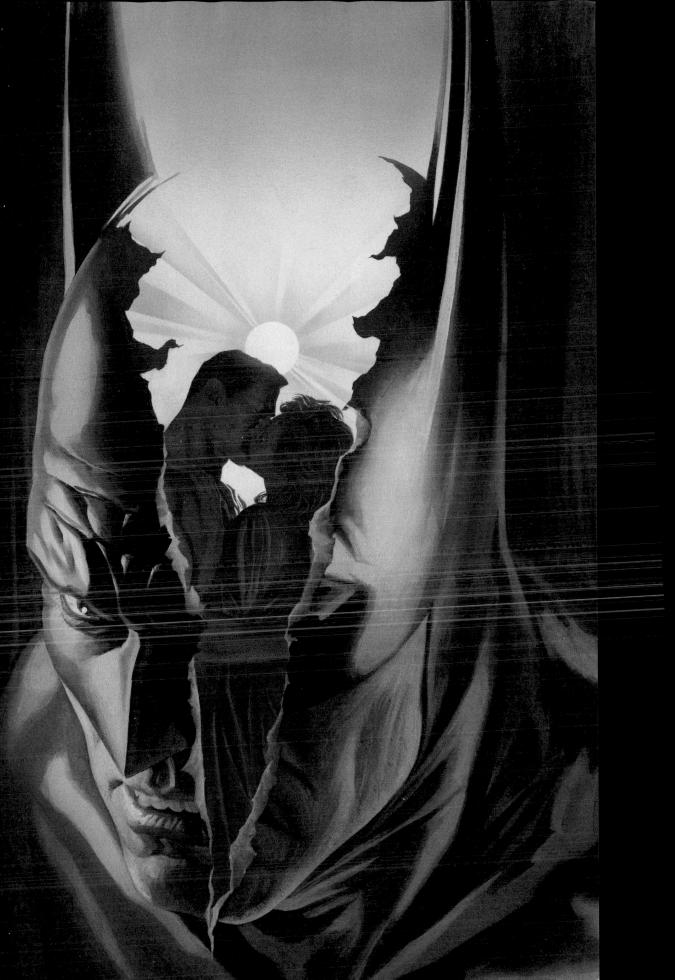

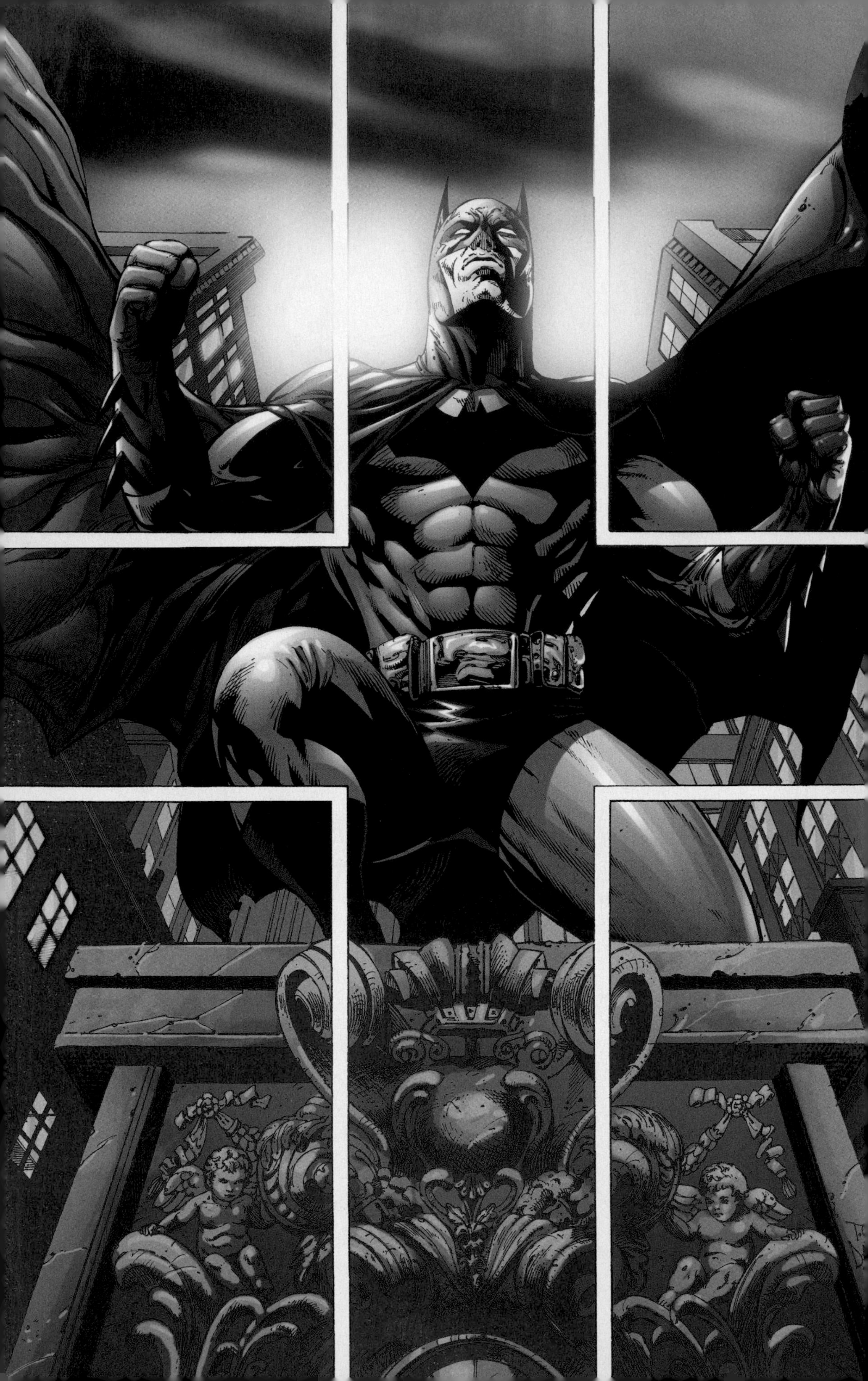

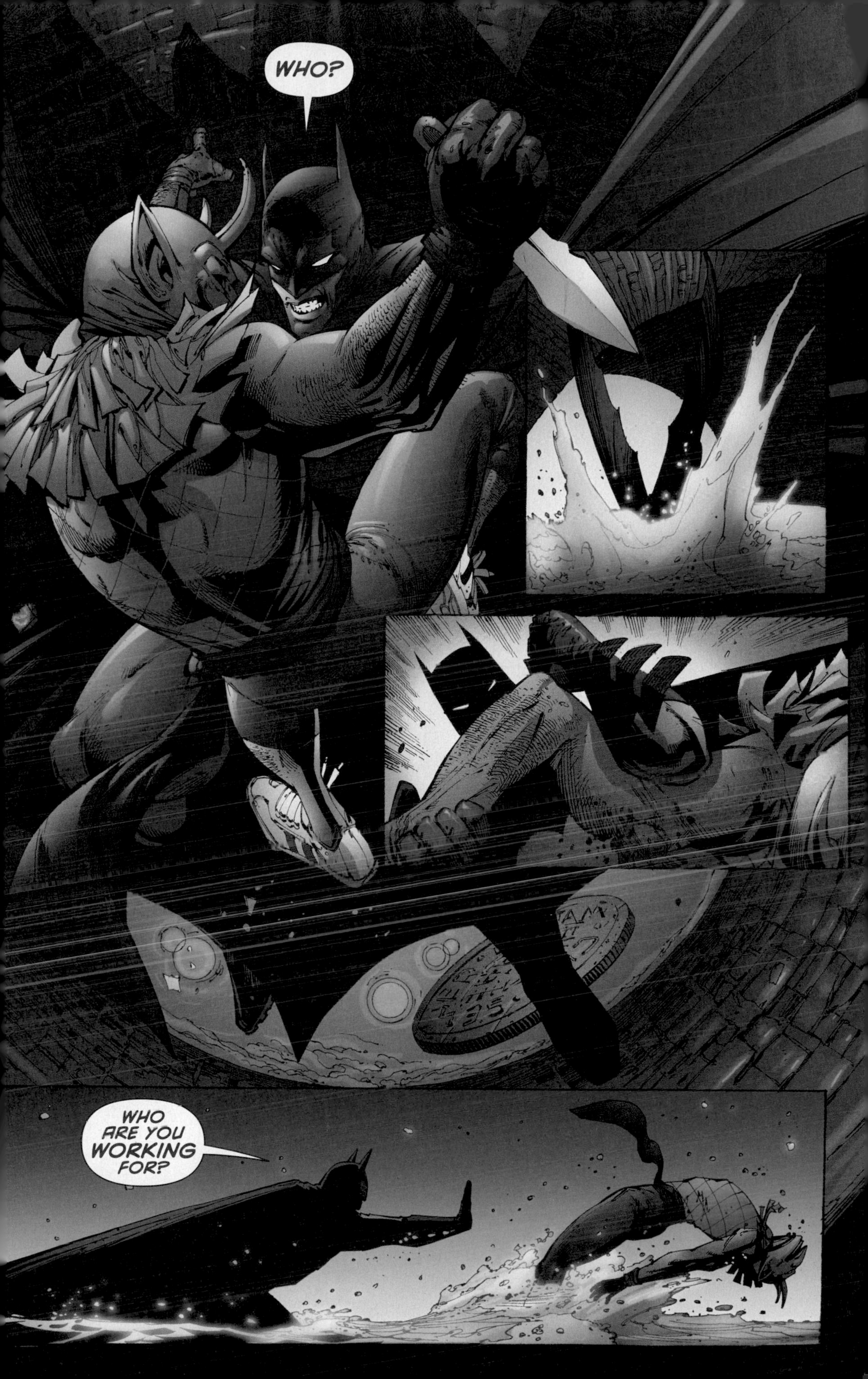
WHO?
WHO ARE YOU WORKING FOR?

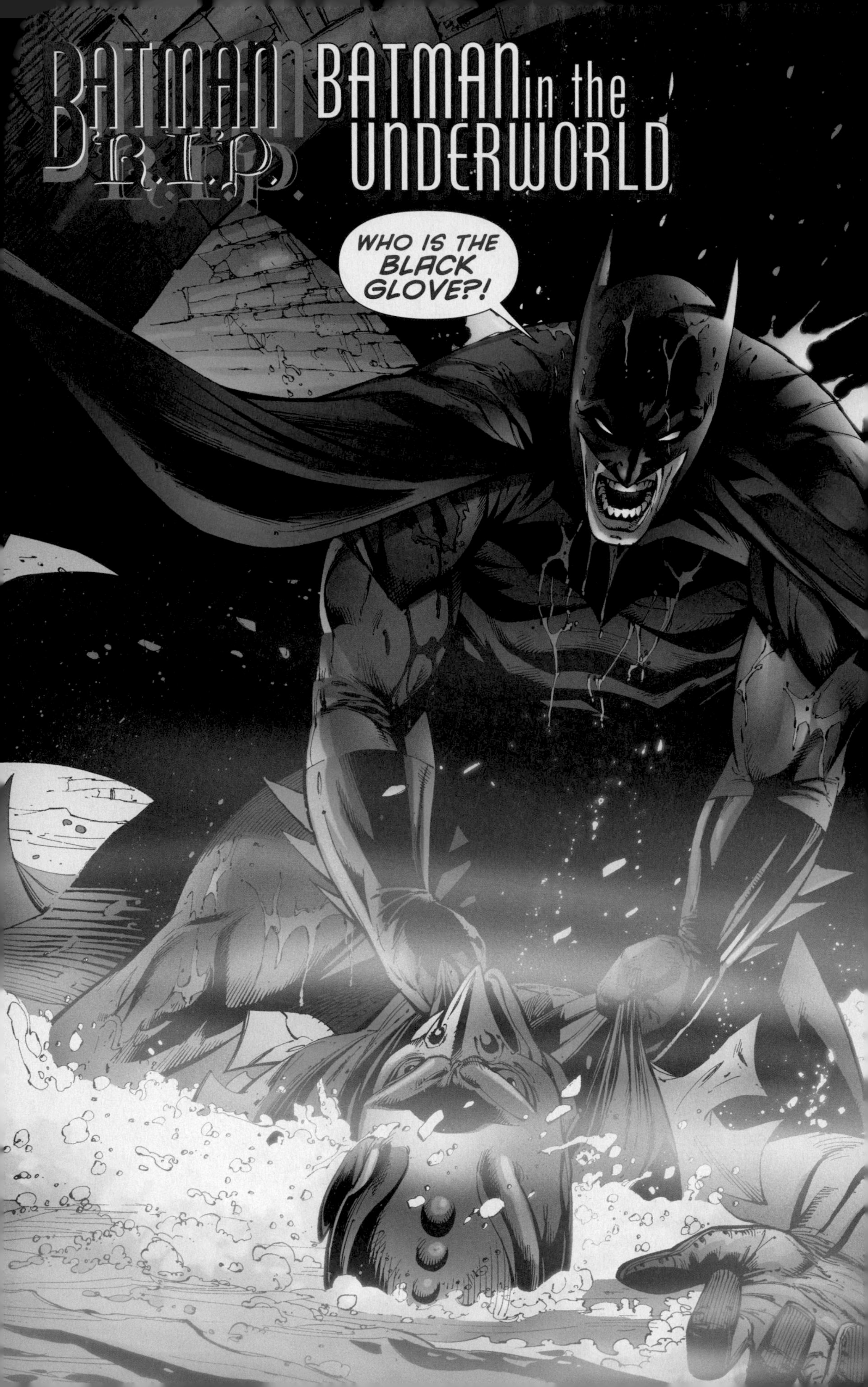
BATMAN R.I.P.
BATMAN in the UNDERWORLD
WHO IS THE BLACK GLOVE?!

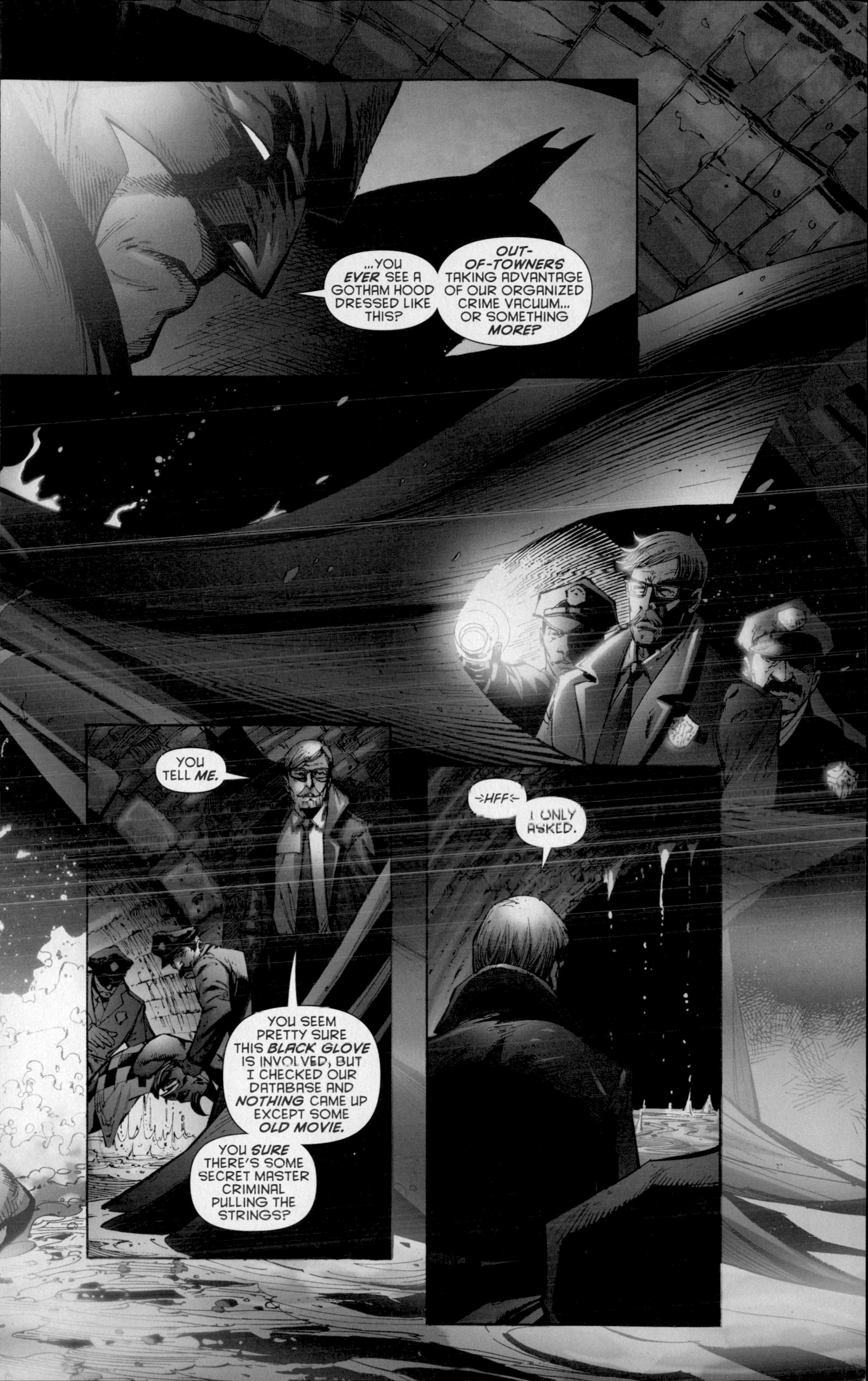
...YOU EVER SEE A GOTHAM HOOD DRESSED LIKE THIS?
OUT-OF-TOWNERS TAKING ADVANTAGE OF OUR ORGANIZED CRIME VACUUM... OR SOMETHING MORE?
YOU TELL ME.
-HFF-
I ONLY ASKED.
YOU SEEM PRETTY SURE THIS BLACK GLOVE IS INVOLVED, BUT I CHECKED OUR DATABASE AND NOTHING CAME UP EXCEPT SOME OLD MOVIE.
YOU SURE THERE'S SOME SECRET MASTER CRIMINAL PULLING THE STRINGS?

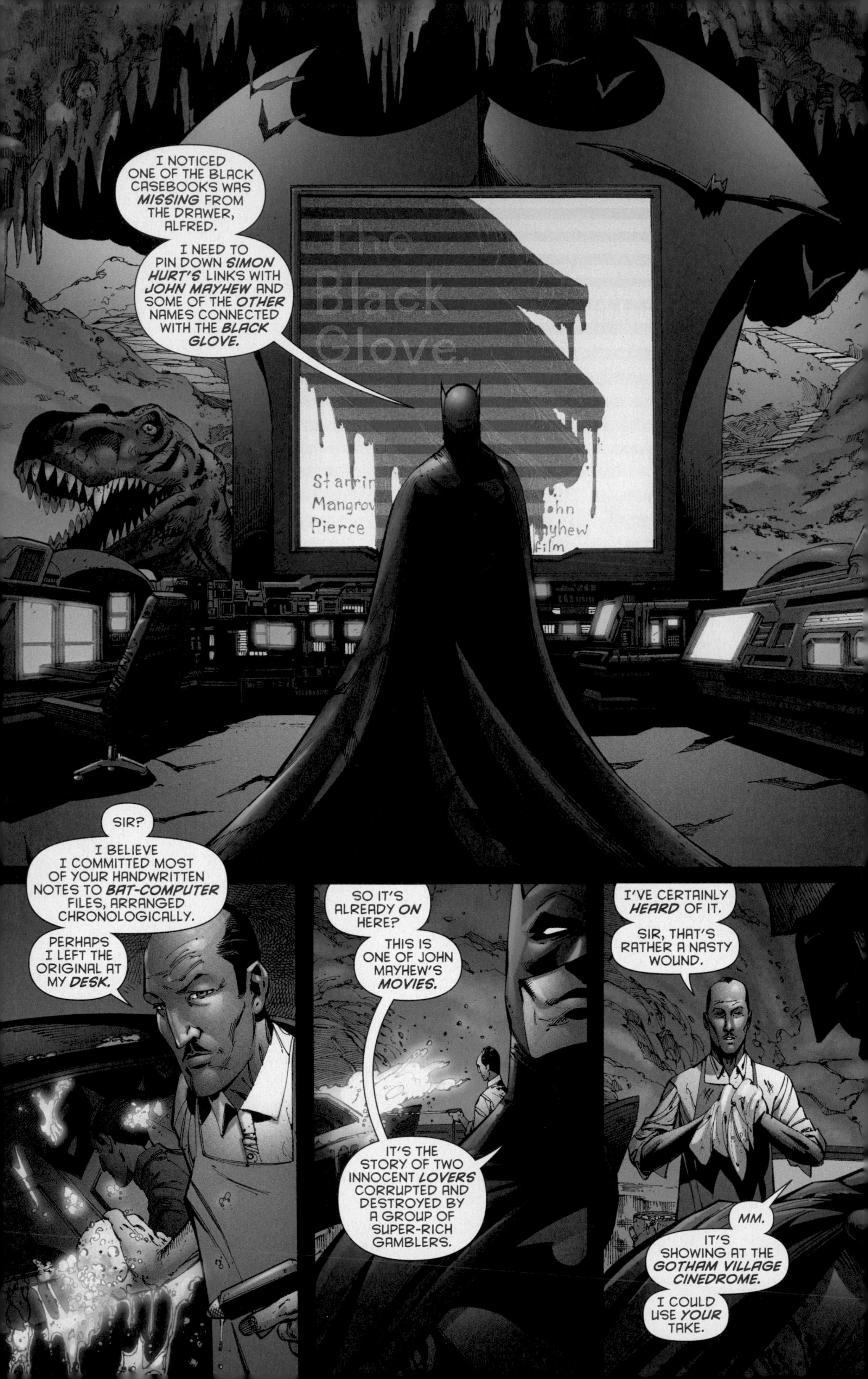

I NOTICED ONE OF THE BLACK CASEBOOKS WAS MISSING FROM THE DRAWER, ALFRED.
I NEED TO PIN DOWN SIMON HURT'S LINKS WITH JOHN MAYHEW AND SOME OF THE OTHER NAMES CONNECTED WITH THE BLACK GLOVE.
The Black Glove.
Starrin
Mangrov
Pierce
John
Mayhew
film
SIR?
I BELIEVE I COMMITTED MOST OF YOUR HANDWRITTEN NOTES TO BAT-COMPUTER FILES, ARRANGED CHRONOLOGICALLY.
PERHAPS I LEFT THE ORIGINAL AT MY DESK.
SO IT'S ALREADY ON HERE?
THIS IS ONE OF JOHN MAYHEW'S MOVIES.
IT'S THE STORY OF TWO INNOCENT LOVERS CORRUPTED AND DESTROYED BY A GROUP OF SUPER-RICH GAMBLERS.
I'VE CERTAINLY HEARD OF IT.
SIR, THAT'S RATHER A NASTY WOUND.
MM.
IT'S SHOWING AT THE GOTHAM VILLAGE CINEDROME.
I COULD USE YOUR TAKE.

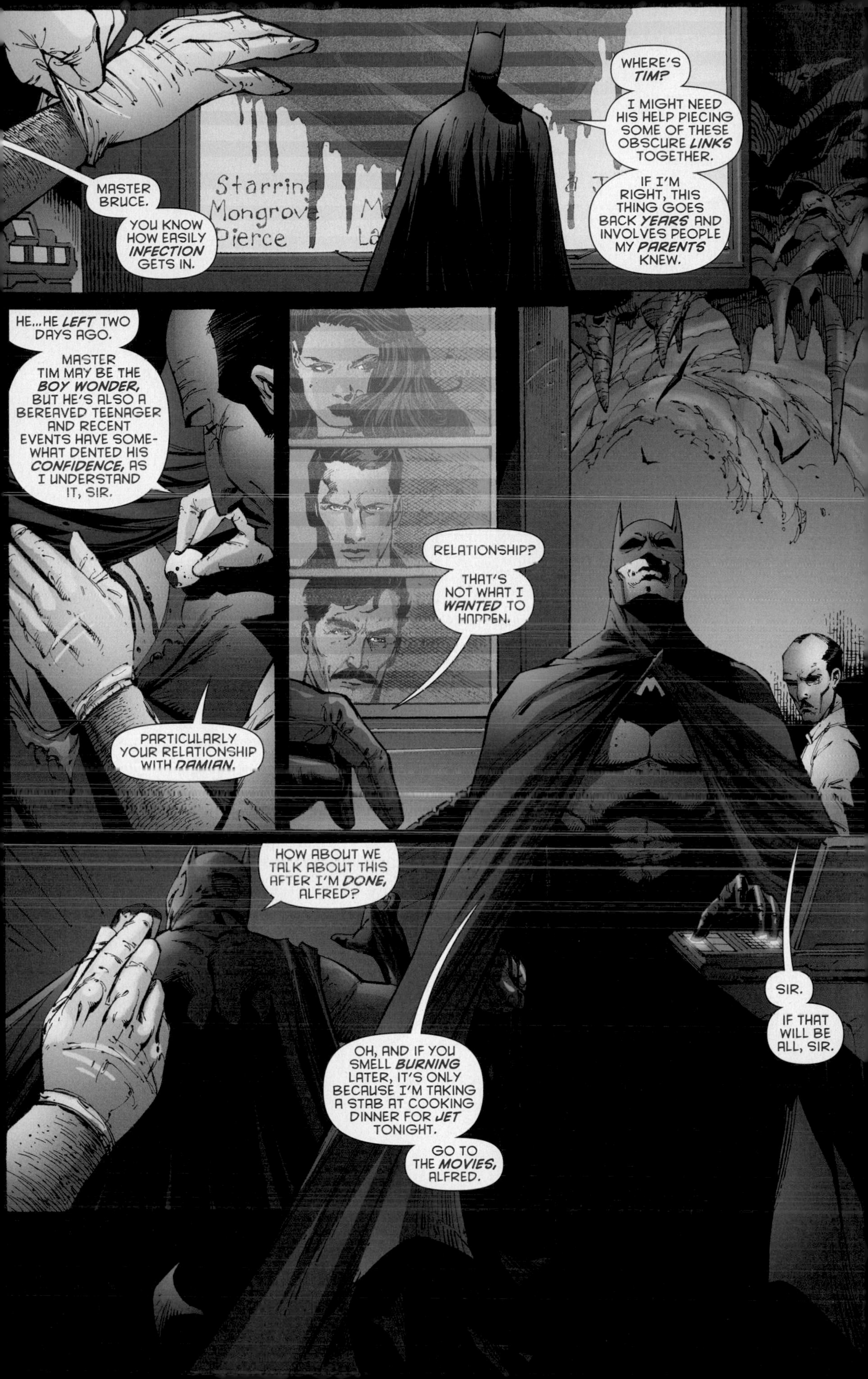
MASTER BRUCE.
YOU KNOW HOW EASILY INFECTION GETS IN.
Starring Mongrove Pierce
WHERE'S TIM?
I MIGHT NEED HIS HELP PIECING SOME OF THESE OBSCURE LINKS TOGETHER.
IF I'M RIGHT, THIS THING GOES BACK YEARS AND INVOLVES PEOPLE MY PARENTS KNEW.
HE...HE LEFT TWO DAYS AGO.
MASTER TIM MAY BE THE BOY WONDER, BUT HE'S ALSO A BEREAVED TEENAGER AND RECENT EVENTS HAVE SOMEWHAT DENTED HIS CONFIDENCE, AS I UNDERSTAND IT, SIR.
PARTICULARLY YOUR RELATIONSHIP WITH DAMIAN.
RELATIONSHIP?
THAT'S NOT WHAT I WANTED TO HAPPEN.
HOW ABOUT WE TALK ABOUT THIS AFTER I'M DONE, ALFRED?
SIR.
IF THAT WILL BE ALL, SIR.
OH, AND IF YOU SMELL BURNING LATER, IT'S ONLY BECAUSE I'M TAKING A STAB AT COOKING DINNER FOR JET TONIGHT.
GO TO THE MOVIES, ALFRED.

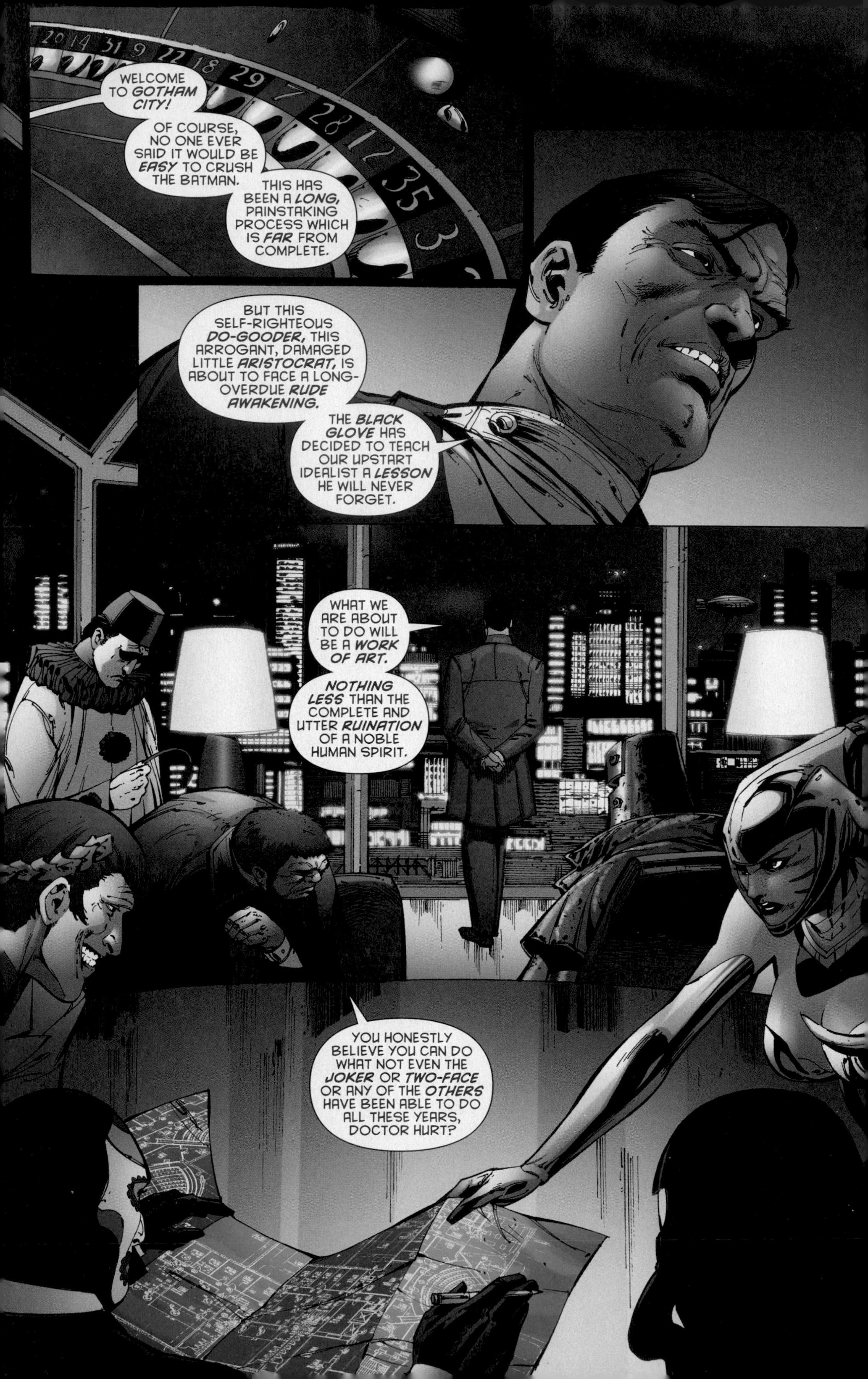
WELCOME TO GOTHAM CITY!
OF COURSE, NO ONE EVER SAID IT WOULD BE EASY TO CRUSH THE BATMAN.
THIS HAS BEEN A LONG, PAINSTAKING PROCESS WHICH IS FAR FROM COMPLETE.
BUT THIS SELF-RIGHTEOUS DO-GOODER, THIS ARROGANT, DAMAGED LITTLE ARISTOCRAT, IS ABOUT TO FACE A LONG-OVERDUE RUDE AWAKENING.
THE BLACK GLOVE HAS DECIDED TO TEACH OUR UPSTART IDEALIST A LESSON HE WILL NEVER FORGET.
WHAT WE ARE ABOUT TO DO WILL BE A WORK OF ART.
NOTHING LESS THAN THE COMPLETE AND UTTER RUINATION OF A NOBLE HUMAN SPIRIT.
YOU HONESTLY BELIEVE YOU CAN DO WHAT NOT EVEN THE JOKER OR TWO-FACE OR ANY OF THE OTHERS HAVE BEEN ABLE TO DO ALL THESE YEARS, DOCTOR HURT?

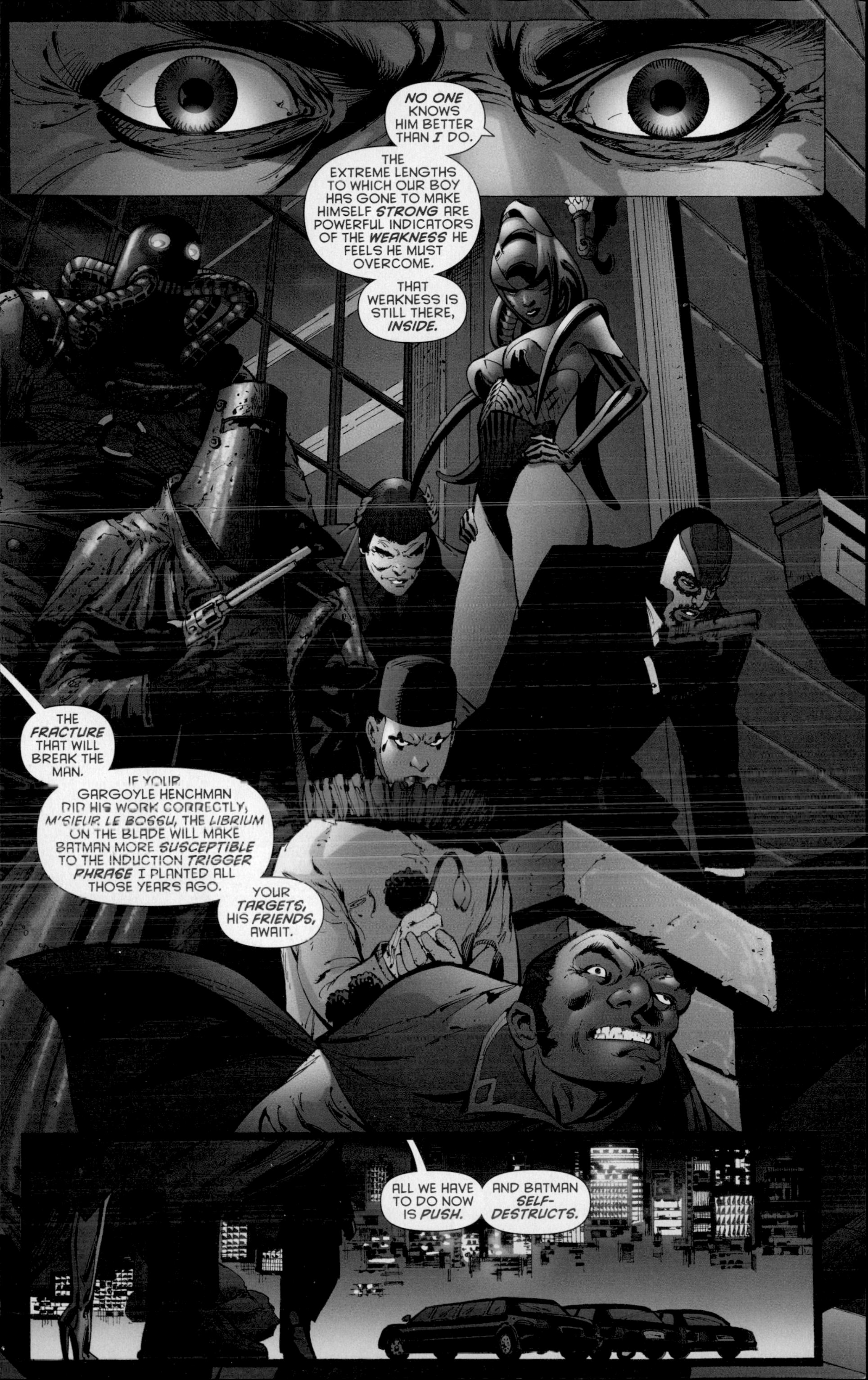
NO ONE KNOWS HIM BETTER THAN I DO.
THE EXTREME LENGTHS TO WHICH OUR BOY HAS GONE TO MAKE HIMSELF STRONG ARE POWERFUL INDICATORS OF THE WEAKNESS HE FEELS HE MUST OVERCOME.
THAT WEAKNESS IS STILL THERE, INSIDE.
THE FRACTURE THAT WILL BREAK THE MAN.
IF YOUR GARGOYLE HENCHMAN DID HIS WORK CORRECTLY, M'SIEUR LE BOSSU, THE LIBRIUM ON THE BLADE WILL MAKE BATMAN MORE SUSCEPTIBLE TO THE INDUCTION TRIGGER PHRASE I PLANTED ALL THOSE YEARS AGO.
YOUR TARGETS, HIS FRIENDS, AWAIT.
ALL WE HAVE TO DO NOW IS PUSH.
AND BATMAN SELF-DESTRUCTS.

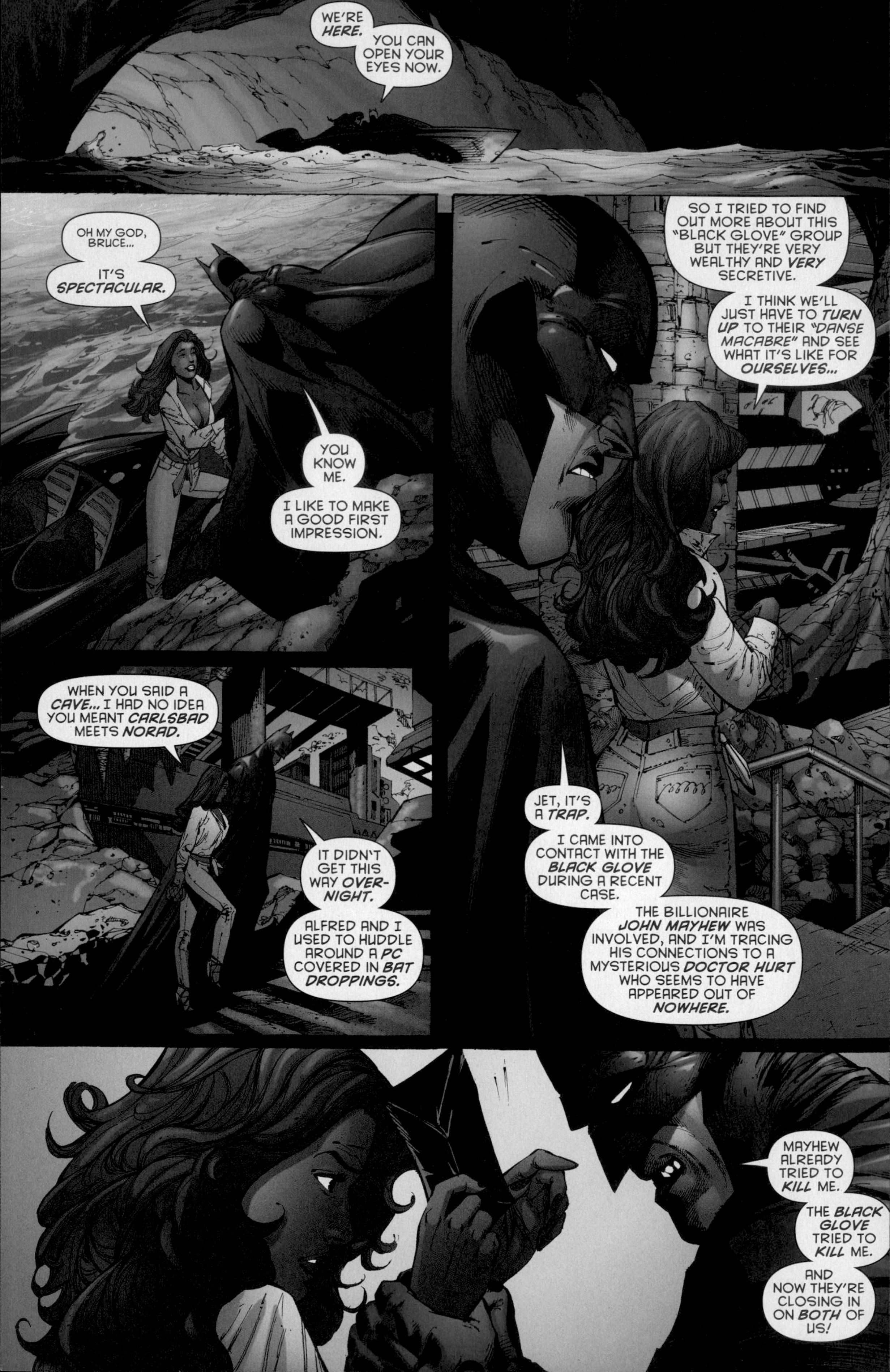
WE'RE HERE.
YOU CAN OPEN YOUR EYES NOW.
OH MY GOD, BRUCE...
IT'S SPECTACULAR.
YOU KNOW ME.
I LIKE TO MAKE A GOOD FIRST IMPRESSION.
SO I TRIED TO FIND OUT MORE ABOUT THIS "BLACK GLOVE" GROUP BUT THEY'RE VERY WEALTHY AND VERY SECRETIVE.
I THINK WE'LL JUST HAVE TO TURN UP TO THEIR "DANSE MACABRE" AND SEE WHAT IT'S LIKE FOR OURSELVES...
WHEN YOU SAID A CAVE... I HAD NO IDEA YOU MEANT CARLSBAD MEETS NORAD.
IT DIDN'T GET THIS WAY OVER-NIGHT.
ALFRED AND I USED TO HUDDLE AROUND A PC COVERED IN BAT DROPPINGS.
JET, IT'S A TRAP.
I CAME INTO CONTACT WITH THE BLACK GLOVE DURING A RECENT CASE.
THE BILLIONAIRE JOHN MAYHEW WAS INVOLVED, AND I'M TRACING HIS CONNECTIONS TO A MYSTERIOUS DOCTOR HURT WHO SEEMS TO HAVE APPEARED OUT OF NOWHERE.
MAYHEW ALREADY TRIED TO KILL ME.
THE BLACK GLOVE TRIED TO KILL ME.
AND NOW THEY'RE CLOSING IN ON BOTH OF US!

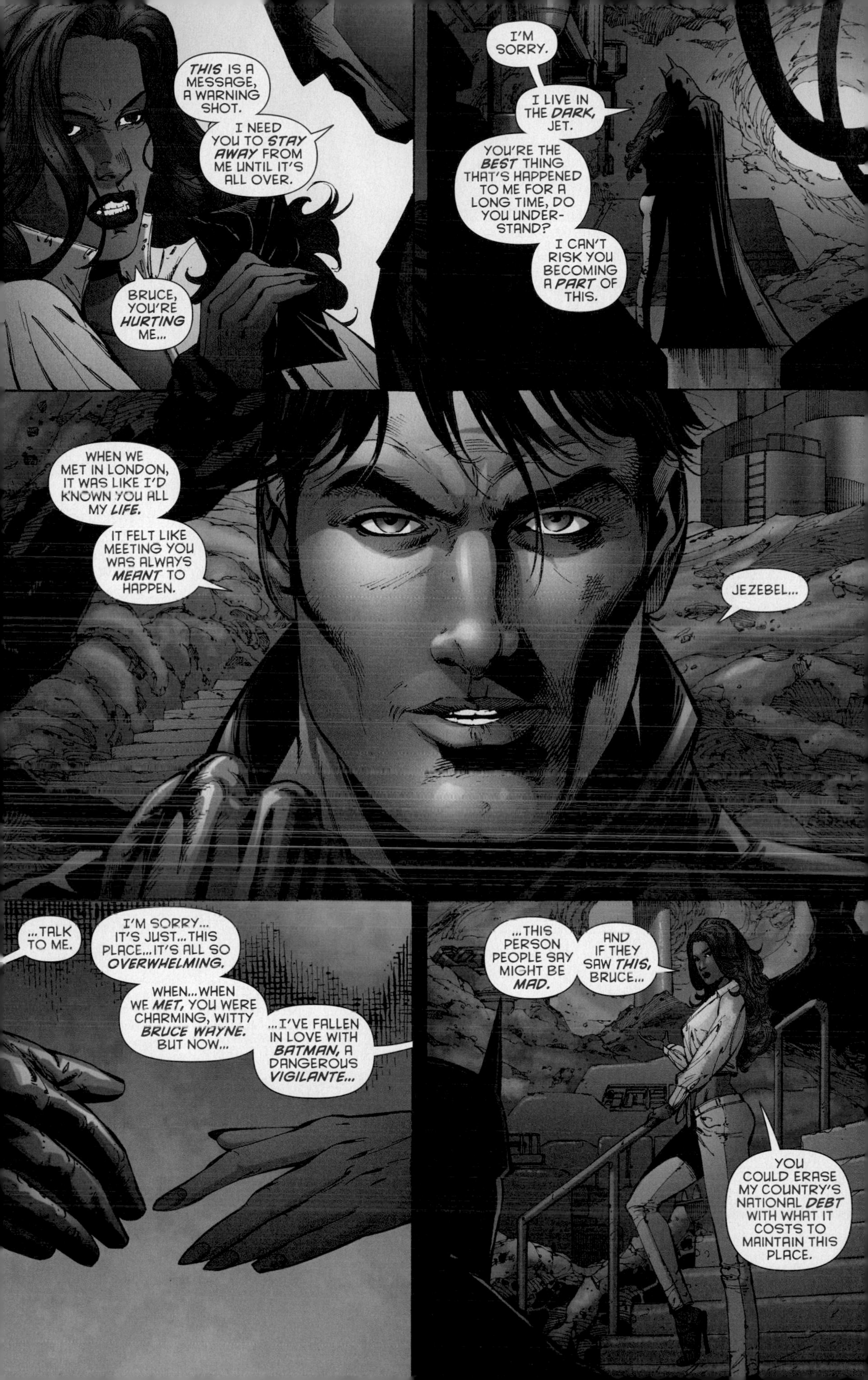
THIS IS A MESSAGE, A WARNING SHOT.
I NEED YOU TO STAY AWAY FROM ME UNTIL IT'S ALL OVER.
BRUCE, YOU'RE HURTING ME...
I'M SORRY.
I LIVE IN THE DARK, JET.
YOU'RE THE BEST THING THAT'S HAPPENED TO ME FOR A LONG TIME, DO YOU UNDER-STAND?
I CAN'T RISK YOU BECOMING A PART OF THIS.
WHEN WE MET IN LONDON, IT WAS LIKE I'D KNOWN YOU ALL MY LIFE.
IT FELT LIKE MEETING YOU WAS ALWAYS MEANT TO HAPPEN.
JEZEBEL...
...TALK TO ME.
I'M SORRY... IT'S JUST... THIS PLACE... IT'S ALL SO OVERWHELMING.
WHEN... WHEN WE MET, YOU WERE CHARMING, WITTY BRUCE WAYNE. BUT NOW...
...I'VE FALLEN IN LOVE WITH BATMAN, A DANGEROUS VIGILANTE...
...THIS PERSON PEOPLE SAY MIGHT BE MAD.
AND IF THEY SAW THIS, BRUCE...
YOU COULD ERASE MY COUNTRY'S NATIONAL DEBT WITH WHAT IT COSTS TO MAINTAIN THIS PLACE.

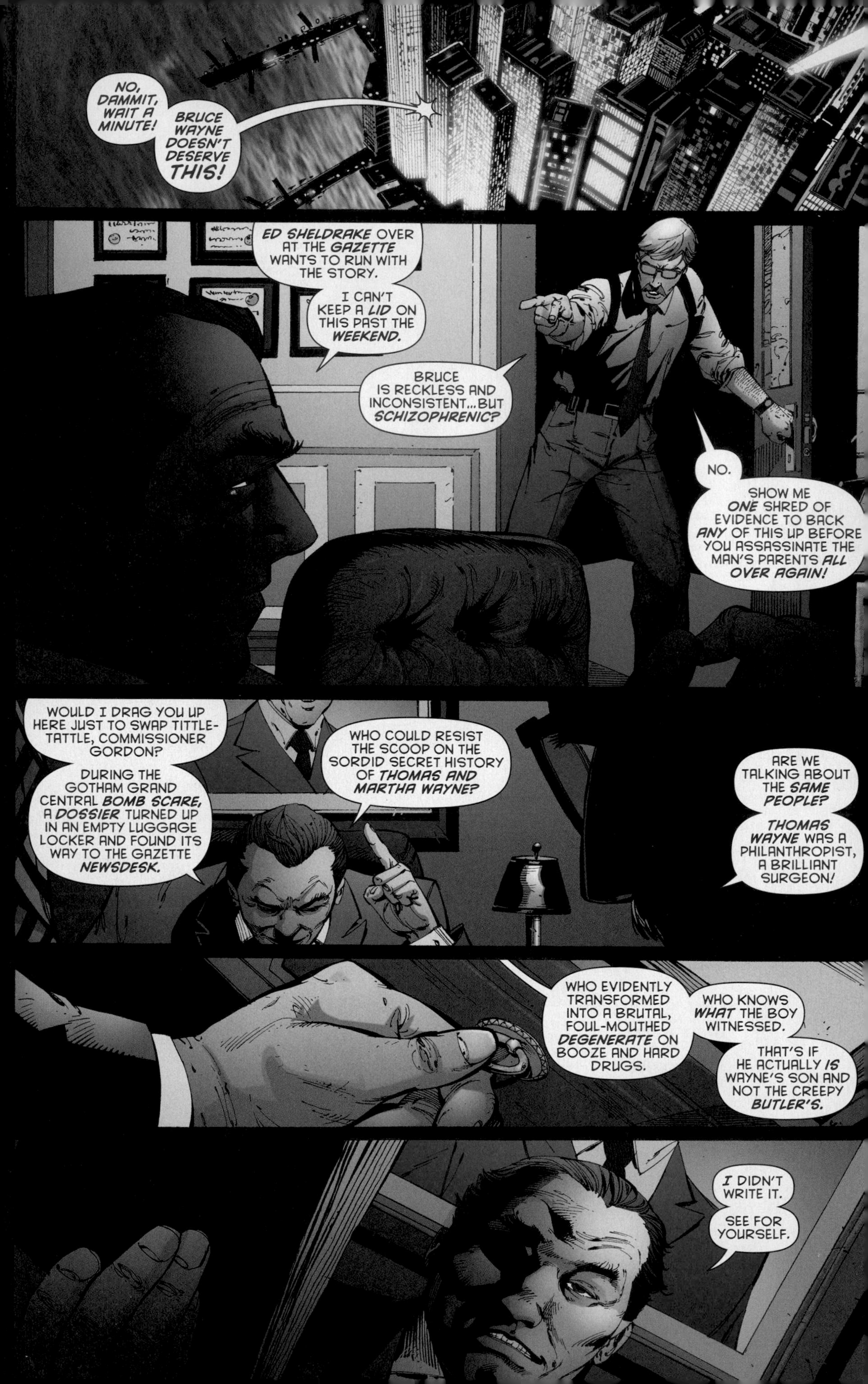
NO, DAMMIT, WAIT A MINUTE!
BRUCE WAYNE DOESN'T DESERVE THIS!
ED SHELDRAKE OVER AT THE GAZETTE WANTS TO RUN WITH THE STORY.
I CAN'T KEEP A LID ON THIS PAST THE WEEKEND.
BRUCE IS RECKLESS AND INCONSISTENT...BUT SCHIZOPHRENIC?
NO.
SHOW ME ONE SHRED OF EVIDENCE TO BACK ANY OF THIS UP BEFORE YOU ASSASSINATE THE MAN'S PARENTS ALL OVER AGAIN!
WOULD I DRAG YOU UP HERE JUST TO SWAP TITTLE-TATTLE, COMMISSIONER GORDON?
DURING THE GOTHAM GRAND CENTRAL BOMB SCARE, A DOSSIER TURNED UP IN AN EMPTY LUGGAGE LOCKER AND FOUND ITS WAY TO THE GAZETTE NEWSDESK.
WHO COULD RESIST THE SCOOP ON THE SORDID SECRET HISTORY OF THOMAS AND MARTHA WAYNE?
ARE WE TALKING ABOUT THE SAME PEOPLE?
THOMAS WAYNE WAS A PHILANTHROPIST, A BRILLIANT SURGEON!
WHO EVIDENTLY TRANSFORMED INTO A BRUTAL, FOUL-MOUTHED DEGENERATE ON BOOZE AND HARD DRUGS.
WHO KNOWS WHAT THE BOY WITNESSED.
THAT'S IF HE ACTUALLY IS WAYNE'S SON AND NOT THE CREEPY BUTLER'S.
I DIDN'T WRITE IT.
SEE FOR YOURSELF.

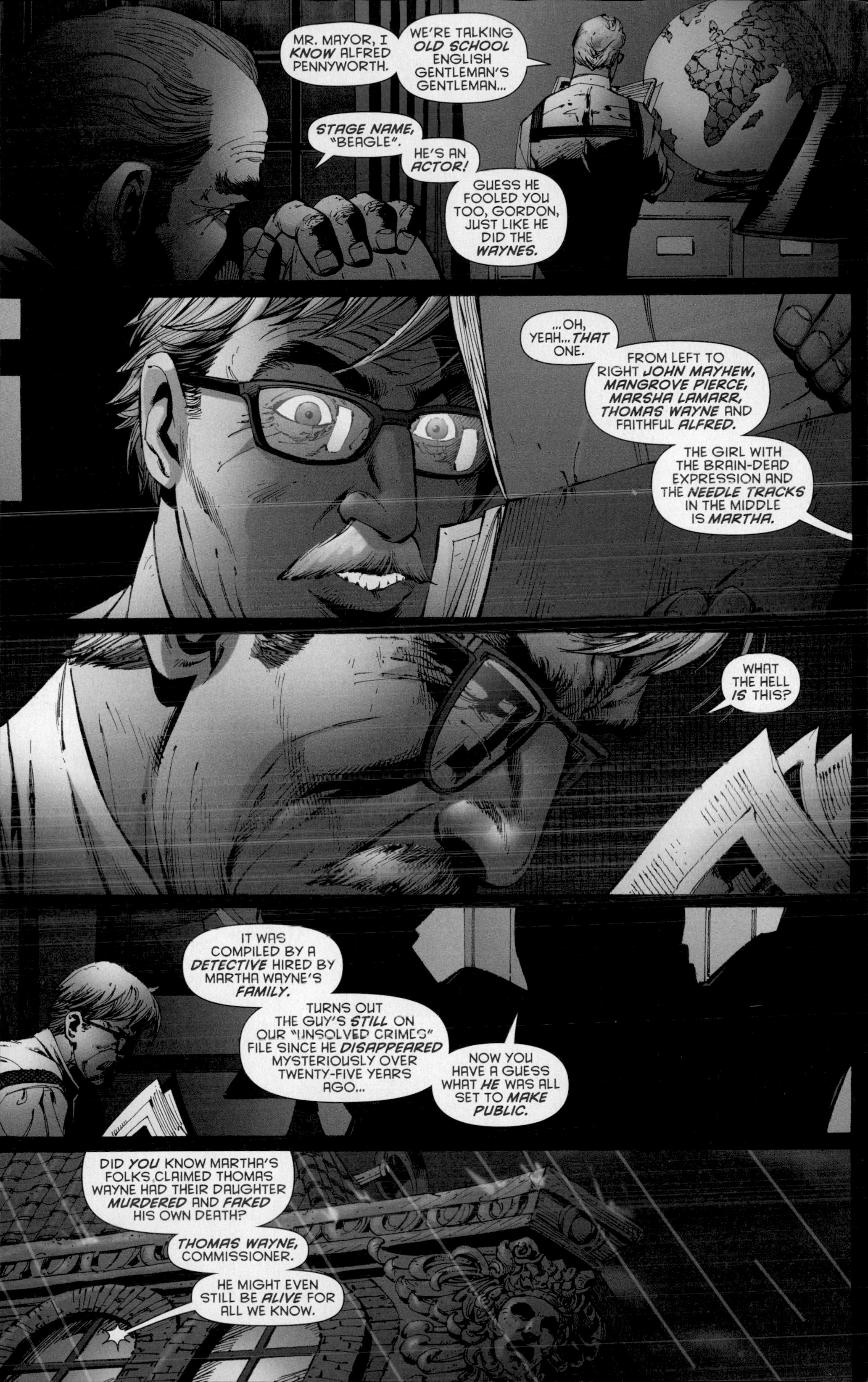
MR. MAYOR, I KNOW ALFRED PENNYWORTH.
WE'RE TALKING OLD SCHOOL ENGLISH GENTLEMAN'S GENTLEMAN...
STAGE NAME, "BEAGLE".
HE'S AN ACTOR!
GUESS HE FOOLED YOU TOO, GORDON, JUST LIKE HE DID THE WAYNES.
...OH, YEAH...THAT ONE.
FROM LEFT TO RIGHT JOHN MAYHEW, MANGROVE PIERCE, MARSHA LAMARR, THOMAS WAYNE AND FAITHFUL ALFRED.
THE GIRL WITH THE BRAIN-DEAD EXPRESSION AND THE NEEDLE TRACKS IN THE MIDDLE IS MARTHA.
WHAT THE HELL IS THIS?
IT WAS COMPILED BY A DETECTIVE HIRED BY MARTHA WAYNE'S FAMILY.
TURNS OUT THE GUY'S STILL ON OUR "UNSOLVED CRIMES" FILE SINCE HE DISAPPEARED MYSTERIOUSLY OVER TWENTY-FIVE YEARS AGO...
NOW YOU HAVE A GUESS WHAT HE WAS ALL SET TO MAKE PUBLIC.
DID YOU KNOW MARTHA'S FOLKS CLAIMED THOMAS WAYNE HAD THEIR DAUGHTER MURDERED AND FAKED HIS OWN DEATH?
THOMAS WAYNE, COMMISSIONER.
HE MIGHT EVEN STILL BE ALIVE FOR ALL WE KNOW.

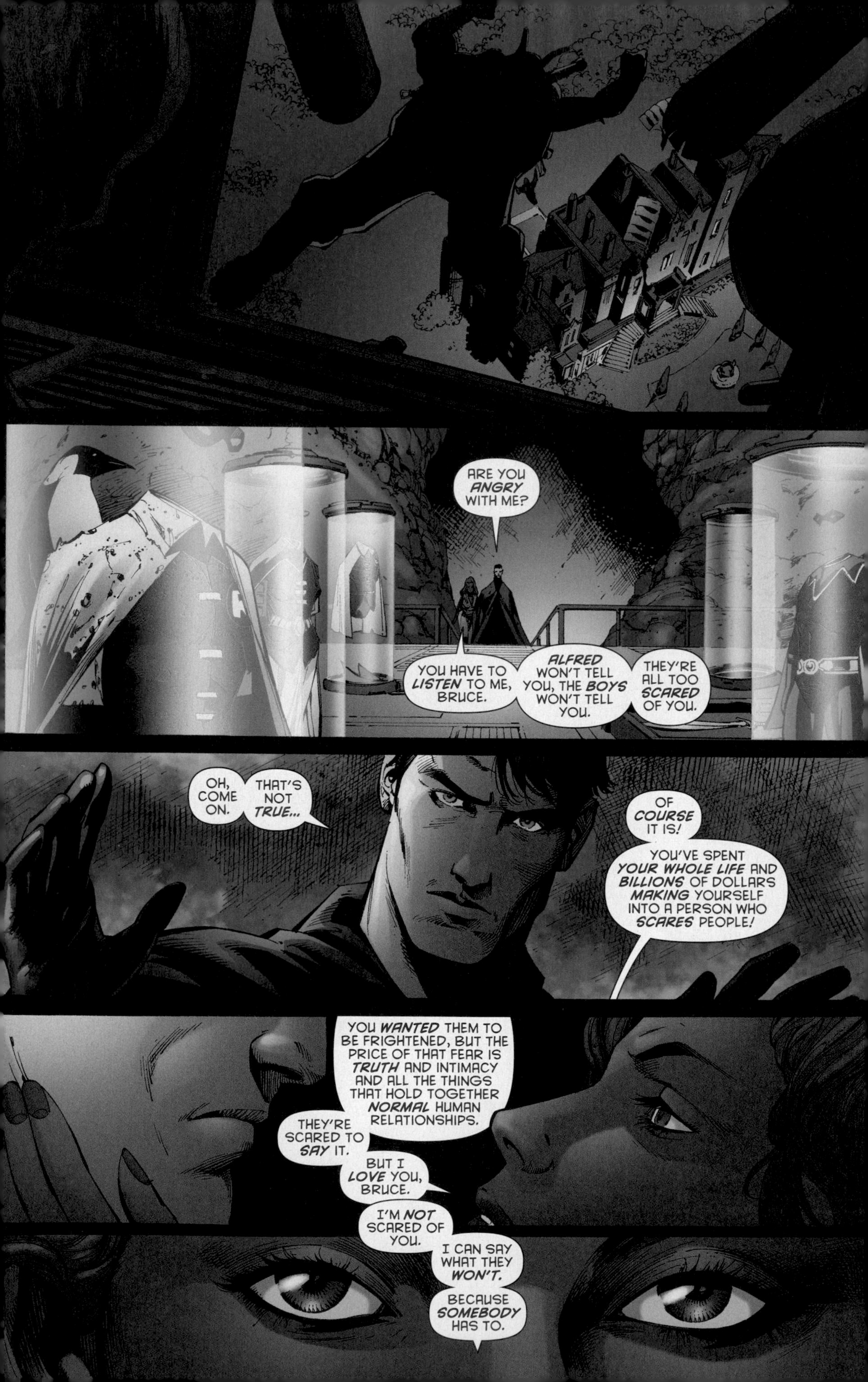
ARE YOU ANGRY WITH ME?
YOU HAVE TO LISTEN TO ME, BRUCE.
ALFRED WON'T TELL YOU, THE BOYS WON'T TELL YOU.
THEY'RE ALL TOO SCARED OF YOU.
OH, COME ON.
THAT'S NOT TRUE...
OF COURSE IT IS!
YOU'VE SPENT YOUR WHOLE LIFE AND BILLIONS OF DOLLARS MAKING YOURSELF INTO A PERSON WHO SCARES PEOPLE!
YOU WANTED THEM TO BE FRIGHTENED, BUT THE PRICE OF THAT FEAR IS TRUTH AND INTIMACY AND ALL THE THINGS THAT HOLD TOGETHER NORMAL HUMAN RELATIONSHIPS.
THEY'RE SCARED TO SAY IT.
BUT I LOVE YOU, BRUCE.
I'M NOT SCARED OF YOU.
I CAN SAY WHAT THEY WON'T.
BECAUSE SOMEBODY HAS TO.

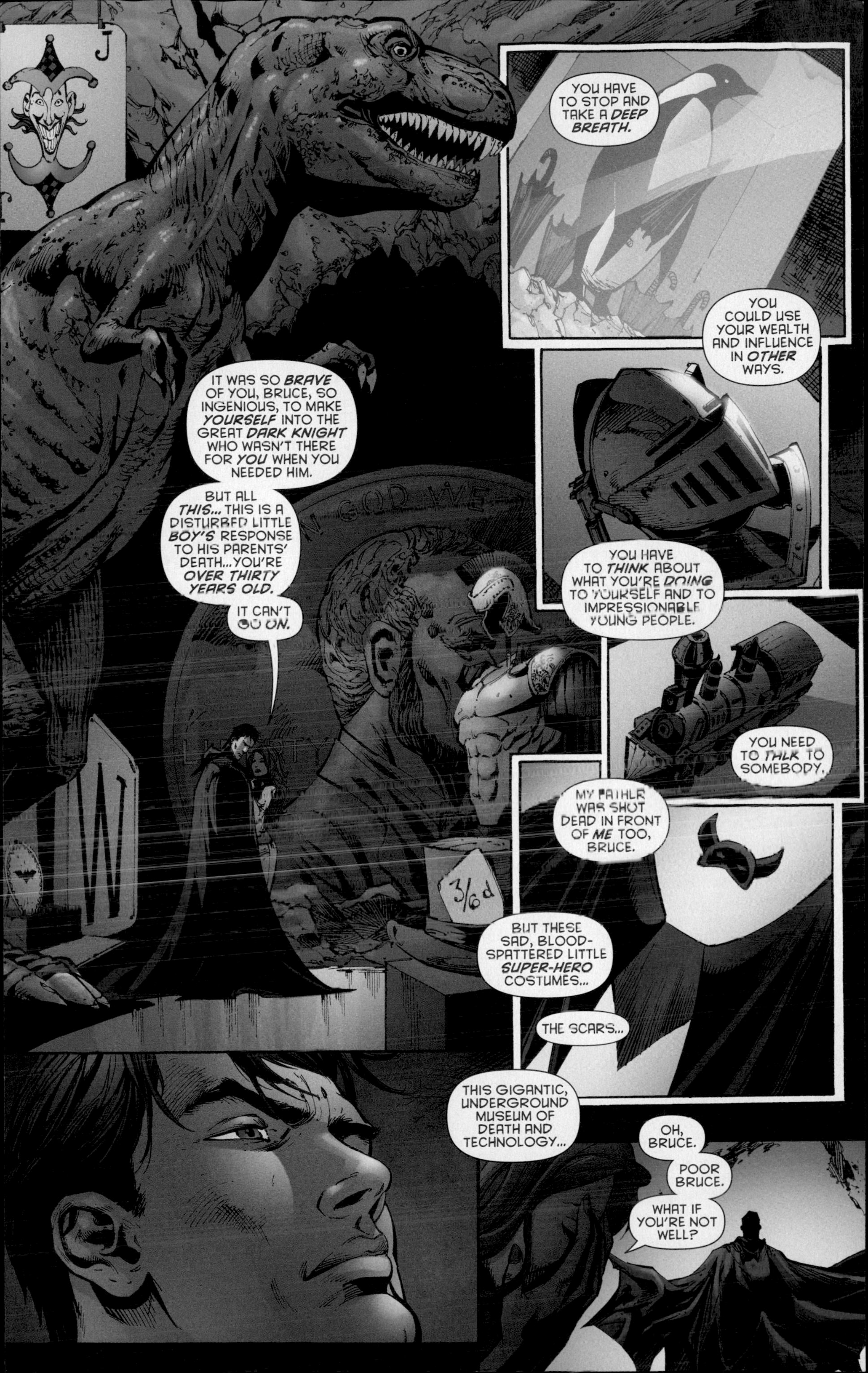
YOU HAVE TO STOP AND TAKE A DEEP BREATH.
YOU COULD USE YOUR WEALTH AND INFLUENCE IN OTHER WAYS.
IT WAS SO BRAVE OF YOU, BRUCE, SO INGENIOUS, TO MAKE YOURSELF INTO THE GREAT DARK KNIGHT WHO WASN'T THERE FOR YOU WHEN YOU NEEDED HIM.
BUT ALL THIS... THIS IS A DISTURBED LITTLE BOY'S RESPONSE TO HIS PARENTS' DEATH...YOU'RE OVER THIRTY YEARS OLD.
IT CAN'T GO ON.
YOU HAVE TO THINK ABOUT WHAT YOU'RE DOING TO YOURSELF AND TO IMPRESSIONABLE YOUNG PEOPLE.
YOU NEED TO TALK TO SOMEBODY.
MY FATHER WAS SHOT DEAD IN FRONT OF ME TOO, BRUCE.
BUT THESE SAD, BLOOD-SPATTERED LITTLE SUPER-HERO COSTUMES...
THE SCARS...
THIS GIGANTIC, UNDERGROUND MUSEUM OF DEATH AND TECHNOLOGY...
OH, BRUCE.
POOR BRUCE.
WHAT IF YOU'RE NOT WELL?

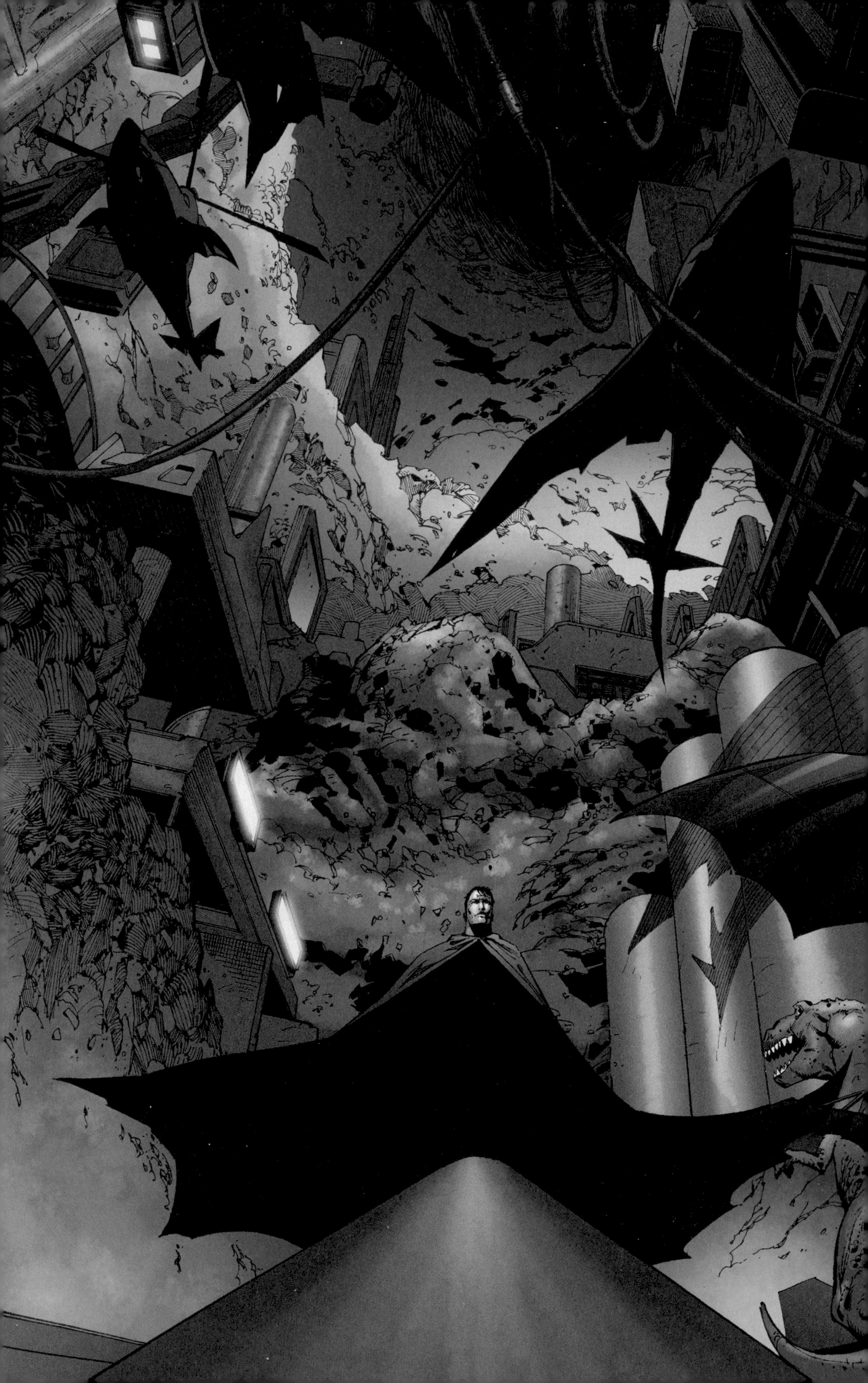

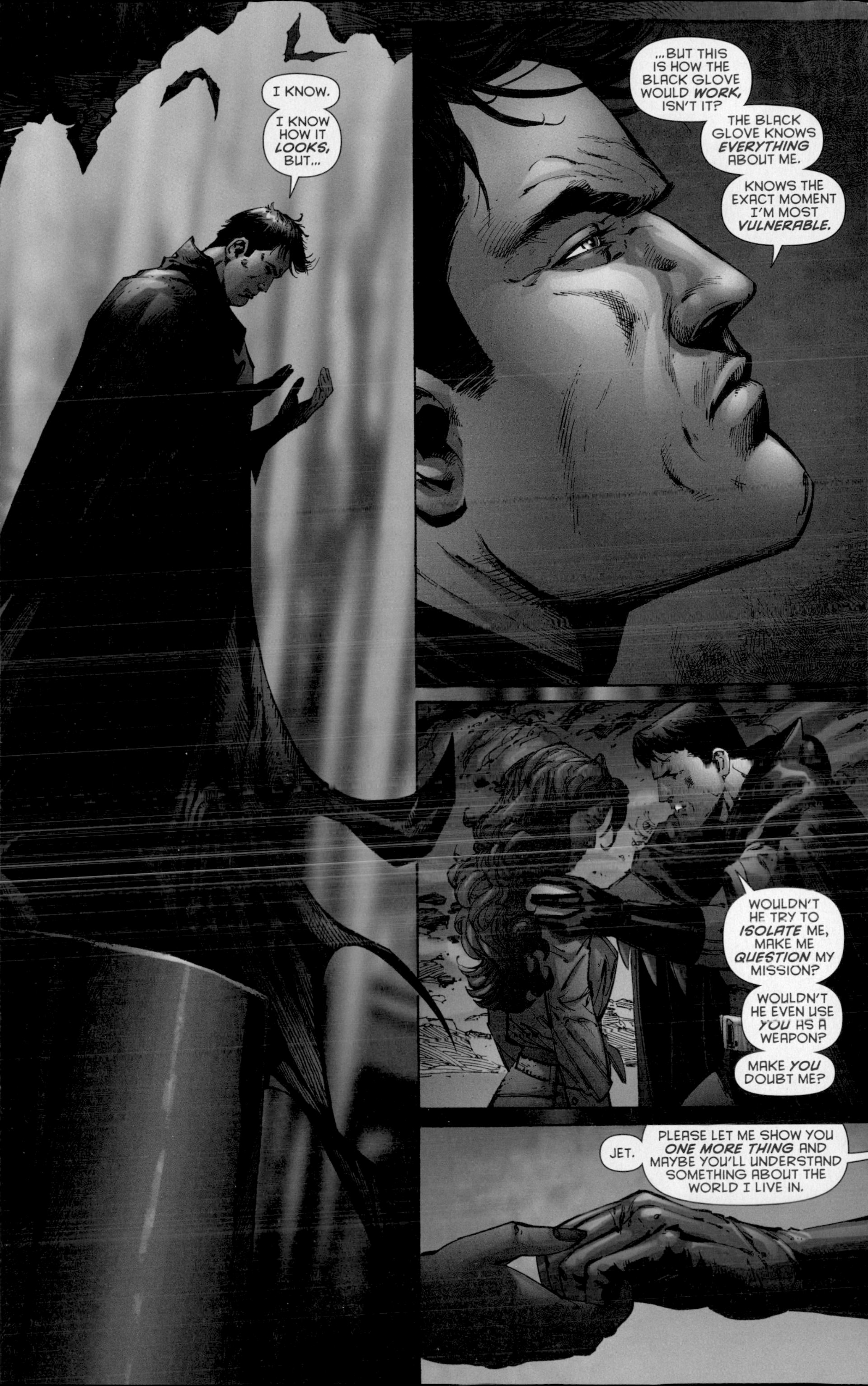
I KNOW.
I KNOW HOW IT *LOOKS,* BUT...
...BUT THIS IS HOW THE BLACK GLOVE WOULD *WORK,* ISN'T IT?
THE BLACK GLOVE KNOWS *EVERYTHING* ABOUT ME.
KNOWS THE EXACT MOMENT I'M MOST *VULNERABLE.*
WOULDN'T HE TRY TO *ISOLATE* ME, MAKE ME *QUESTION* MY MISSION?
WOULDN'T HE EVEN USE *YOU* AS A WEAPON?
MAKE *YOU* DOUBT ME?
JET.
PLEASE LET ME SHOW YOU *ONE MORE THING* AND MAYBE YOU'LL UNDERSTAND SOMETHING ABOUT THE WORLD I LIVE IN.

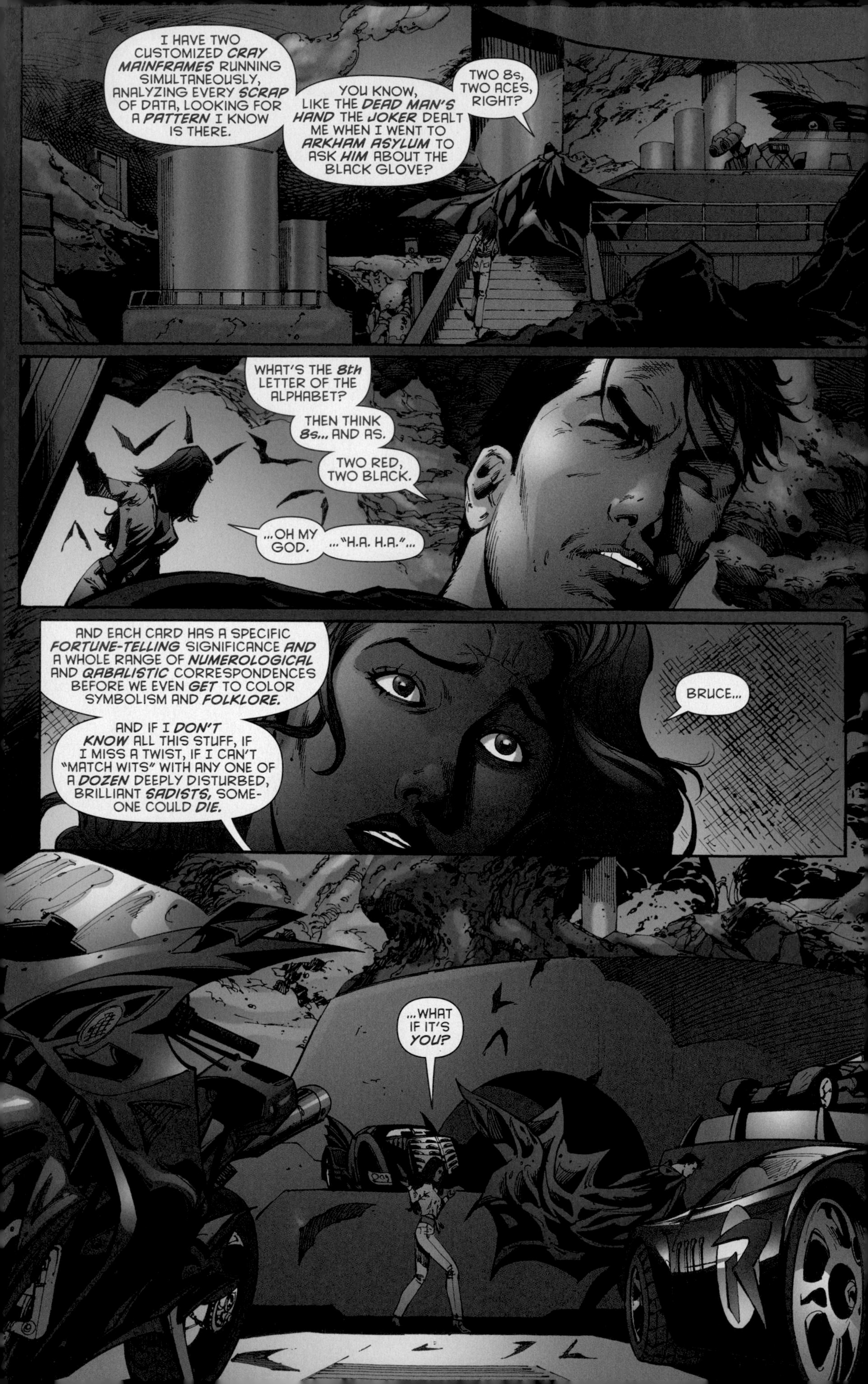
I HAVE TWO CUSTOMIZED CRAY MAINFRAMES RUNNING SIMULTANEOUSLY, ANALYZING EVERY SCRAP OF DATA, LOOKING FOR A PATTERN I KNOW IS THERE.
YOU KNOW, LIKE THE DEAD MAN'S HAND THE JOKER DEALT ME WHEN I WENT TO ARKHAM ASYLUM TO ASK HIM ABOUT THE BLACK GLOVE?
TWO 8s, TWO ACES, RIGHT?
WHAT'S THE 8th LETTER OF THE ALPHABET?
THEN THINK 8s... AND AS.
TWO RED, TWO BLACK.
...OH MY GOD.
..."H.A. H.A."...
AND EACH CARD HAS A SPECIFIC FORTUNE-TELLING SIGNIFICANCE AND A WHOLE RANGE OF NUMEROLOGICAL AND QABALISTIC CORRESPONDENCES BEFORE WE EVEN GET TO COLOR SYMBOLISM AND FOLKLORE.
AND IF I DON'T KNOW ALL THIS STUFF, IF I MISS A TWIST, IF I CAN'T "MATCH WITS" WITH ANY ONE OF A DOZEN DEEPLY DISTURBED, BRILLIANT SADISTS, SOME-ONE COULD DIE.
BRUCE...
...WHAT IF IT'S YOU?

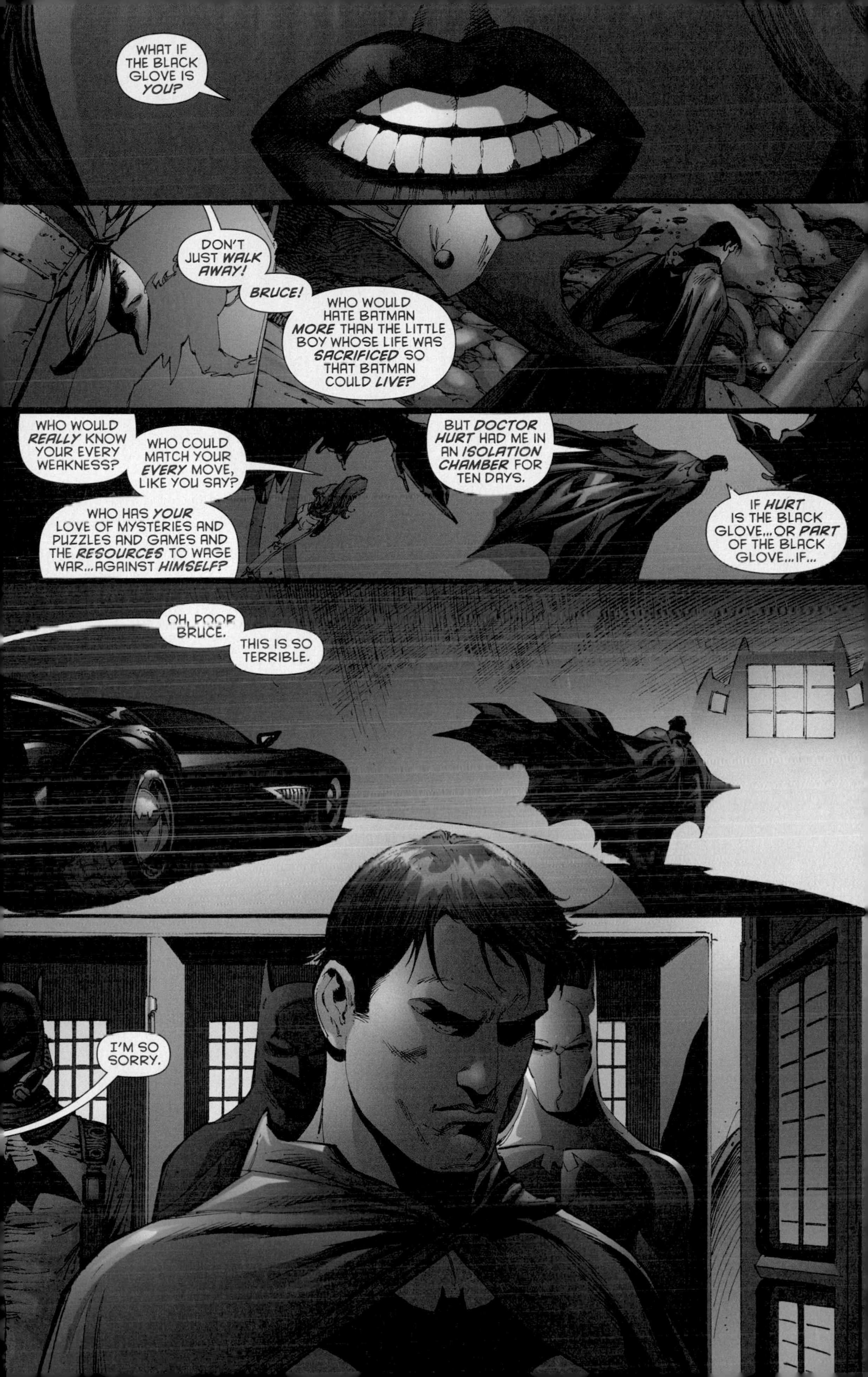
WHAT IF THE BLACK GLOVE IS YOU?
DON'T JUST WALK AWAY!
BRUCE!
WHO WOULD HATE BATMAN MORE THAN THE LITTLE BOY WHOSE LIFE WAS SACRIFICED SO THAT BATMAN COULD LIVE?
WHO WOULD REALLY KNOW YOUR EVERY WEAKNESS?
WHO COULD MATCH YOUR EVERY MOVE, LIKE YOU SAY?
WHO HAS YOUR LOVE OF MYSTERIES AND PUZZLES AND GAMES AND THE RESOURCES TO WAGE WAR...AGAINST HIMSELF?
BUT DOCTOR HURT HAD ME IN AN ISOLATION CHAMBER FOR TEN DAYS.
IF HURT IS THE BLACK GLOVE...OR PART OF THE BLACK GLOVE...IF...
OH, POOR BRUCE.
THIS IS SO TERRIBLE.
I'M SO SORRY.

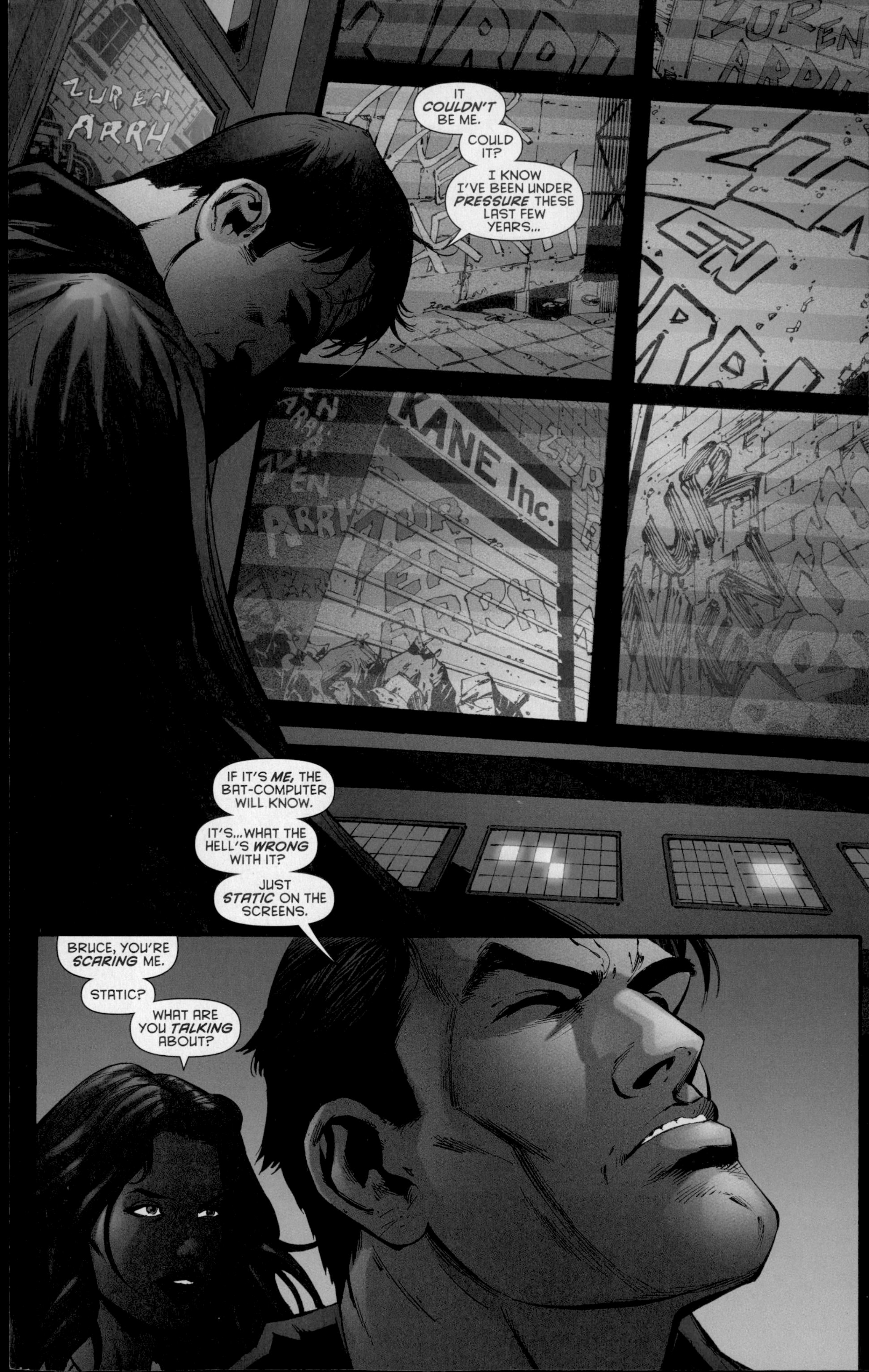
ZUR EN ARRH
IT COULDN'T BE ME.
COULD IT?
I KNOW I'VE BEEN UNDER PRESSURE THESE LAST FEW YEARS...
KANE Inc.
IF IT'S ME, THE BAT-COMPUTER WILL KNOW.
IT'S...WHAT THE HELL'S WRONG WITH IT?
JUST STATIC ON THE SCREENS.
BRUCE, YOU'RE SCARING ME.
STATIC?
WHAT ARE YOU TALKING ABOUT?

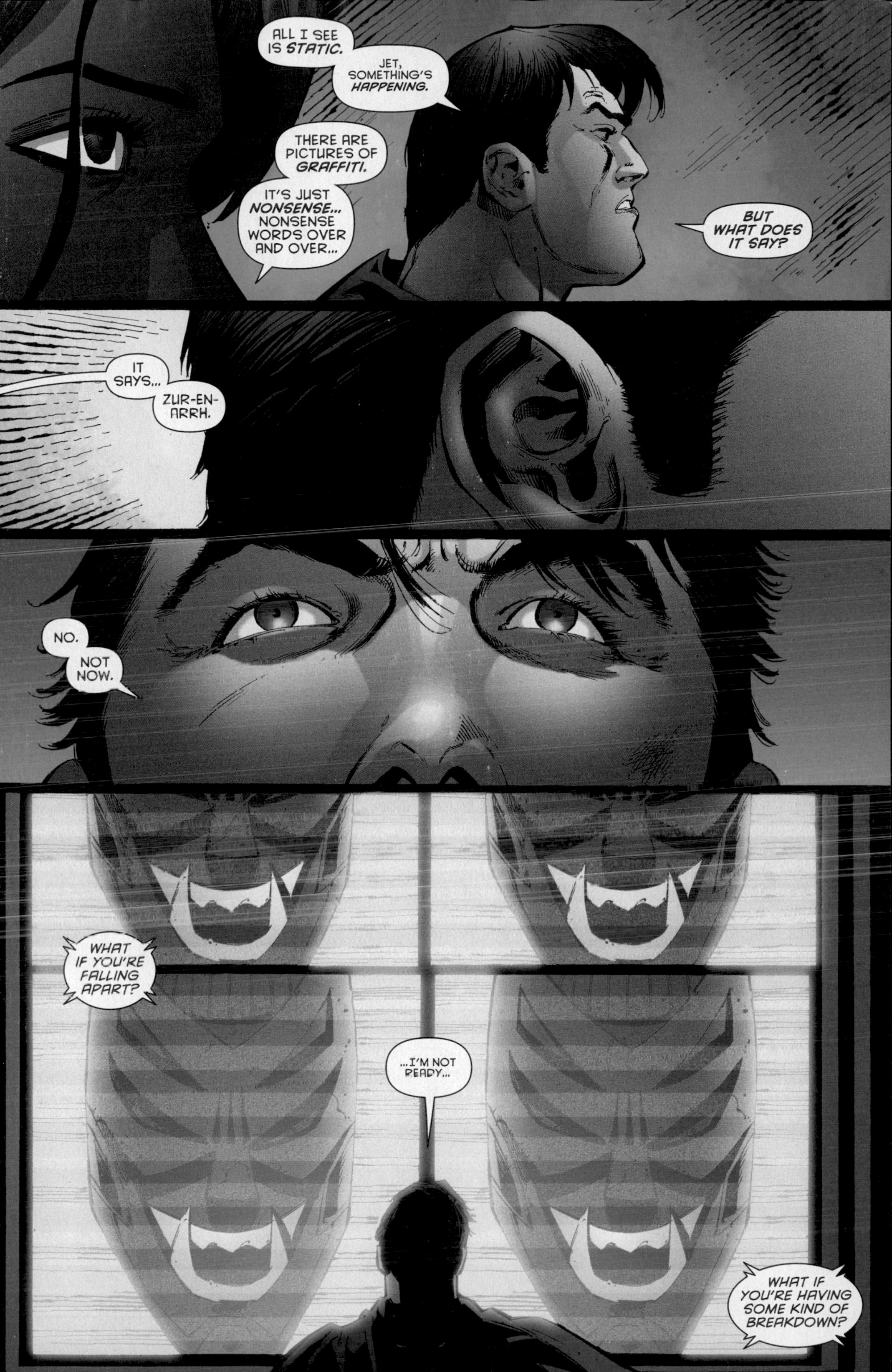
ALL I SEE IS *STATIC.*
JET, SOMETHING'S *HAPPENING.*
THERE ARE PICTURES OF *GRAFFITI.*
IT'S JUST *NONSENSE...* NONSENSE WORDS OVER AND OVER...
BUT WHAT DOES IT SAY?
IT SAYS...
ZUR-EN-ARRH.
NO.
NOT NOW.
WHAT IF YOU'RE FALLING APART?
...I'M NOT READY...
WHAT IF YOU'RE HAVING SOME KIND OF BREAKDOWN?

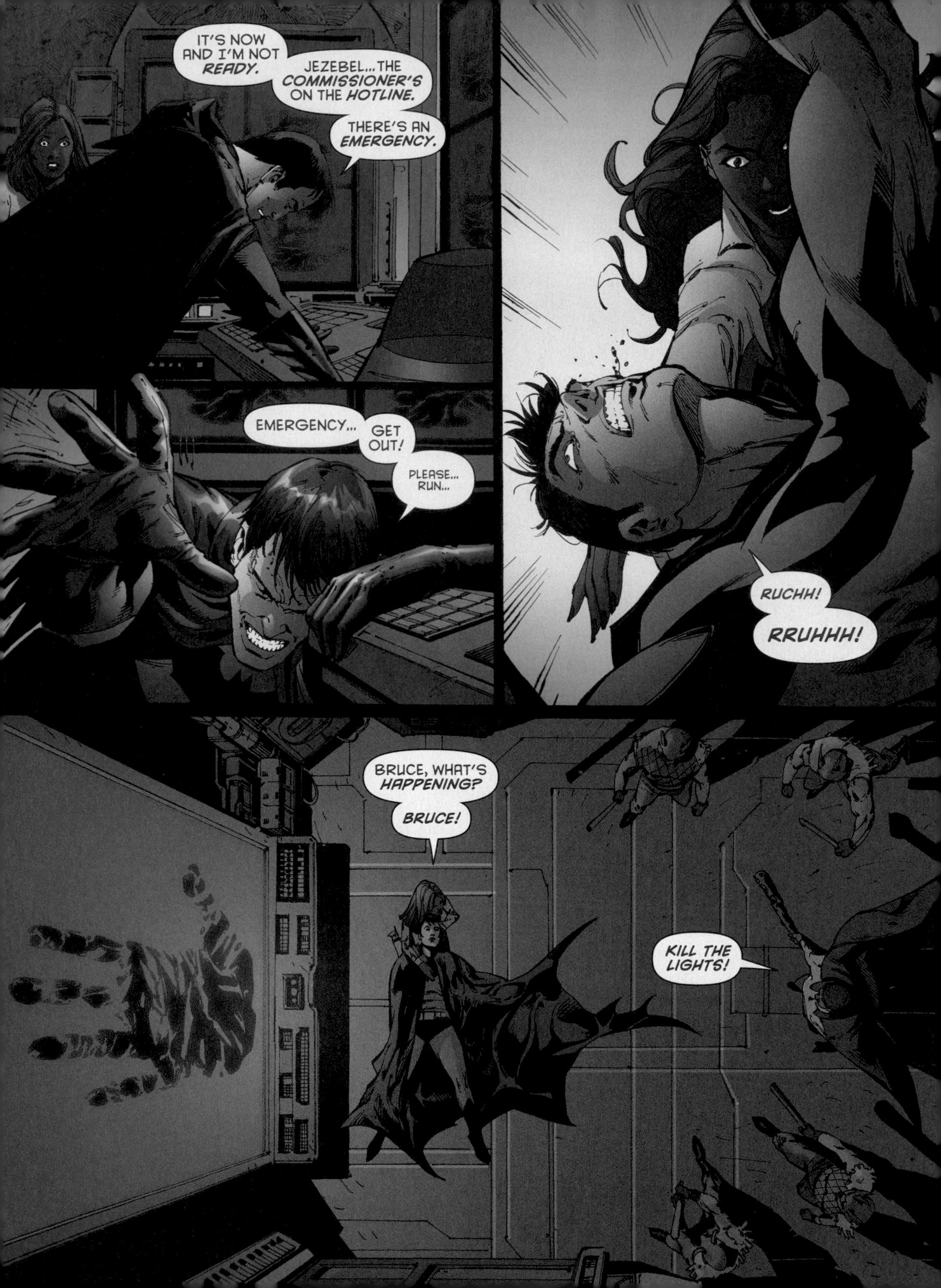

IT'S NOW AND I'M NOT *READY.*
JEZEBEL... THE *COMMISSIONER'S* ON THE *HOTLINE.*
THERE'S AN *EMERGENCY.*
EMERGENCY...
GET OUT!
PLEASE... RUN...
RUCHH!
RRUHHH!
BRUCE, WHAT'S *HAPPENING?*
BRUCE!
KILL THE LIGHTS!

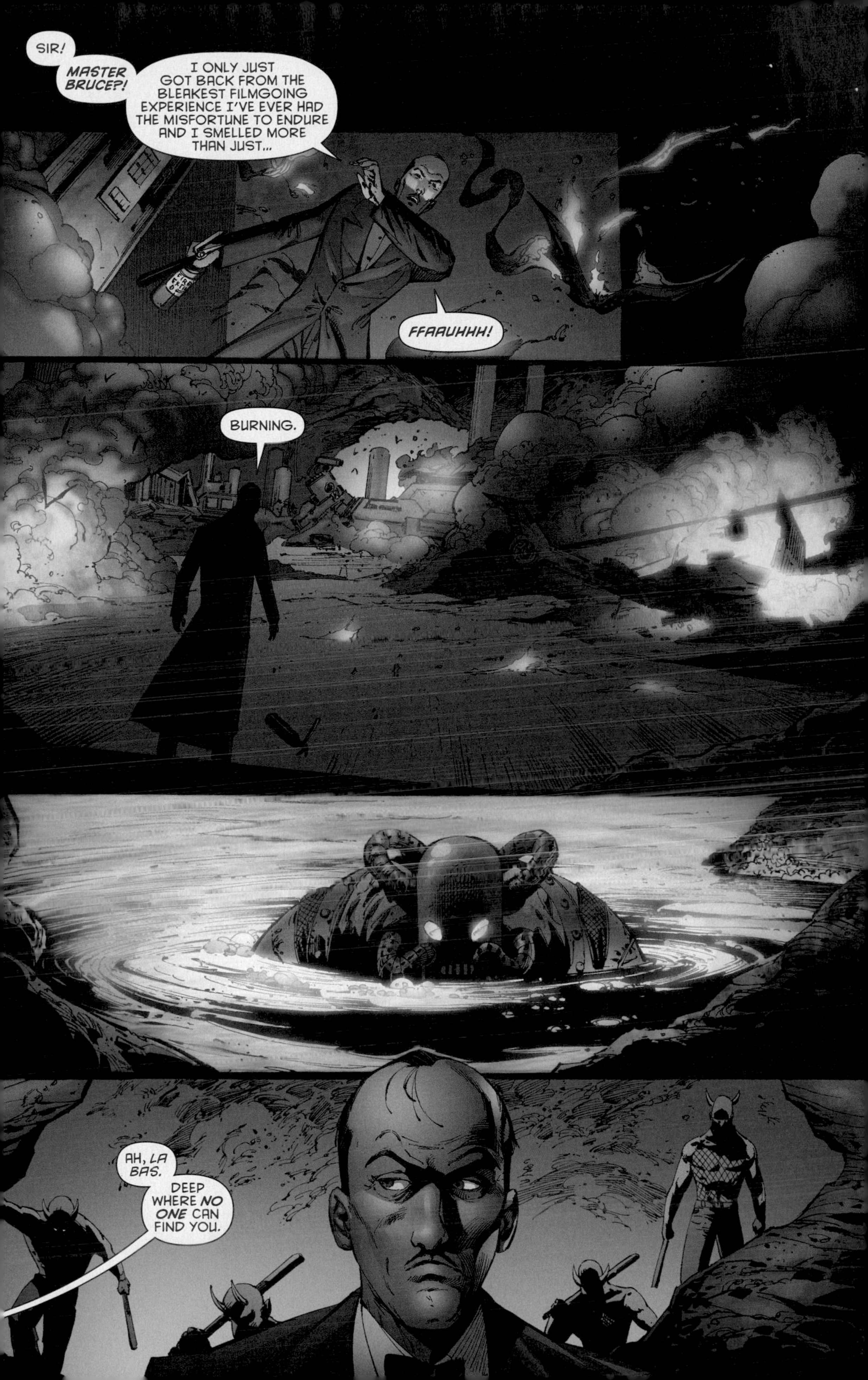
SIR!
MASTER BRUCE?!
I ONLY JUST GOT BACK FROM THE BLEAKEST FILMGOING EXPERIENCE I'VE EVER HAD THE MISFORTUNE TO ENDURE AND I SMELLED MORE THAN JUST...
FFAAUHHH!
BURNING.
AH, *LA BAS.*
DEEP WHERE *NO ONE* CAN FIND YOU.

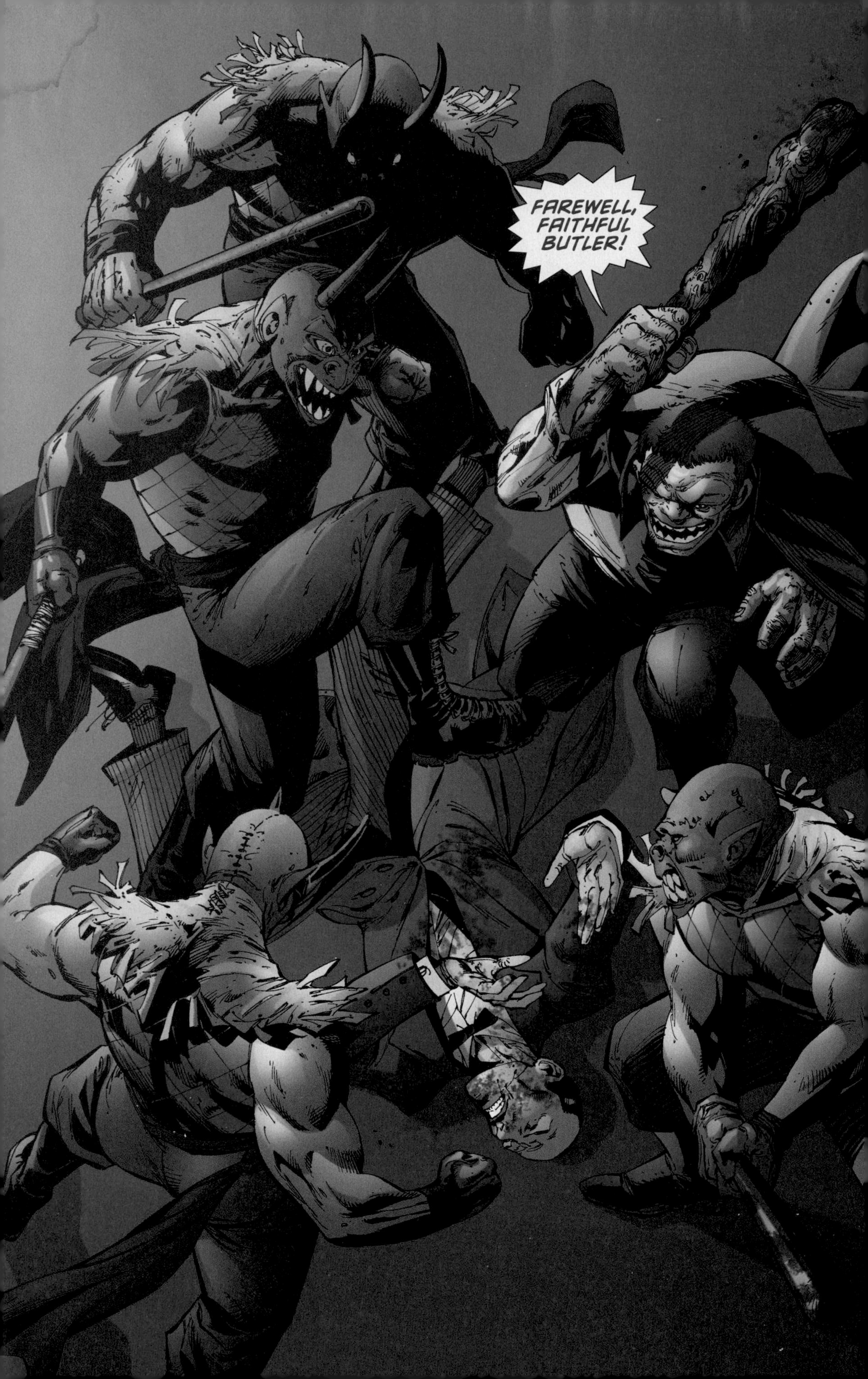
FAREWELL, FAITHFUL BUTLER!

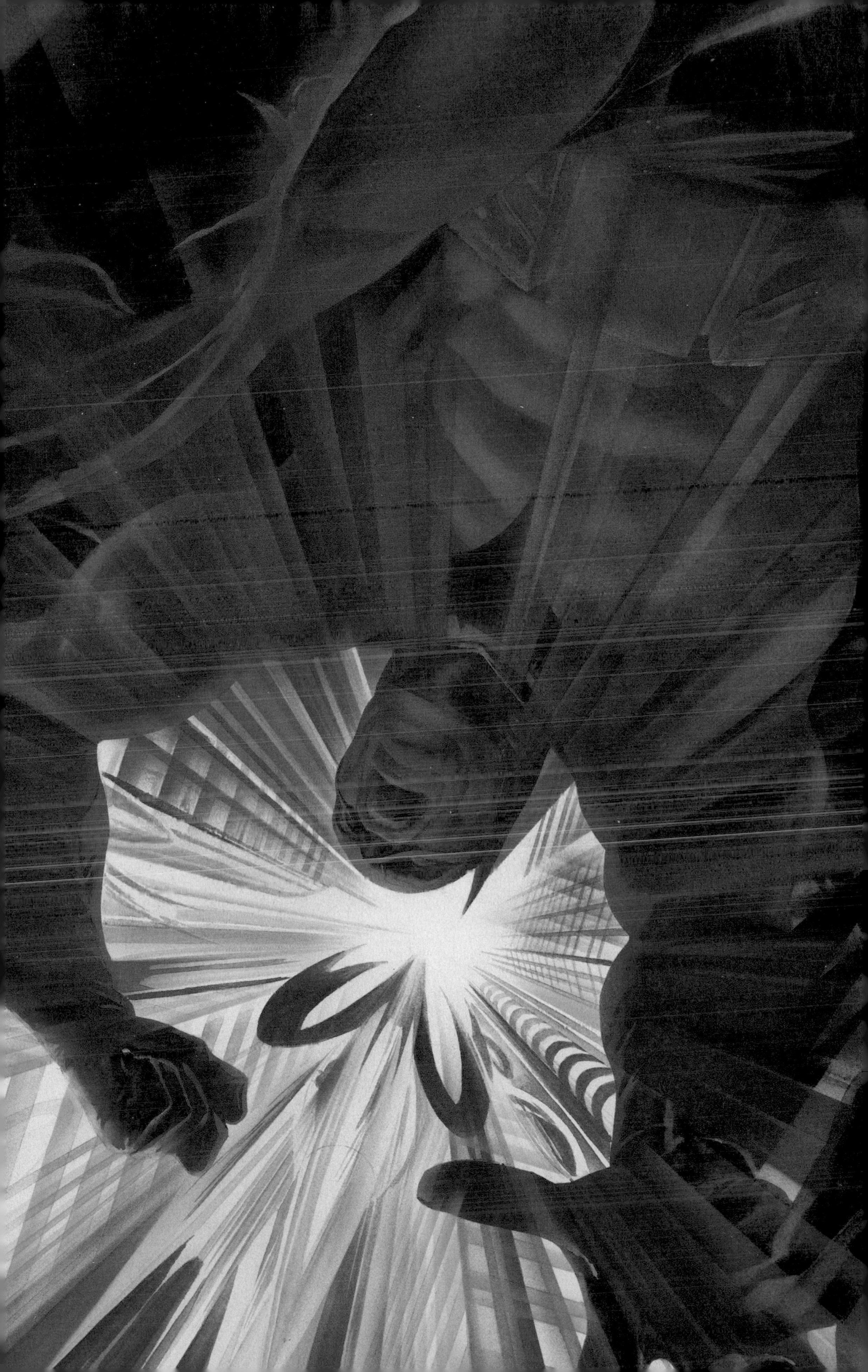

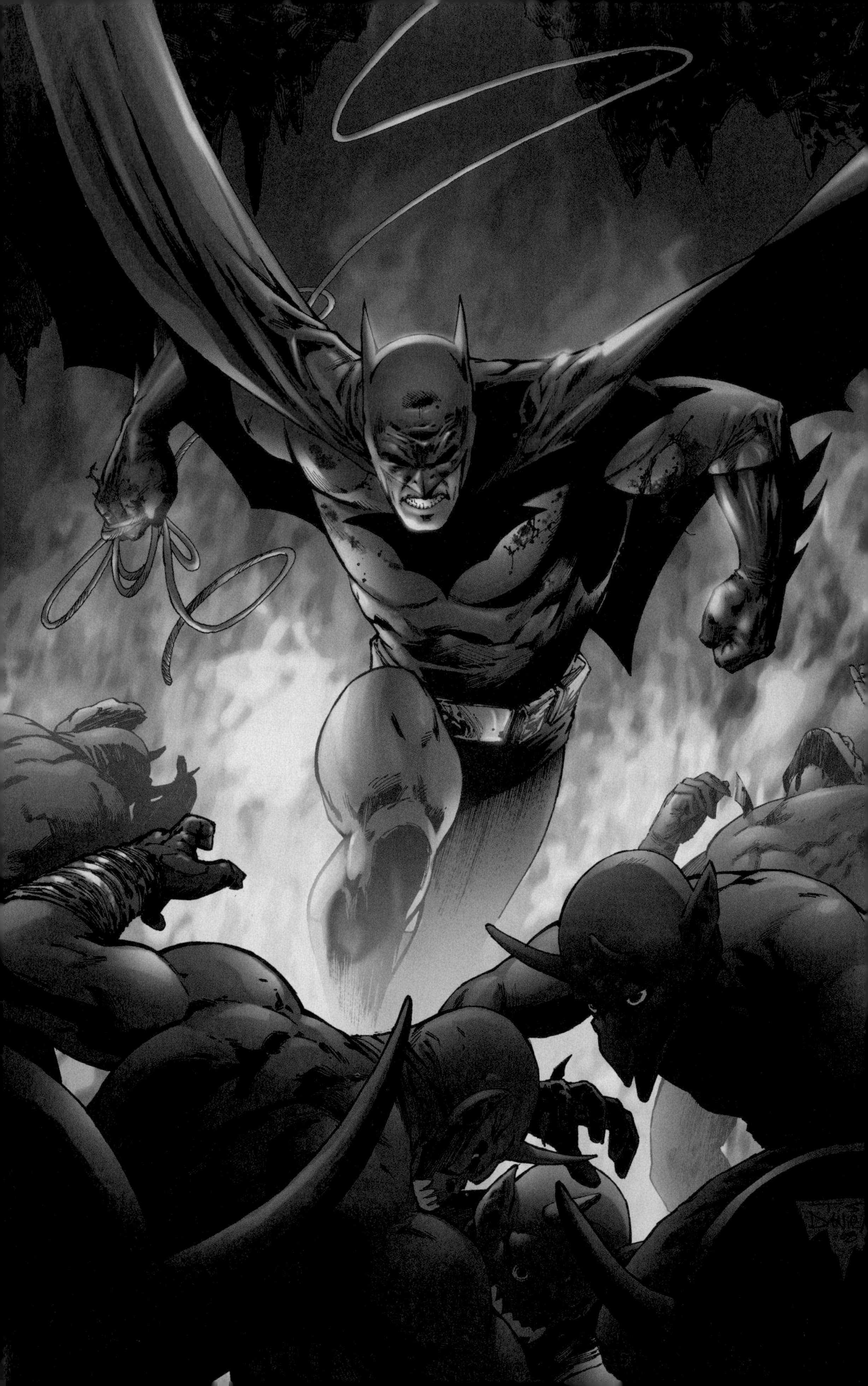

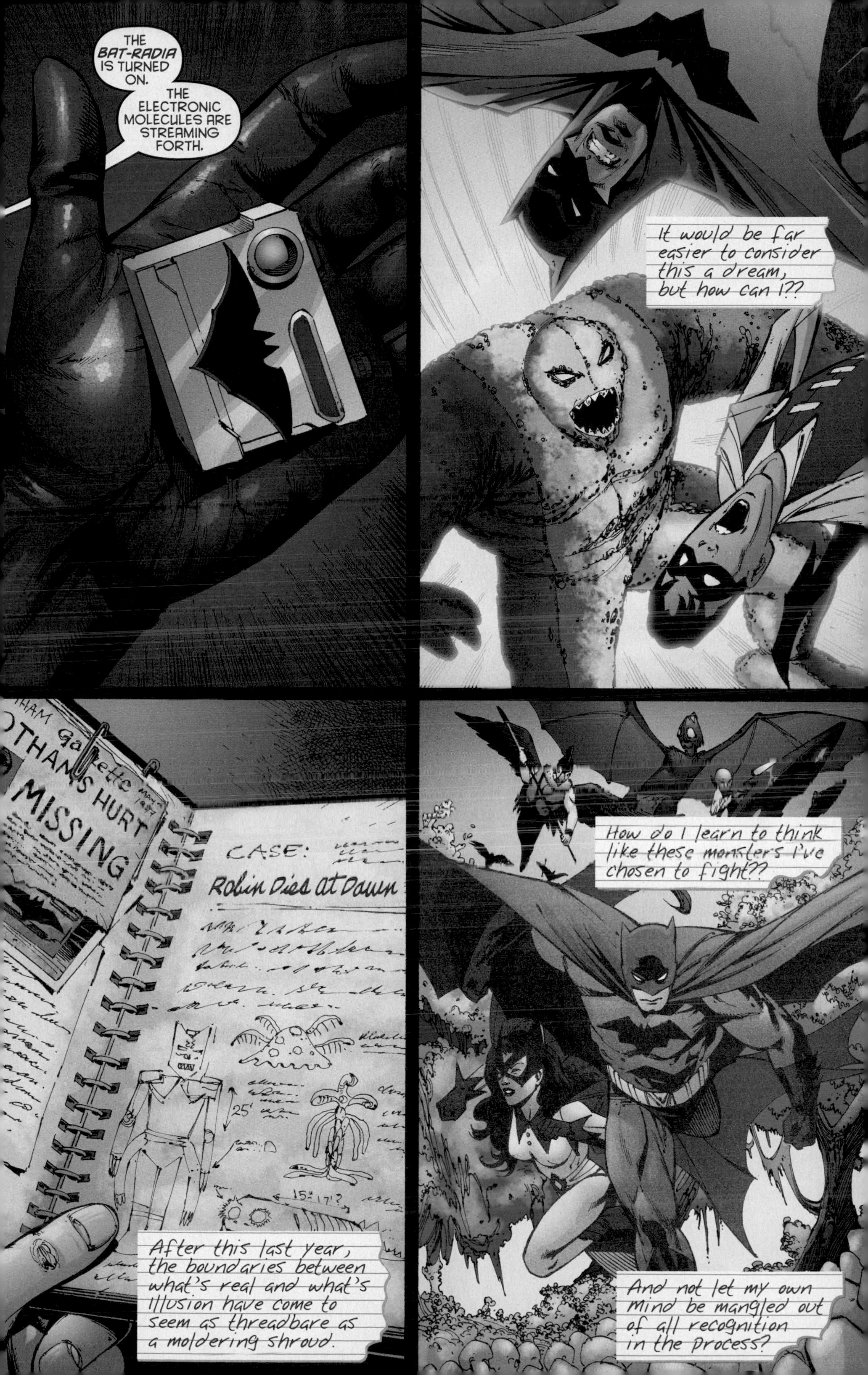
THE BAT-RADIA IS TURNED ON.
THE ELECTRONIC MOLECULES ARE STREAMING FORTH.
It would be far easier to consider this a dream, but how can I??
MISSING
CASE:
Robin Dies at Dawn
After this last year, the boundaries between what's real and what's illusion have come to seem as threadbare as a moldering shroud.
How do I learn to think like these monsters I've chosen to fight??
And not let my own mind be mangled out of all recognition in the process?

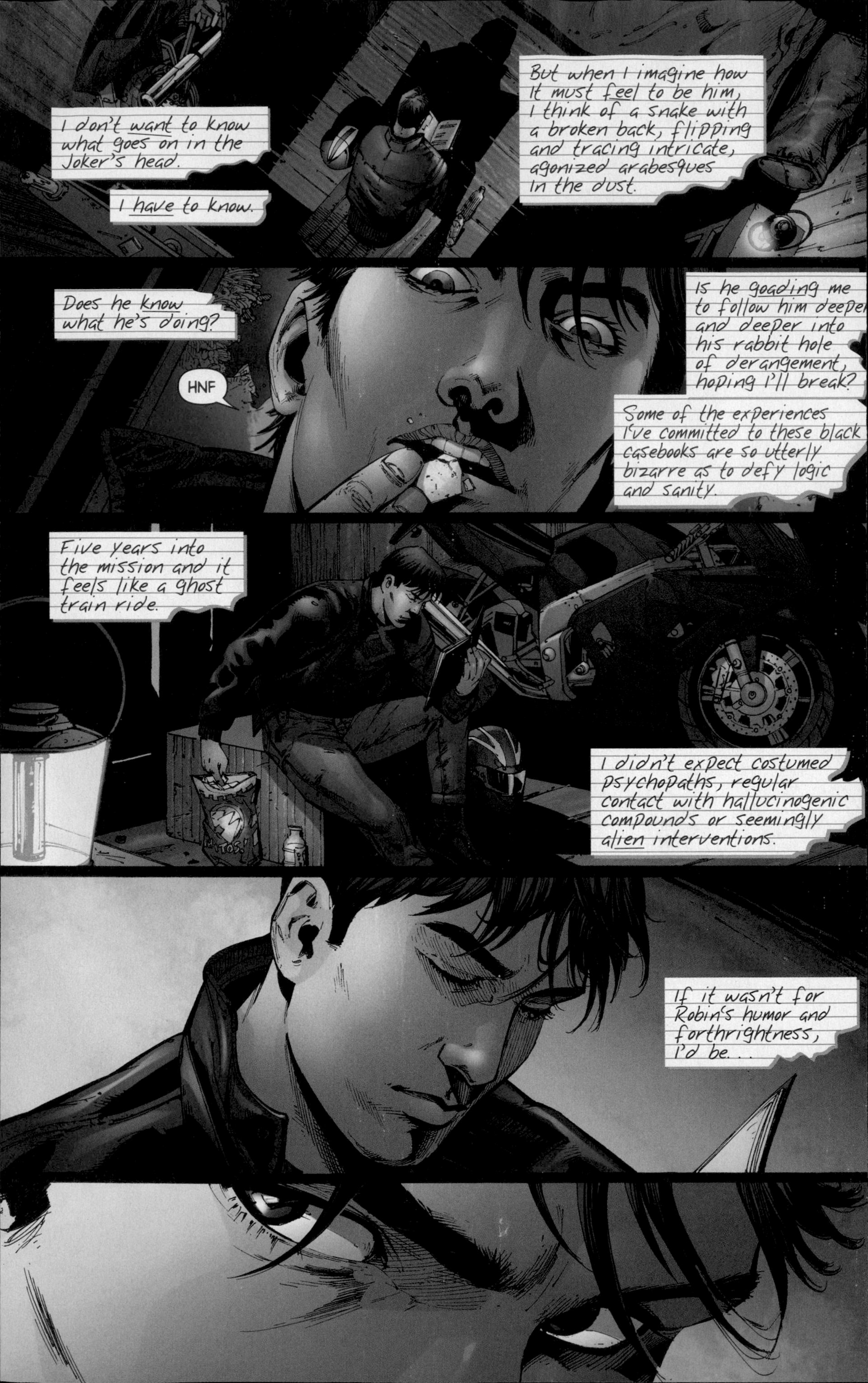
I don't want to know what goes on in the Joker's head.
I have to know.
But when I imagine how it must feel to be him, I think of a snake with a broken back, flipping and tracing intricate, agonized arabesques in the dust.
Does he know what he's doing?
HNF
Is he goading me to follow him deeper and deeper into his rabbit hole of derangement, hoping I'll break?
Some of the experiences I've committed to these black casebooks are so utterly bizarre as to defy logic and sanity.
Five years into the mission and it feels like a ghost train ride.
I didn't expect costumed psychopaths, regular contact with hallucinogenic compounds or seemingly alien interventions.
If it wasn't for Robin's humor and forthrightness, I'd be...

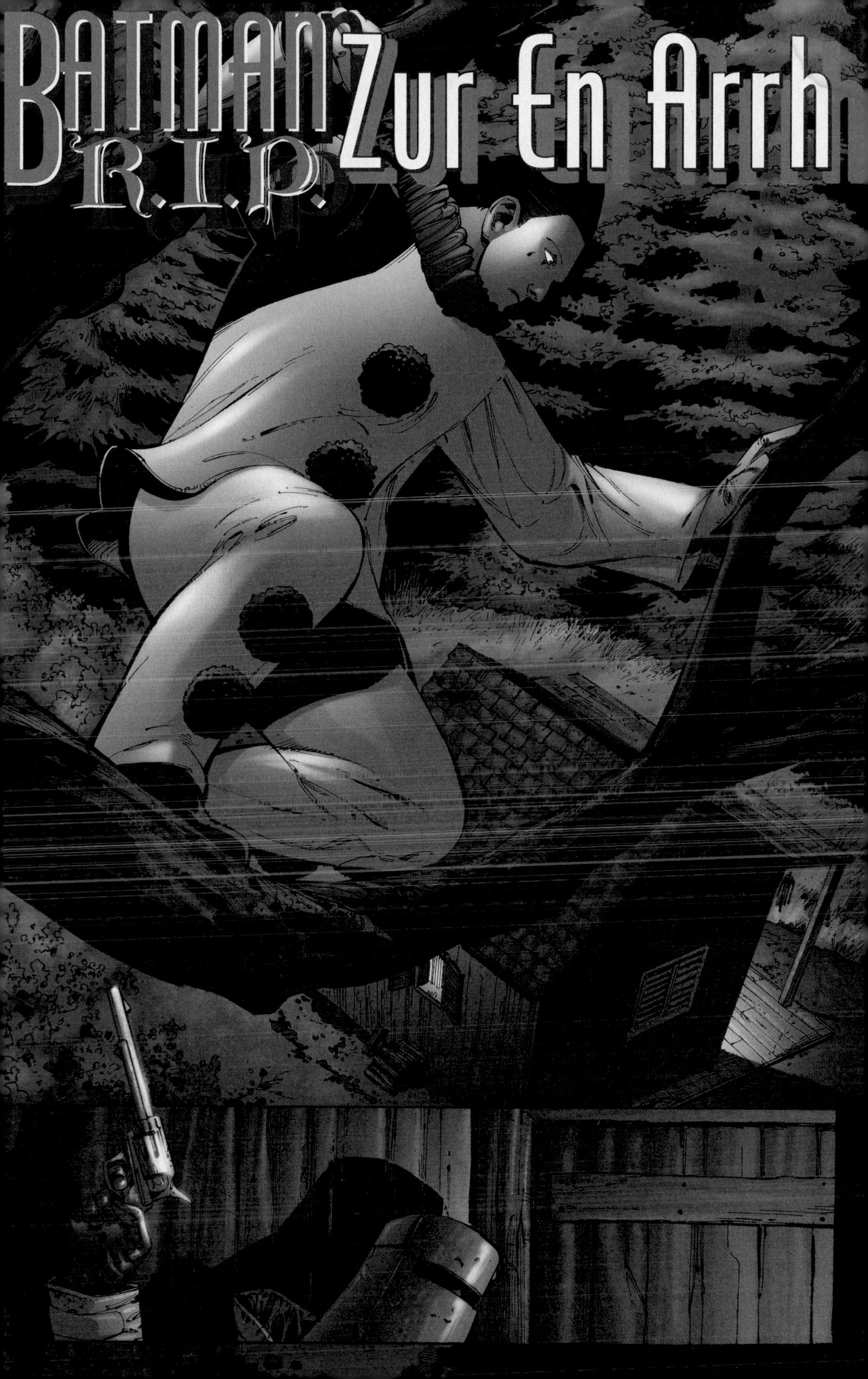
BATMAN R.I.P.
Zur En Arrh

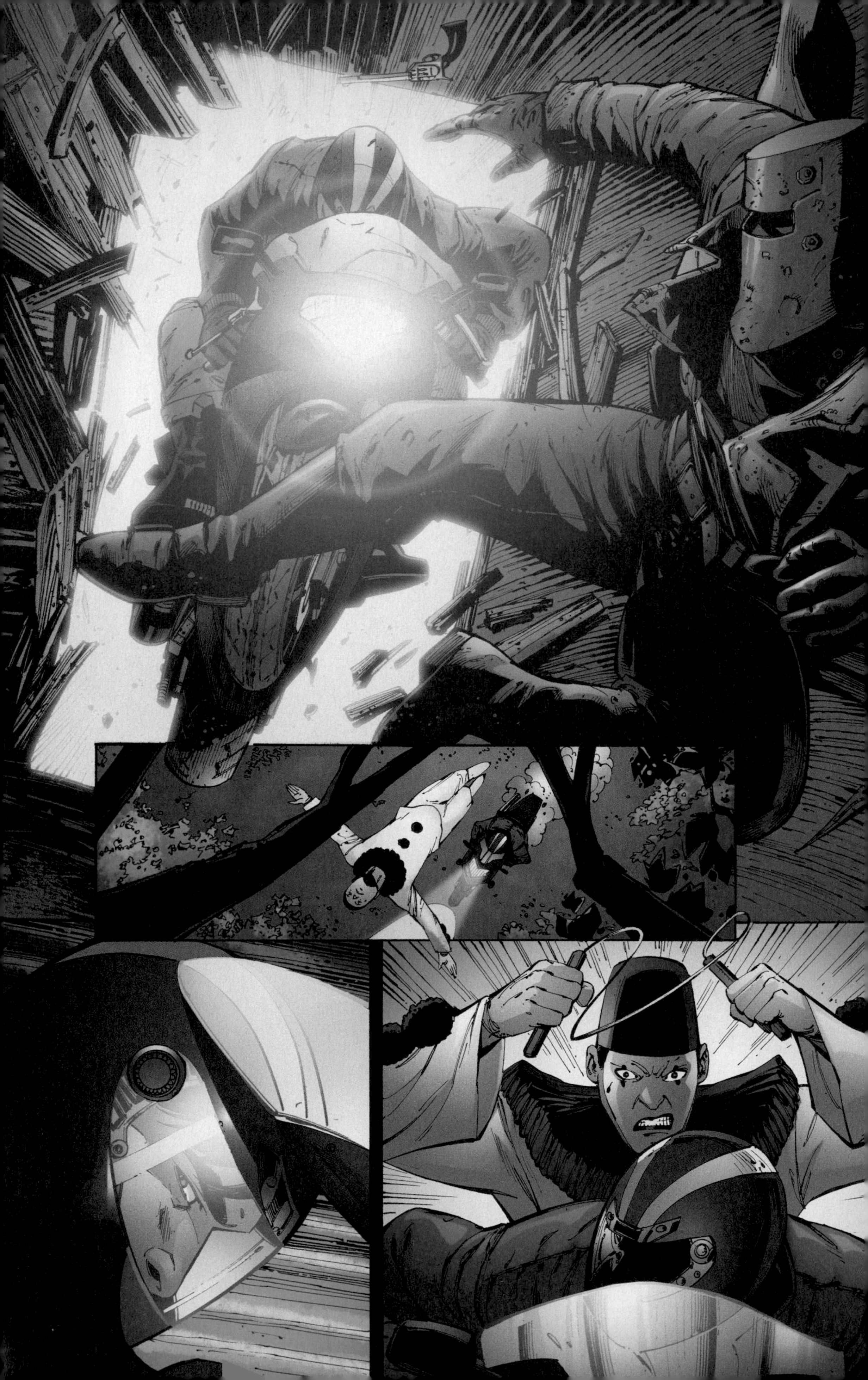

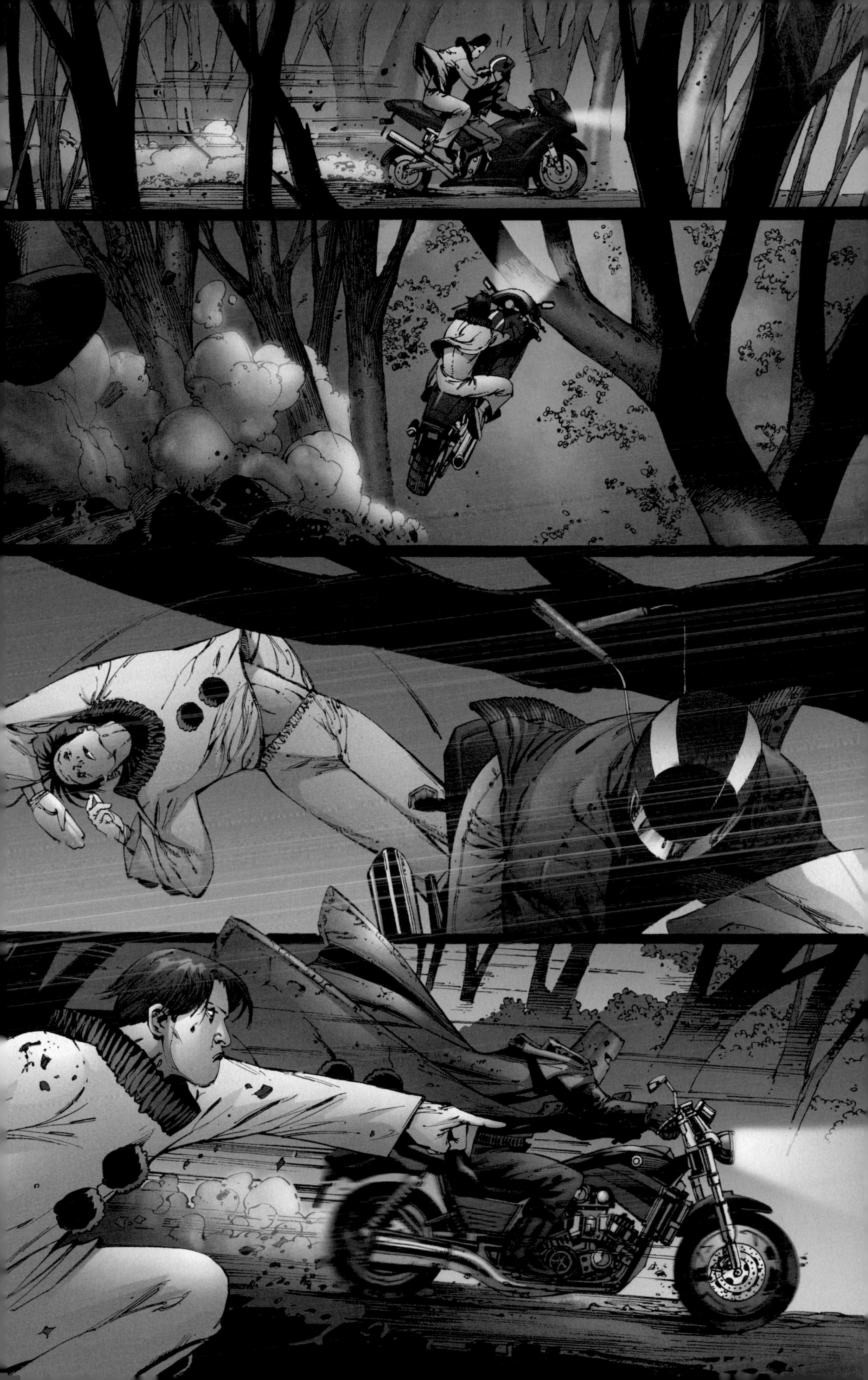

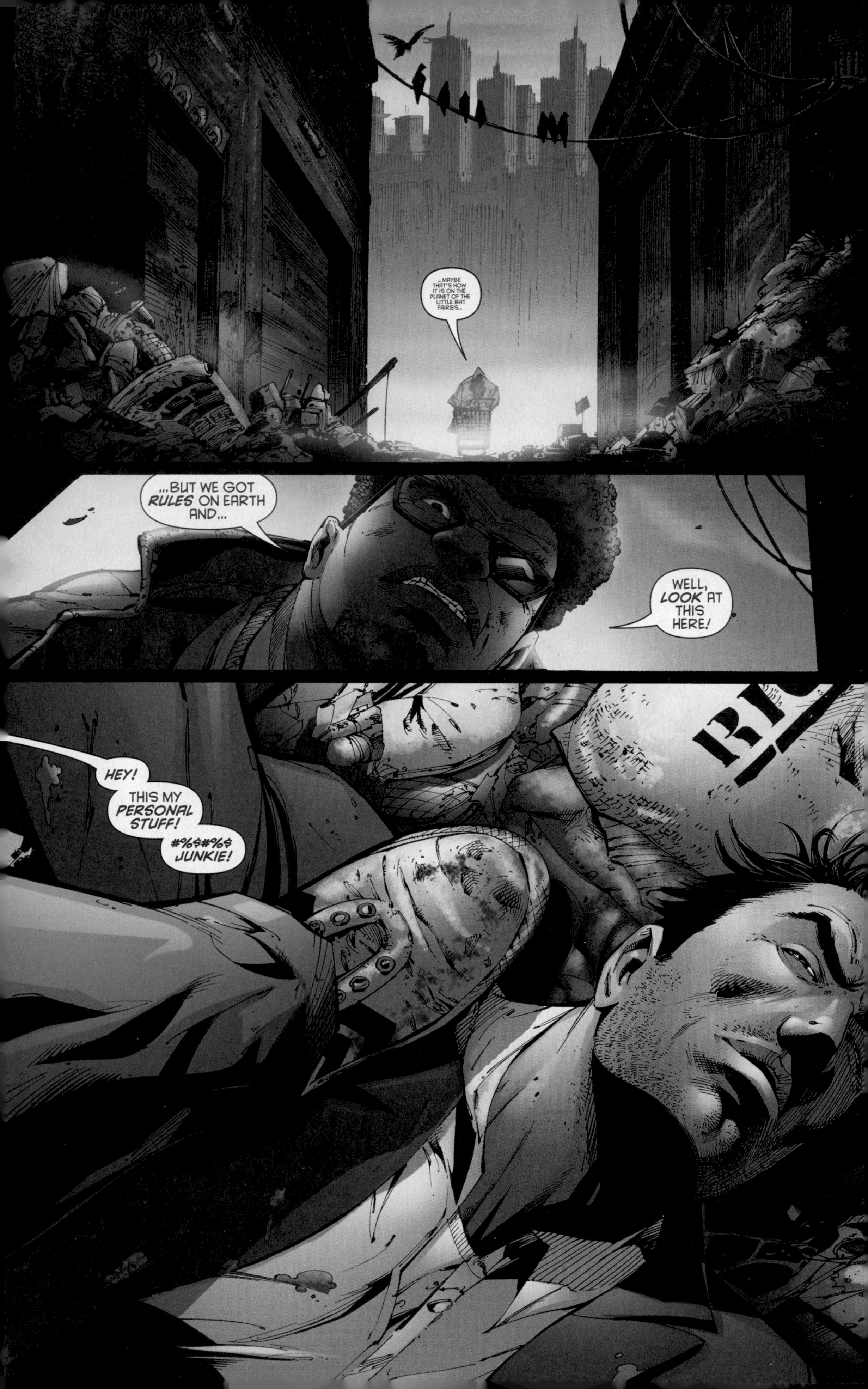
...MAYBE THAT'S HOW IT IS ON THE PLANET OF THE LITTLE BAT FAIRIES...
...BUT WE GOT RULES ON EARTH AND...
WELL, LOOK AT THIS HERE!
HEY! THIS MY PERSONAL STUFF!
#%$#%$ JUNKIE!

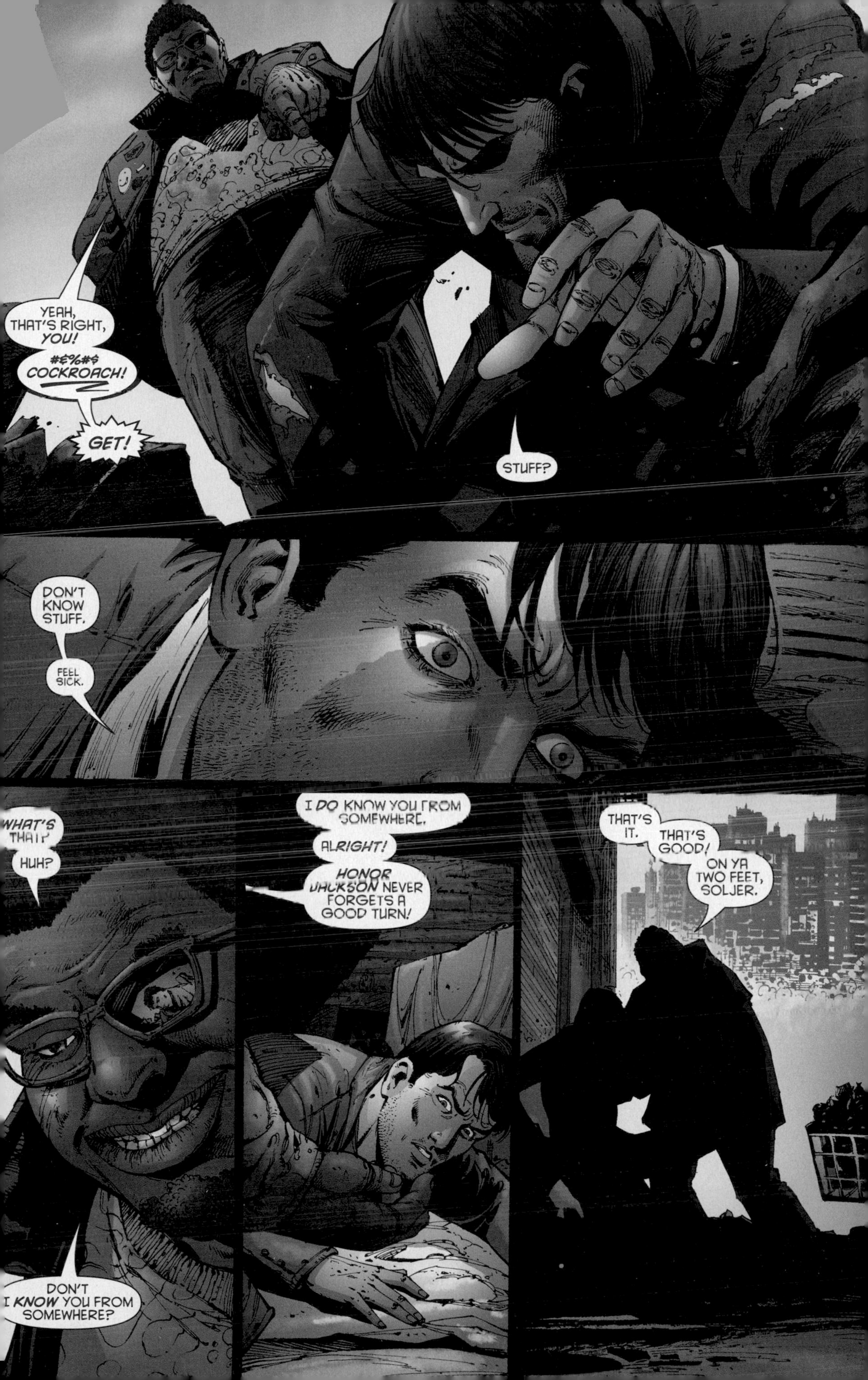
YEAH, THAT'S RIGHT, YOU!
#£%#$ COCKROACH!
GET!
STUFF?
DON'T KNOW STUFF.
FEEL SICK.
WHAT'S THAT?
HUH?
DON'T I KNOW YOU FROM SOMEWHERE?
I DO KNOW YOU FROM SOMEWHERE.
ALRIGHT!
HONOR JACKSON NEVER FORGETS A GOOD TURN!
THAT'S IT.
THAT'S GOOD!
ON YA TWO FEET, SOLJER.

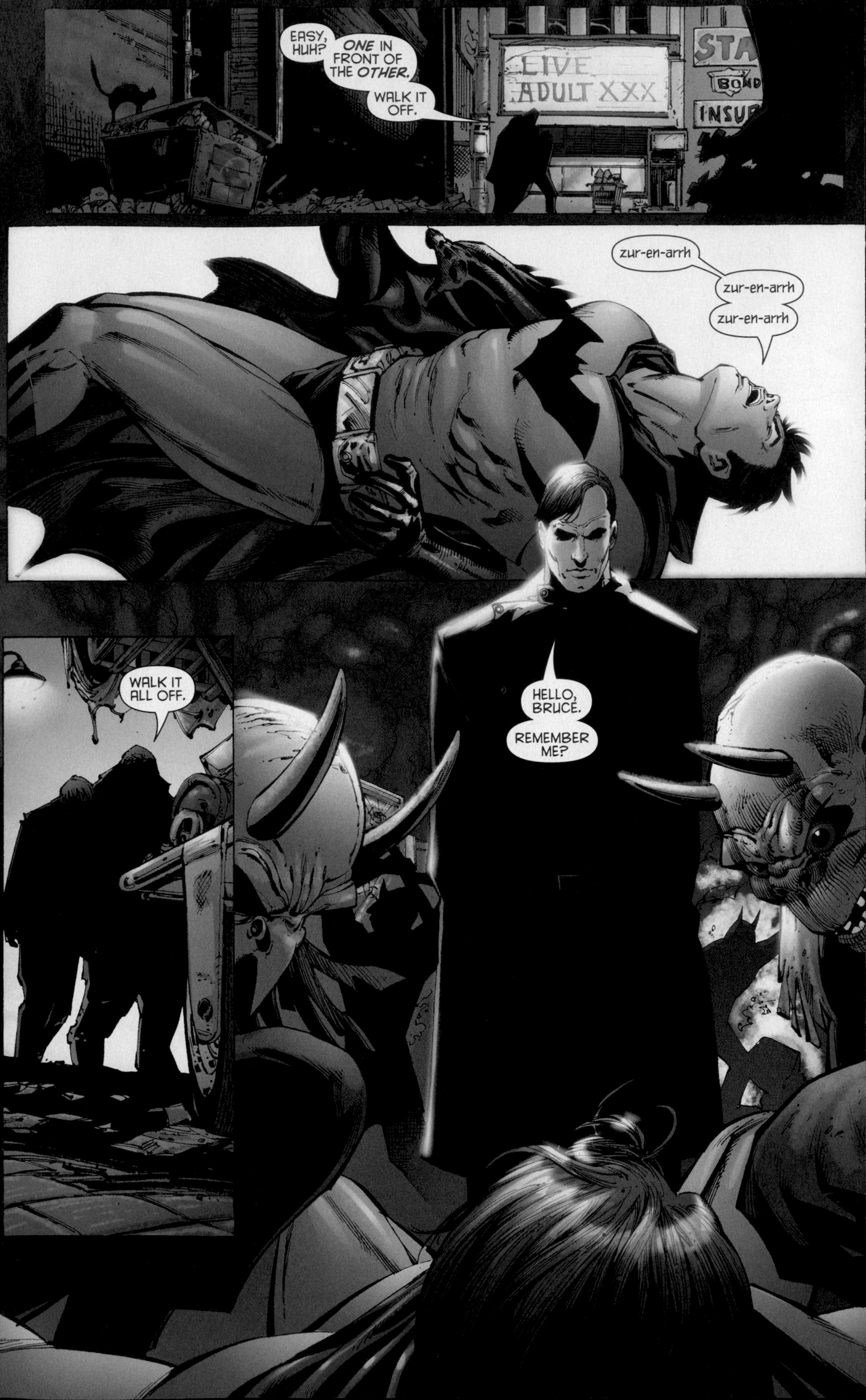
LIVE
ADULT XXX
STA
BOND
INSUR
EASY, HUH? ONE IN FRONT OF THE OTHER.
WALK IT OFF.
zur-en-arrh
zur-en-arrh
zur-en-arrh
WALK IT ALL OFF.
HELLO, BRUCE.
REMEMBER ME?

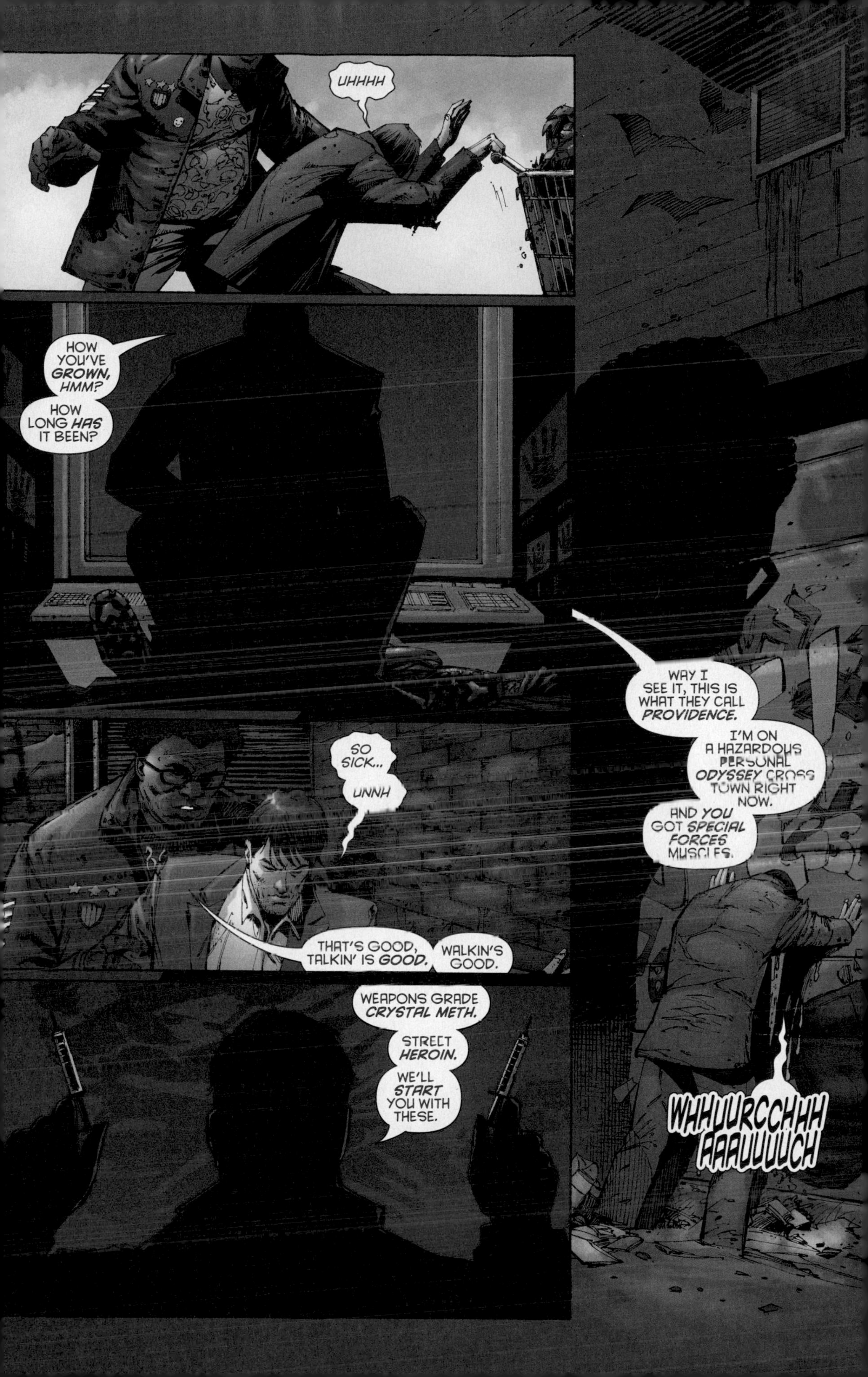
UHHHH
HOW YOU'VE GROWN, HMM?
HOW LONG HAS IT BEEN?
WAY I SEE IT, THIS IS WHAT THEY CALL PROVIDENCE.
I'M ON A HAZARDOUS PERSONAL ODYSSEY CROSS TOWN RIGHT NOW.
AND YOU GOT SPECIAL FORCES MUSCLES.
SO SICK...
UNNH
THAT'S GOOD, TALKIN' IS GOOD.
WALKIN'S GOOD.
WEAPONS GRADE CRYSTAL METH.
STREET HEROIN.
WE'LL START YOU WITH THESE.
WHHUURCCHHH AAAUUUUCH

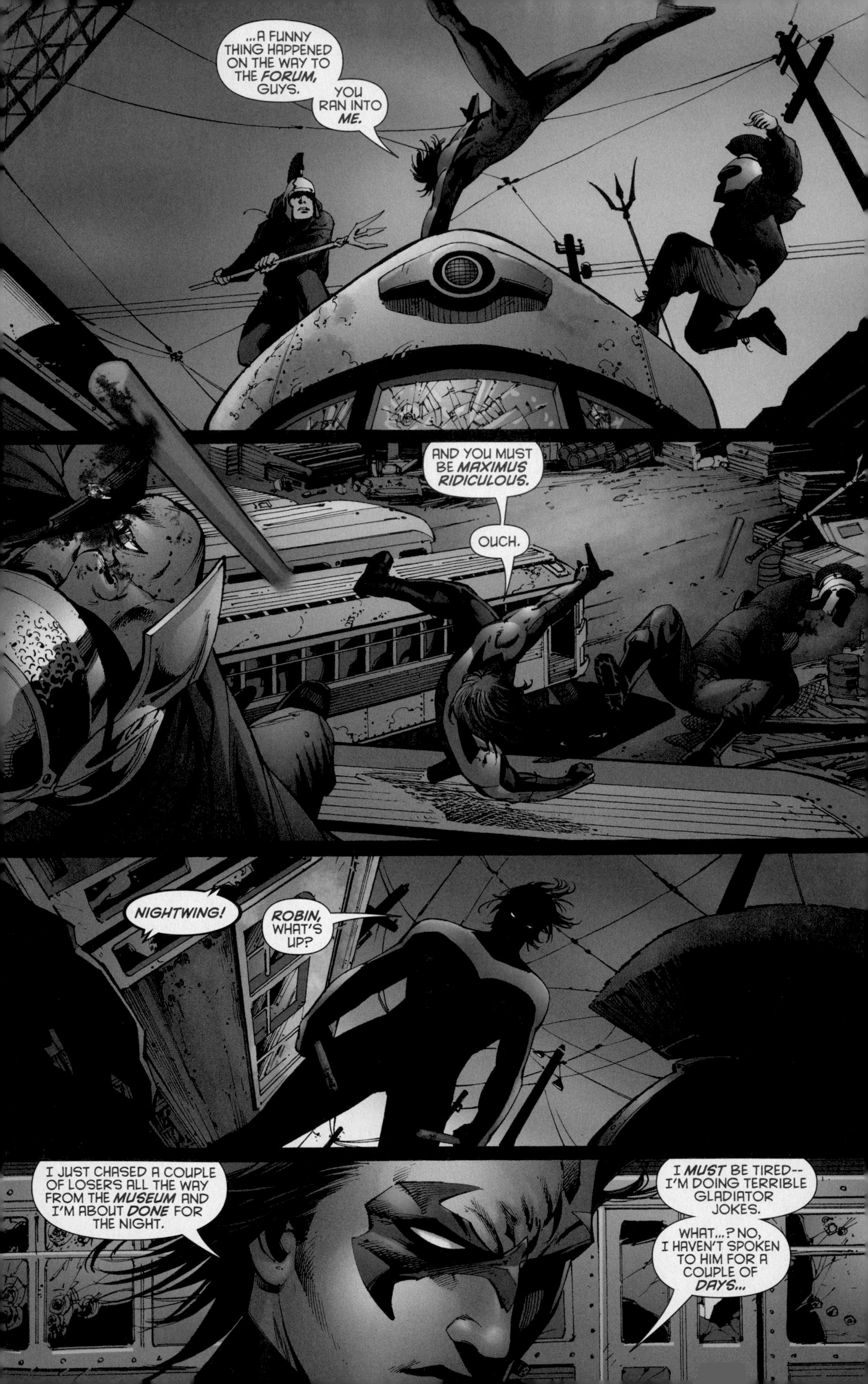
...A FUNNY THING HAPPENED ON THE WAY TO THE FORUM, GUYS.
YOU RAN INTO ME.
AND YOU MUST BE MAXIMUS RIDICULOUS.
OUCH.
NIGHTWING!
ROBIN, WHAT'S UP?
I JUST CHASED A COUPLE OF LOSERS ALL THE WAY FROM THE MUSEUM AND I'M ABOUT DONE FOR THE NIGHT.
I MUST BE TIRED-- I'M DOING TERRIBLE GLADIATOR JOKES.
WHAT...? NO, I HAVEN'T SPOKEN TO HIM FOR A COUPLE OF DAYS...

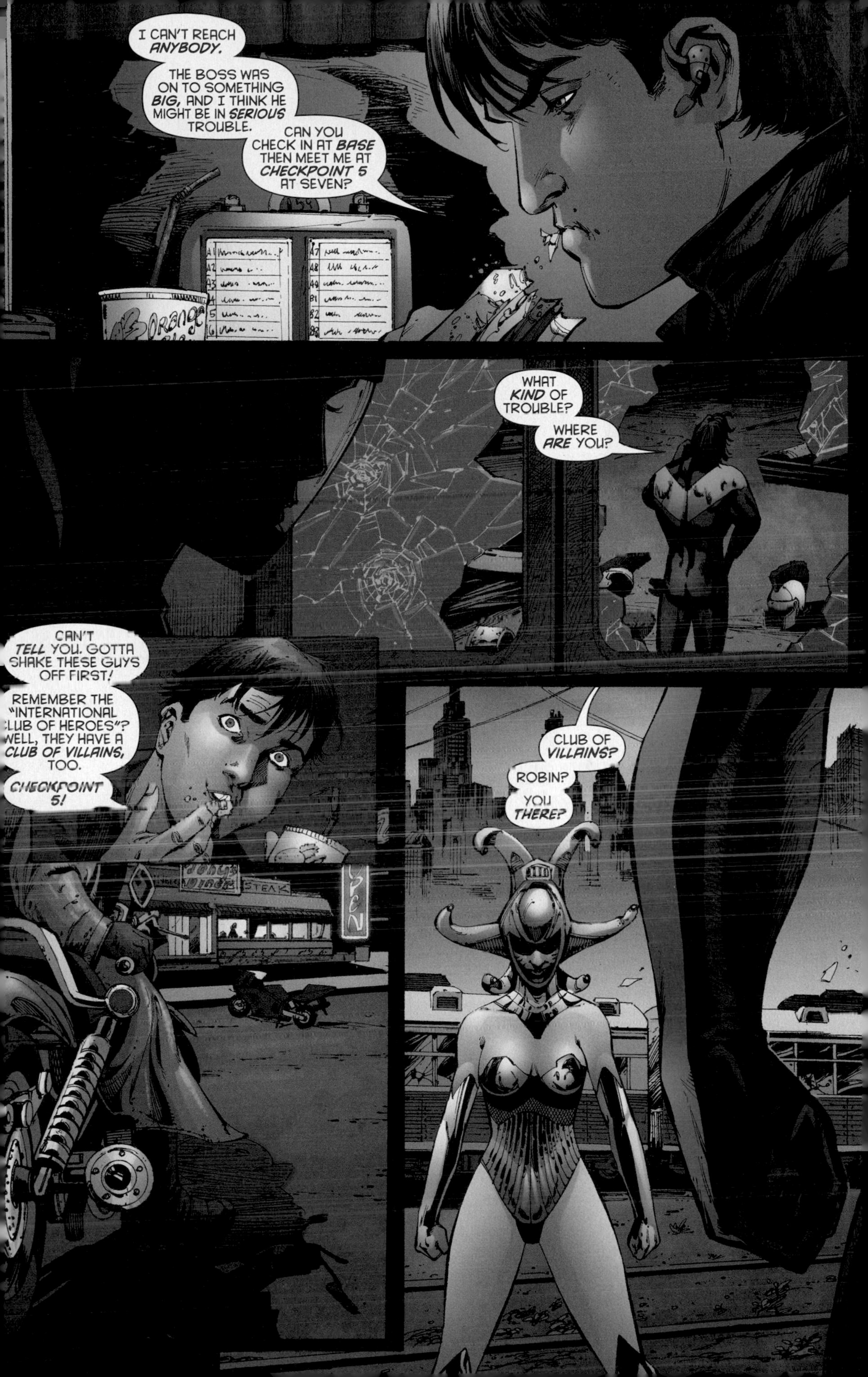
I CAN'T REACH ANYBODY.
THE BOSS WAS ON TO SOMETHING BIG, AND I THINK HE MIGHT BE IN SERIOUS TROUBLE.
CAN YOU CHECK IN AT BASE THEN MEET ME AT CHECKPOINT 5 AT SEVEN?
WHAT KIND OF TROUBLE?
WHERE ARE YOU?
CAN'T TELL YOU. GOTTA SHAKE THESE GUYS OFF FIRST!
REMEMBER THE "INTERNATIONAL CLUB OF HEROES"? WELL, THEY HAVE A CLUB OF VILLAINS, TOO.
CHECKPOINT 5!
CLUB OF VILLAINS?
ROBIN?
YOU THERE?
STEAK
OPEN

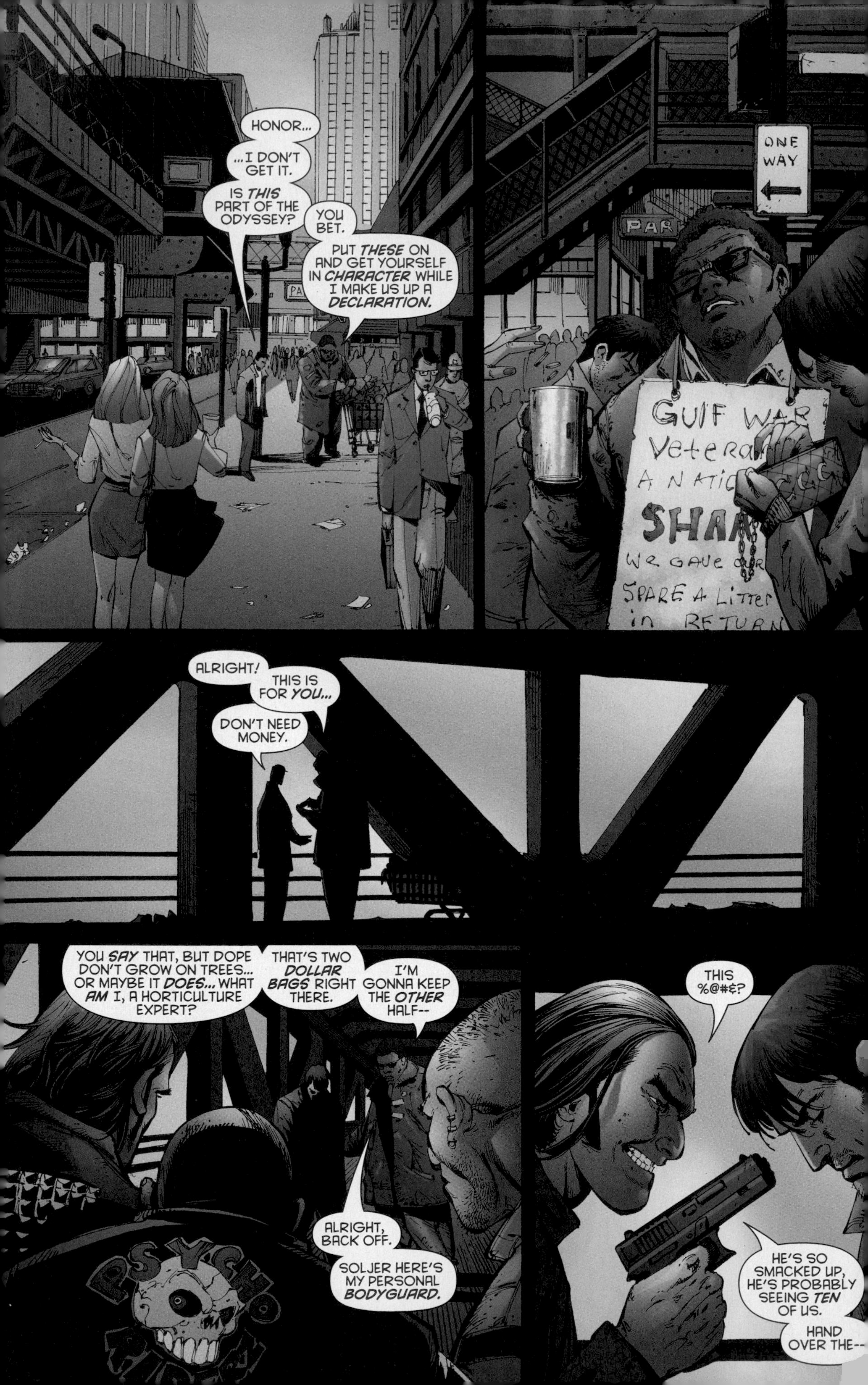
HONOR...
...I DON'T GET IT.
IS THIS PART OF THE ODYSSEY?
YOU BET.
PUT THESE ON AND GET YOURSELF IN CHARACTER WHILE I MAKE US UP A DECLARATION.
ONE WAY
ALRIGHT!
THIS IS FOR YOU...
DON'T NEED MONEY.
YOU SAY THAT, BUT DOPE DON'T GROW ON TREES... OR MAYBE IT DOES... WHAT AM I, A HORTICULTURE EXPERT?
THAT'S TWO DOLLAR BAGS RIGHT THERE.
I'M GONNA KEEP THE OTHER HALF--
ALRIGHT, BACK OFF.
SOLJER HERE'S MY PERSONAL BODYGUARD.
PSYCHO
THIS %@#&?
HE'S SO SMACKED UP, HE'S PROBABLY SEEING TEN OF US.
HAND OVER THE--

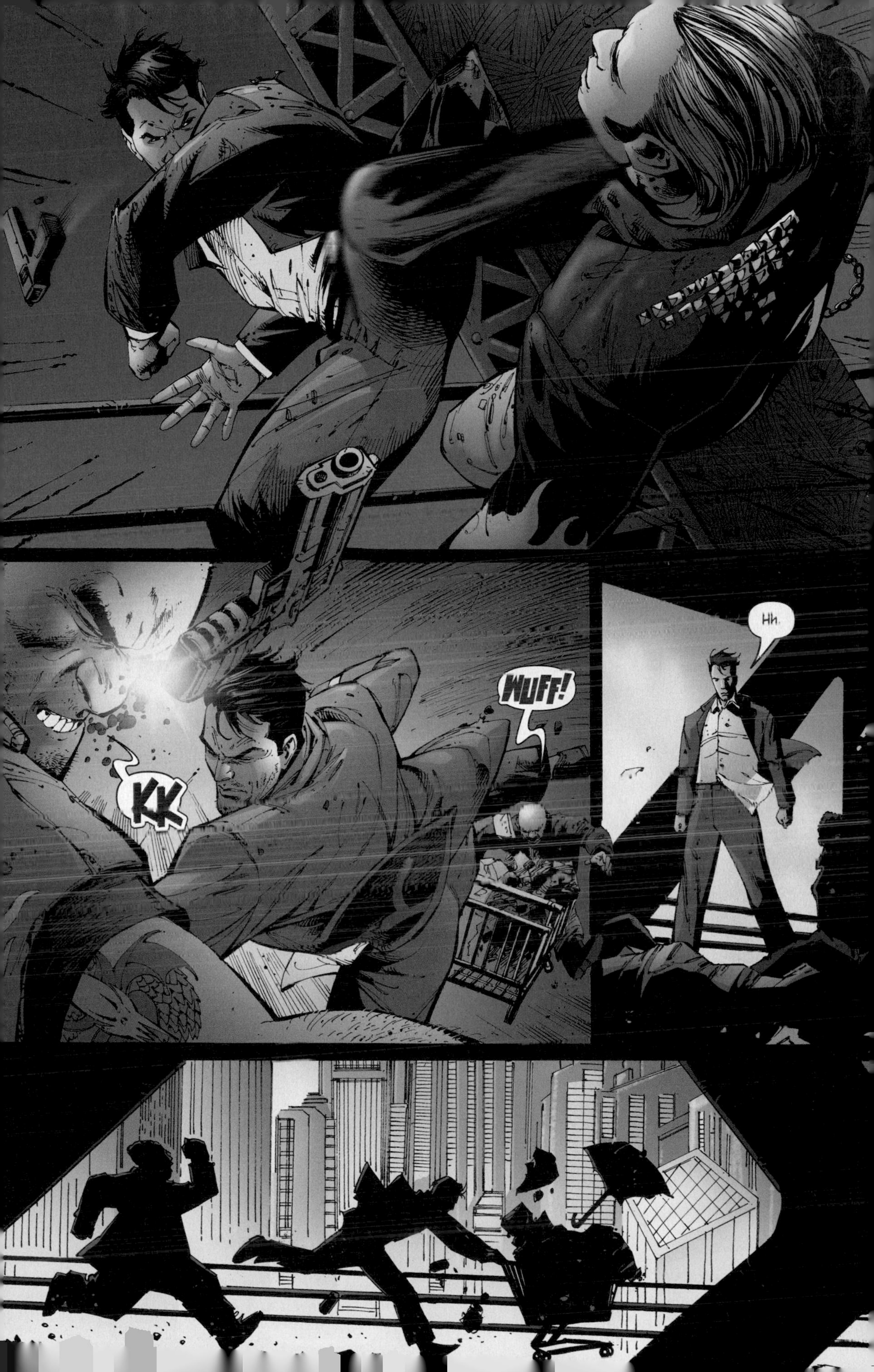
WUFF!
KK
Hh.

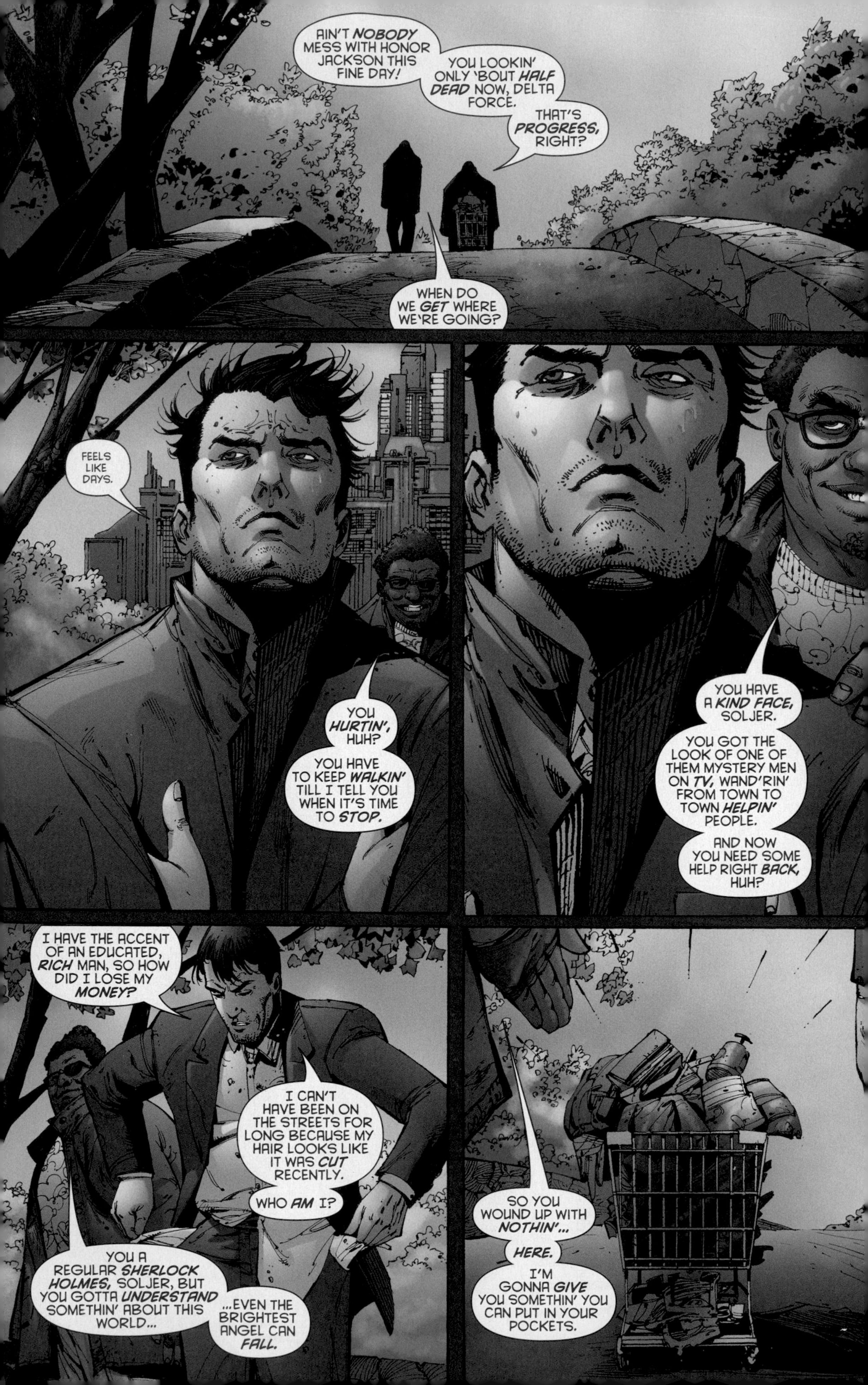
AIN'T NOBODY MESS WITH HONOR JACKSON THIS FINE DAY!
YOU LOOKIN' ONLY 'BOUT HALF DEAD NOW, DELTA FORCE.
THAT'S PROGRESS, RIGHT?
WHEN DO WE GET WHERE WE'RE GOING?
FEELS LIKE DAYS.
YOU HURTIN', HUH?
YOU HAVE TO KEEP WALKIN' TILL I TELL YOU WHEN IT'S TIME TO STOP.
YOU HAVE A KIND FACE, SOLJER.
YOU GOT THE LOOK OF ONE OF THEM MYSTERY MEN ON TV, WAND'RIN' FROM TOWN TO TOWN HELPIN' PEOPLE.
AND NOW YOU NEED SOME HELP RIGHT BACK, HUH?
I HAVE THE ACCENT OF AN EDUCATED, RICH MAN, SO HOW DID I LOSE MY MONEY?
I CAN'T HAVE BEEN ON THE STREETS FOR LONG BECAUSE MY HAIR LOOKS LIKE IT WAS CUT RECENTLY.
WHO AM I?
YOU A REGULAR SHERLOCK HOLMES, SOLJER, BUT YOU GOTTA UNDERSTAND SOMETHIN' ABOUT THIS WORLD...
...EVEN THE BRIGHTEST ANGEL CAN FALL.
SO YOU WOUND UP WITH NOTHIN'...
HERE.
I'M GONNA GIVE YOU SOMETHIN' YOU CAN PUT IN YOUR POCKETS.

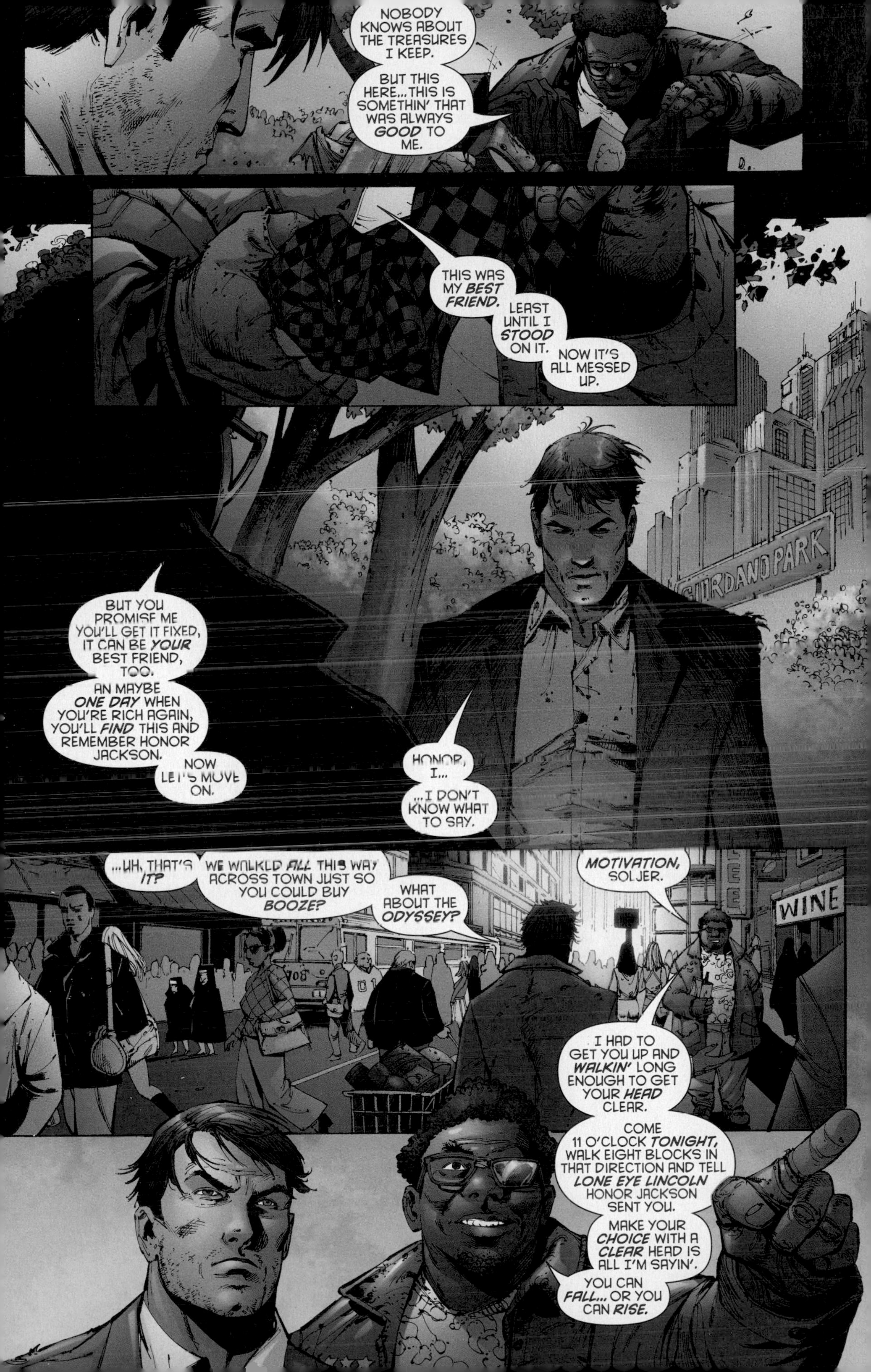
NOBODY KNOWS ABOUT THE TREASURES I KEEP.
BUT THIS HERE... THIS IS SOMETHIN' THAT WAS ALWAYS GOOD TO ME.
THIS WAS MY BEST FRIEND.
LEAST UNTIL I STOOD ON IT.
NOW IT'S ALL MESSED UP.
GIORDANO PARK
BUT YOU PROMISE ME YOU'LL GET IT FIXED, IT CAN BE YOUR BEST FRIEND, TOO.
AN MAYBE ONE DAY WHEN YOU'RE RICH AGAIN, YOU'LL FIND THIS AND REMEMBER HONOR JACKSON.
NOW LET'S MOVE ON.
HONOR, I...
...I DON'T KNOW WHAT TO SAY.
...UH, THAT'S IT?
WE WALKED ALL THIS WAY ACROSS TOWN JUST SO YOU COULD BUY BOOZE?
WHAT ABOUT THE ODYSSEY?
MOTIVATION, SOLJER.
WINE
I HAD TO GET YOU UP AND WALKIN' LONG ENOUGH TO GET YOUR HEAD CLEAR.
COME 11 O'CLOCK TONIGHT, WALK EIGHT BLOCKS IN THAT DIRECTION AND TELL LONE EYE LINCOLN HONOR JACKSON SENT YOU.
MAKE YOUR CHOICE WITH A CLEAR HEAD IS ALL I'M SAYIN'.
YOU CAN FALL... OR YOU CAN RISE.

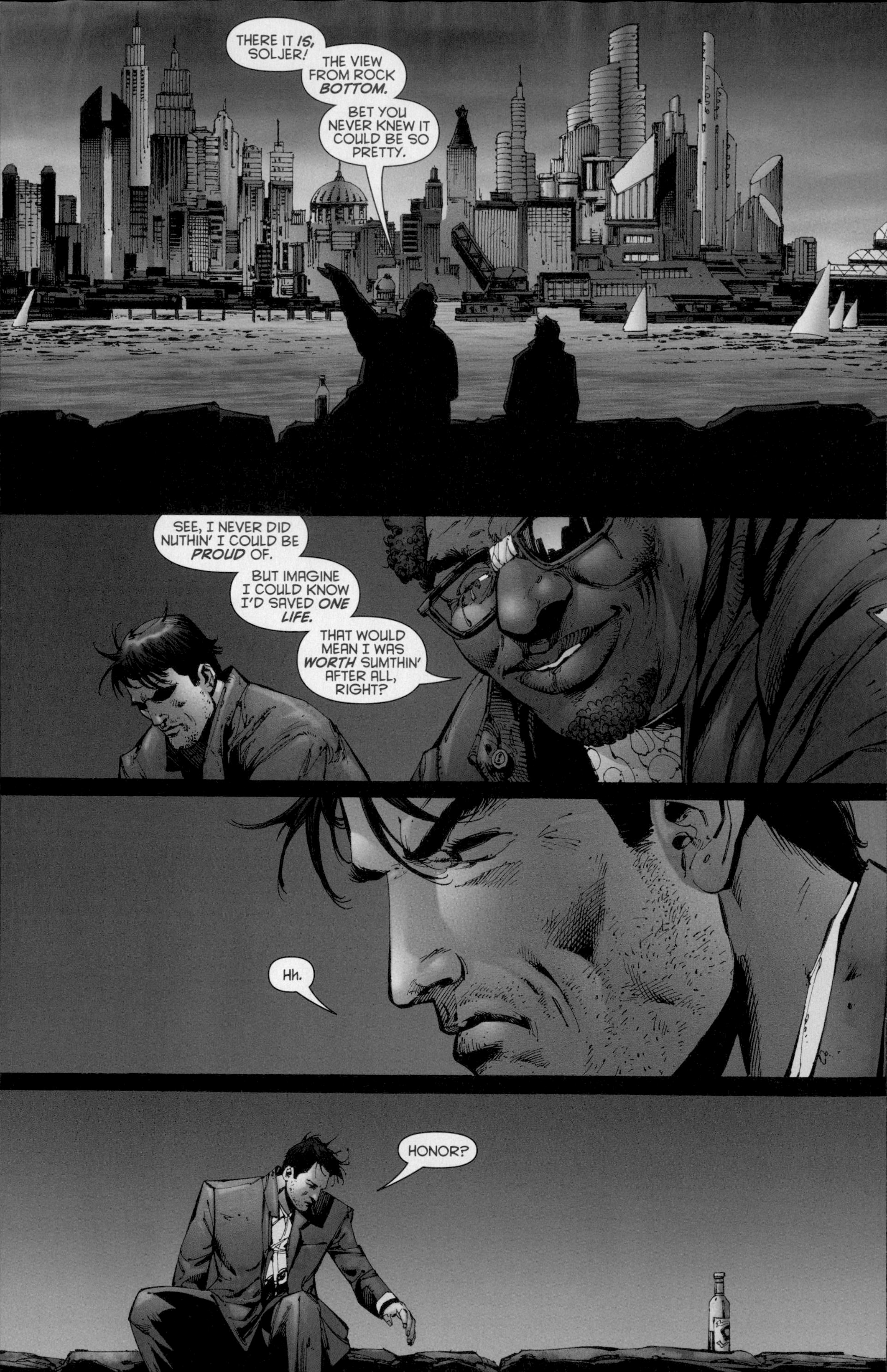
THERE IT IS, SOLJER!
THE VIEW FROM ROCK BOTTOM.
BET YOU NEVER KNEW IT COULD BE SO PRETTY.
SEE, I NEVER DID NUTHIN' I COULD BE PROUD OF.
BUT IMAGINE I COULD KNOW I'D SAVED ONE LIFE.
THAT WOULD MEAN I WAS WORTH SUMTHIN' AFTER ALL, RIGHT?
Hh.
HONOR?

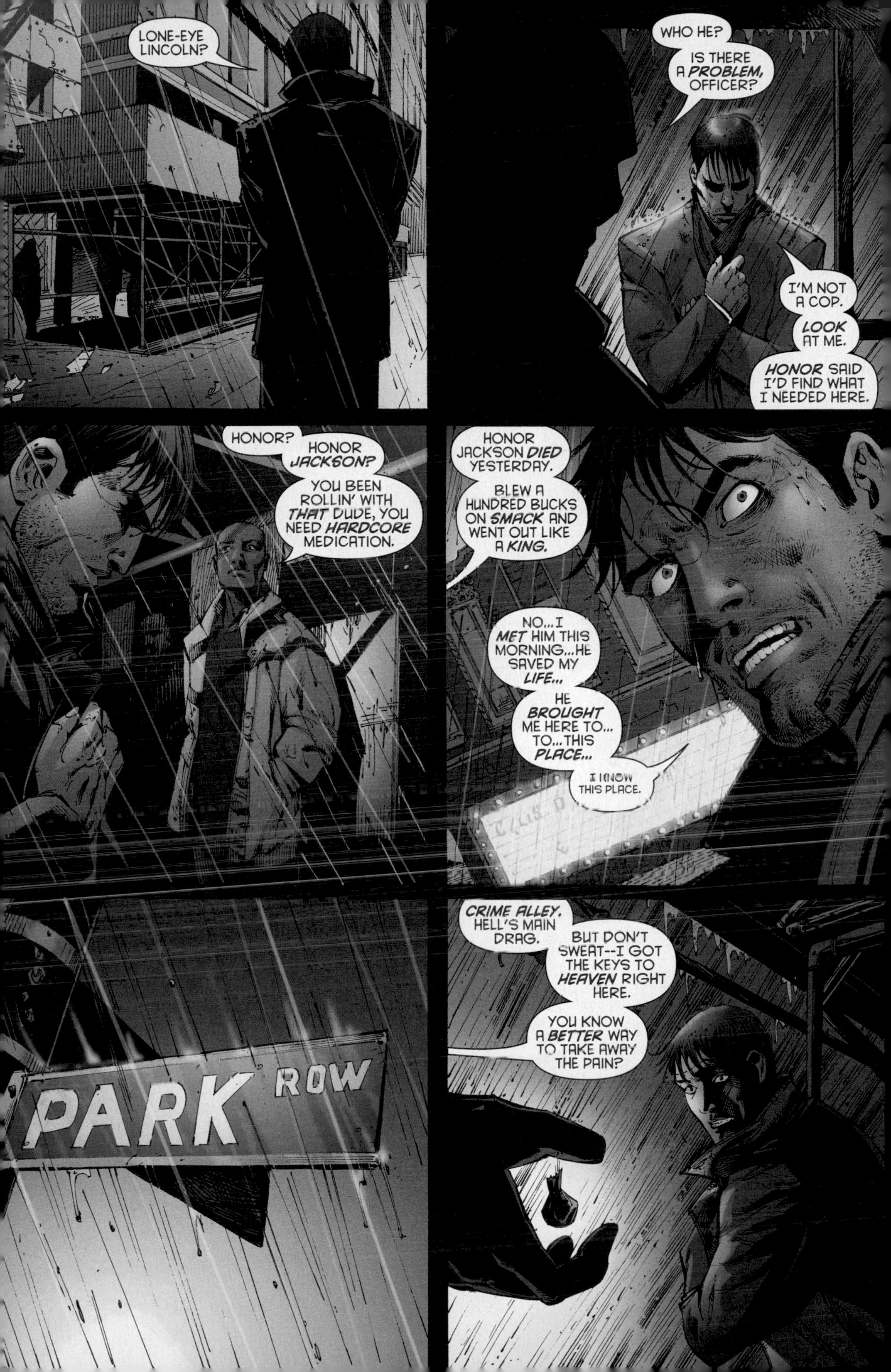
LONE-EYE LINCOLN?
WHO HE?
IS THERE A *PROBLEM,* OFFICER?
I'M NOT A COP.
LOOK AT ME.
HONOR SAID I'D FIND WHAT I NEEDED HERE.
HONOR?
HONOR *JACKSON?*
YOU BEEN ROLLIN' WITH *THAT* DUDE, YOU NEED *HARDCORE* MEDICATION.
HONOR JACKSON *DIED* YESTERDAY.
BLEW A HUNDRED BUCKS ON *SMACK* AND WENT OUT LIKE A *KING.*
NO...I *MET* HIM THIS MORNING...HE SAVED MY *LIFE...*
HE *BROUGHT* ME HERE TO... TO...THIS *PLACE...*
I KNOW THIS PLACE.
PARK ROW
CRIME ALLEY. HELL'S MAIN DRAG.
BUT DON'T SWEAT--I GOT THE KEYS TO *HEAVEN* RIGHT HERE.
YOU KNOW A *BETTER* WAY TO TAKE AWAY THE PAIN?

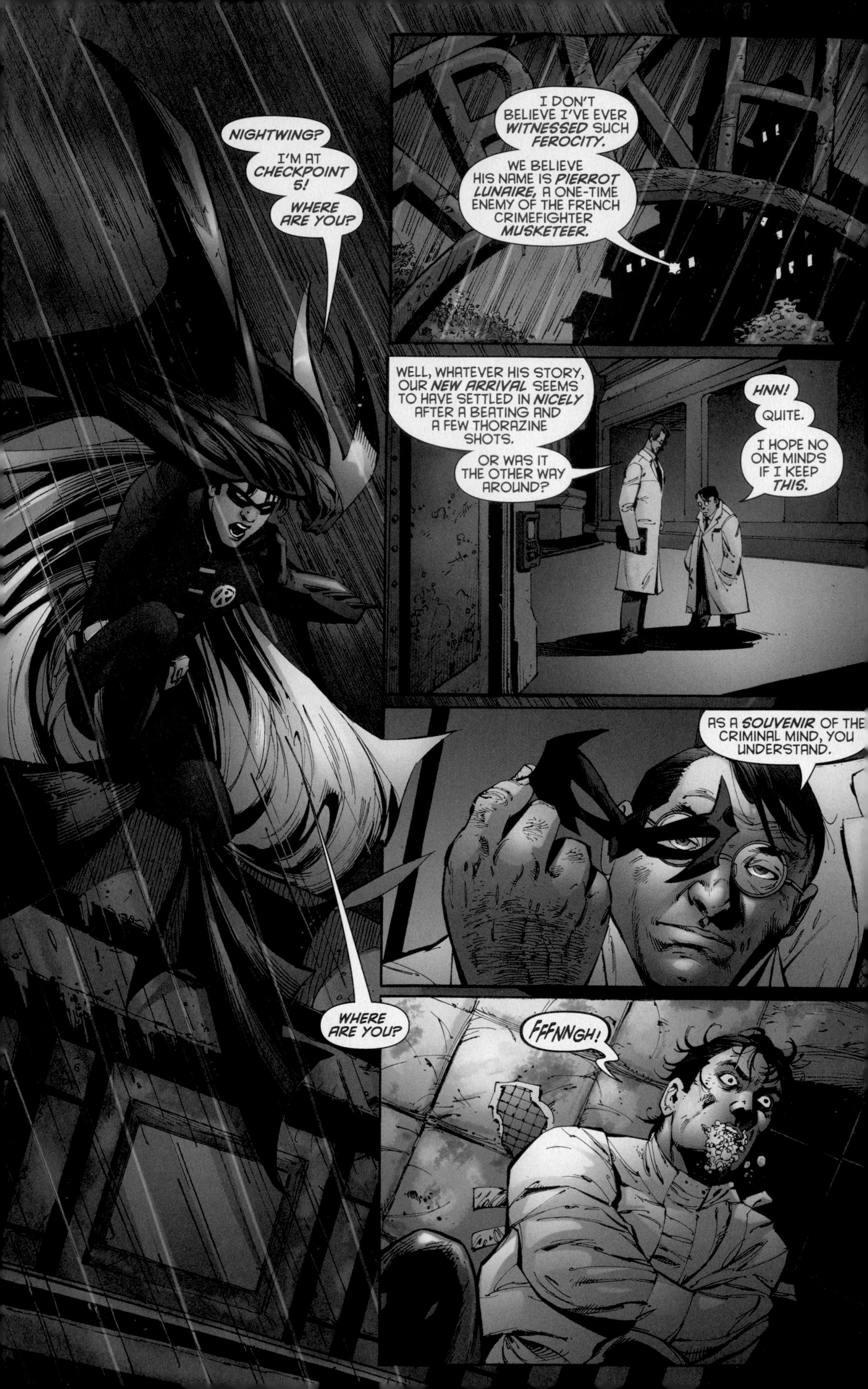
NIGHTWING?
I'M AT CHECKPOINT 5!
WHERE ARE YOU?
I DON'T BELIEVE I'VE EVER WITNESSED SUCH FEROCITY.
WE BELIEVE HIS NAME IS PIERROT LUNAIRE, A ONE-TIME ENEMY OF THE FRENCH CRIMEFIGHTER MUSKETEER.
WELL, WHATEVER HIS STORY, OUR NEW ARRIVAL SEEMS TO HAVE SETTLED IN NICELY AFTER A BEATING AND A FEW THORAZINE SHOTS.
OR WAS IT THE OTHER WAY AROUND?
HNN!
QUITE.
I HOPE NO ONE MINDS IF I KEEP THIS.
AS A SOUVENIR OF THE CRIMINAL MIND, YOU UNDERSTAND.
WHERE ARE YOU?
FFFNNGH!

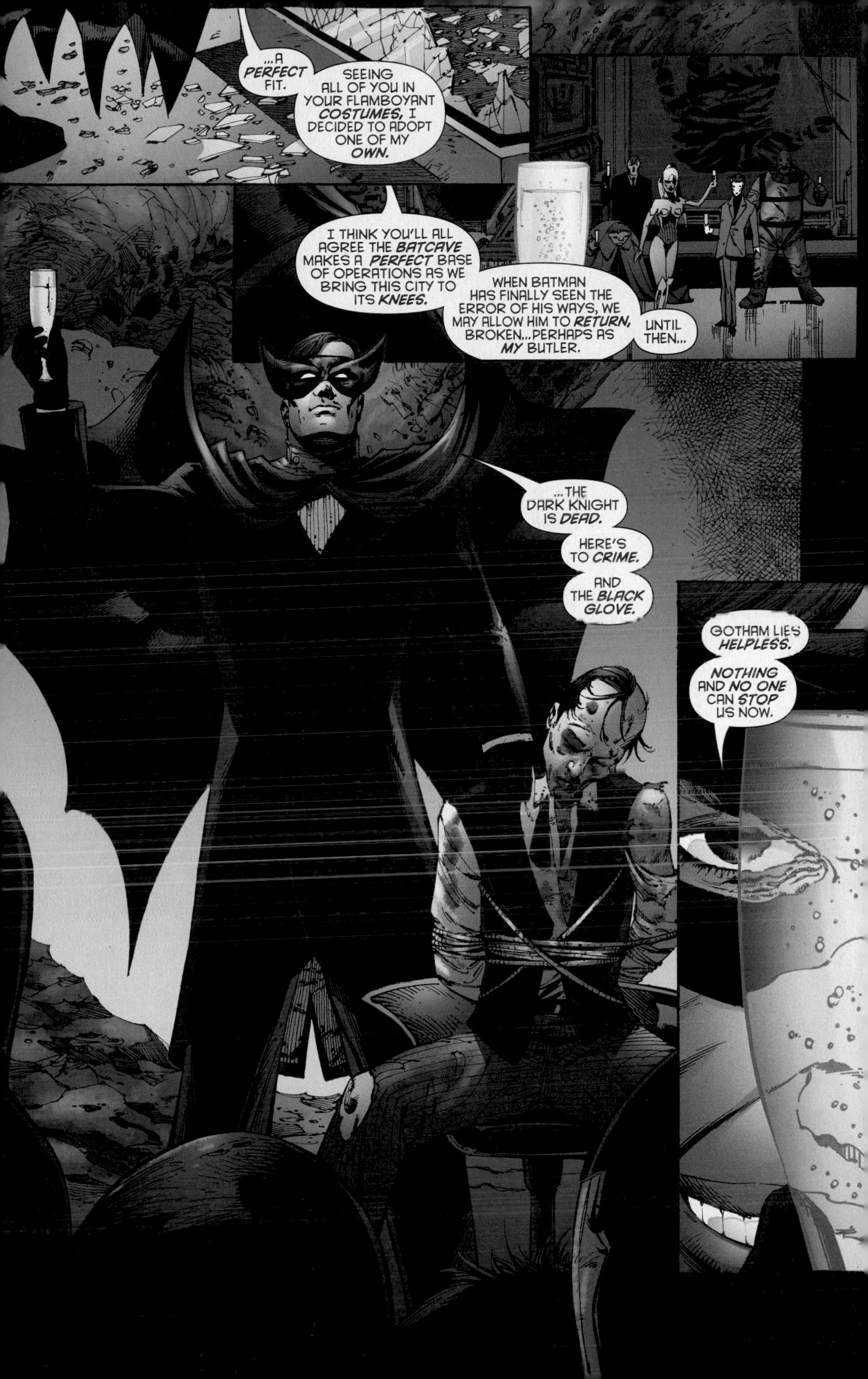
...A *PERFECT* FIT.
SEEING ALL OF YOU IN YOUR FLAMBOYANT *COSTUMES,* I DECIDED TO ADOPT ONE OF MY *OWN.*
I THINK YOU'LL ALL AGREE THE *BATCAVE* MAKES A *PERFECT* BASE OF OPERATIONS AS WE BRING THIS CITY TO ITS *KNEES.*
WHEN BATMAN HAS FINALLY SEEN THE ERROR OF HIS WAYS, WE MAY ALLOW HIM TO *RETURN,* BROKEN...PERHAPS AS *MY* BUTLER.
UNTIL THEN...
...THE DARK KNIGHT IS *DEAD.*
HERE'S TO *CRIME.*
AND THE *BLACK GLOVE.*
GOTHAM LIES *HELPLESS.*
NOTHING AND *NO ONE* CAN *STOP* US NOW.

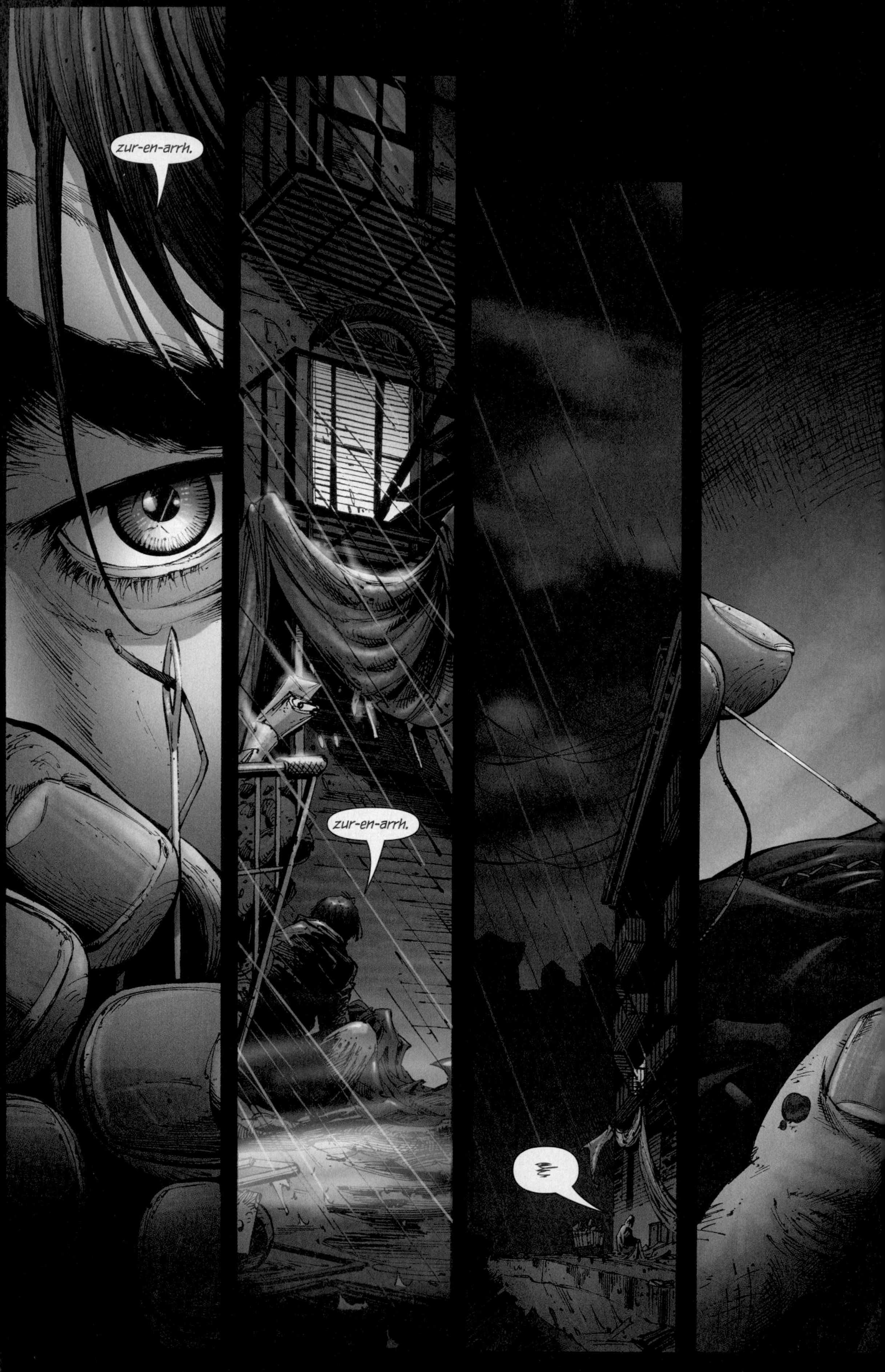
zur-en-arrh.
zur-en-arrh.

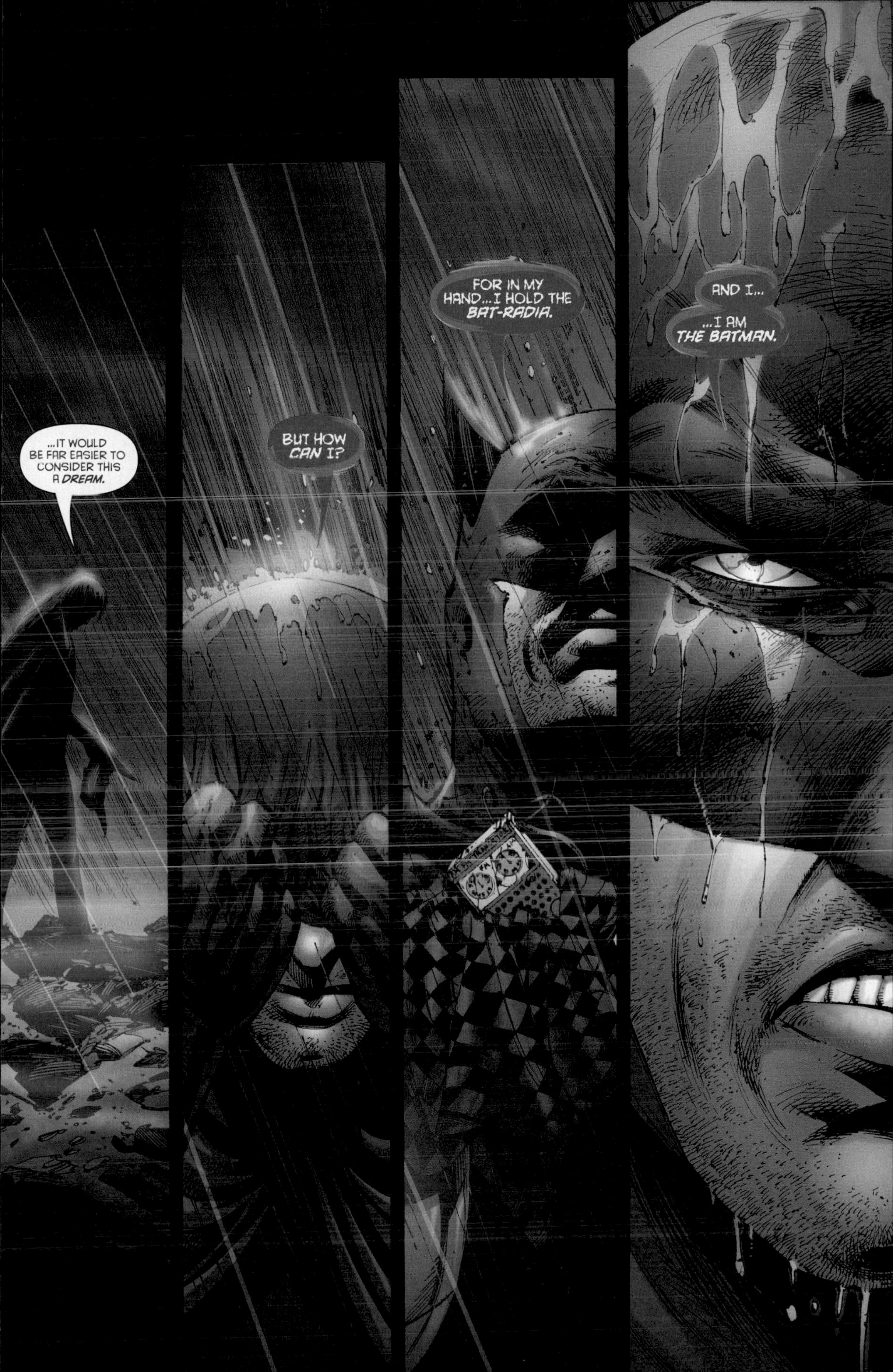
...IT WOULD BE FAR EASIER TO CONSIDER THIS A DREAM.
BUT HOW CAN I?
FOR IN MY HAND...I HOLD THE BAT-RADIA.
AND I...
...I AM THE BATMAN.

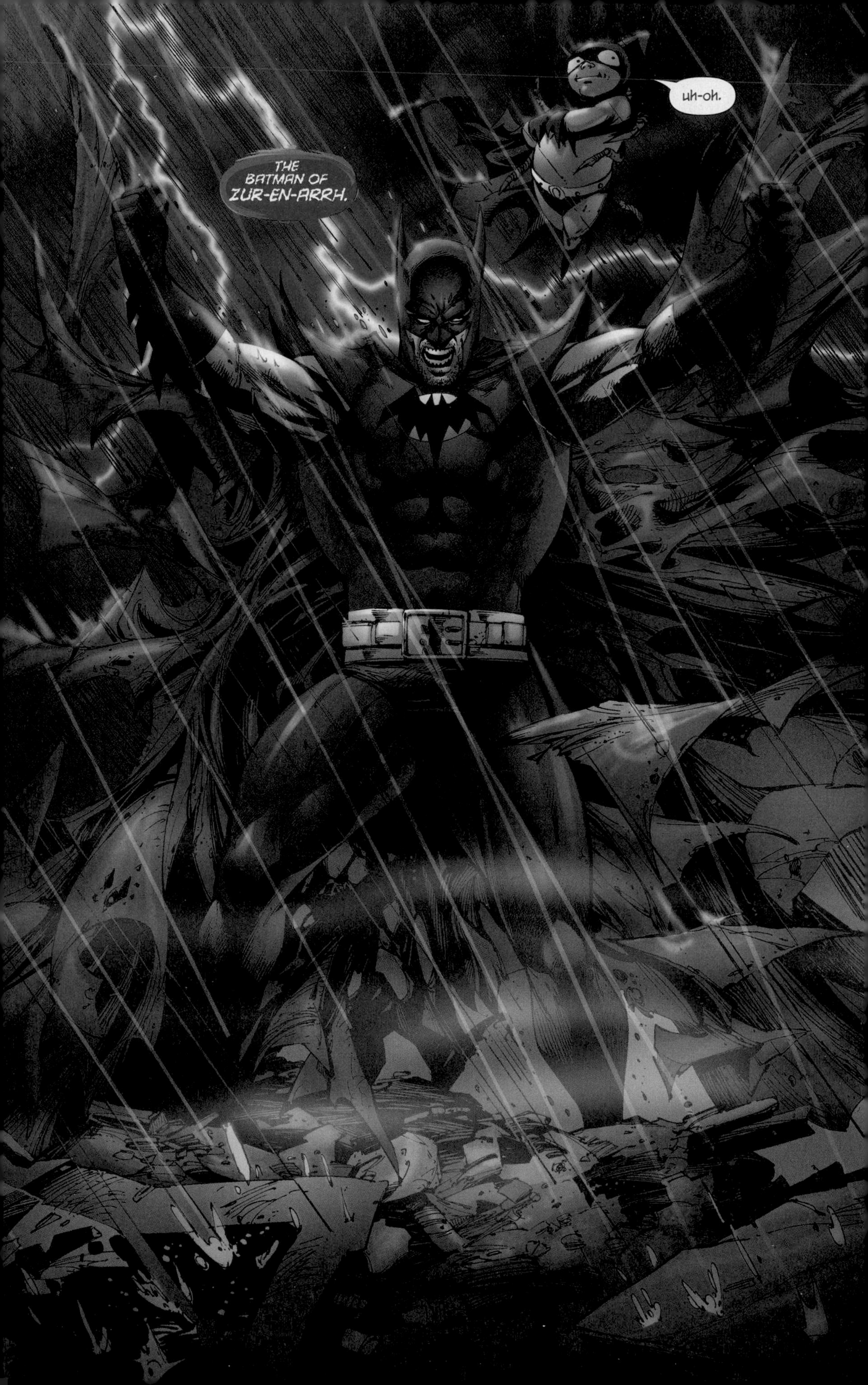
THE BATMAN OF ZUR-EN-ARRH.
uh-oh.

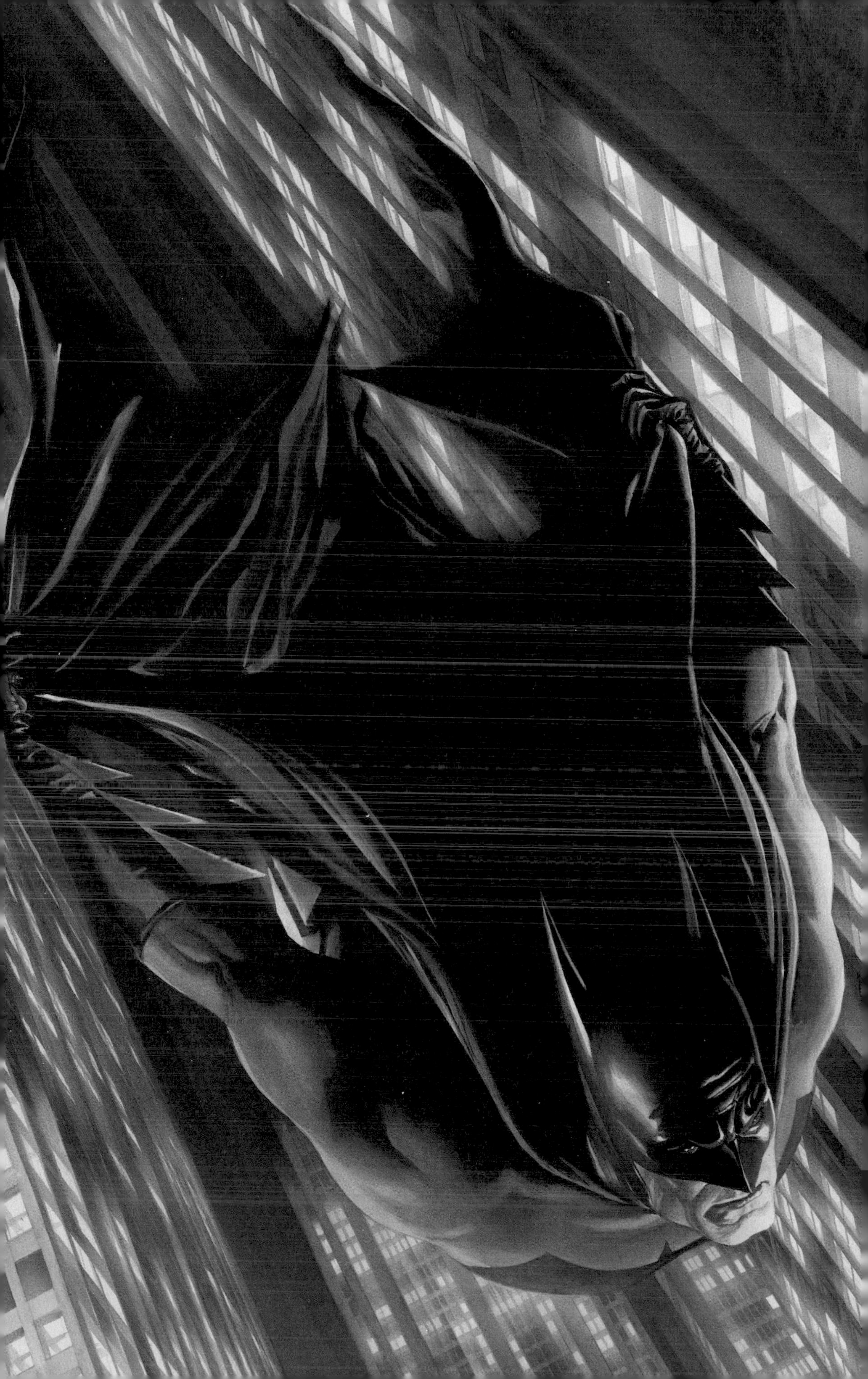

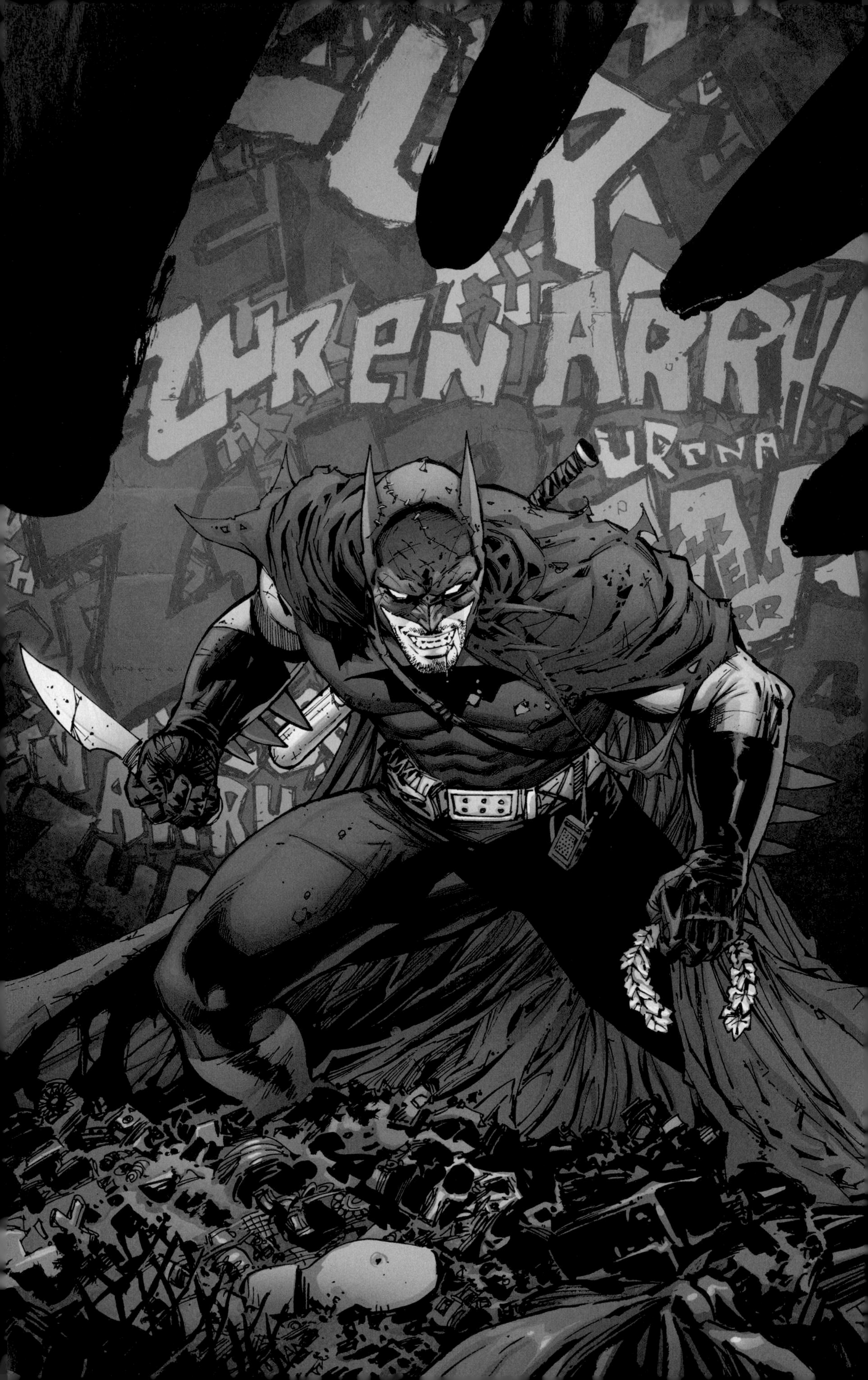

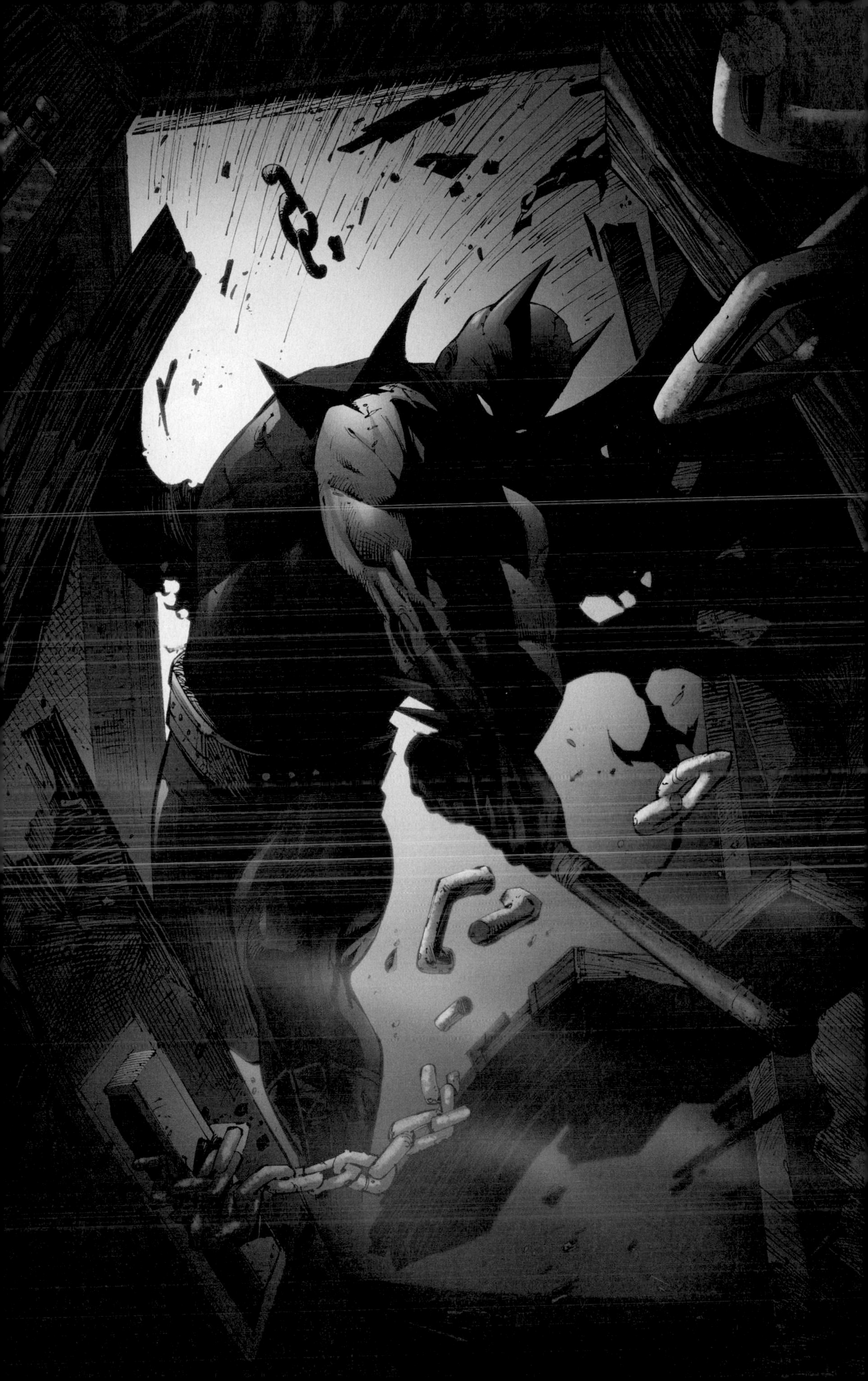

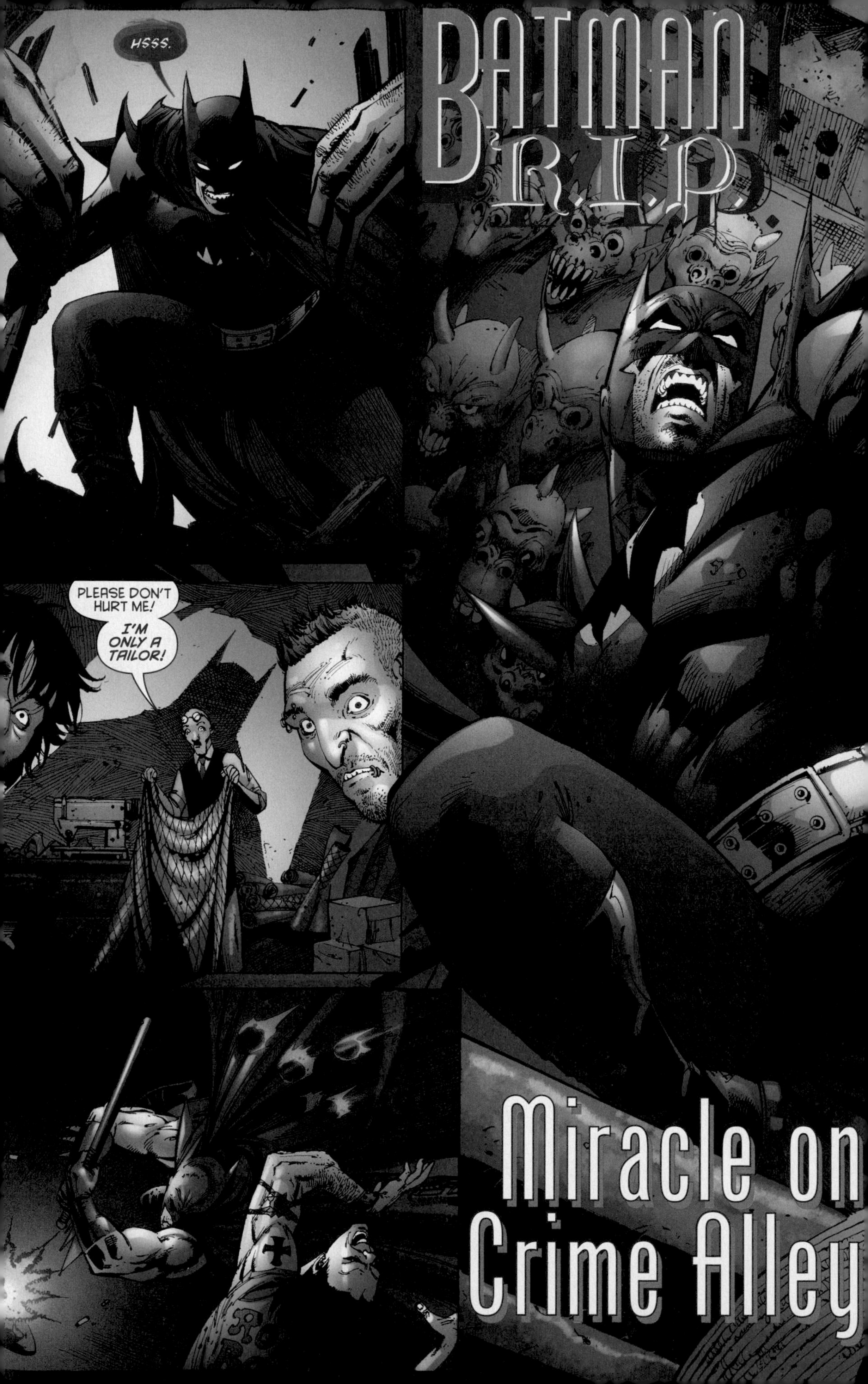
HSSS.
BATMAN R.I.P.
PLEASE DON'T HURT ME!
I'M ONLY A TAILOR!
Miracle on Crime Alley

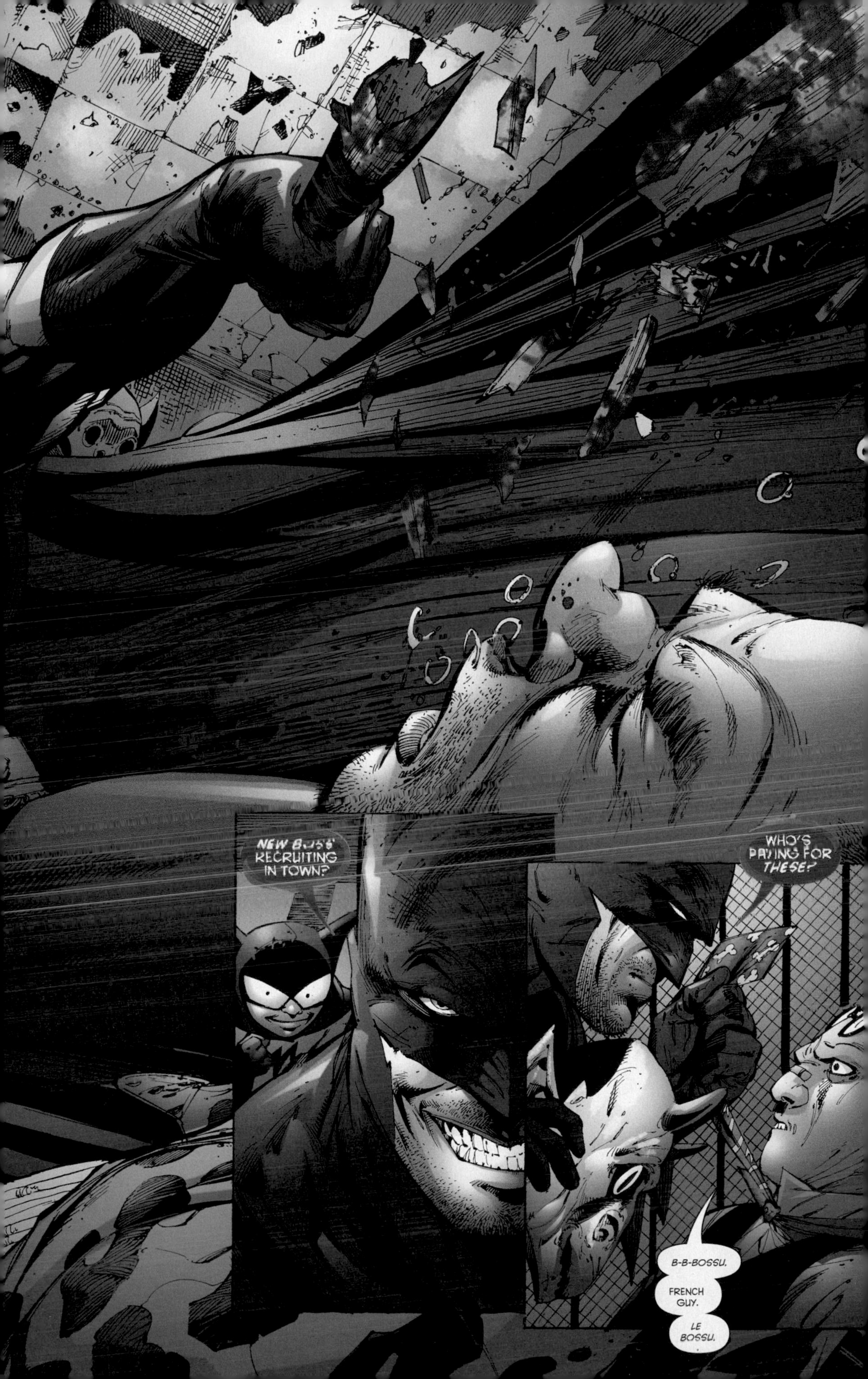
NEW BOSS' RECRUITING IN TOWN?
WHO'S PAYING FOR THESE?
B-B-BOSSU.
FRENCH GUY.
LE BOSSU.

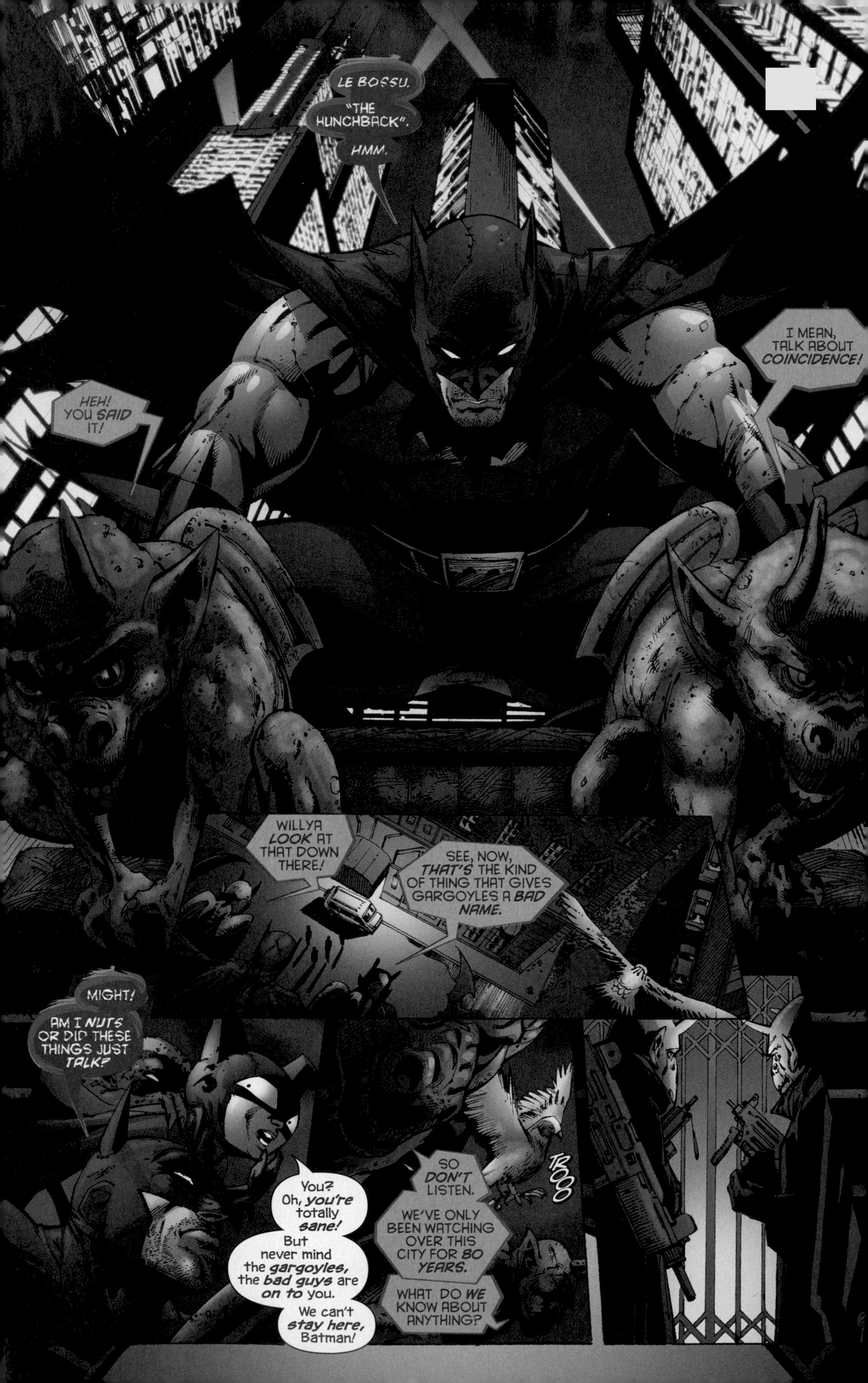
LE BOSSU.
"THE HUNCHBACK".
HMM.
HEH! YOU SAID IT!
I MEAN, TALK ABOUT COINCIDENCE!
WILLYA LOOK AT THAT DOWN THERE!
SEE, NOW, THAT'S THE KIND OF THING THAT GIVES GARGOYLES A BAD NAME.
MIGHT!
AM I NUTS OR DID THESE THINGS JUST TALK?
You? Oh, you're totally sane! But never mind the gargoyles, the bad guys are on to you.
We can't stay here, Batman!
SO DON'T LISTEN.
WE'VE ONLY BEEN WATCHING OVER THIS CITY FOR 80 YEARS.
WHAT DO WE KNOW ABOUT ANYTHING?

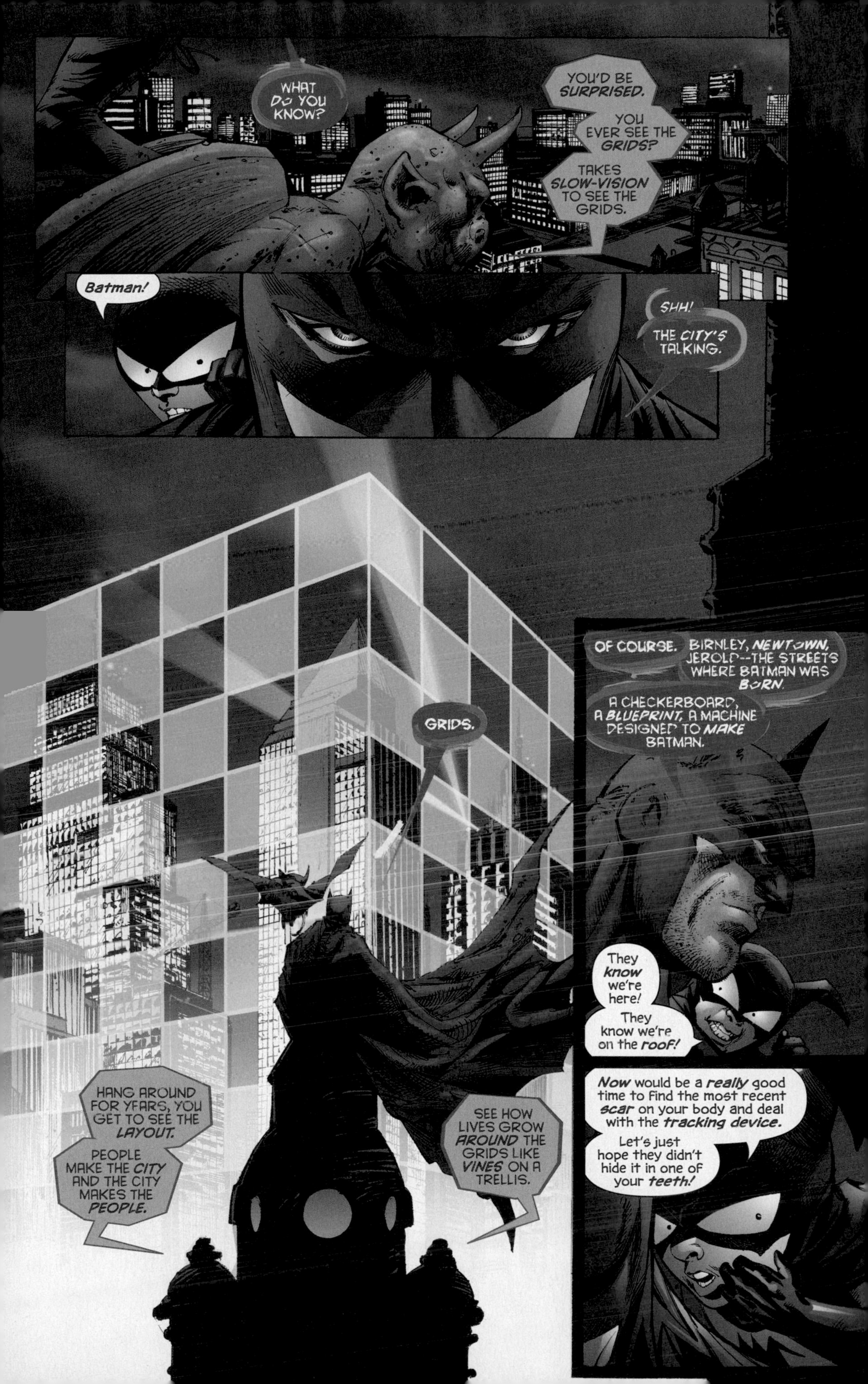
WHAT DO YOU KNOW?
YOU'D BE SURPRISED.
YOU EVER SEE THE GRIDS?
TAKES SLOW-VISION TO SEE THE GRIDS.
Batman!
SHH!
THE CITY'S TALKING.
GRIDS.
OF COURSE.
BIRNLEY, NEWTOWN, JEROLD--THE STREETS WHERE BATMAN WAS BORN.
A CHECKERBOARD, A BLUEPRINT, A MACHINE DESIGNED TO MAKE BATMAN.
They know we're here!
They know we're on the roof!
HANG AROUND FOR YEARS, YOU GET TO SEE THE LAYOUT.
PEOPLE MAKE THE CITY AND THE CITY MAKES THE PEOPLE.
SEE HOW LIVES GROW AROUND THE GRIDS LIKE VINES ON A TRELLIS.
Now would be a really good time to find the most recent scar on your body and deal with the tracking device.
Let's just hope they didn't hide it in one of your teeth!

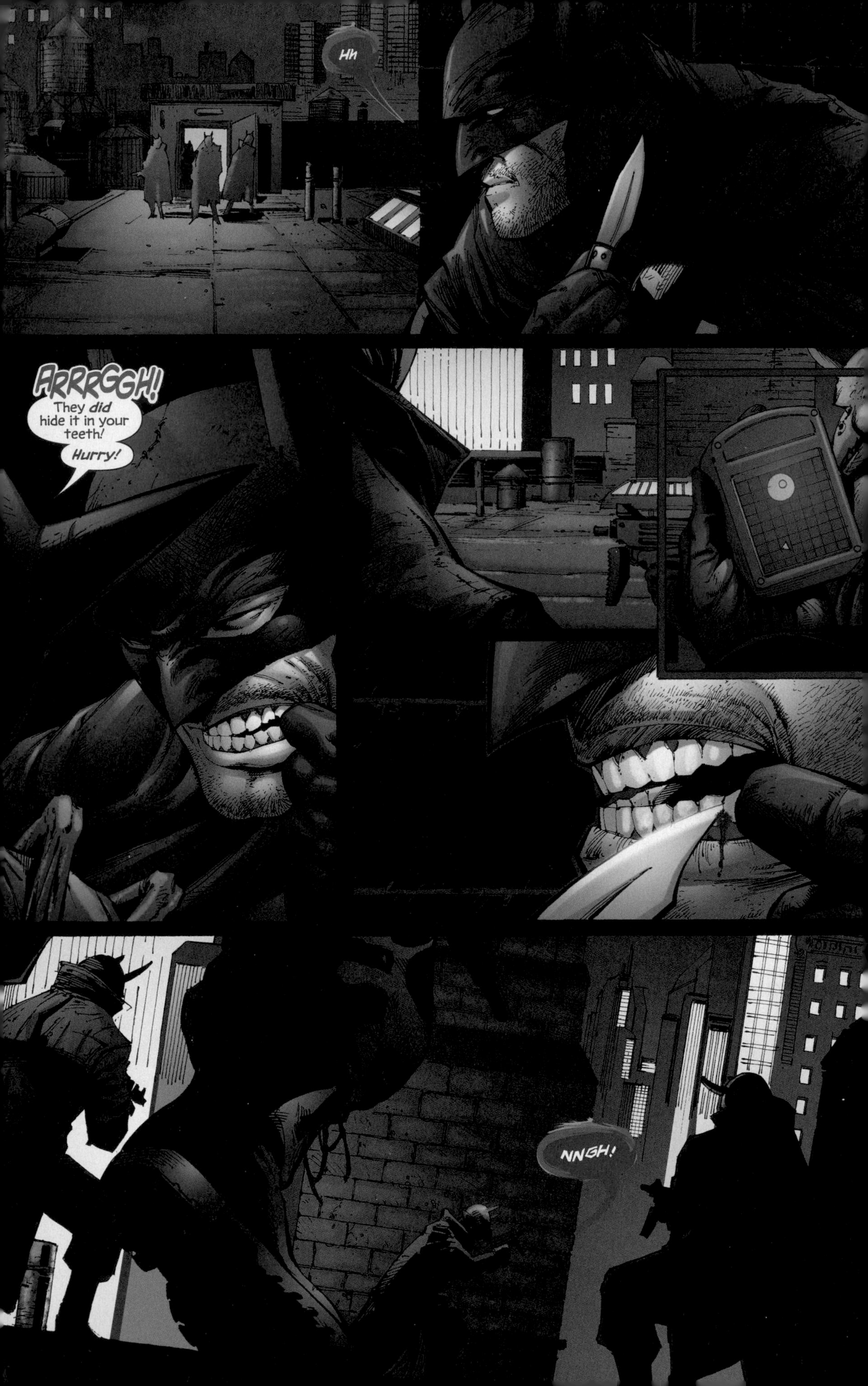
Hh
ARRRGGH!
They did hide it in your teeth!
Hurry!
NNGH!

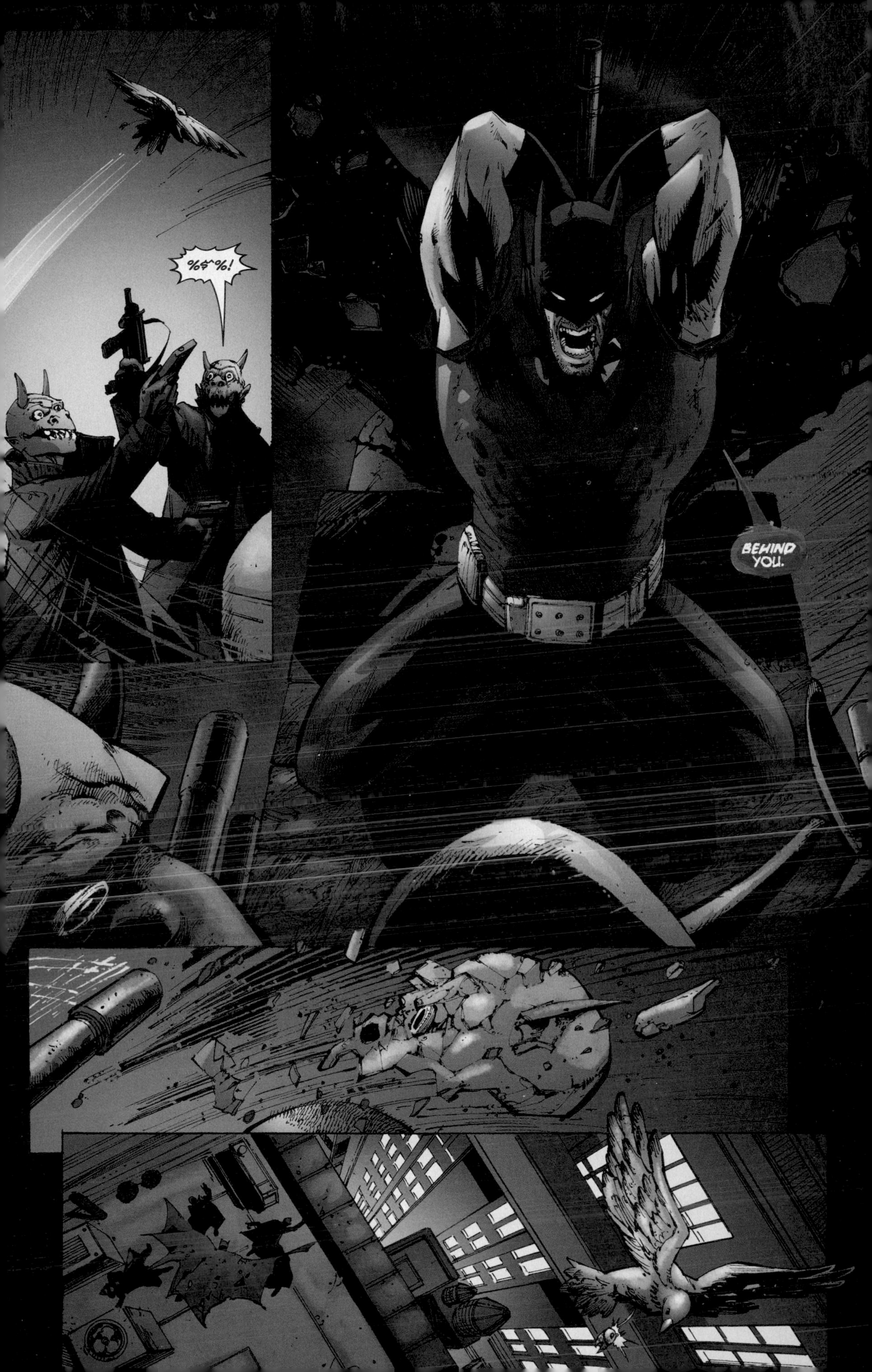
%$^%!
BEHIND YOU.

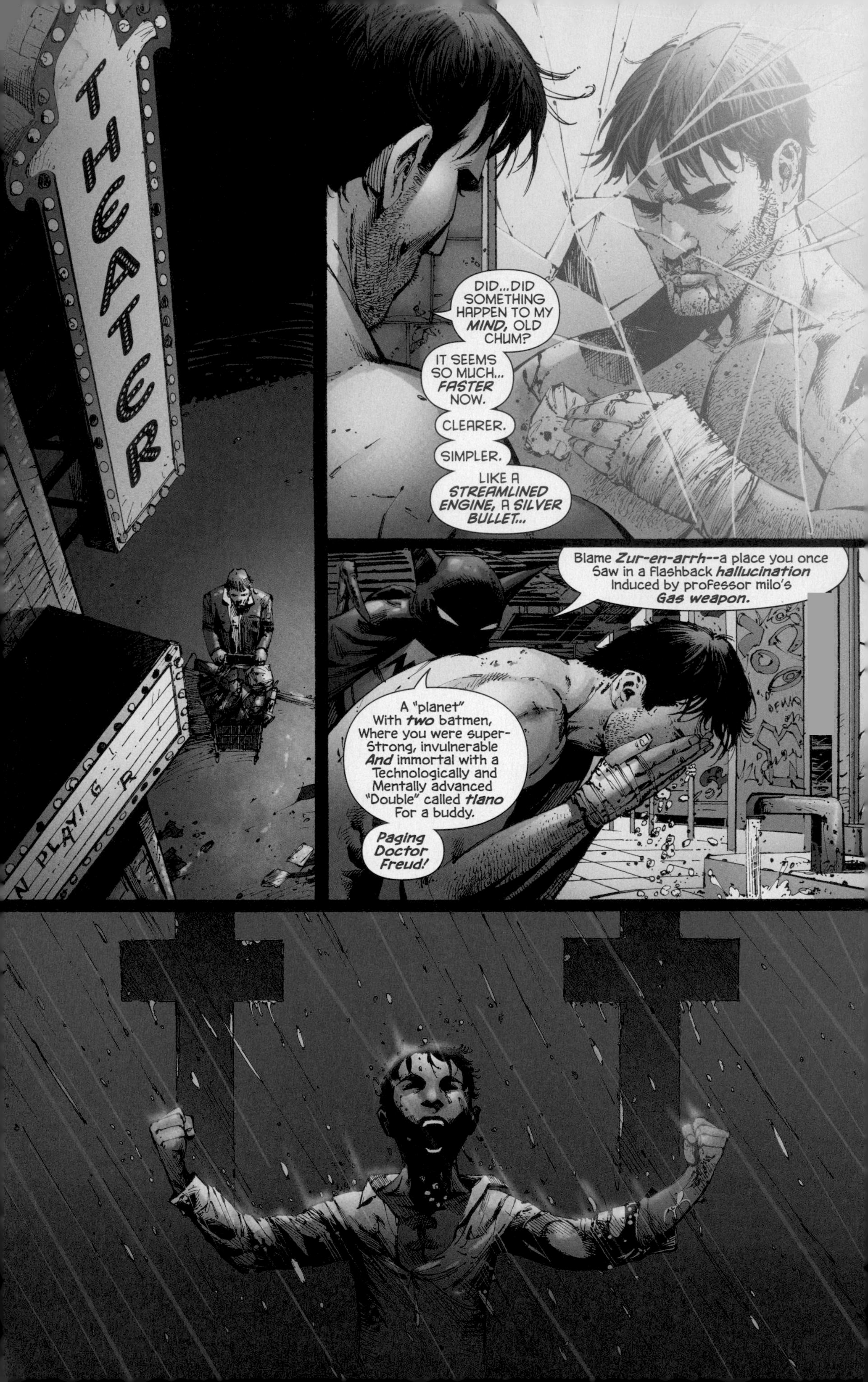
THEATER
DID...DID SOMETHING HAPPEN TO MY MIND, OLD CHUM?
IT SEEMS SO MUCH... FASTER NOW.
CLEARER.
SIMPLER.
LIKE A STREAMLINED ENGINE, A SILVER BULLET...
Blame Zur-en-arrh--a place you once Saw in a Flashback hallucination Induced by professor milo's Gas weapon.
A "planet" With two batmen, Where you were super-Strong, invulnerable And immortal with a Technologically and Mentally advanced "Double" called tlano For a buddy.
Paging Doctor Freud!

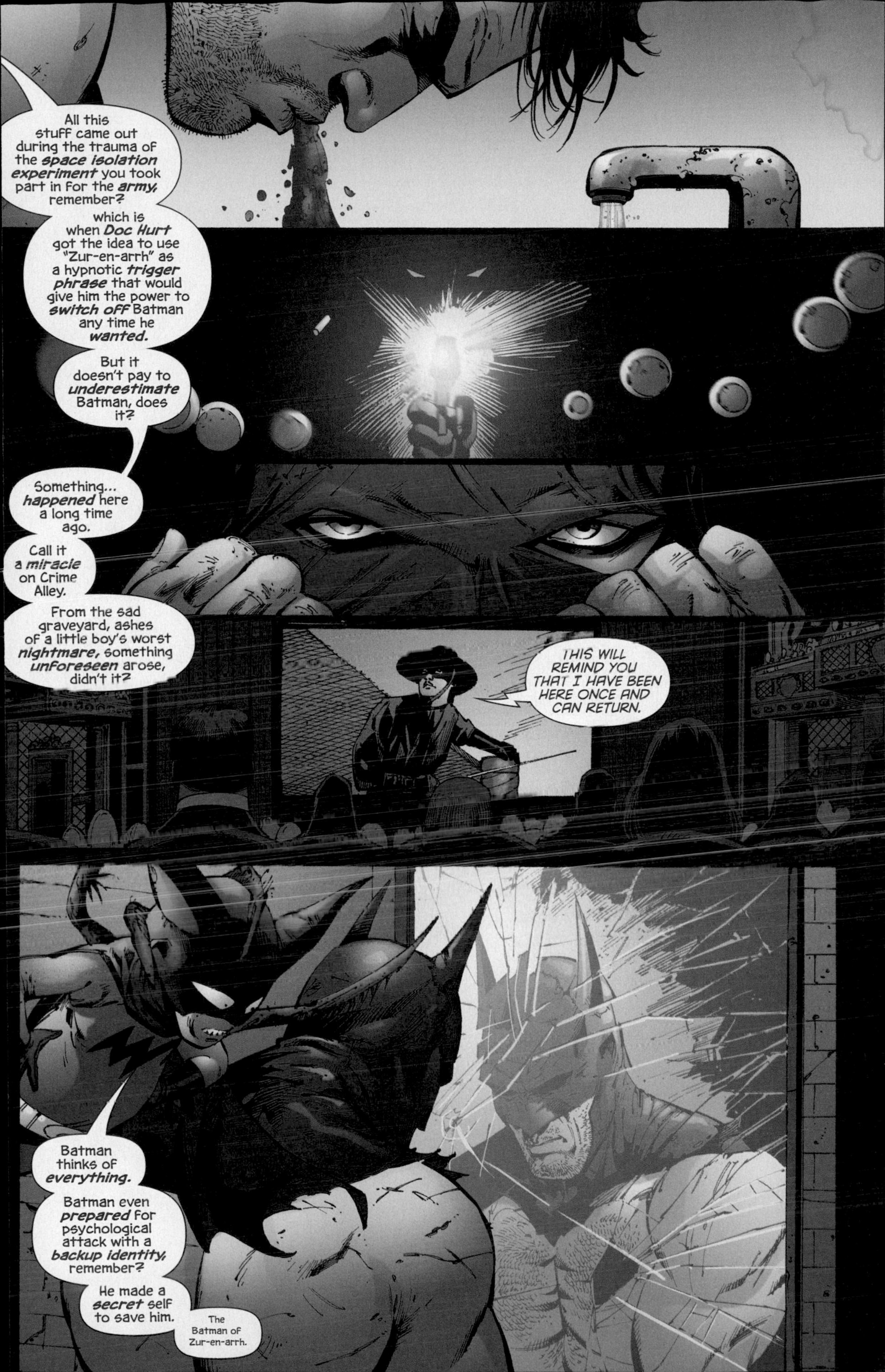
All this stuff came out during the trauma of the *space isolation experiment* you took part in for the *army,* remember?
which is when *Doc Hurt* got the idea to use "Zur-en-arrh" as a hypnotic *trigger phrase* that would give him the power to *switch off* Batman any time he *wanted.*
But it doesn't pay to *underestimate* Batman, does it?
Something... *happened* here a long time ago.
Call it a *miracle* on Crime Alley.
From the sad graveyard, ashes of a little boy's worst *nightmare,* something *unforeseen* arose, didn't it?
THIS WILL REMIND YOU THAT I HAVE BEEN HERE ONCE AND CAN RETURN.
Batman thinks of *everything.*
Batman even *prepared* for psychological attack with a *backup identity,* remember?
He made a *secret* self to save him.
The Batman of Zur-en-arrh.

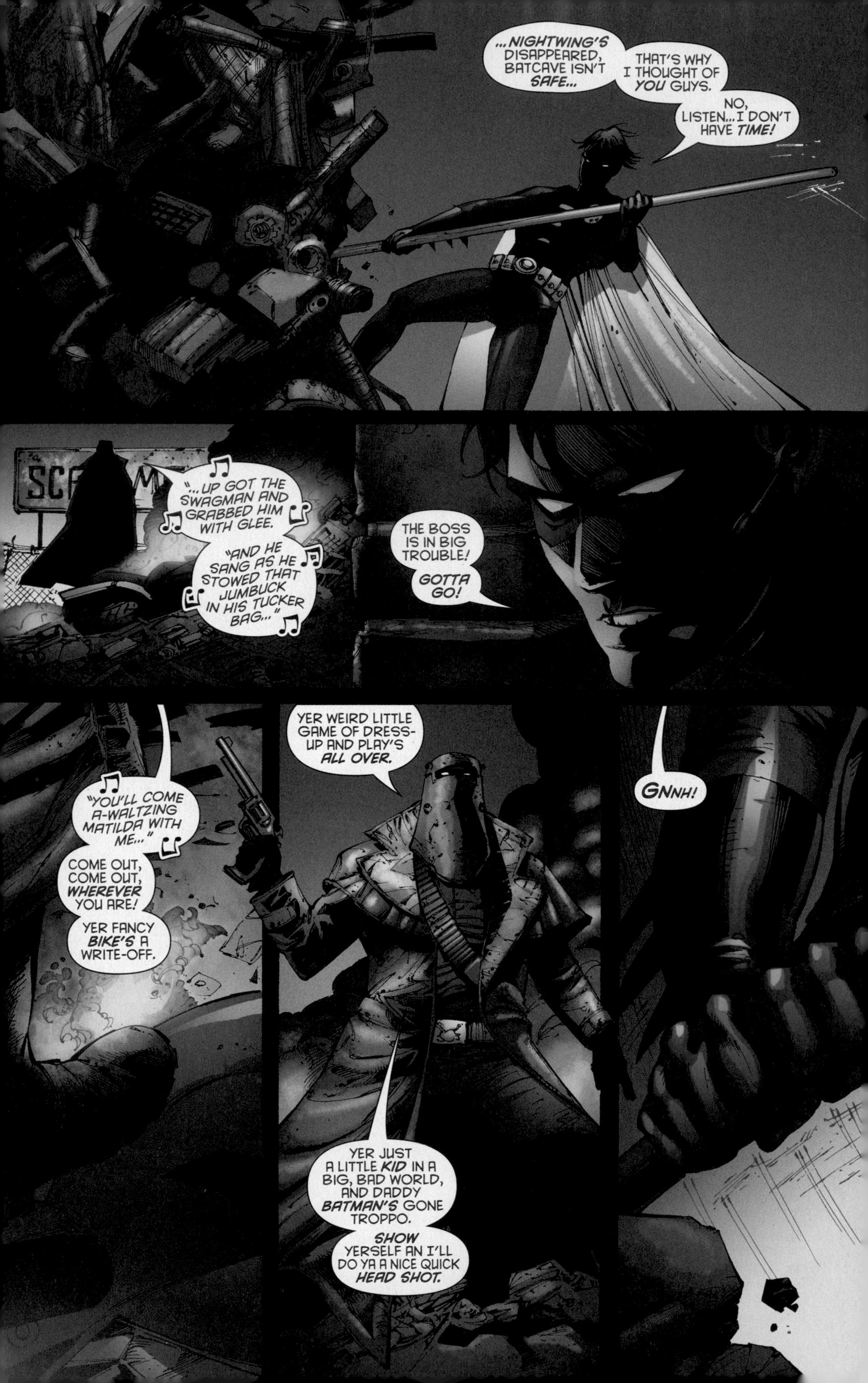

...NIGHTWING'S DISAPPEARED, BATCAVE ISN'T SAFE...
THAT'S WHY I THOUGHT OF YOU GUYS.
NO, LISTEN...I DON'T HAVE TIME!
"...UP GOT THE SWAGMAN AND GRABBED HIM WITH GLEE.
"AND HE SANG AS HE STOWED THAT JUMBUCK IN HIS TUCKER BAG..."
THE BOSS IS IN BIG TROUBLE!
GOTTA GO!
"YOU'LL COME A-WALTZING MATILDA WITH ME..."
COME OUT, COME OUT, WHEREVER YOU ARE!
YER FANCY BIKE'S A WRITE-OFF.
YER WEIRD LITTLE GAME OF DRESS-UP AND PLAY'S ALL OVER.
YER JUST A LITTLE KID IN A BIG, BAD WORLD, AND DADDY BATMAN'S GONE TROPPO.
SHOW YERSELF AN I'LL DO YA A NICE QUICK HEAD SHOT.
GNNH!

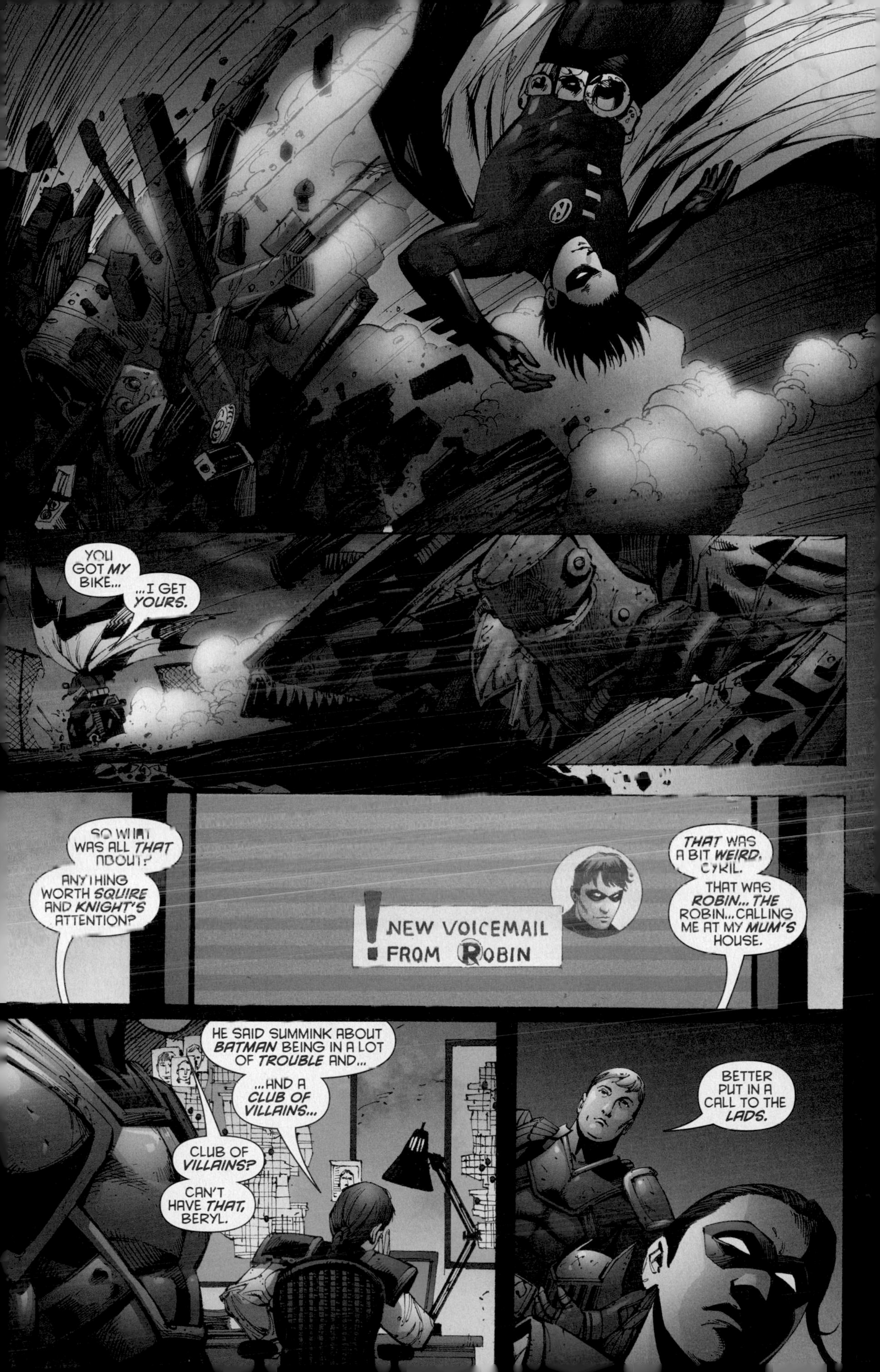

YOU GOT MY BIKE...
...I GET YOURS.
SO WHAT WAS ALL THAT ABOUT?
ANYTHING WORTH SQUIRE AND KNIGHT'S ATTENTION?
NEW VOICEMAIL FROM ROBIN
THAT WAS A BIT WEIRD, CYRIL.
THAT WAS ROBIN... THE ROBIN...CALLING ME AT MY MUM'S HOUSE.
HE SAID SUMMINK ABOUT BATMAN BEING IN A LOT OF TROUBLE AND...
...AND A CLUB OF VILLAINS...
CLUB OF VILLAINS?
CAN'T HAVE THAT, BERYL.
BETTER PUT IN A CALL TO THE LADS.

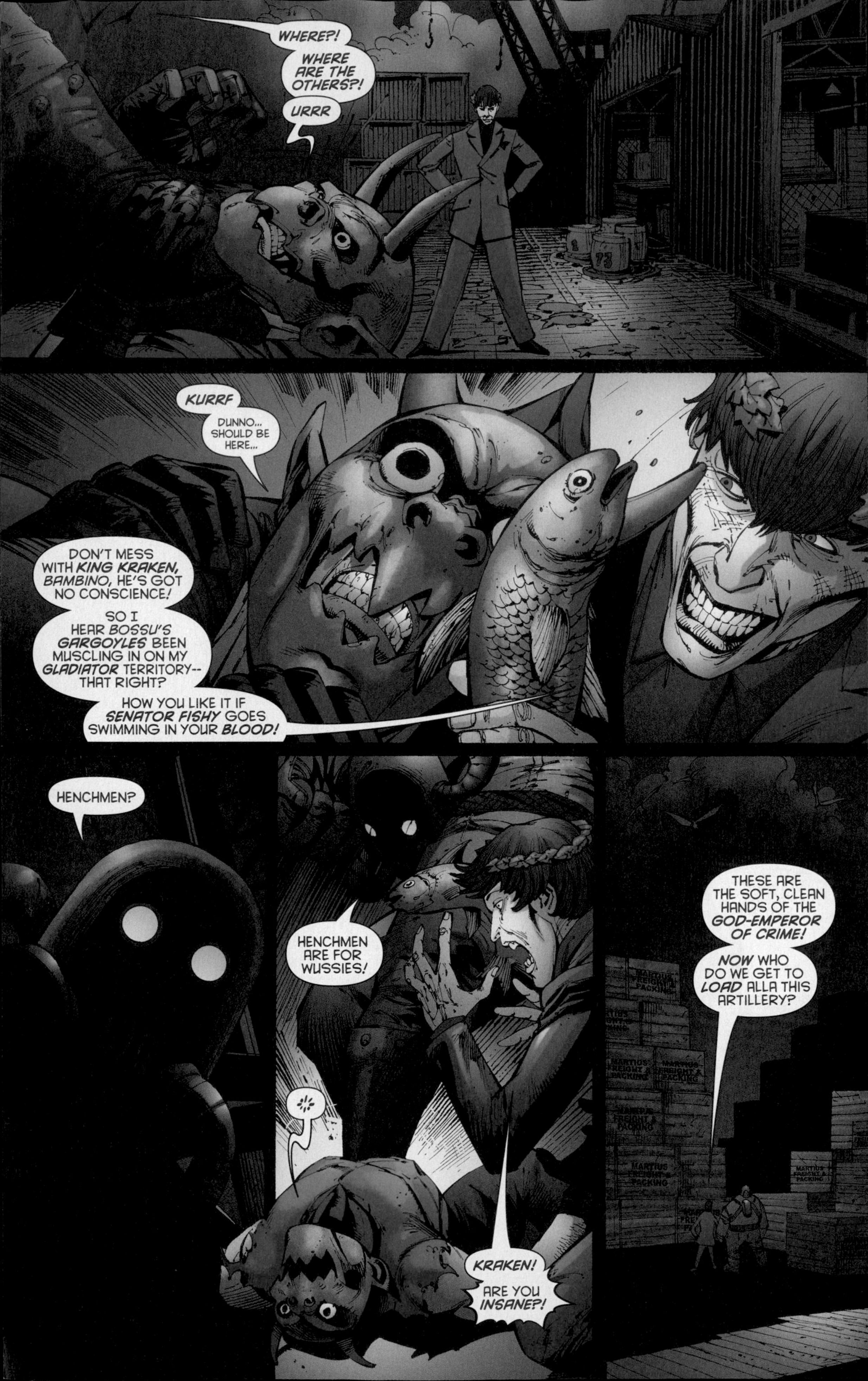
WHERE?!
WHERE ARE THE OTHERS?!
URRR
KURRF
DUNNO... SHOULD BE HERE...
DON'T MESS WITH KING KRAKEN, BAMBINO, HE'S GOT NO CONSCIENCE!
SO I HEAR BOSSU'S GARGOYLES BEEN MUSCLING IN ON MY GLADIATOR TERRITORY-- THAT RIGHT?
HOW YOU LIKE IT IF SENATOR FISHY GOES SWIMMING IN YOUR BLOOD!
HENCHMEN?
HENCHMEN ARE FOR WUSSIES!
KRAKEN!
ARE YOU INSANE?!
THESE ARE THE SOFT, CLEAN HANDS OF THE GOD-EMPEROR OF CRIME!
NOW WHO DO WE GET TO LOAD ALLA THIS ARTILLERY?

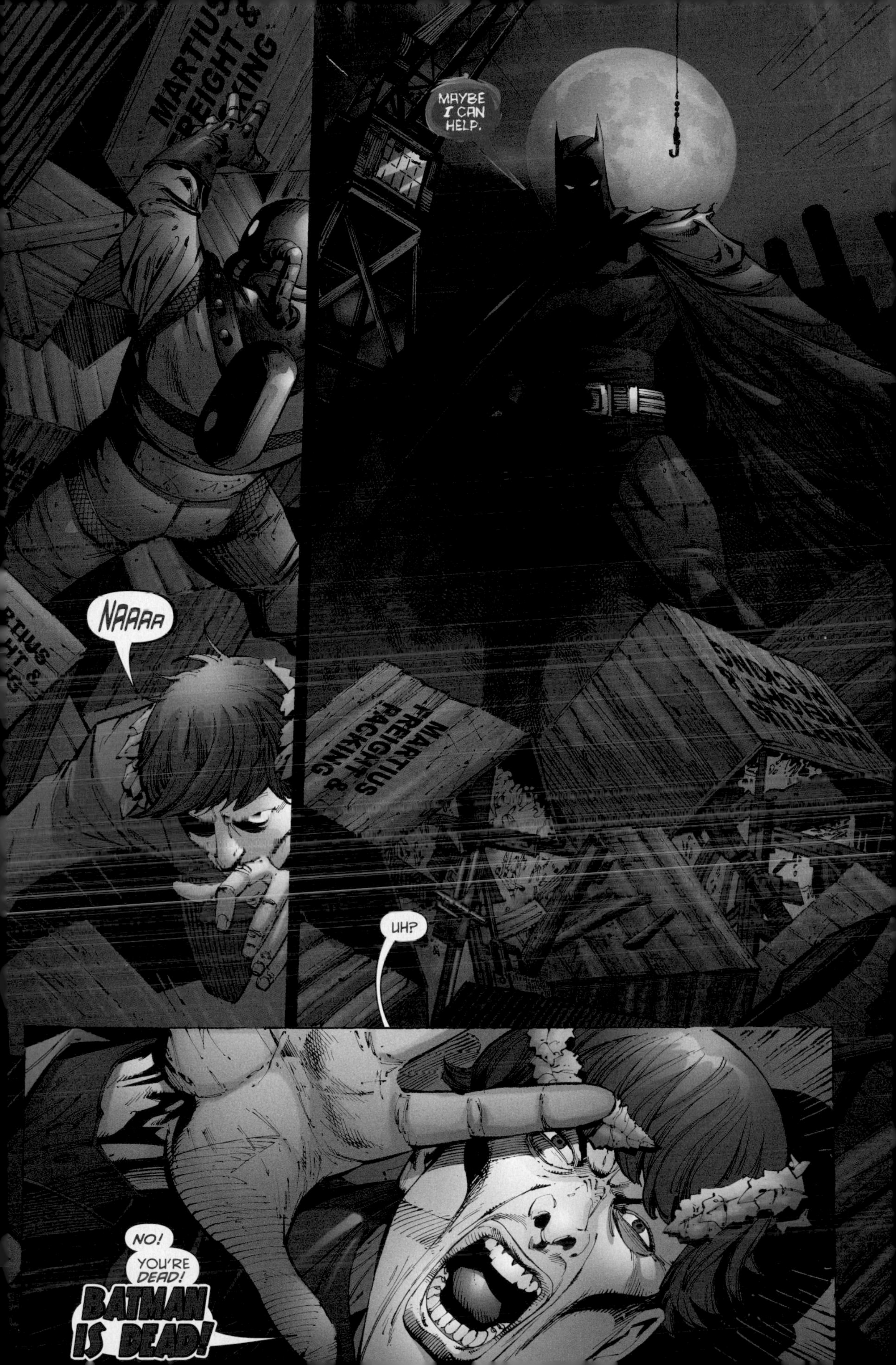
MARTIUS FREIGHT & PACKING
MAYBE I CAN HELP.
NAAAA
MARTIUS FREIGHT & PACKING
UH?
NO!
YOU'RE DEAD!
BATMAN IS DEAD!

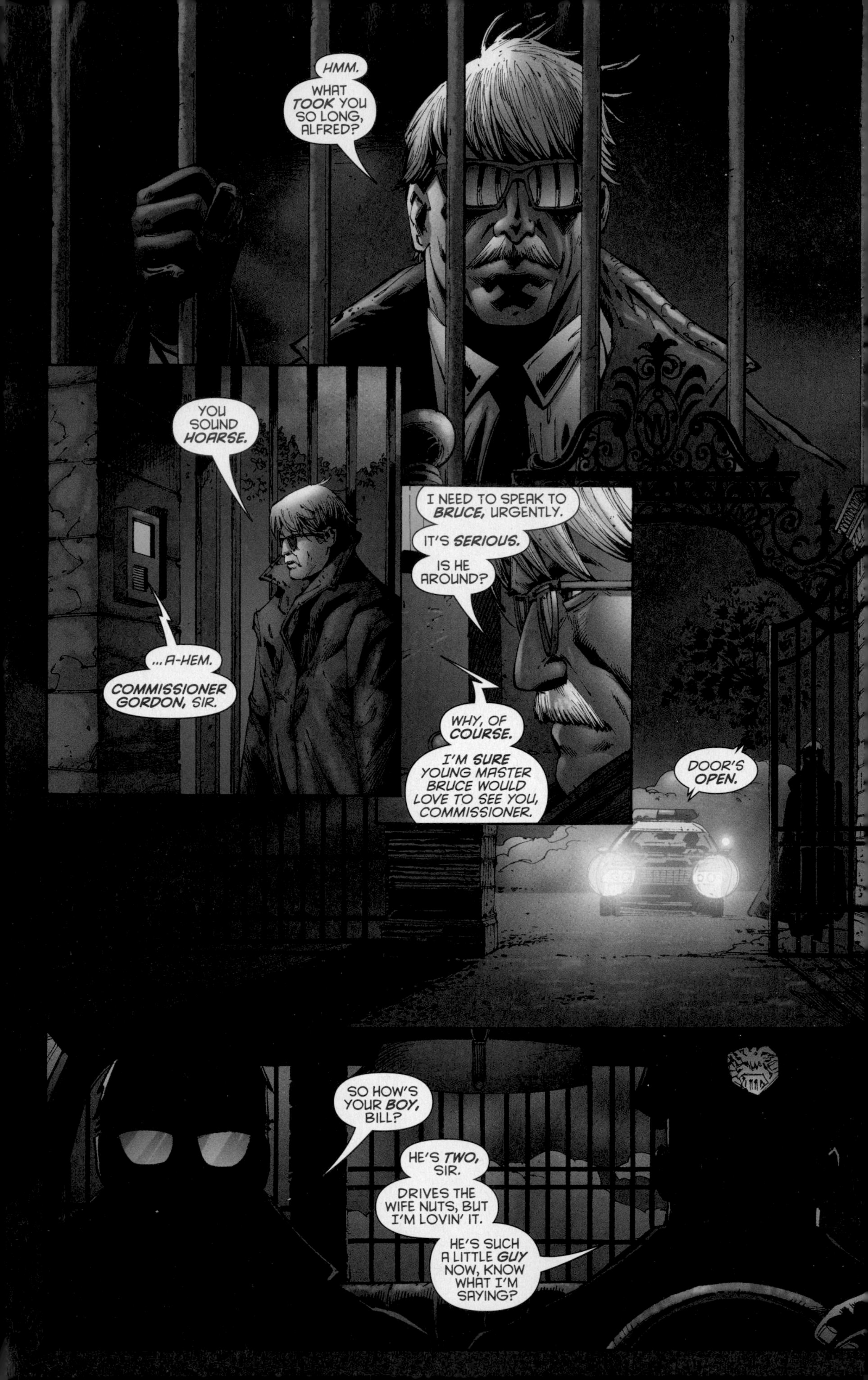
HMM.
WHAT TOOK YOU SO LONG, ALFRED?
YOU SOUND HOARSE.
...A-HEM.
COMMISSIONER GORDON, SIR.
I NEED TO SPEAK TO BRUCE, URGENTLY.
IT'S SERIOUS.
IS HE AROUND?
WHY, OF COURSE.
I'M SURE YOUNG MASTER BRUCE WOULD LOVE TO SEE YOU, COMMISSIONER.
DOOR'S OPEN.
SO HOW'S YOUR BOY, BILL?
HE'S TWO, SIR.
DRIVES THE WIFE NUTS, BUT I'M LOVIN' IT.
HE'S SUCH A LITTLE GUY NOW, KNOW WHAT I'M SAYING?

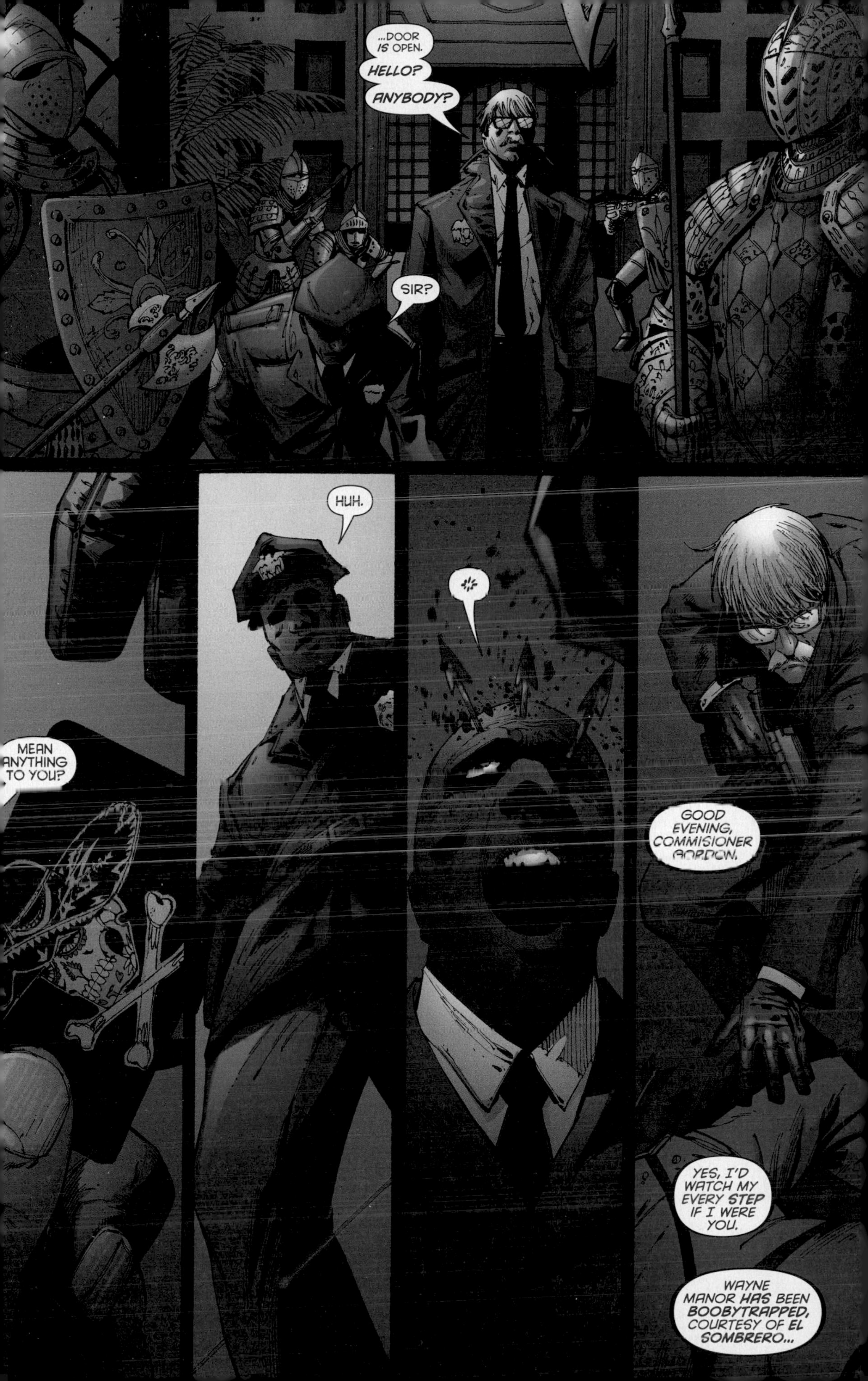
...DOOR IS OPEN.
HELLO?
ANYBODY?
SIR?
HUH.
MEAN ANYTHING TO YOU?
GOOD EVENING, COMMISIONER GORDON.
YES, I'D WATCH MY EVERY STEP IF I WERE YOU.
WAYNE MANOR HAS BEEN BOOBYTRAPPED, COURTESY OF EL SOMBRERO...

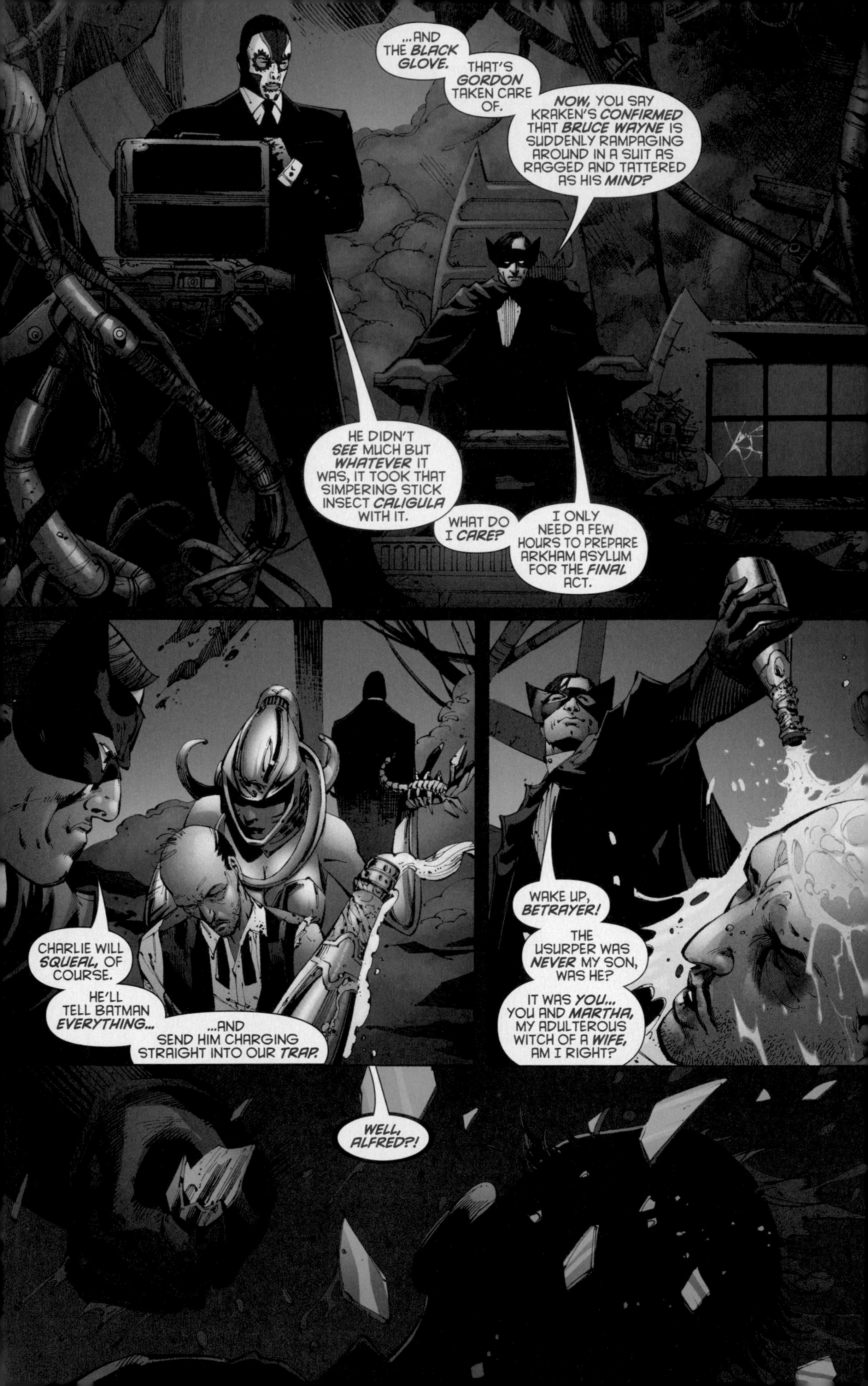

...AND THE BLACK GLOVE.
THAT'S GORDON TAKEN CARE OF.
NOW, YOU SAY KRAKEN'S CONFIRMED THAT BRUCE WAYNE IS SUDDENLY RAMPAGING AROUND IN A SUIT AS RAGGED AND TATTERED AS HIS MIND?
HE DIDN'T SEE MUCH BUT WHATEVER IT WAS, IT TOOK THAT SIMPERING STICK INSECT CALIGULA WITH IT.
WHAT DO I CARE?
I ONLY NEED A FEW HOURS TO PREPARE ARKHAM ASYLUM FOR THE FINAL ACT.
CHARLIE WILL SQUEAL, OF COURSE.
HE'LL TELL BATMAN EVERYTHING...
...AND SEND HIM CHARGING STRAIGHT INTO OUR TRAP.
WAKE UP, BETRAYER!
THE USURPER WAS NEVER MY SON, WAS HE?
IT WAS YOU... YOU AND MARTHA, MY ADULTEROUS WITCH OF A WIFE, AM I RIGHT?
WELL, ALFRED?!

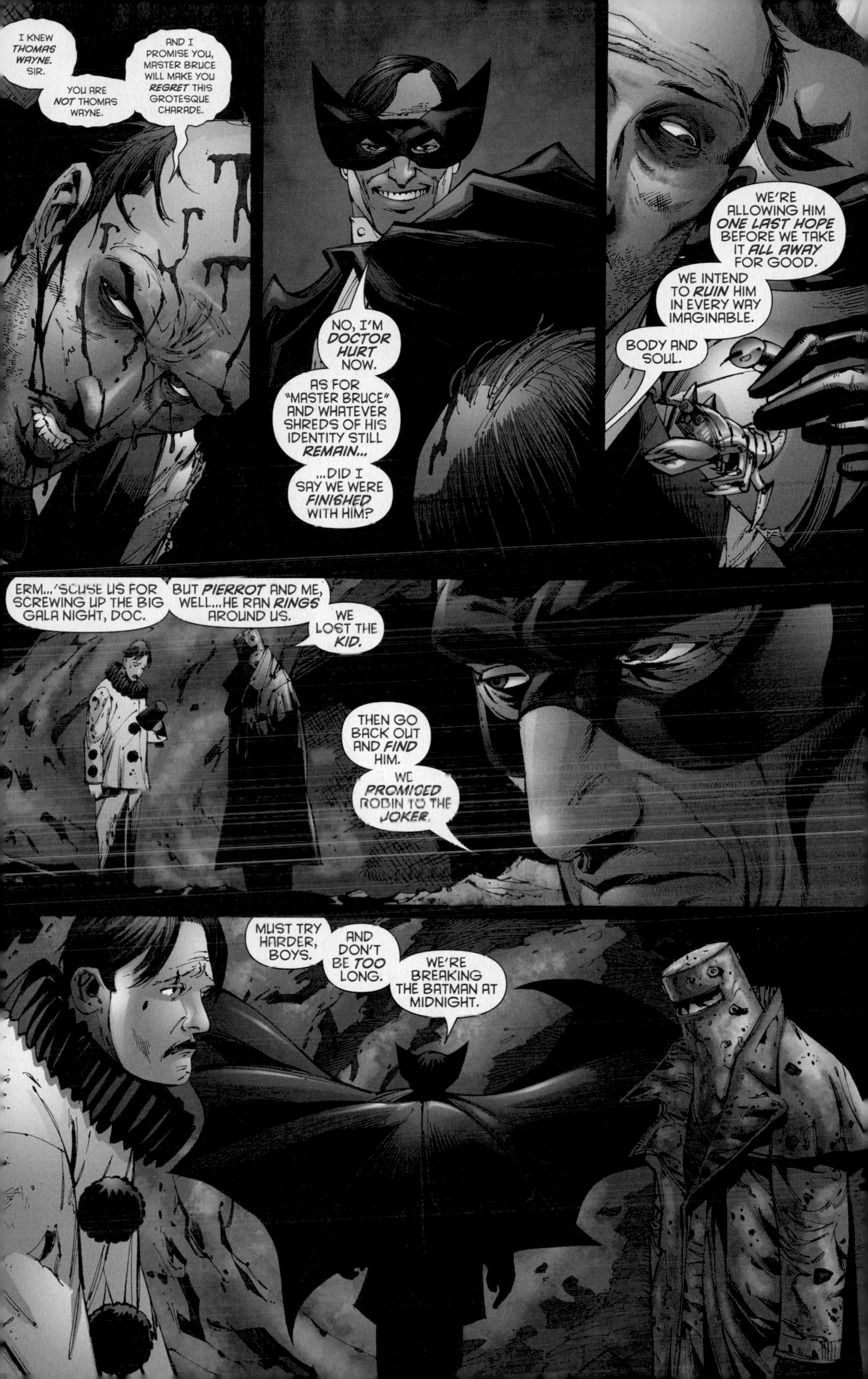
I KNEW THOMAS WAYNE. SIR.
YOU ARE NOT THOMAS WAYNE.
AND I PROMISE YOU, MASTER BRUCE WILL MAKE YOU REGRET THIS GROTESQUE CHARADE.
NO, I'M DOCTOR HURT NOW.
AS FOR "MASTER BRUCE" AND WHATEVER SHREDS OF HIS IDENTITY STILL REMAIN...
...DID I SAY WE WERE FINISHED WITH HIM?
WE'RE ALLOWING HIM ONE LAST HOPE BEFORE WE TAKE IT ALL AWAY FOR GOOD.
WE INTEND TO RUIN HIM IN EVERY WAY IMAGINABLE.
BODY AND SOUL.
ERM...'SCUSE US FOR SCREWING UP THE BIG GALA NIGHT, DOC.
BUT PIERROT AND ME, WELL...HE RAN RINGS AROUND US.
WE LOST THE KID.
THEN GO BACK OUT AND FIND HIM.
WE PROMISED ROBIN TO THE JOKER.
MUST TRY HARDER, BOYS.
AND DON'T BE TOO LONG.
WE'RE BREAKING THE BATMAN AT MIDNIGHT.

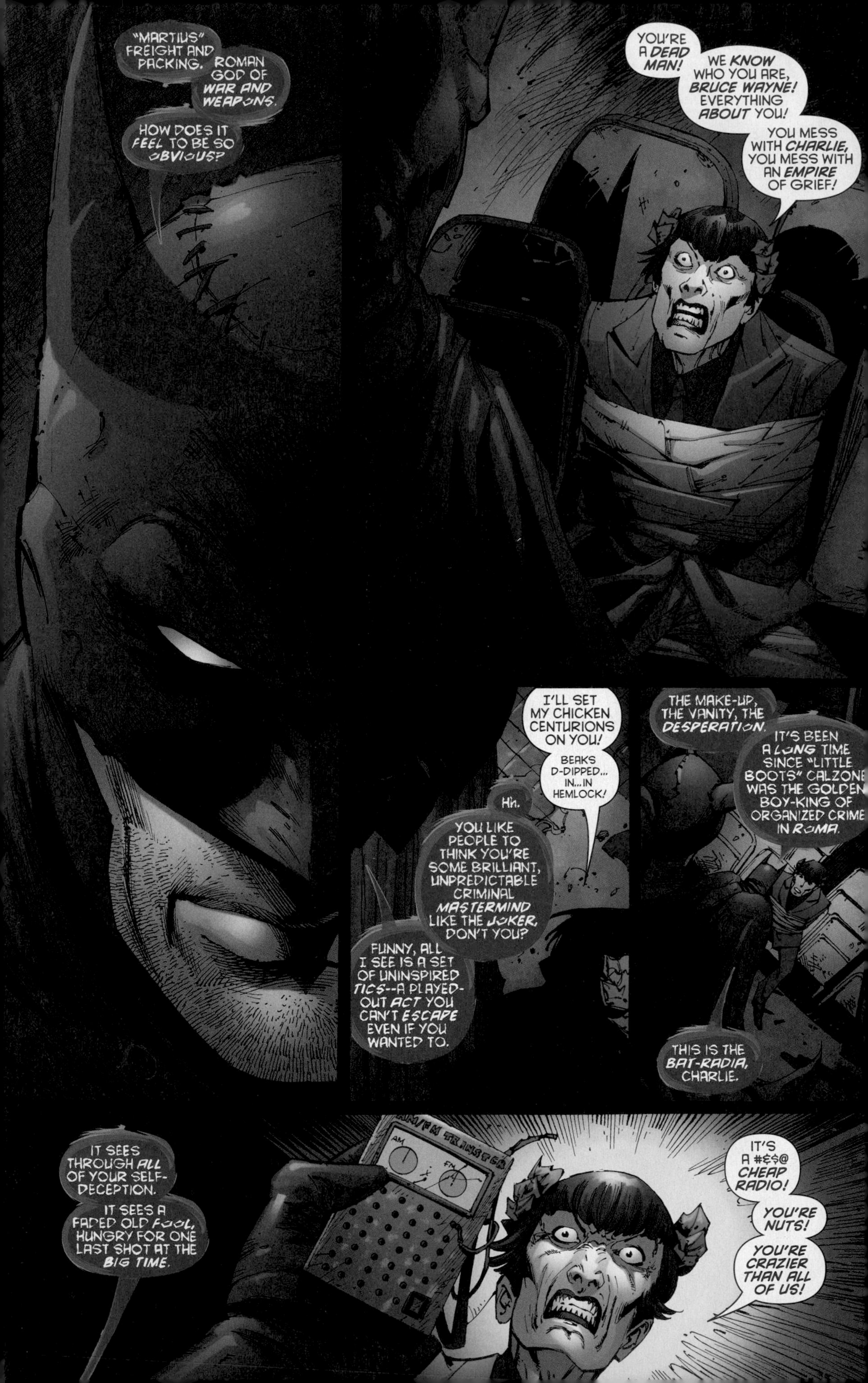
"MARTIUS" FREIGHT AND PACKING.
ROMAN GOD OF WAR AND WEAPONS.
HOW DOES IT FEEL TO BE SO OBVIOUS?
YOU'RE A DEAD MAN!
WE KNOW WHO YOU ARE, BRUCE WAYNE! EVERYTHING ABOUT YOU!
YOU MESS WITH CHARLIE, YOU MESS WITH AN EMPIRE OF GRIEF!
I'LL SET MY CHICKEN CENTURIONS ON YOU!
BEAKS D-DIPPED... IN... IN HEMLOCK!
Hh.
YOU LIKE PEOPLE TO THINK YOU'RE SOME BRILLIANT, UNPREDICTABLE CRIMINAL MASTERMIND LIKE THE JOKER, DON'T YOU?
FUNNY, ALL I SEE IS A SET OF UNINSPIRED TICS--A PLAYED-OUT ACT YOU CAN'T ESCAPE EVEN IF YOU WANTED TO.
THE MAKE-UP, THE VANITY, THE DESPERATION.
IT'S BEEN A LONG TIME SINCE "LITTLE BOOTS" CALZONE WAS THE GOLDEN BOY-KING OF ORGANIZED CRIME IN ROMA.
THIS IS THE BAT-RADIA, CHARLIE.
IT SEES THROUGH ALL OF YOUR SELF-DECEPTION.
IT SEES A FADED OLD FOOL, HUNGRY FOR ONE LAST SHOT AT THE BIG TIME.
IT'S A #€$@ CHEAP RADIO!
YOU'RE NUTS!
YOU'RE CRAZIER THAN ALL OF US!

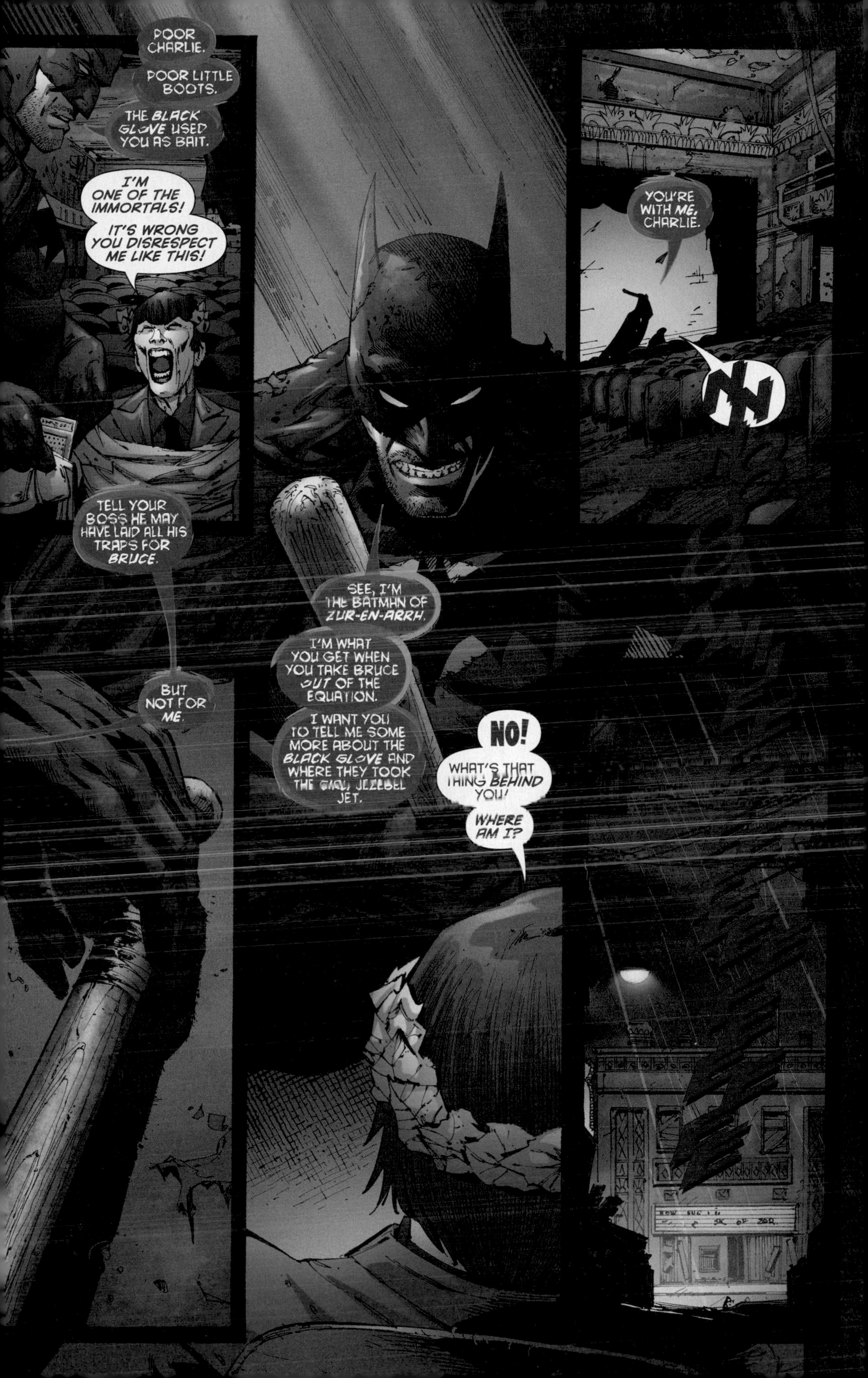

POOR CHARLIE.
POOR LITTLE BOOTS.
THE BLACK GLOVE USED YOU AS BAIT.
I'M ONE OF THE IMMORTALS!
IT'S WRONG YOU DISRESPECT ME LIKE THIS!
YOU'RE WITH ME, CHARLIE.
NN
TELL YOUR BOSS HE MAY HAVE LAID ALL HIS TRAPS FOR BRUCE.
BUT NOT FOR ME.
SEE, I'M THE BATMAN OF ZUR-EN-ARRH.
I'M WHAT YOU GET WHEN YOU TAKE BRUCE OUT OF THE EQUATION.
I WANT YOU TO TELL ME SOME MORE ABOUT THE BLACK GLOVE AND WHERE THEY TOOK THE JEZEBEL JET.
NO!
WHAT'S THAT THING BEHIND YOU!
WHERE AM I?

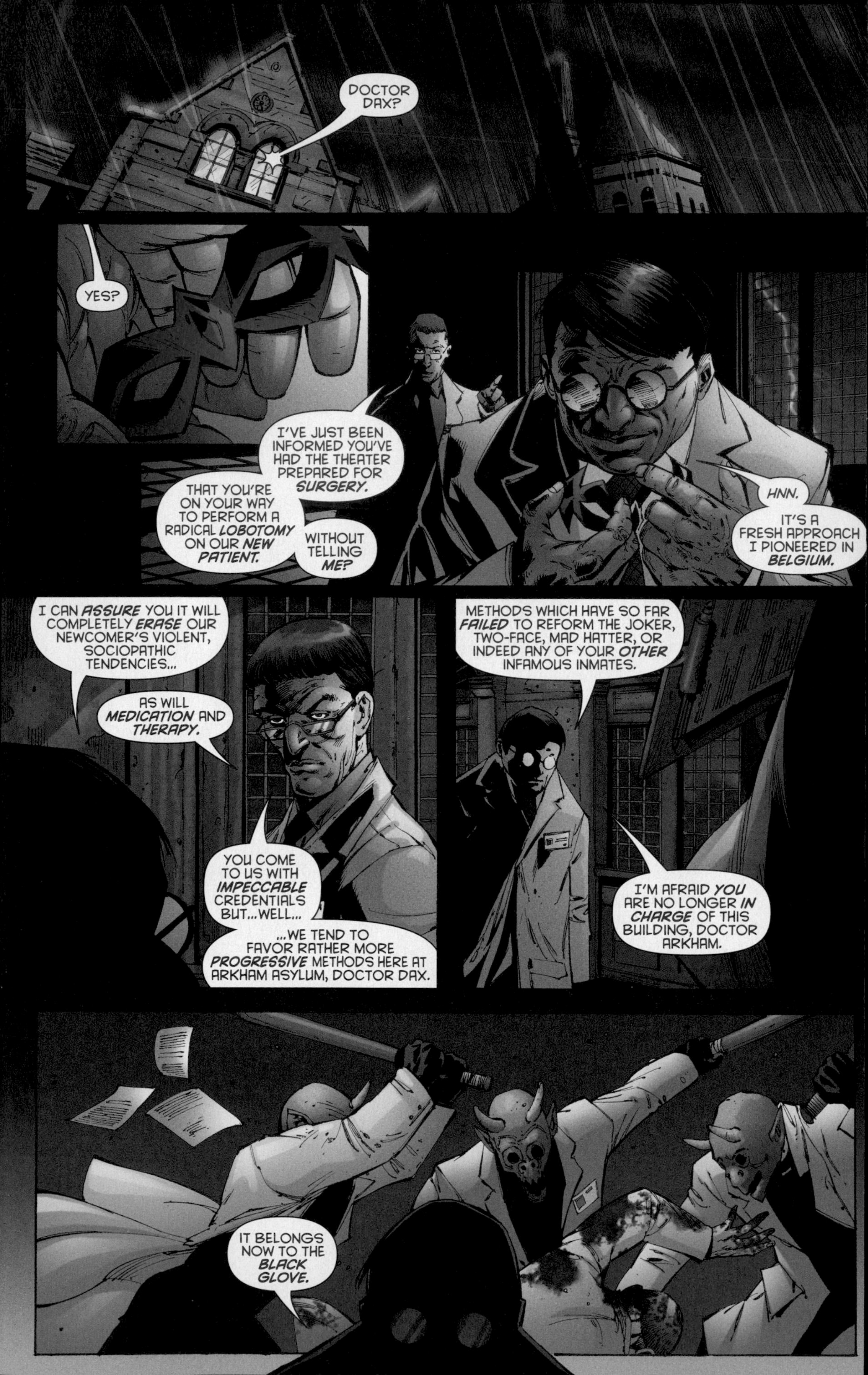
DOCTOR DAX?
YES?
I'VE JUST BEEN INFORMED YOU'VE HAD THE THEATER PREPARED FOR *SURGERY.*
THAT YOU'RE ON YOUR WAY TO PERFORM A RADICAL *LOBOTOMY* ON OUR *NEW PATIENT.*
WITHOUT TELLING *ME?*
HNN.
IT'S A FRESH APPROACH I PIONEERED IN *BELGIUM.*
I CAN *ASSURE* YOU IT WILL COMPLETELY *ERASE* OUR NEWCOMER'S VIOLENT, SOCIOPATHIC TENDENCIES...
AS WILL *MEDICATION* AND *THERAPY.*
YOU COME TO US WITH *IMPECCABLE* CREDENTIALS BUT...WELL...
...WE TEND TO FAVOR RATHER MORE *PROGRESSIVE* METHODS HERE AT ARKHAM ASYLUM, DOCTOR DAX.
METHODS WHICH HAVE SO FAR *FAILED* TO REFORM THE JOKER, TWO-FACE, MAD HATTER, OR INDEED ANY OF YOUR *OTHER* INFAMOUS INMATES.
I'M AFRAID *YOU* ARE NO LONGER *IN CHARGE* OF THIS BUILDING, DOCTOR ARKHAM.
IT BELONGS NOW TO THE *BLACK GLOVE.*

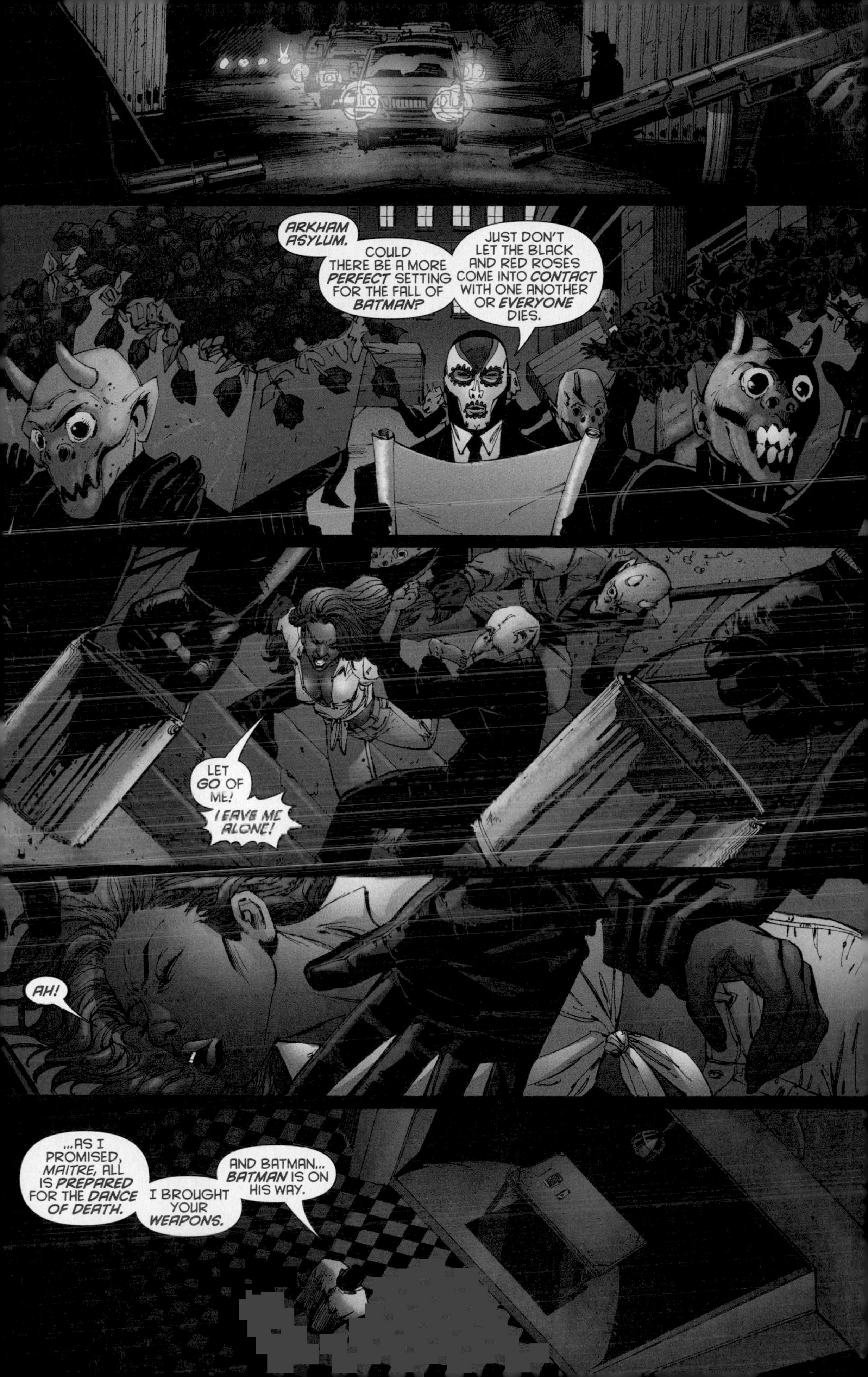
ARKHAM ASYLUM.
COULD THERE BE A MORE PERFECT SETTING FOR THE FALL OF BATMAN?
JUST DON'T LET THE BLACK AND RED ROSES COME INTO CONTACT WITH ONE ANOTHER OR EVERYONE DIES.
LET GO OF ME!
LEAVE ME ALONE!
AH!
...AS I PROMISED, MAITRE, ALL IS PREPARED FOR THE DANCE OF DEATH.
I BROUGHT YOUR WEAPONS.
AND BATMAN... BATMAN IS ON HIS WAY.

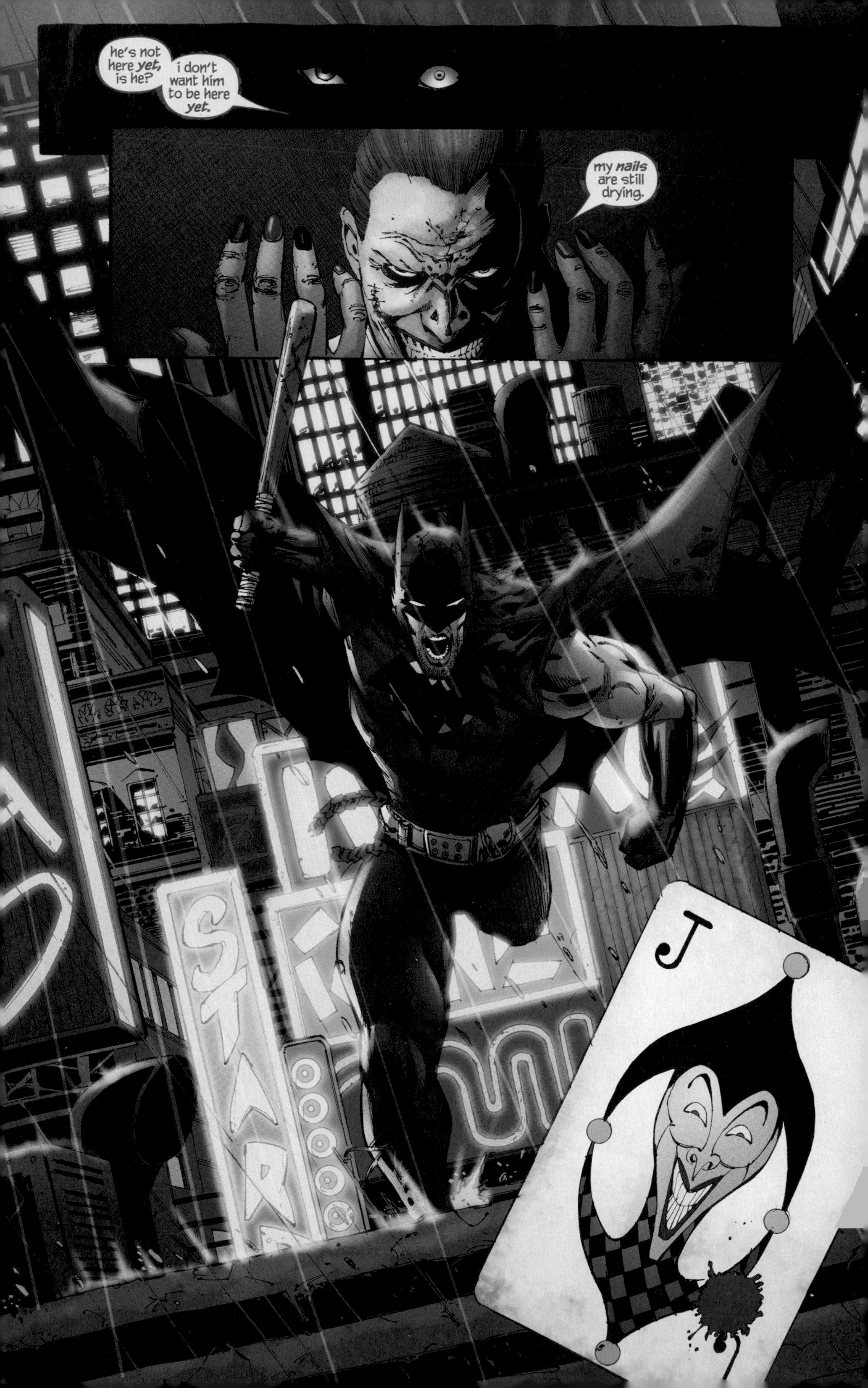
he's not here *yet,* is he?
i don't want him to be here *yet.*
my *nails* are still drying.

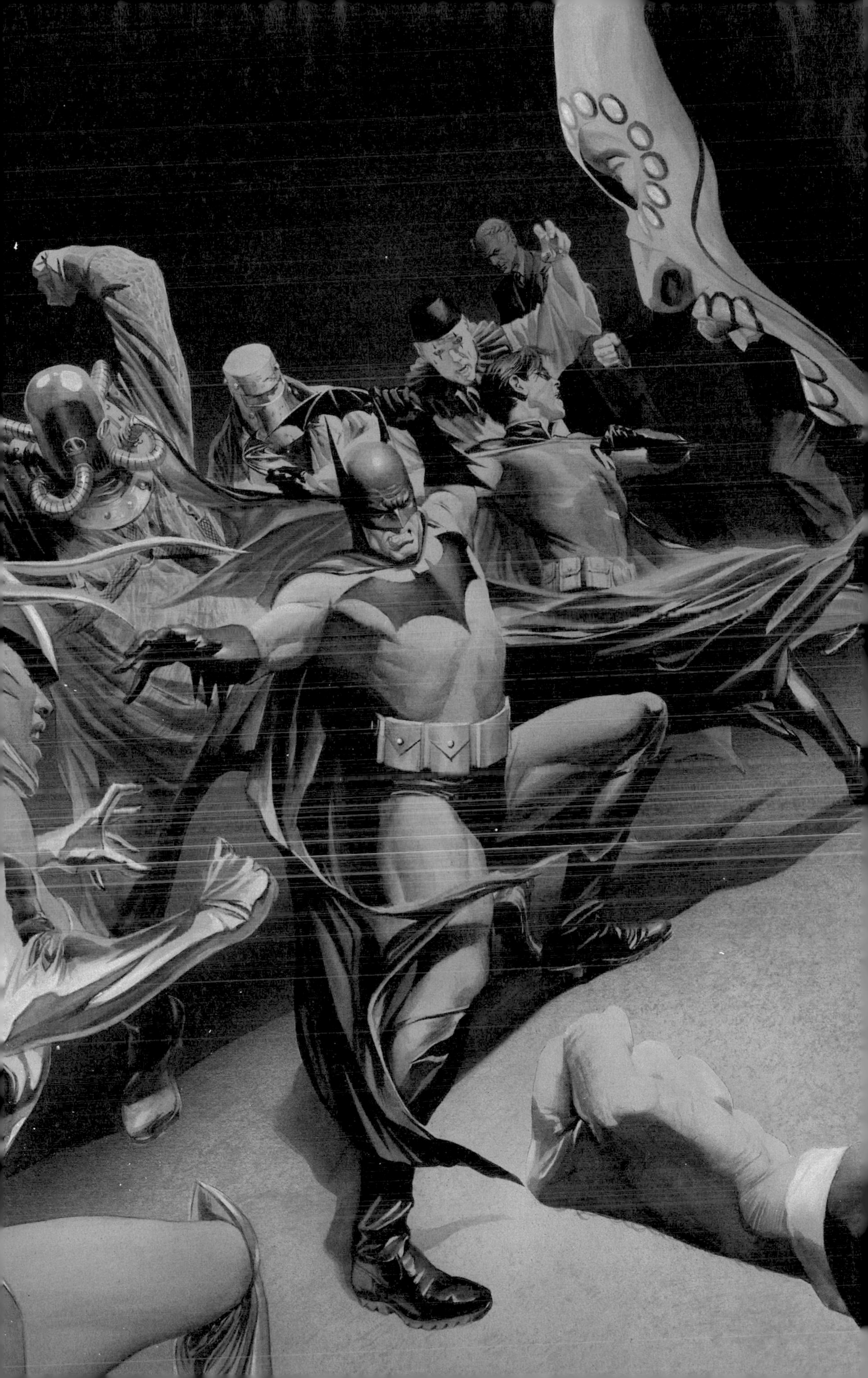

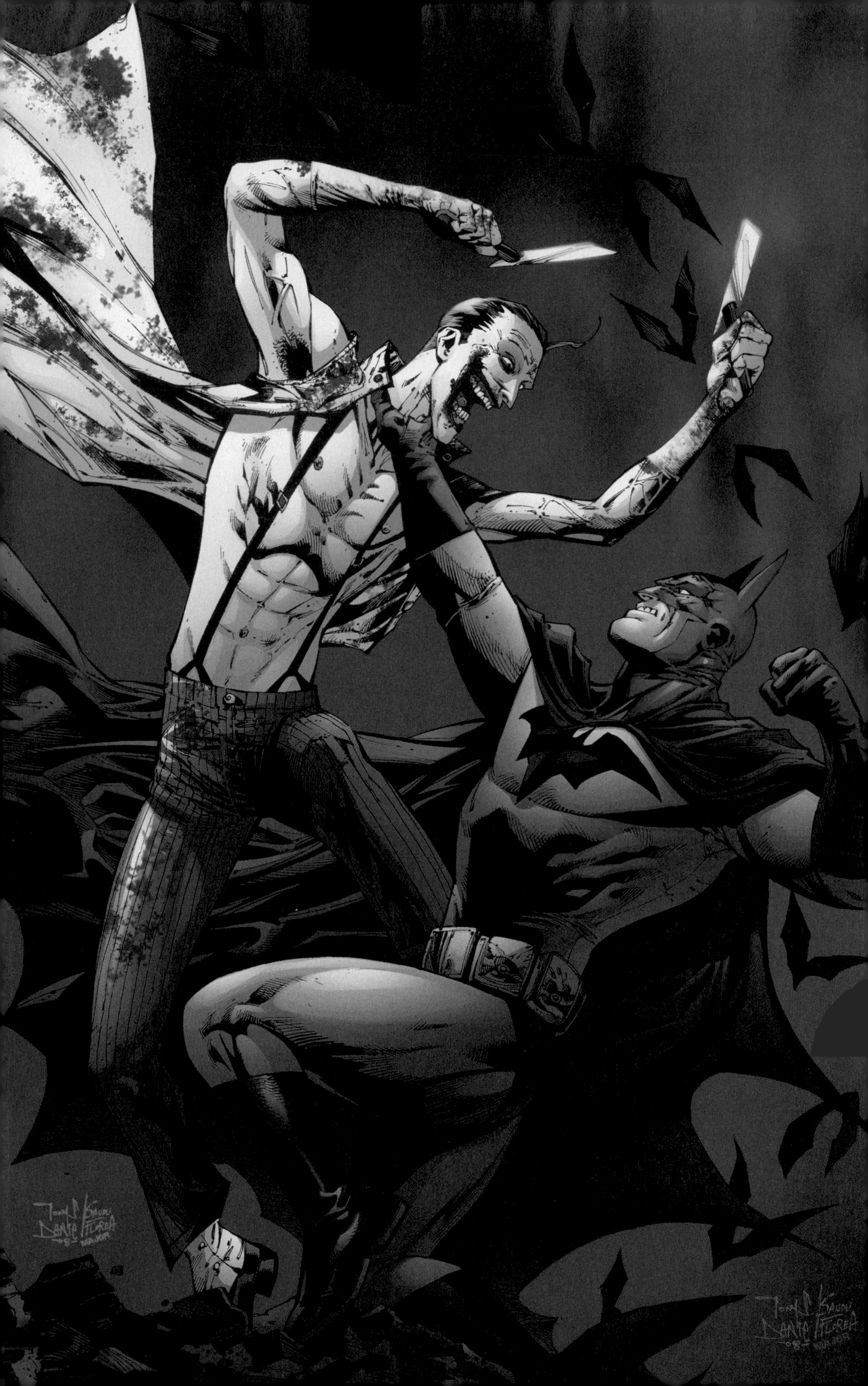

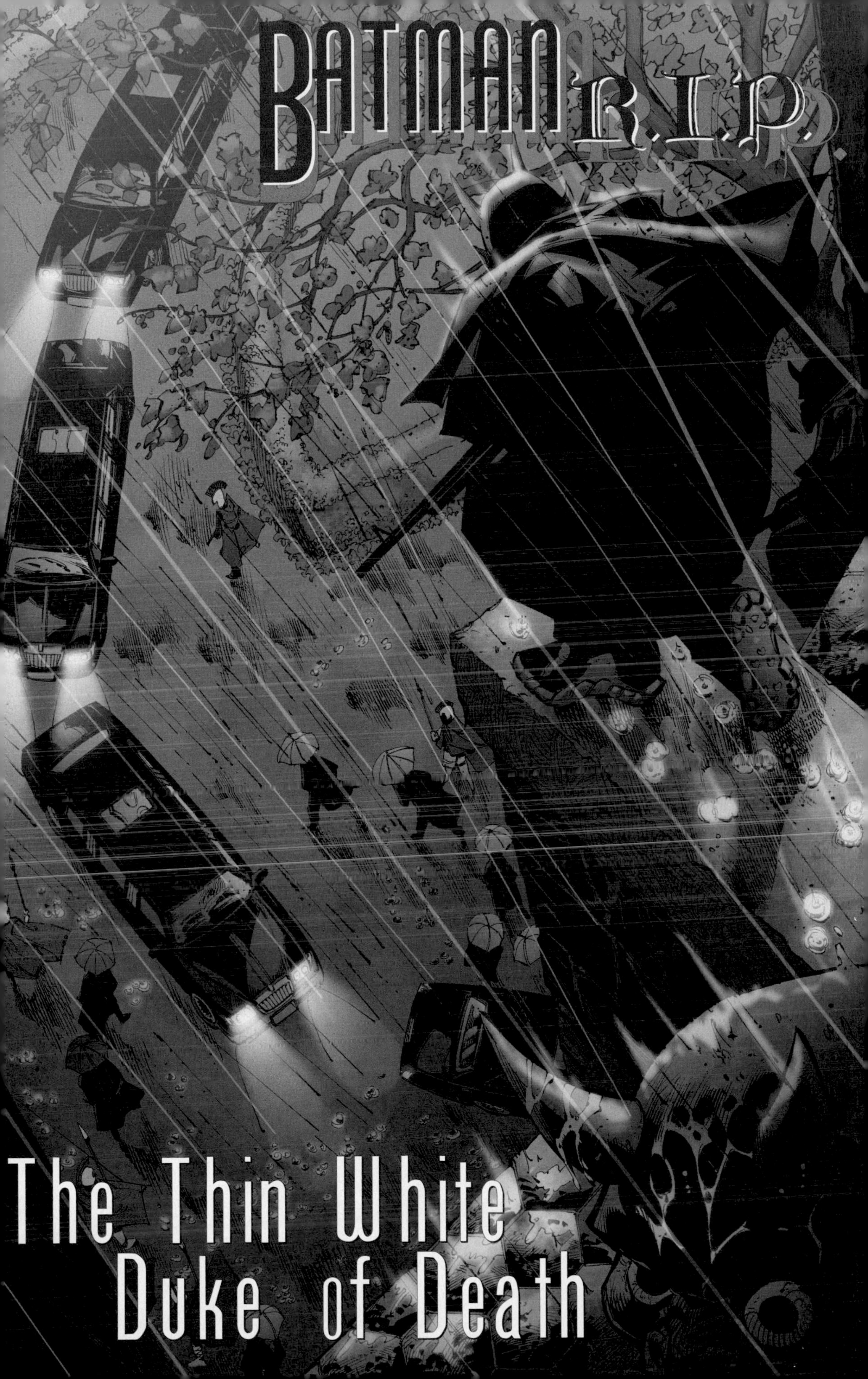
BATMAN R.I.P.
The Thin White Duke of Death

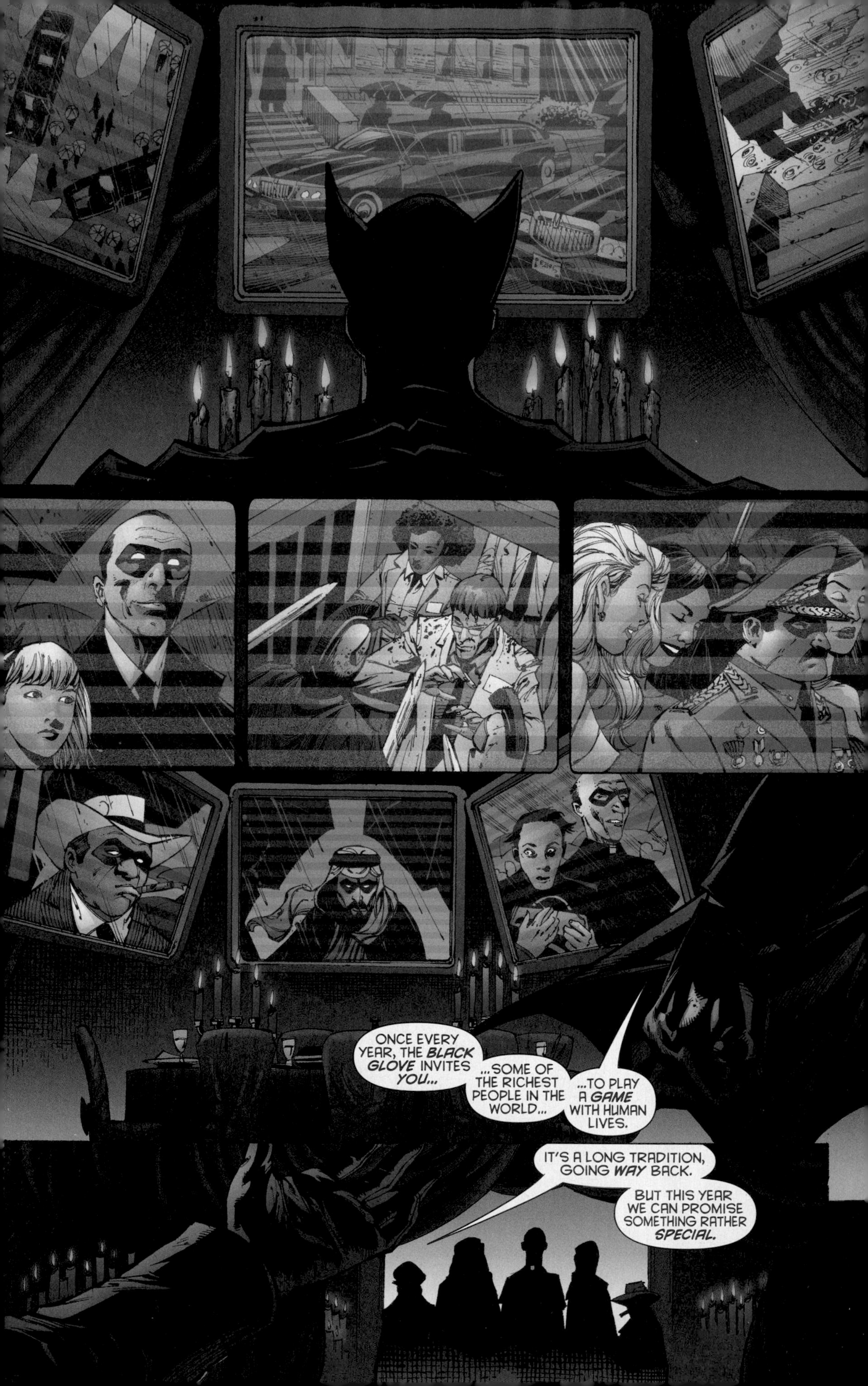
ONCE EVERY YEAR, THE BLACK GLOVE INVITES YOU...
...SOME OF THE RICHEST PEOPLE IN THE WORLD...
...TO PLAY A GAME WITH HUMAN LIVES.
IT'S A LONG TRADITION, GOING WAY BACK.
BUT THIS YEAR WE CAN PROMISE SOMETHING RATHER SPECIAL.

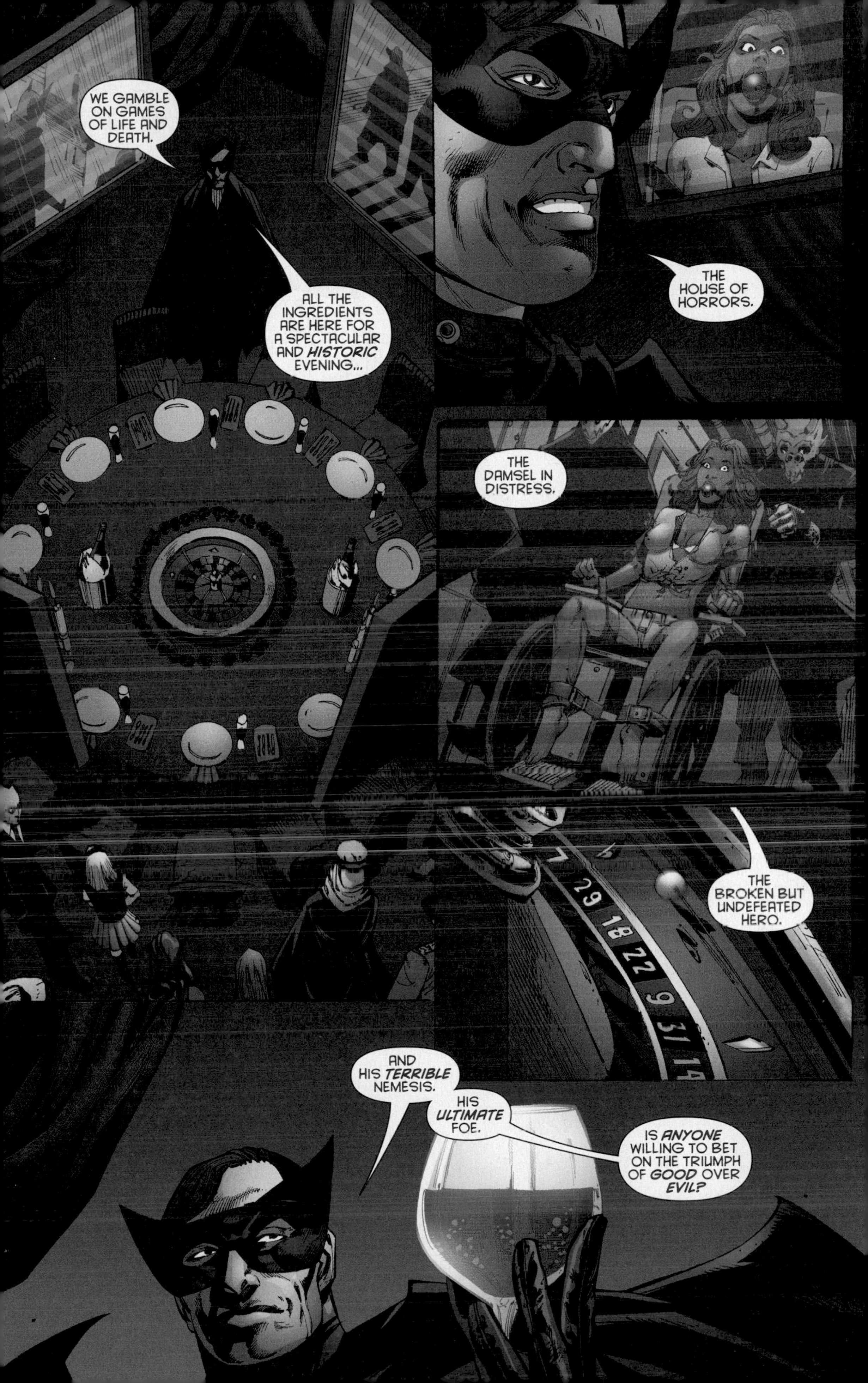
WE GAMBLE ON GAMES OF LIFE AND DEATH.
THE HOUSE OF HORRORS.
ALL THE INGREDIENTS ARE HERE FOR A SPECTACULAR AND HISTORIC EVENING...
THE DAMSEL IN DISTRESS.
THE BROKEN BUT UNDEFEATED HERO.
AND HIS TERRIBLE NEMESIS.
HIS ULTIMATE FOE.
IS ANYONE WILLING TO BET ON THE TRIUMPH OF GOOD OVER EVIL?

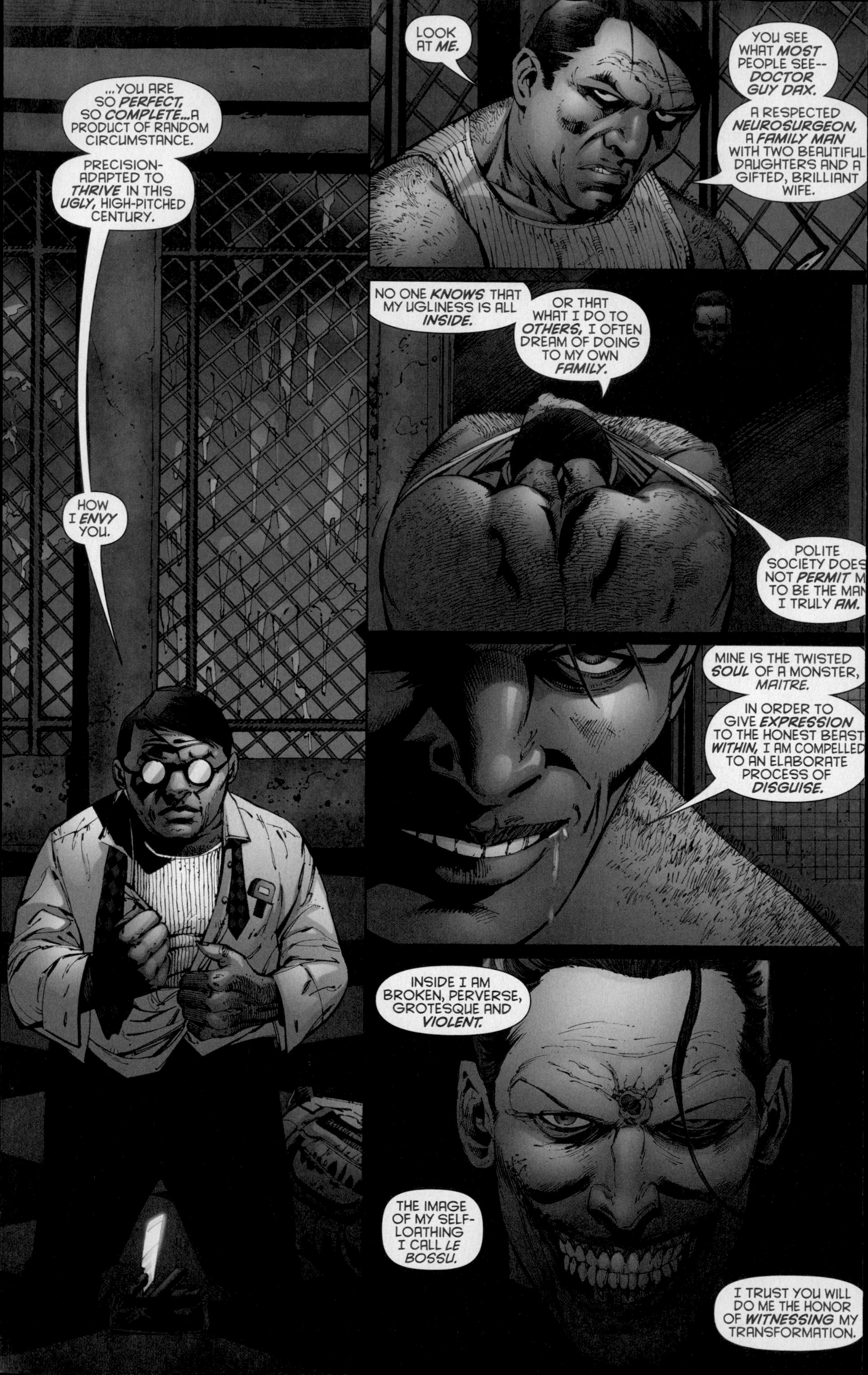
...YOU ARE SO PERFECT, SO COMPLETE...A PRODUCT OF RANDOM CIRCUMSTANCE.
PRECISION-ADAPTED TO THRIVE IN THIS UGLY, HIGH-PITCHED CENTURY.
HOW I ENVY YOU.
LOOK AT ME.
YOU SEE WHAT MOST PEOPLE SEE-- DOCTOR GUY DAX.
A RESPECTED NEUROSURGEON, A FAMILY MAN WITH TWO BEAUTIFUL DAUGHTERS AND A GIFTED, BRILLIANT WIFE.
NO ONE KNOWS THAT MY UGLINESS IS ALL INSIDE.
OR THAT WHAT I DO TO OTHERS, I OFTEN DREAM OF DOING TO MY OWN FAMILY.
POLITE SOCIETY DOES NOT PERMIT M TO BE THE MAN I TRULY AM.
MINE IS THE TWISTED SOUL OF A MONSTER, MAITRE.
IN ORDER TO GIVE EXPRESSION TO THE HONEST BEAST WITHIN, I AM COMPELLED TO AN ELABORATE PROCESS OF DISGUISE.
INSIDE I AM BROKEN, PERVERSE, GROTESQUE AND VIOLENT.
THE IMAGE OF MY SELF-LOATHING I CALL LE BOSSU.
I TRUST YOU WILL DO ME THE HONOR OF WITNESSING MY TRANSFORMATION.

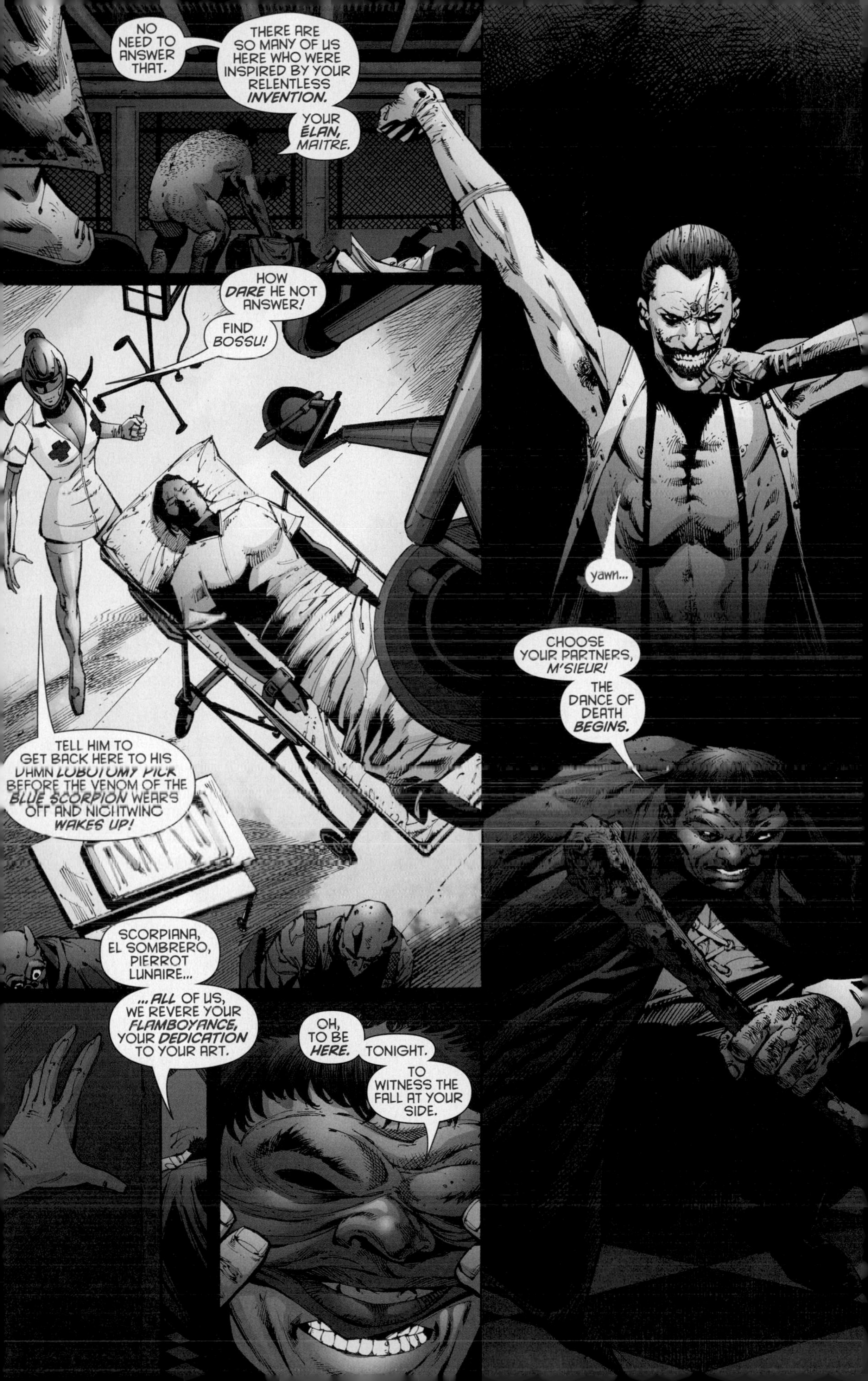
NO NEED TO ANSWER THAT.
THERE ARE SO MANY OF US HERE WHO WERE INSPIRED BY YOUR RELENTLESS INVENTION.
YOUR ÉLAN, MAITRE.
HOW DARE HE NOT ANSWER!
FIND BOSSU!
TELL HIM TO GET BACK HERE TO HIS DAMN LOBOTOMY PICK BEFORE THE VENOM OF THE BLUE SCORPION WEARS OFF AND NIGHTWING WAKES UP!
SCORPIANA, EL SOMBRERO, PIERROT LUNAIRE...
...ALL OF US, WE REVERE YOUR FLAMBOYANCE, YOUR DEDICATION TO YOUR ART.
OH, TO BE HERE.
TONIGHT.
TO WITNESS THE FALL AT YOUR SIDE.
yawn...
CHOOSE YOUR PARTNERS, M'SIEUR!
THE DANCE OF DEATH BEGINS.

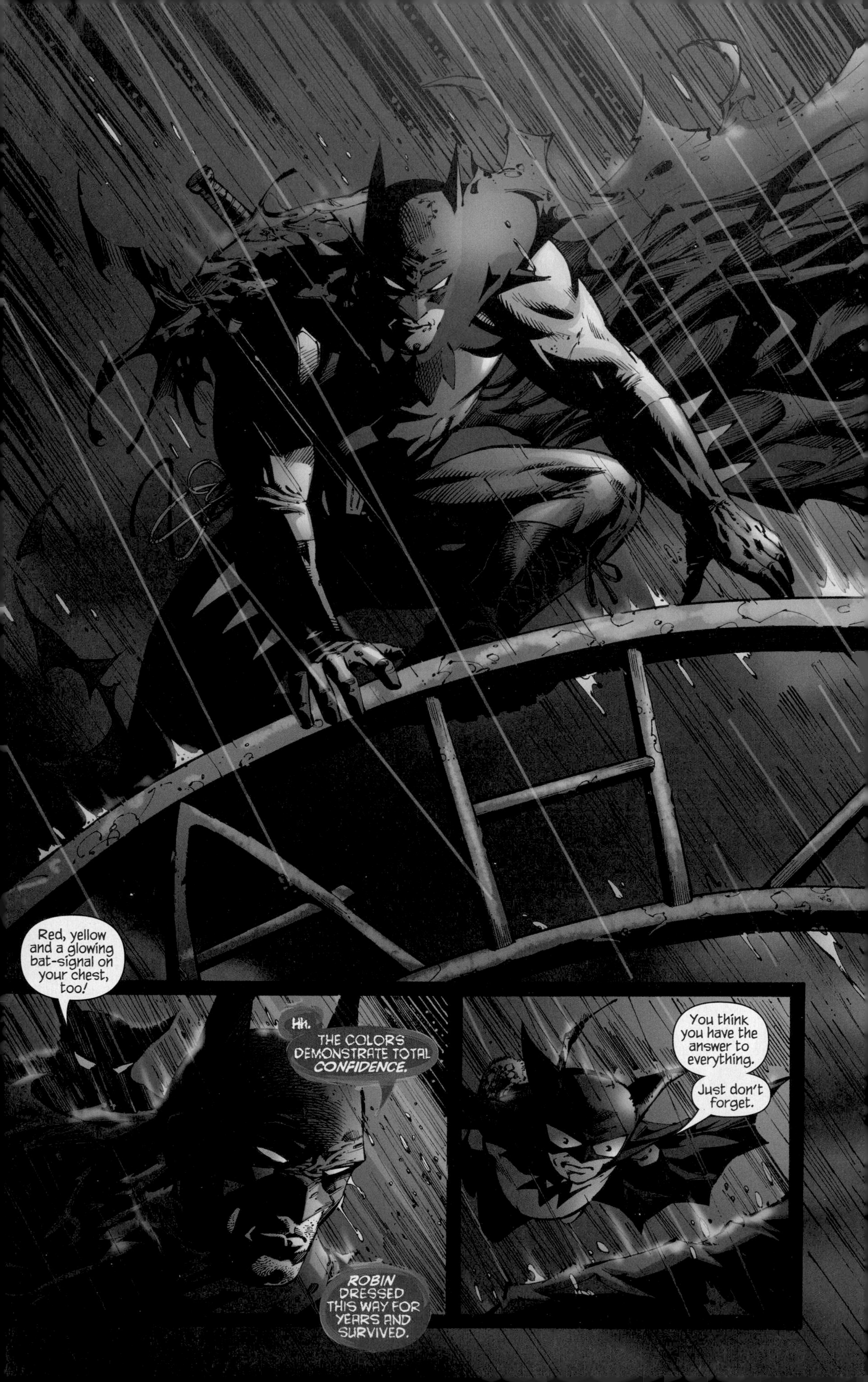

Red, yellow and a glowing bat-signal on your chest, too!
Hh.
THE COLORS DEMONSTRATE TOTAL CONFIDENCE.
ROBIN DRESSED THIS WAY FOR YEARS AND SURVIVED.
You think you have the answer to everything.
Just don't forget.

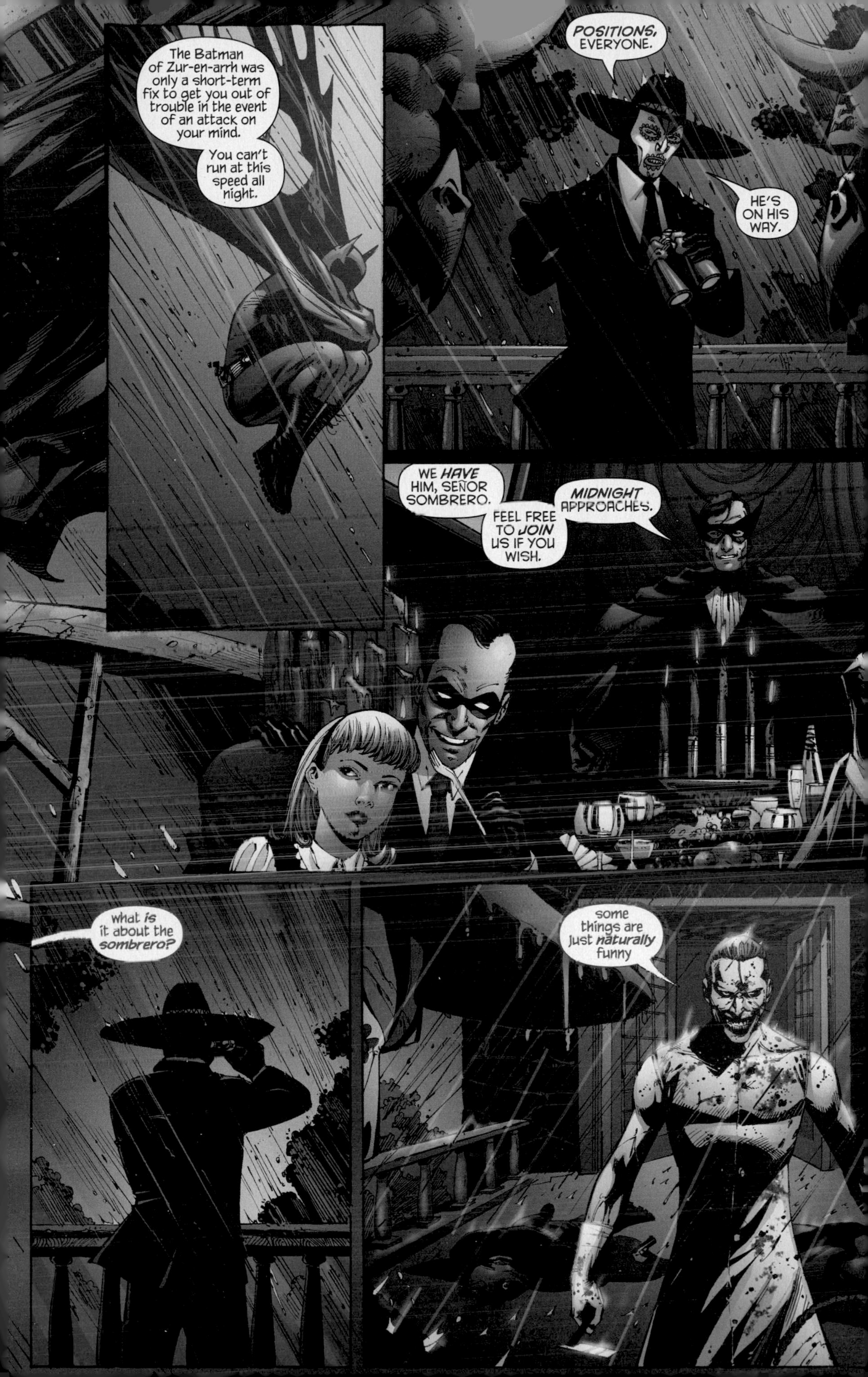
The Batman of Zur-en-arrh was only a short-term fix to get you out of trouble in the event of an attack on your mind.
You can't run at this speed all night.
POSITIONS, EVERYONE.
HE'S ON HIS WAY.
WE HAVE HIM, SEÑOR SOMBRERO.
FEEL FREE TO JOIN US IF YOU WISH.
MIDNIGHT APPROACHES.
what is it about the sombrero?
some things are just naturally funny

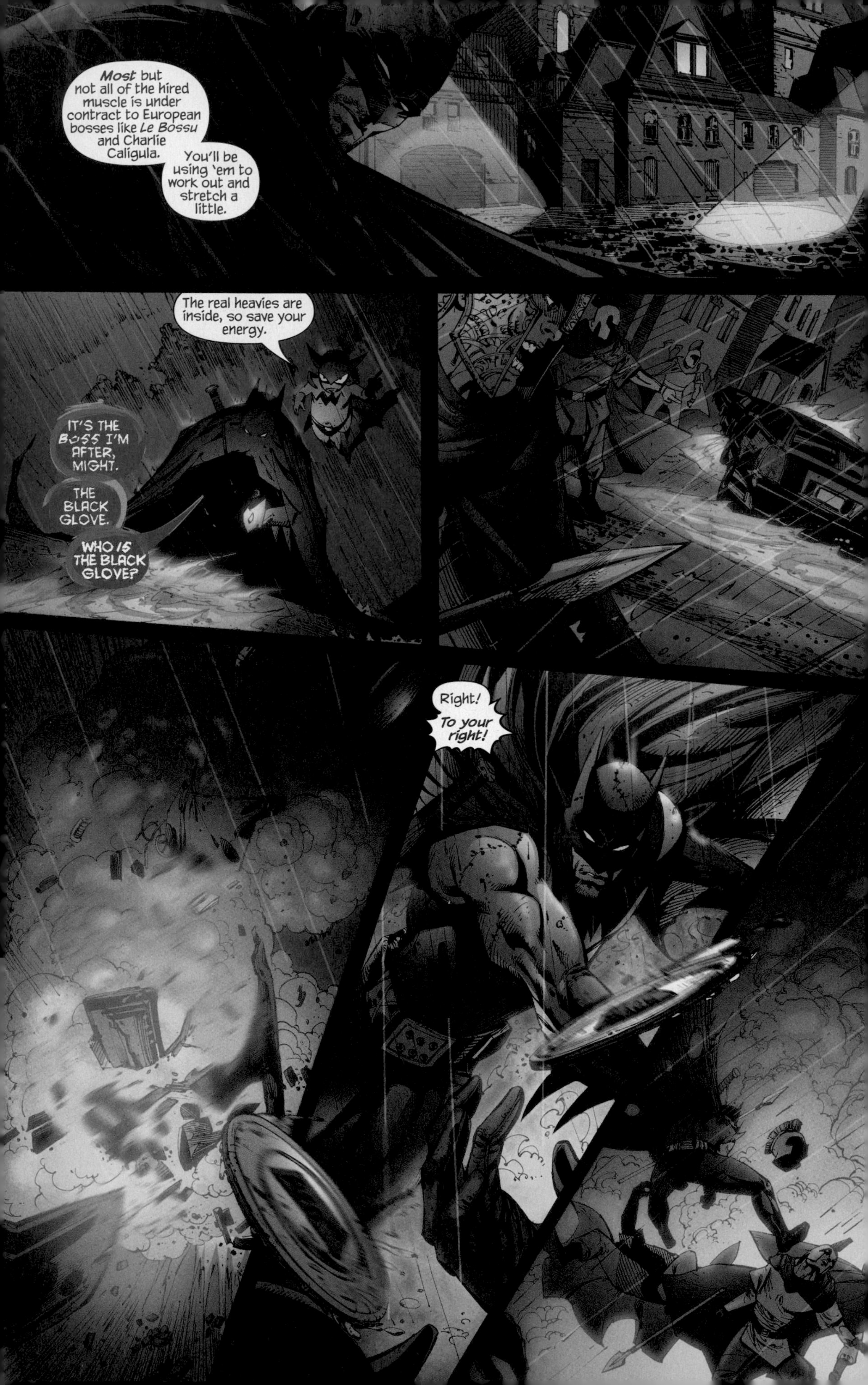
Most but not all of the hired muscle is under contract to European bosses like Le Bossu and Charlie Caligula.
You'll be using 'em to work out and stretch a little.
The real heavies are inside, so save your energy.
IT'S THE BOSS I'M AFTER, MIGHT.
THE BLACK GLOVE.
WHO IS THE BLACK GLOVE?
Right!
To your right!

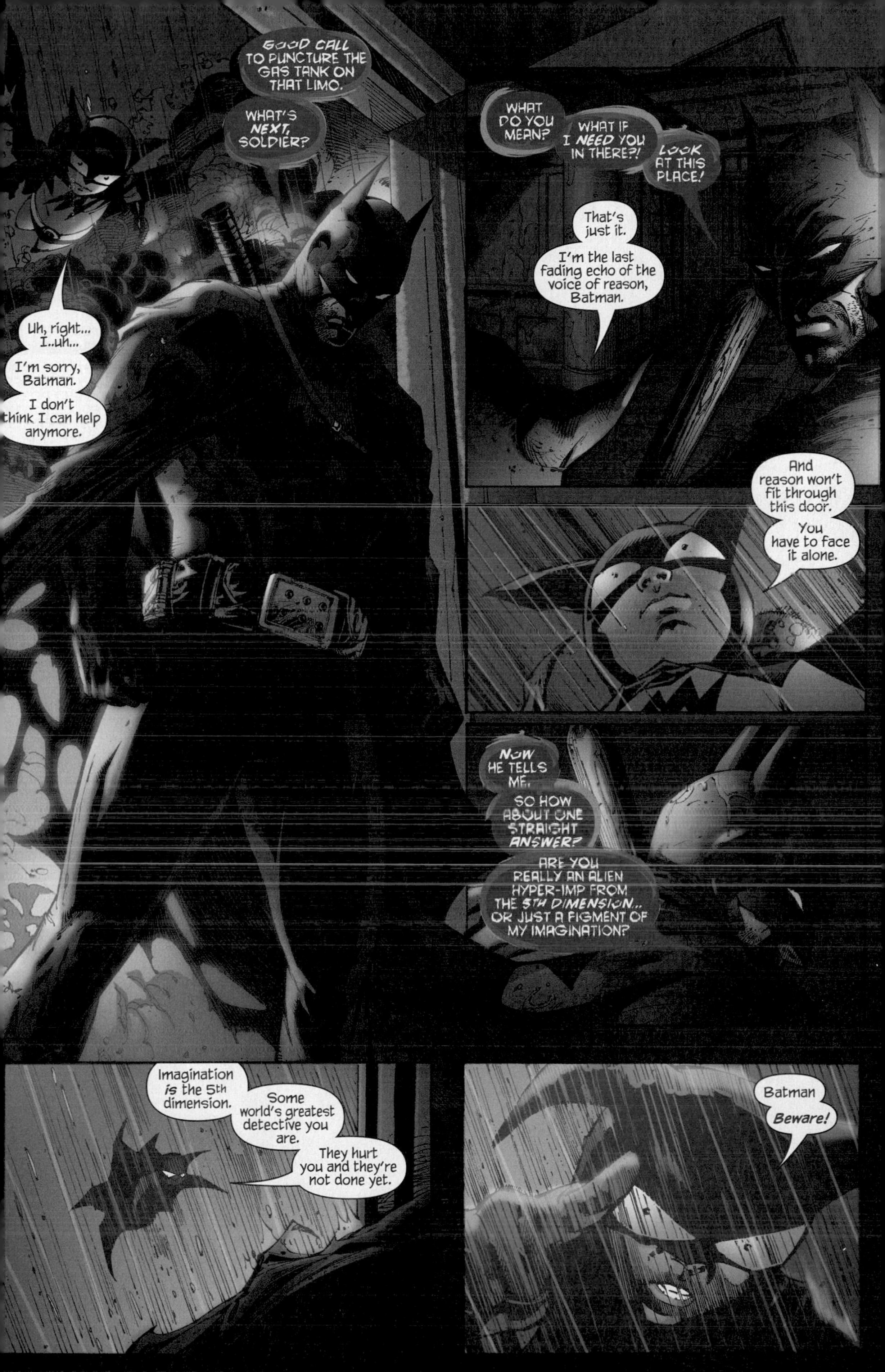
GOOD CALL TO PUNCTURE THE GAS TANK ON THAT LIMO.
WHAT'S NEXT, SOLDIER?
Uh, right... I..uh...
I'm sorry, Batman.
I don't think I can help anymore.
WHAT DO YOU MEAN?
WHAT IF I NEED YOU IN THERE?!
LOOK AT THIS PLACE!
That's just it.
I'm the last fading echo of the voice of reason, Batman.
And reason won't fit through this door.
You have to face it alone.
NOW HE TELLS ME.
SO HOW ABOUT ONE STRAIGHT ANSWER?
ARE YOU REALLY AN ALIEN HYPER-IMP FROM THE 5TH DIMENSION... OR JUST A FIGMENT OF MY IMAGINATION?
Imagination is the 5th dimension.
Some world's greatest detective you are.
They hurt you and they're not done yet.
Batman Beware!

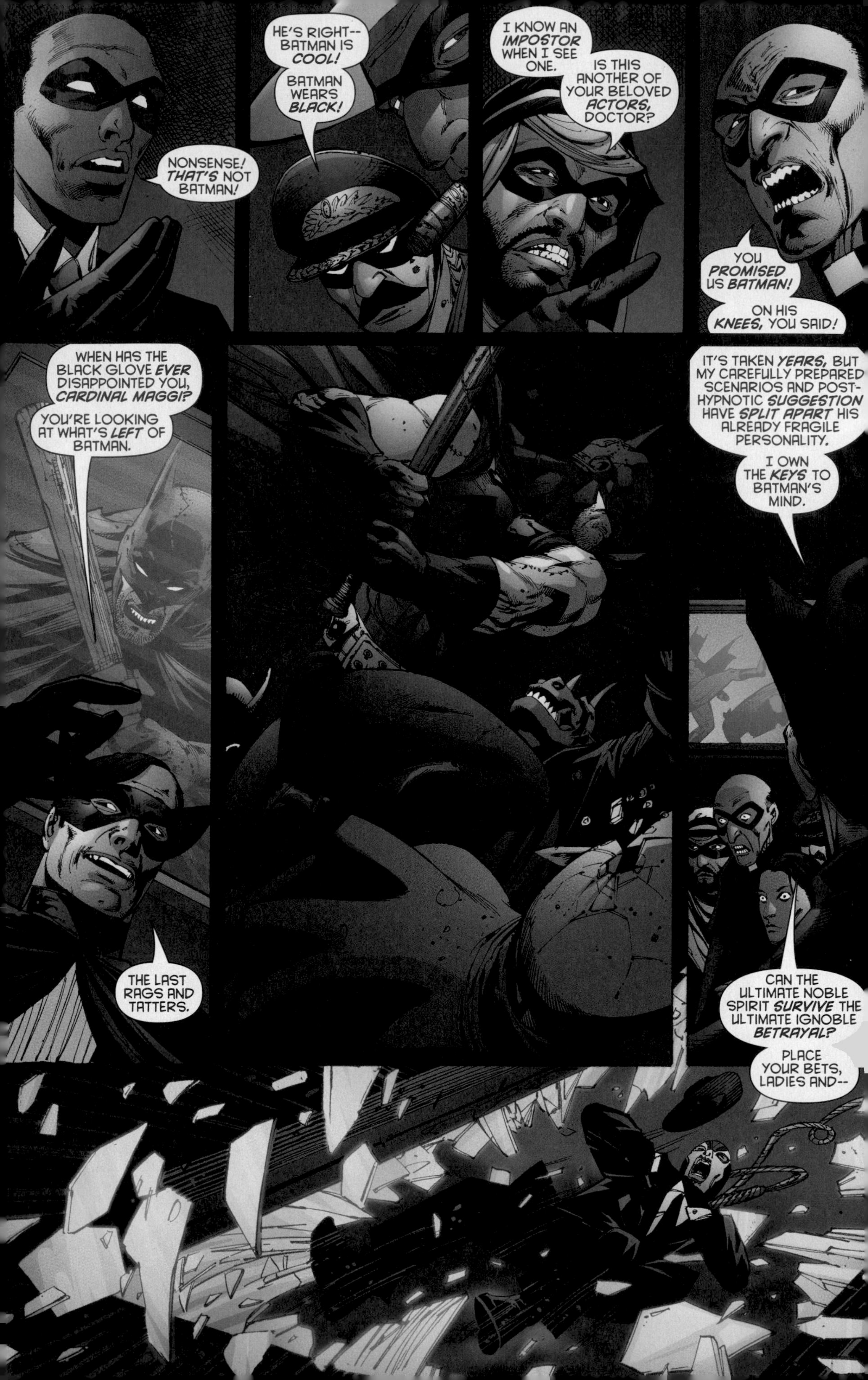
NONSENSE! THAT'S NOT BATMAN!
HE'S RIGHT-- BATMAN IS COOL!
BATMAN WEARS BLACK!
I KNOW AN IMPOSTOR WHEN I SEE ONE.
IS THIS ANOTHER OF YOUR BELOVED ACTORS, DOCTOR?
YOU PROMISED US BATMAN!
ON HIS KNEES, YOU SAID!
WHEN HAS THE BLACK GLOVE EVER DISAPPOINTED YOU, CARDINAL MAGGI?
YOU'RE LOOKING AT WHAT'S LEFT OF BATMAN.
THE LAST RAGS AND TATTERS.
IT'S TAKEN YEARS, BUT MY CAREFULLY PREPARED SCENARIOS AND POST-HYPNOTIC SUGGESTION HAVE SPLIT APART HIS ALREADY FRAGILE PERSONALITY.
I OWN THE KEYS TO BATMAN'S MIND.
CAN THE ULTIMATE NOBLE SPIRIT SURVIVE THE ULTIMATE IGNOBLE BETRAYAL?
PLACE YOUR BETS, LADIES AND--

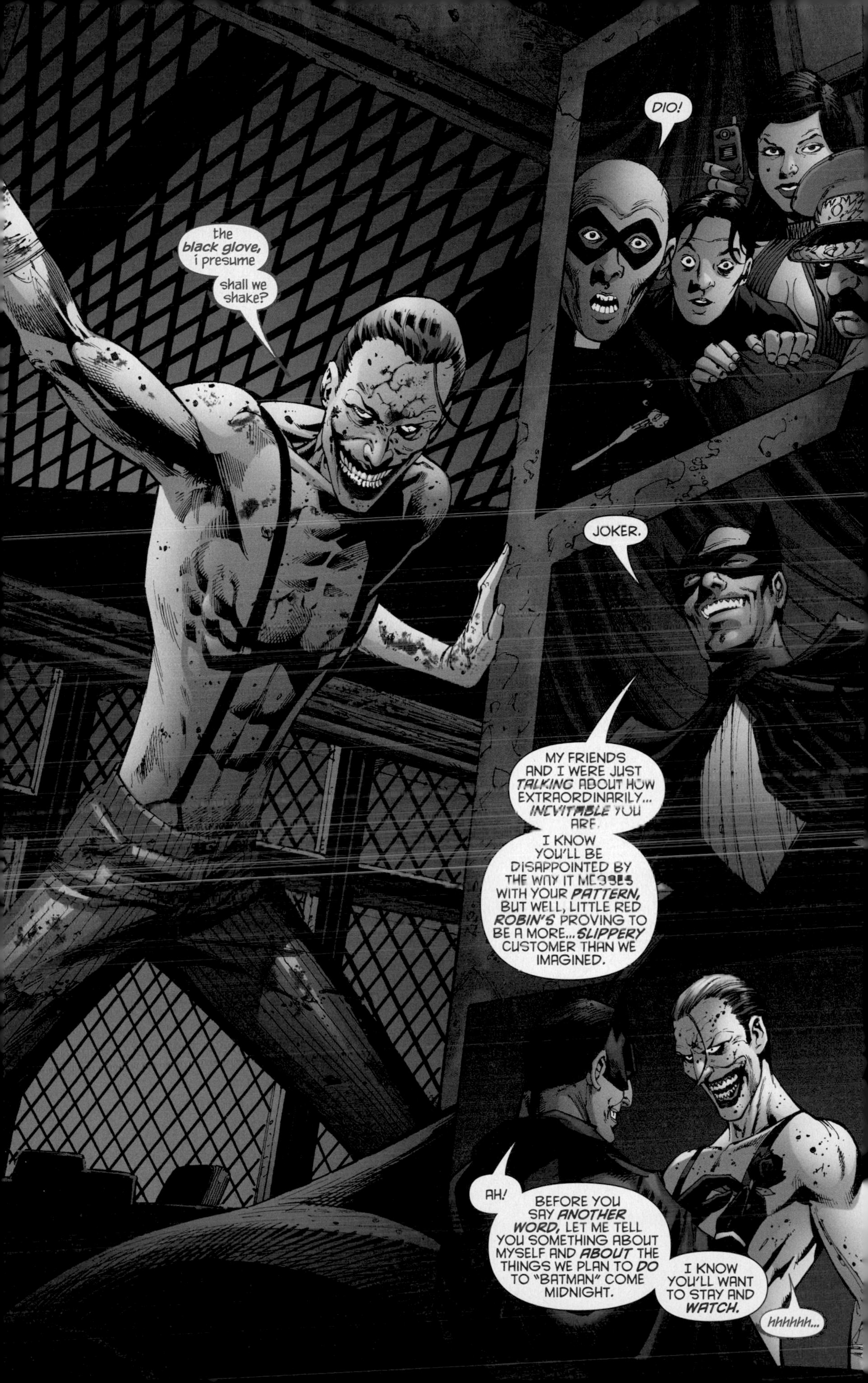
the black glove, i presume
shall we shake?
DIO!
JOKER.
MY FRIENDS AND I WERE JUST TALKING ABOUT HOW EXTRAORDINARILY... INEVITABLE YOU ARE.
I KNOW YOU'LL BE DISAPPOINTED BY THE WAY IT MESSES WITH YOUR PATTERN, BUT WELL, LITTLE RED ROBIN'S PROVING TO BE A MORE... SLIPPERY CUSTOMER THAN WE IMAGINED.
AH!
BEFORE YOU SAY ANOTHER WORD, LET ME TELL YOU SOMETHING ABOUT MYSELF AND ABOUT THE THINGS WE PLAN TO DO TO "BATMAN" COME MIDNIGHT.
I KNOW YOU'LL WANT TO STAY AND WATCH.
hhhhhh...

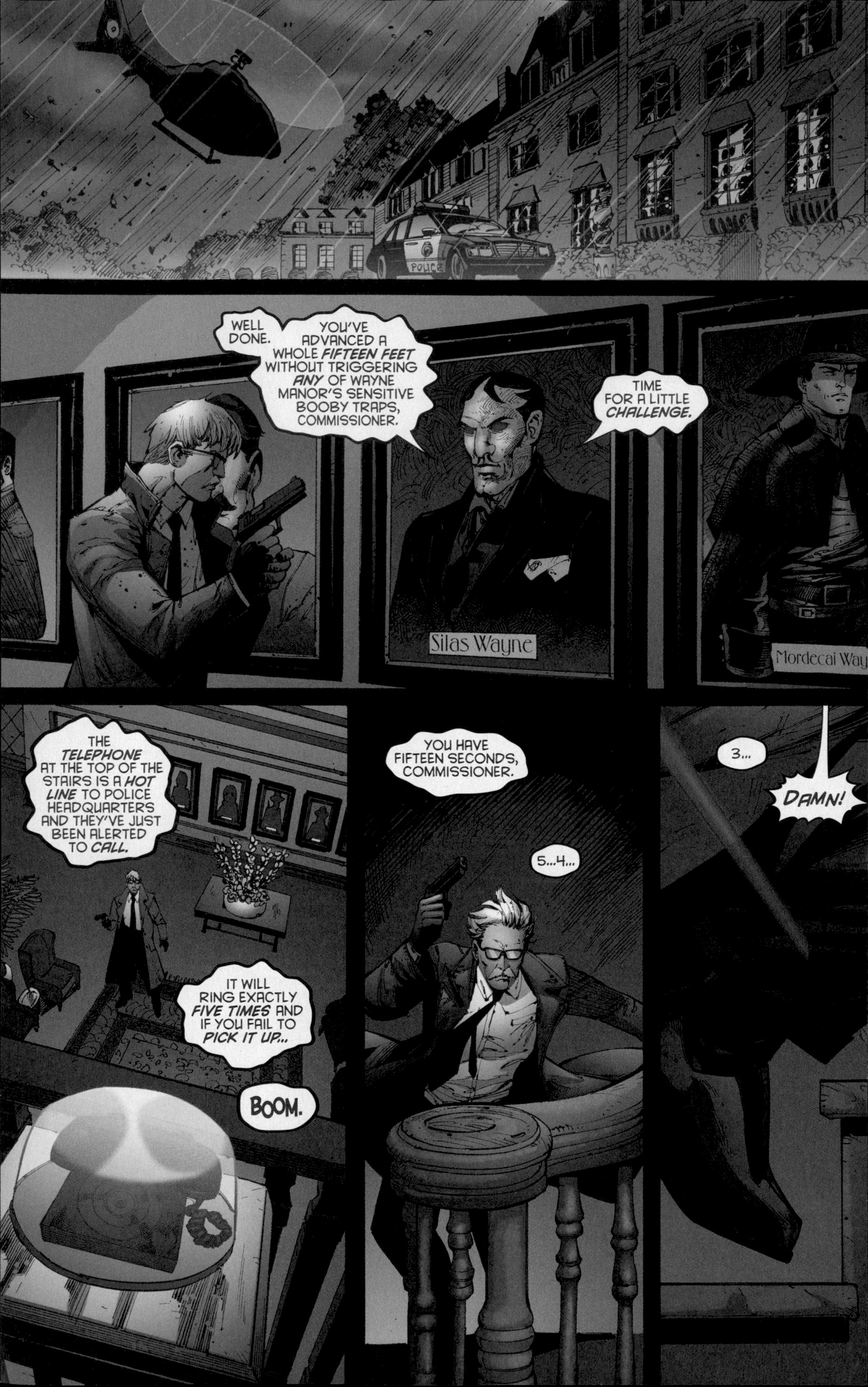
POLICE
WELL DONE.
YOU'VE ADVANCED A WHOLE FIFTEEN FEET WITHOUT TRIGGERING ANY OF WAYNE MANOR'S SENSITIVE BOOBY TRAPS, COMMISSIONER.
TIME FOR A LITTLE CHALLENGE.
Silas Wayne
Mordecai Way
THE TELEPHONE AT THE TOP OF THE STAIRS IS A HOT LINE TO POLICE HEADQUARTERS AND THEY'VE JUST BEEN ALERTED TO CALL.
IT WILL RING EXACTLY FIVE TIMES AND IF YOU FAIL TO PICK IT UP...
BOOM.
YOU HAVE FIFTEEN SECONDS, COMMISSIONER.
5...4...
3...
DAMN!

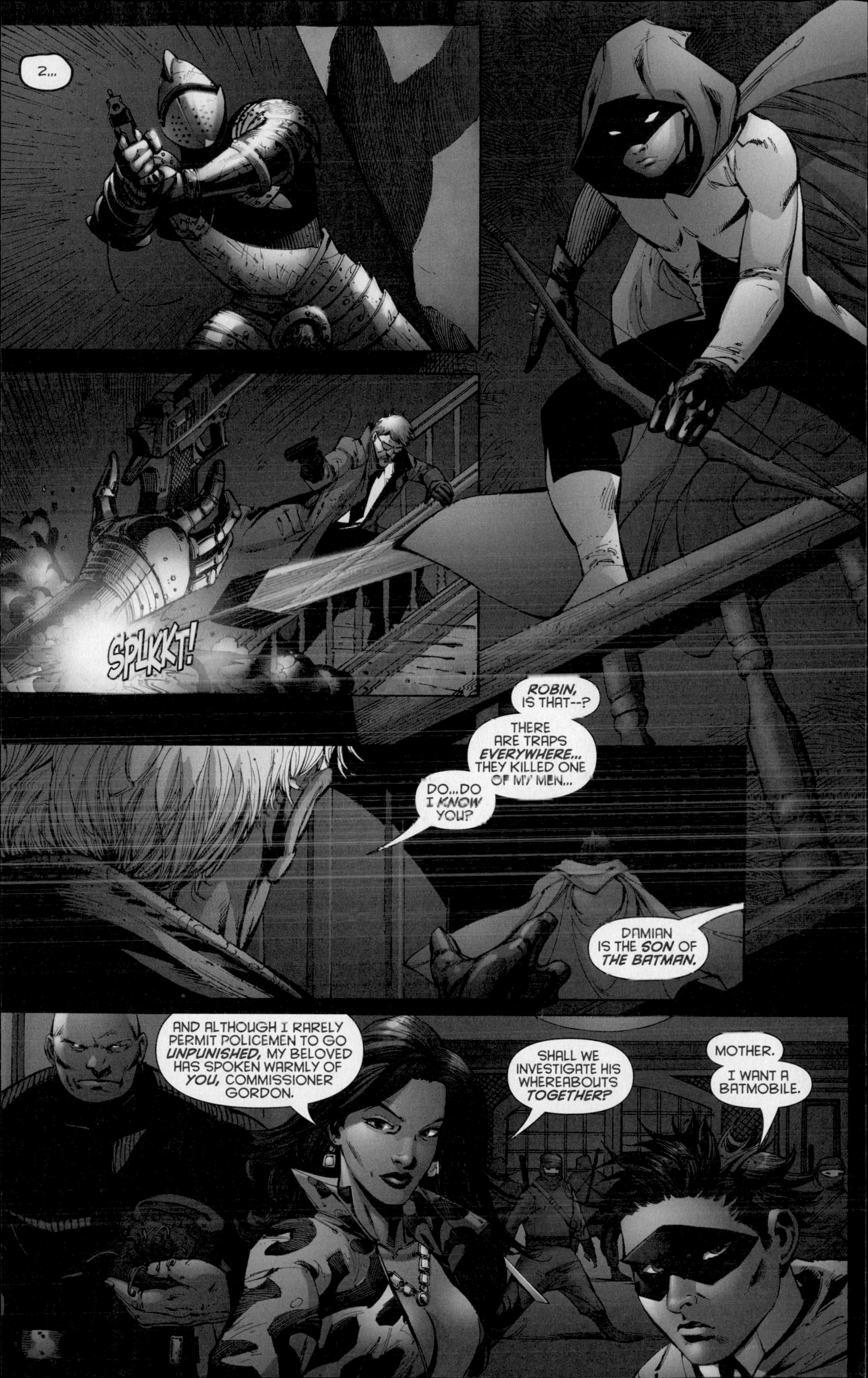

2...
SPLKKT!
ROBIN, IS THAT--?
THERE ARE TRAPS EVERYWHERE... THEY KILLED ONE OF MY MEN...
DO...DO I KNOW YOU?
DAMIAN IS THE SON OF THE BATMAN.
AND ALTHOUGH I RARELY PERMIT POLICEMEN TO GO UNPUNISHED, MY BELOVED HAS SPOKEN WARMLY OF YOU, COMMISSIONER GORDON.
SHALL WE INVESTIGATE HIS WHEREABOUTS TOGETHER?
MOTHER.
I WANT A BATMOBILE.

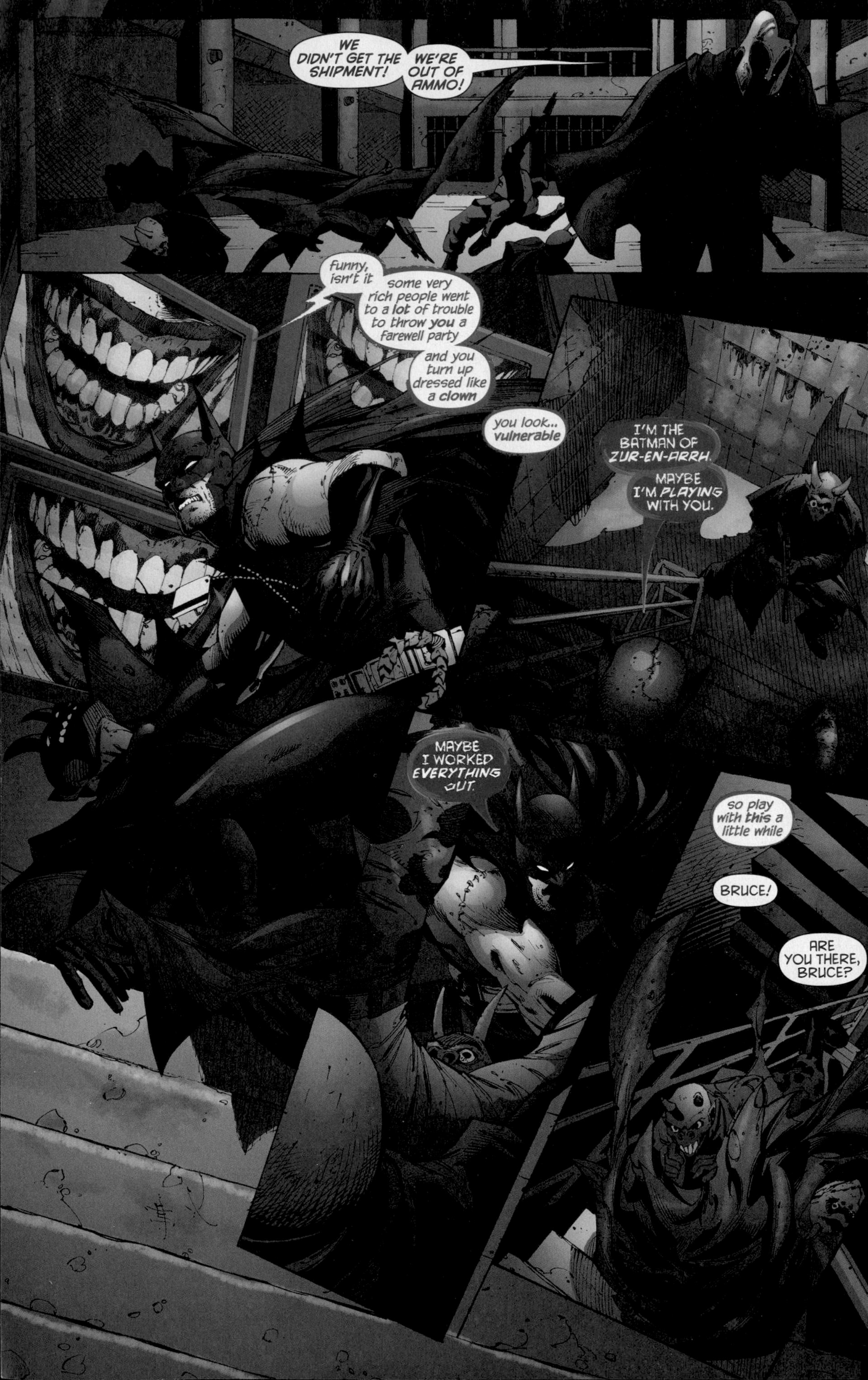
WE DIDN'T GET THE SHIPMENT!
WE'RE OUT OF AMMO!
funny, isn't it
some very rich people went to a lot of trouble to throw you a farewell party
and you turn up dressed like a clown
you look... vulnerable
I'M THE BATMAN OF ZUR-EN-ARRH.
MAYBE I'M PLAYING WITH YOU.
MAYBE I WORKED EVERYTHING OUT.
so play with this a little while
BRUCE!
ARE YOU THERE, BRUCE?

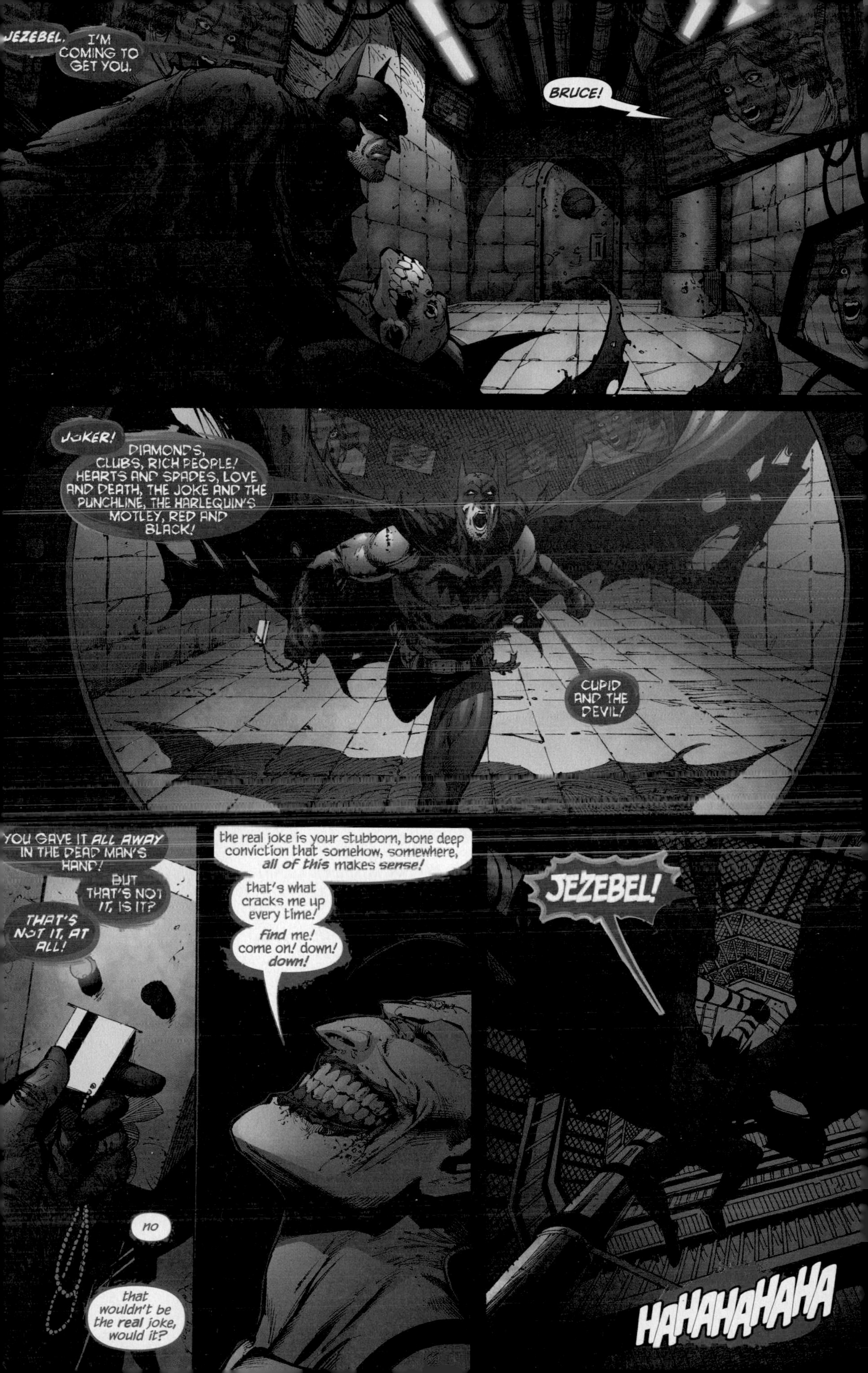
JEZEBEL.
I'M COMING TO GET YOU.
BRUCE!
JOKER!
DIAMONDS, CLUBS, RICH PEOPLE! HEARTS AND SPADES, LOVE AND DEATH, THE JOKE AND THE PUNCHLINE, THE HARLEQUIN'S MOTLEY, RED AND BLACK!
CUPID AND THE DEVIL!
YOU GAVE IT ALL AWAY IN THE DEAD MAN'S HAND!
BUT THAT'S NOT IT, IS IT?
THAT'S NOT IT, AT ALL!
no
that wouldn't be the real joke, would it?
the real joke is your stubborn, bone deep conviction that somehow, somewhere, all of this makes sense!
that's what cracks me up every time!
find me! come on! down! down!
JEZEBEL!
HAHAHAHAHA

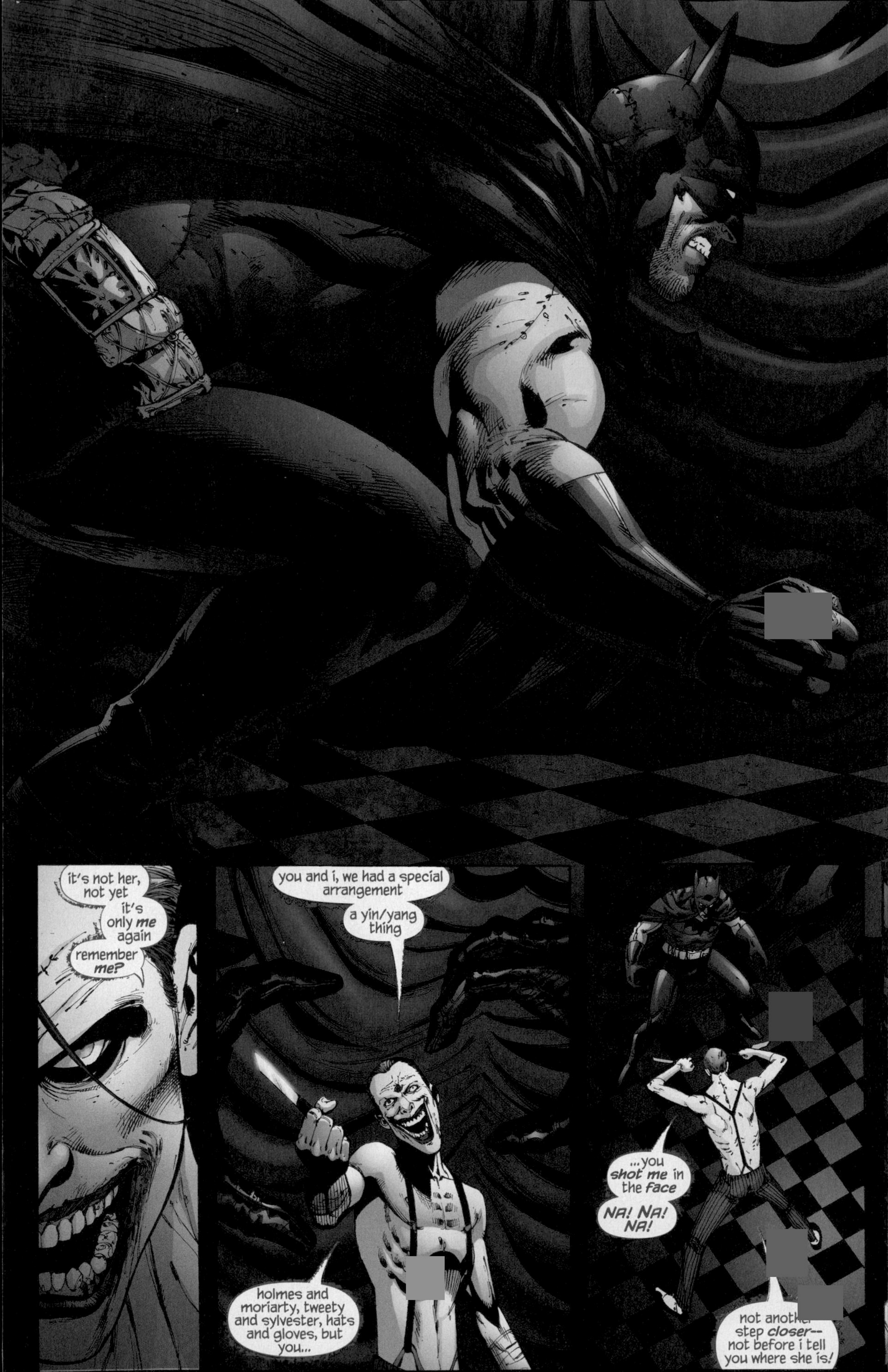
it's not her, not yet
it's only *me* again
remember *me?*
you and i, we had a special arrangement
a yin/yang thing
holmes and moriarty, tweety and sylvester, hats and gloves, but you...
...you *shot me* in the *face*
NA! NA! NA!
not another step *closer--* not before i tell you where she is!

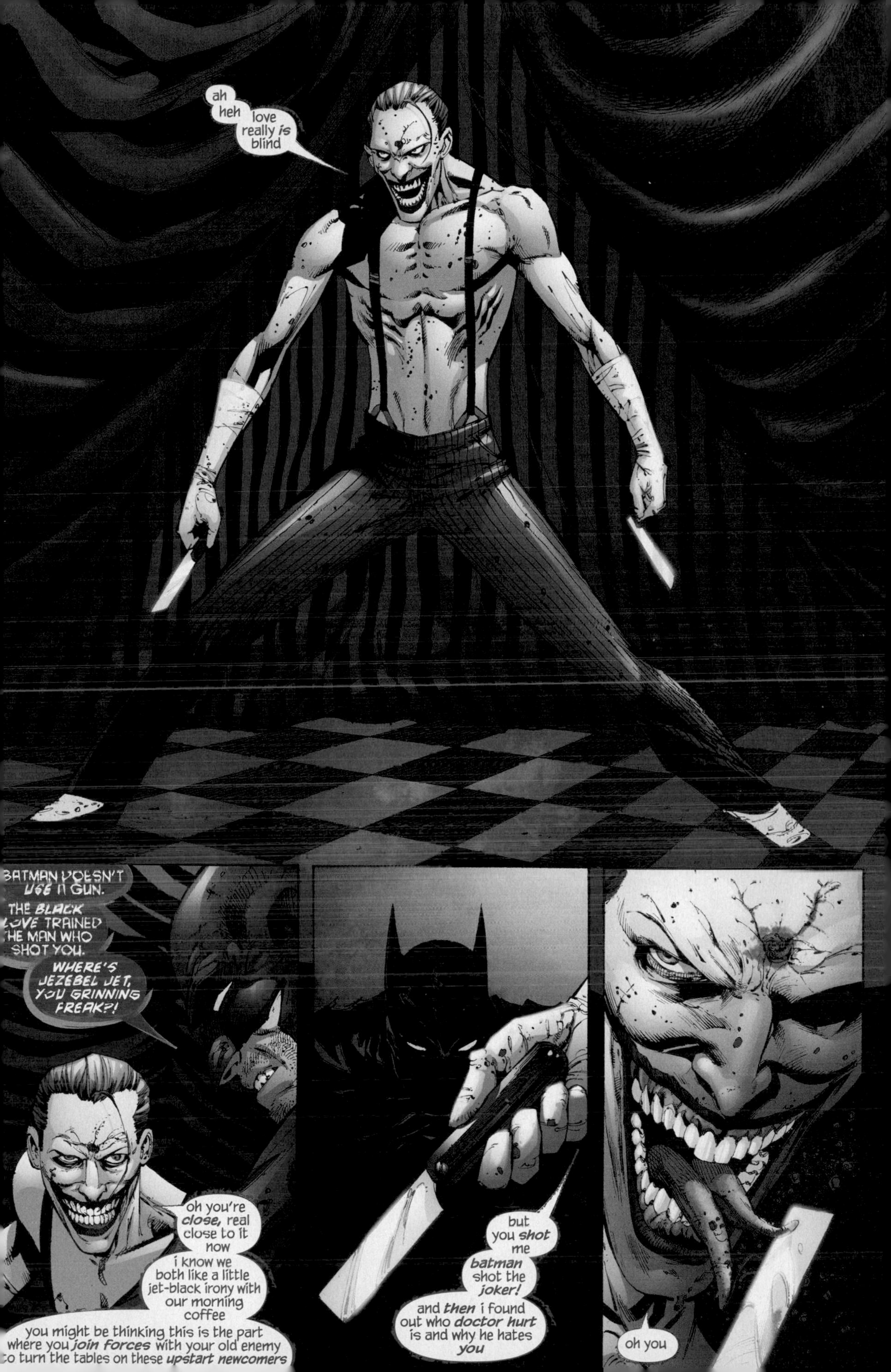
ah heh love really is blind
BATMAN DOESN'T USE A GUN.
THE BLACK GLOVE TRAINED THE MAN WHO SHOT YOU.
WHERE'S JEZEBEL JET, YOU GRINNING FREAK?!
oh you're close, real close to it now
i know we both like a little jet-black irony with our morning coffee
you might be thinking this is the part where you join forces with your old enemy to turn the tables on these upstart newcomers
but you shot me
batman shot the joker!
and then i found out who doctor hurt is and why he hates you
oh you

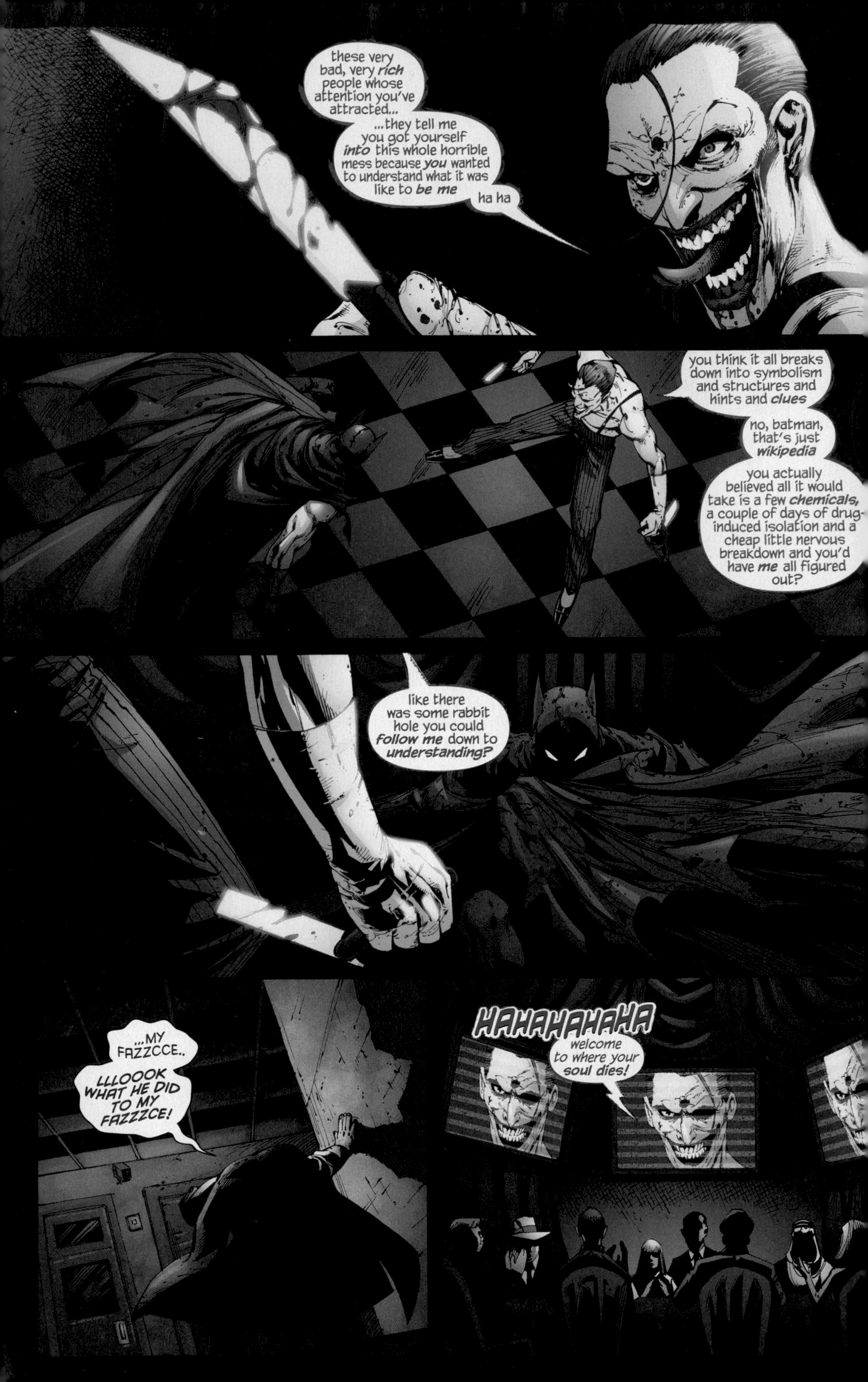

these very bad, very *rich* people whose attention you've attracted...
...they tell me you got yourself *into* this whole horrible mess because *you* wanted to understand what it was like to *be me*
ha ha
you think it all breaks down into symbolism and structures and hints and *clues*
no, batman, that's just *wikipedia*
you actually believed all it would take is a few *chemicals,* a couple of days of drug-induced isolation and a cheap little nervous breakdown and you'd have *me* all figured out?
like there was some rabbit hole you could *follow me* down to *understanding?*
...MY FAZZCCE..
LLLOOOK WHAT HE DID TO MY FAZZZCE!
HAHAHAHAHAHA
welcome to where your *soul dies!*

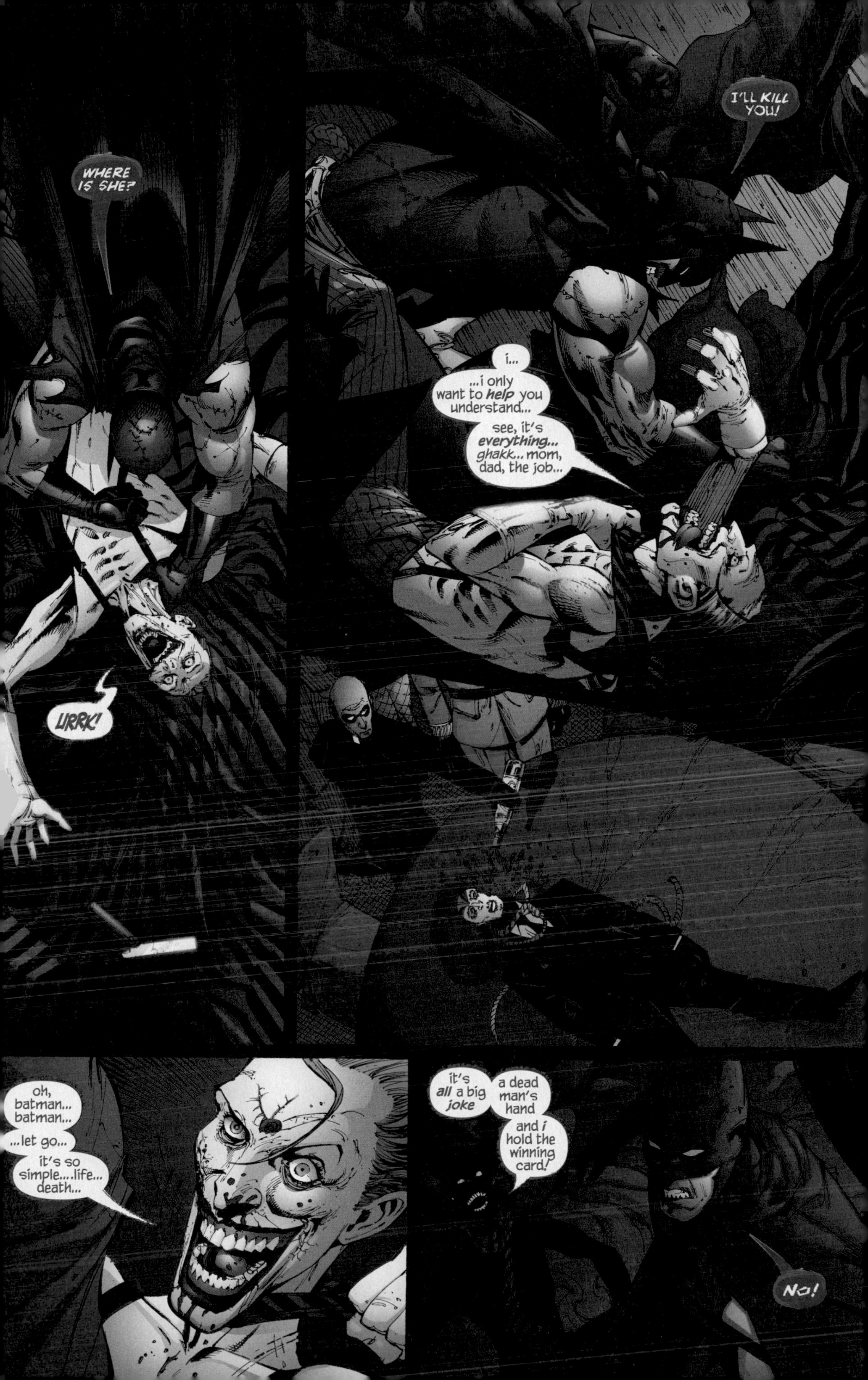
WHERE IS SHE?
URRK!
I'LL KILL YOU!
i... ...i only want to help you understand...
see, it's everything... ghakk... mom, dad, the job...
oh, batman... batman...
...let go...
it's so simple....life... death...
it's all a big joke
a dead man's hand
and i hold the winning card!
No!

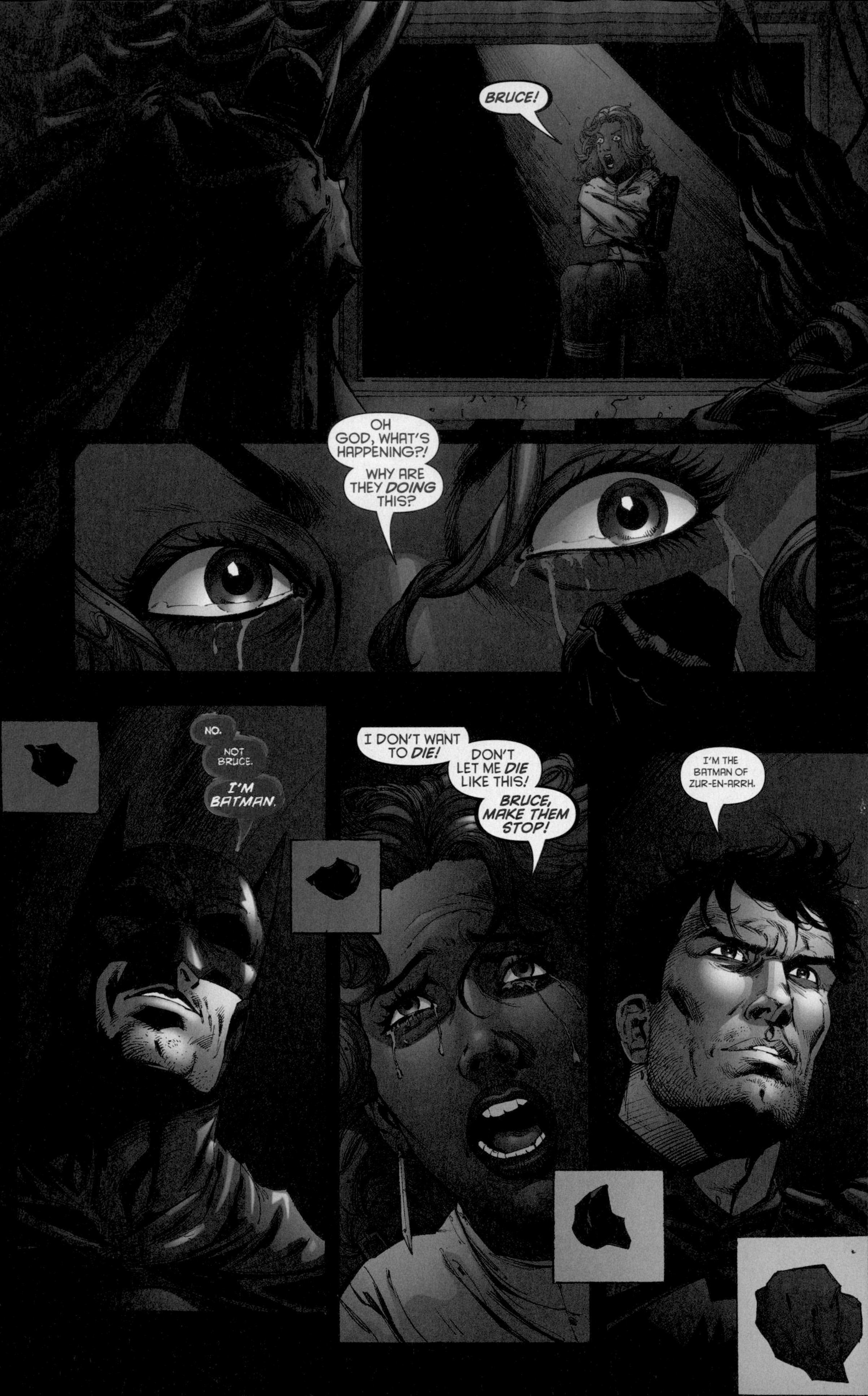
BRUCE!
OH GOD, WHAT'S HAPPENING?!
WHY ARE THEY DOING THIS?
NO.
NOT BRUCE.
I'M BATMAN.
I DON'T WANT TO DIE!
DON'T LET ME DIE LIKE THIS!
BRUCE, MAKE THEM STOP!
I'M THE BATMAN OF ZUR-EN-ARRH.

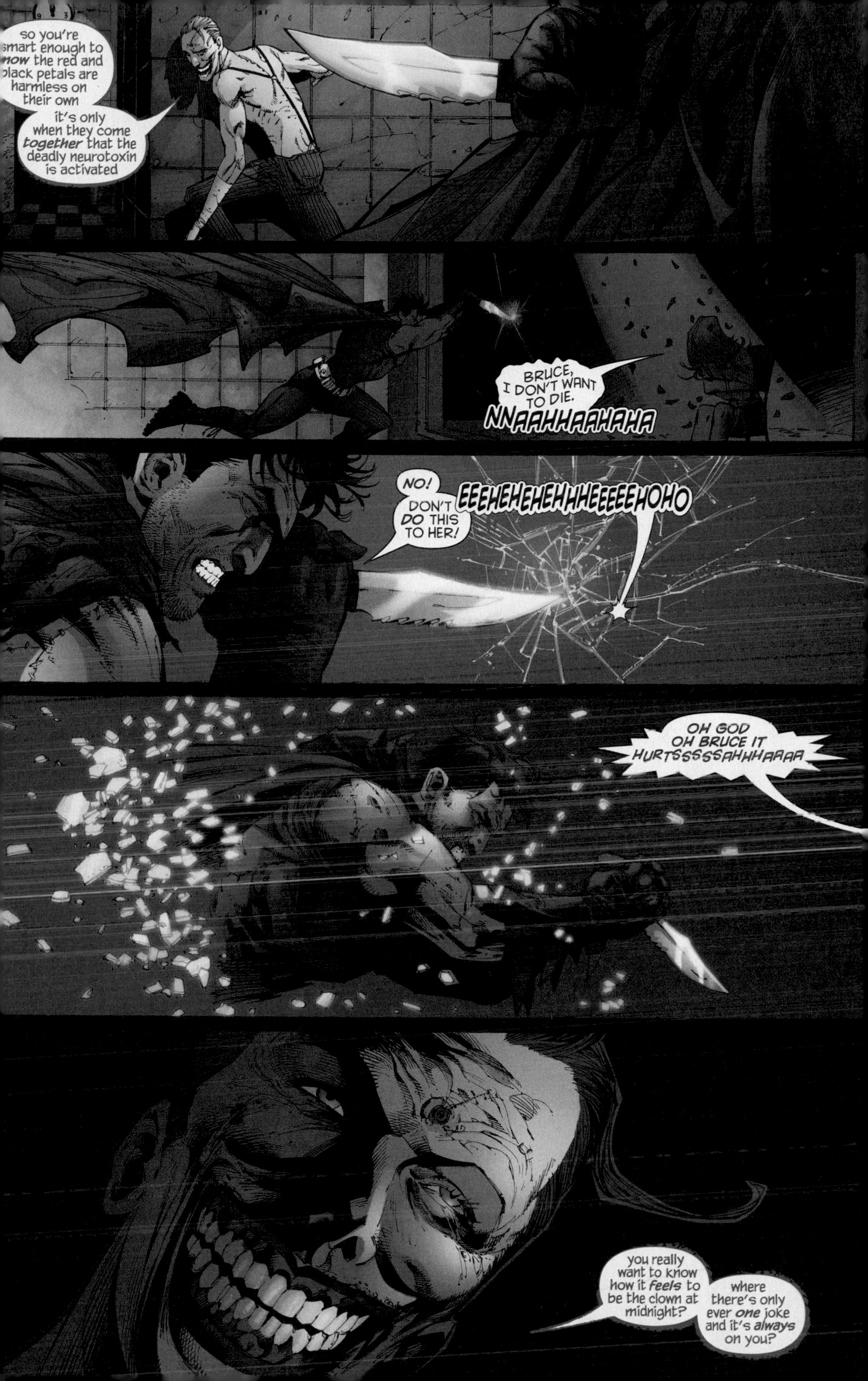
so you're smart enough to know the red and black petals are harmless on their own
it's only when they come together that the deadly neurotoxin is activated
BRUCE, I DON'T WANT TO DIE. NNAAHHAAHAHA
NO! DON'T DO THIS TO HER!
EEEHEHEHEHHHEEEEEHOHO
OH GOD OH BRUCE IT HURTSSSSSAHHHAAAA
you really want to know how it feels to be the clown at midnight?
where there's only ever one joke and it's always on you?

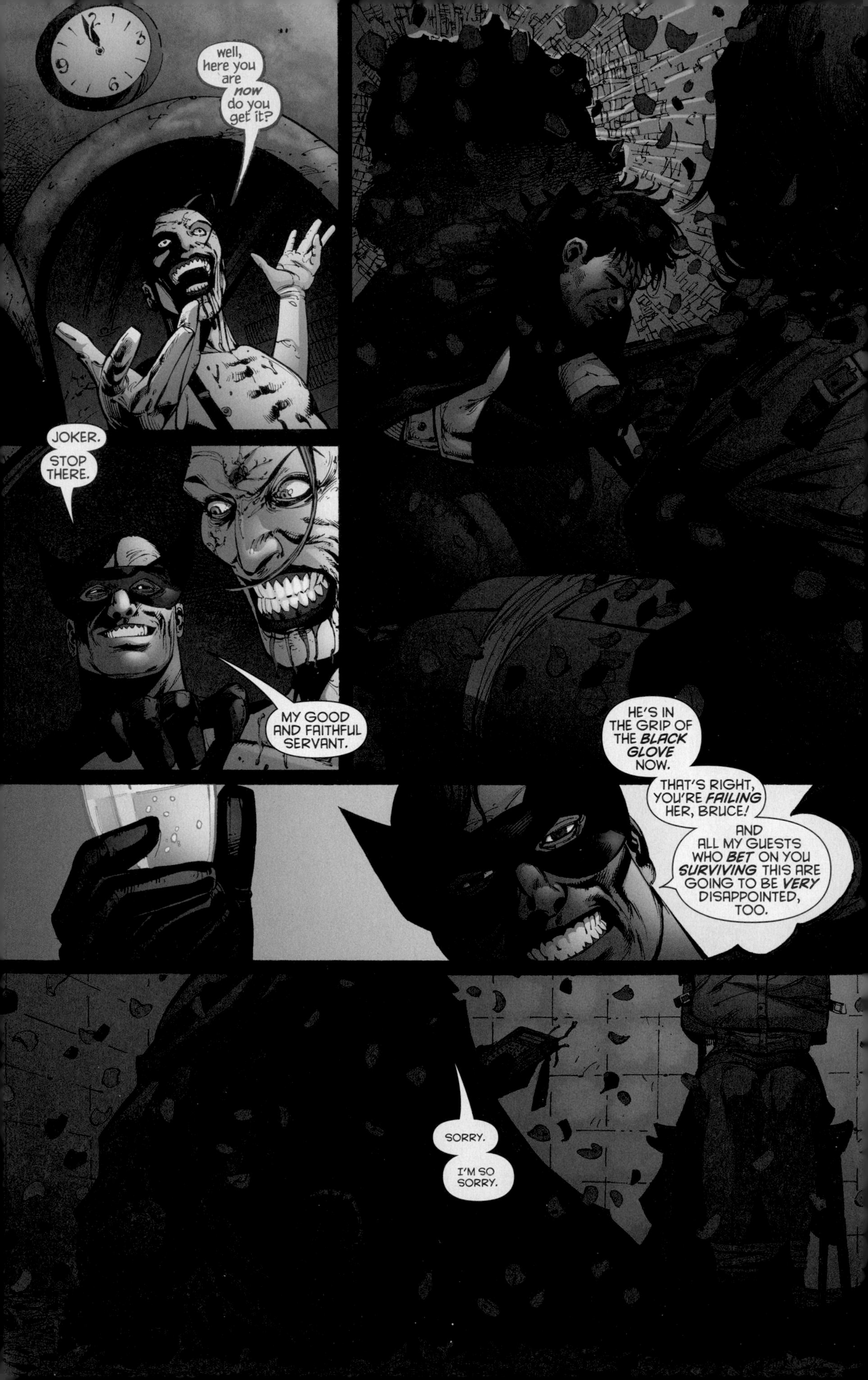
well, here you are now do you get it?
JOKER. STOP THERE.
MY GOOD AND FAITHFUL SERVANT.
HE'S IN THE GRIP OF THE BLACK GLOVE NOW.
THAT'S RIGHT, YOU'RE FAILING HER, BRUCE!
AND ALL MY GUESTS WHO BET ON YOU SURVIVING THIS ARE GOING TO BE VERY DISAPPOINTED, TOO.
SORRY.
I'M SO SORRY.

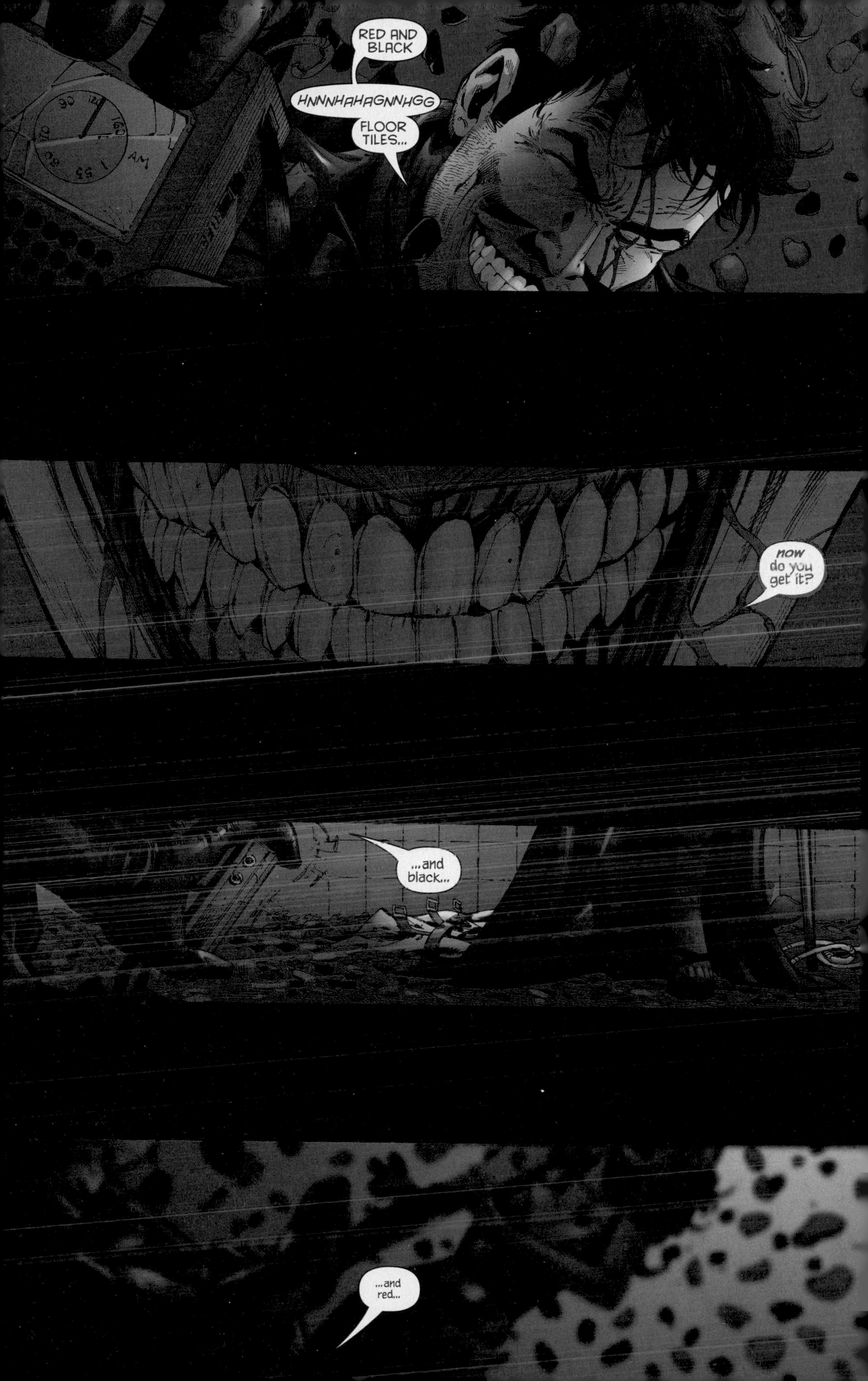
RED AND BLACK
HNNNHAHAGNNHGG
FLOOR TILES...
NOW do you get it?
...and black...
...and red...

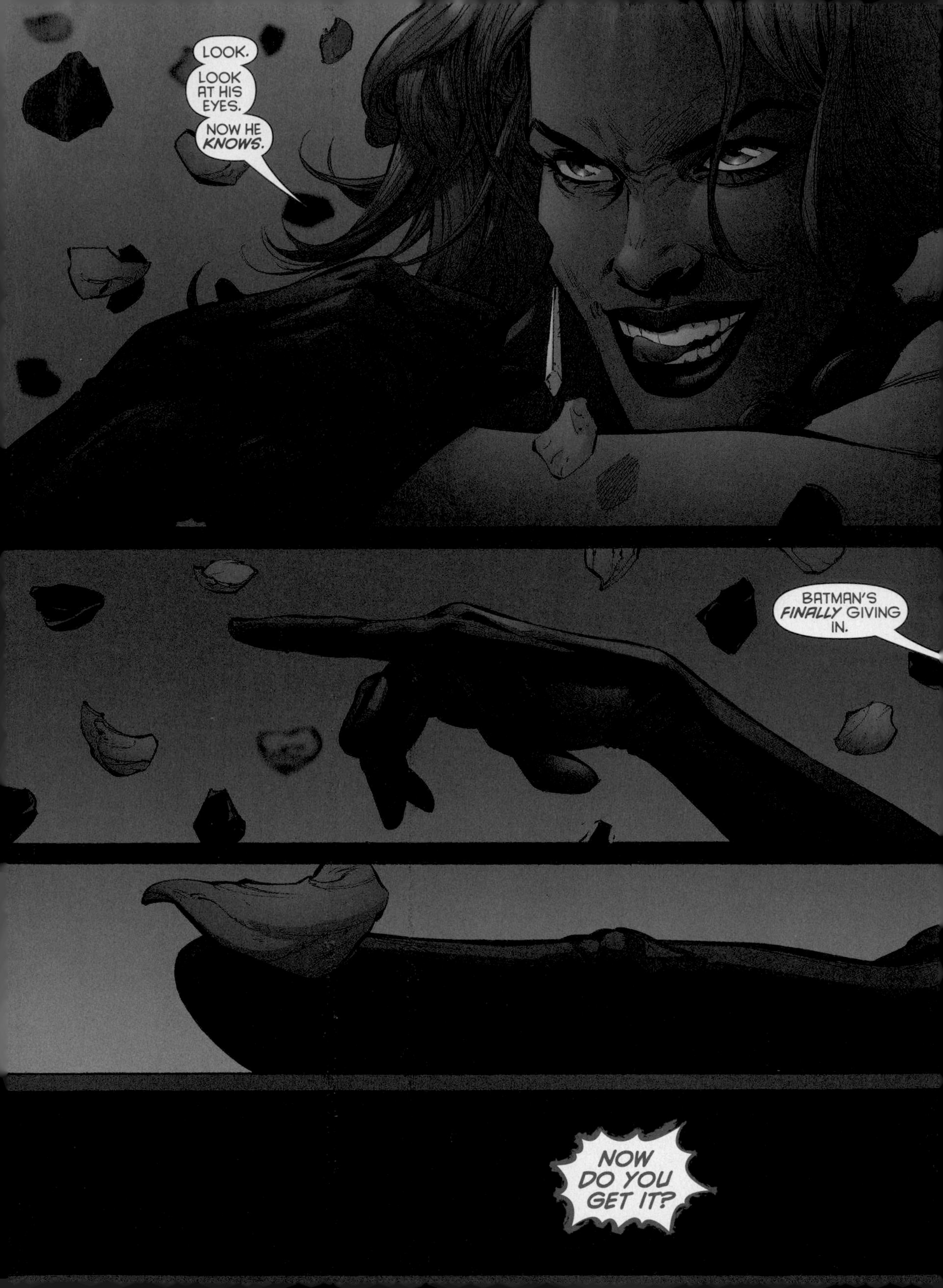
LOOK.
LOOK AT HIS EYES.
NOW HE *KNOWS*.
BATMAN'S *FINALLY* GIVING IN.
NOW DO YOU GET IT?

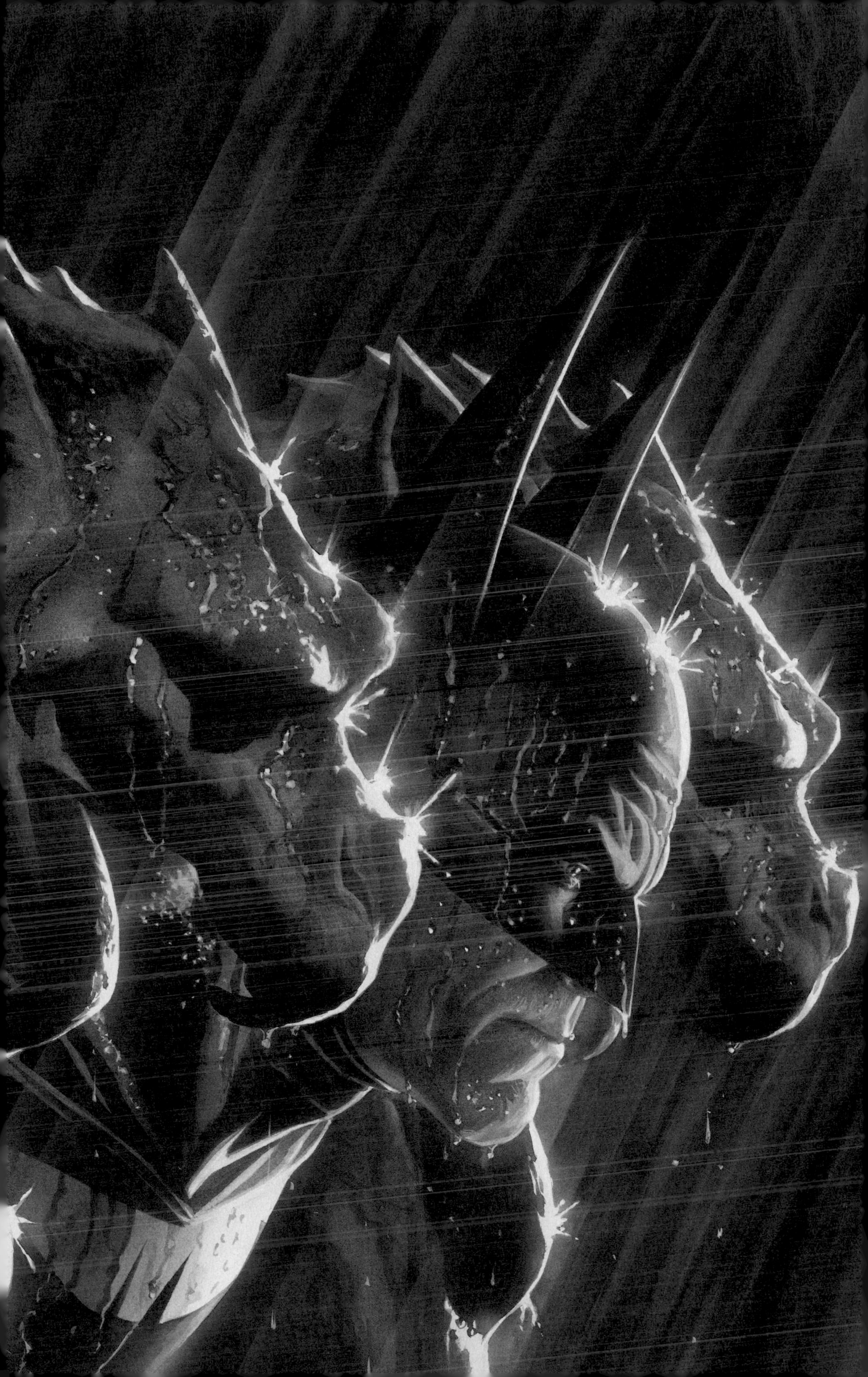

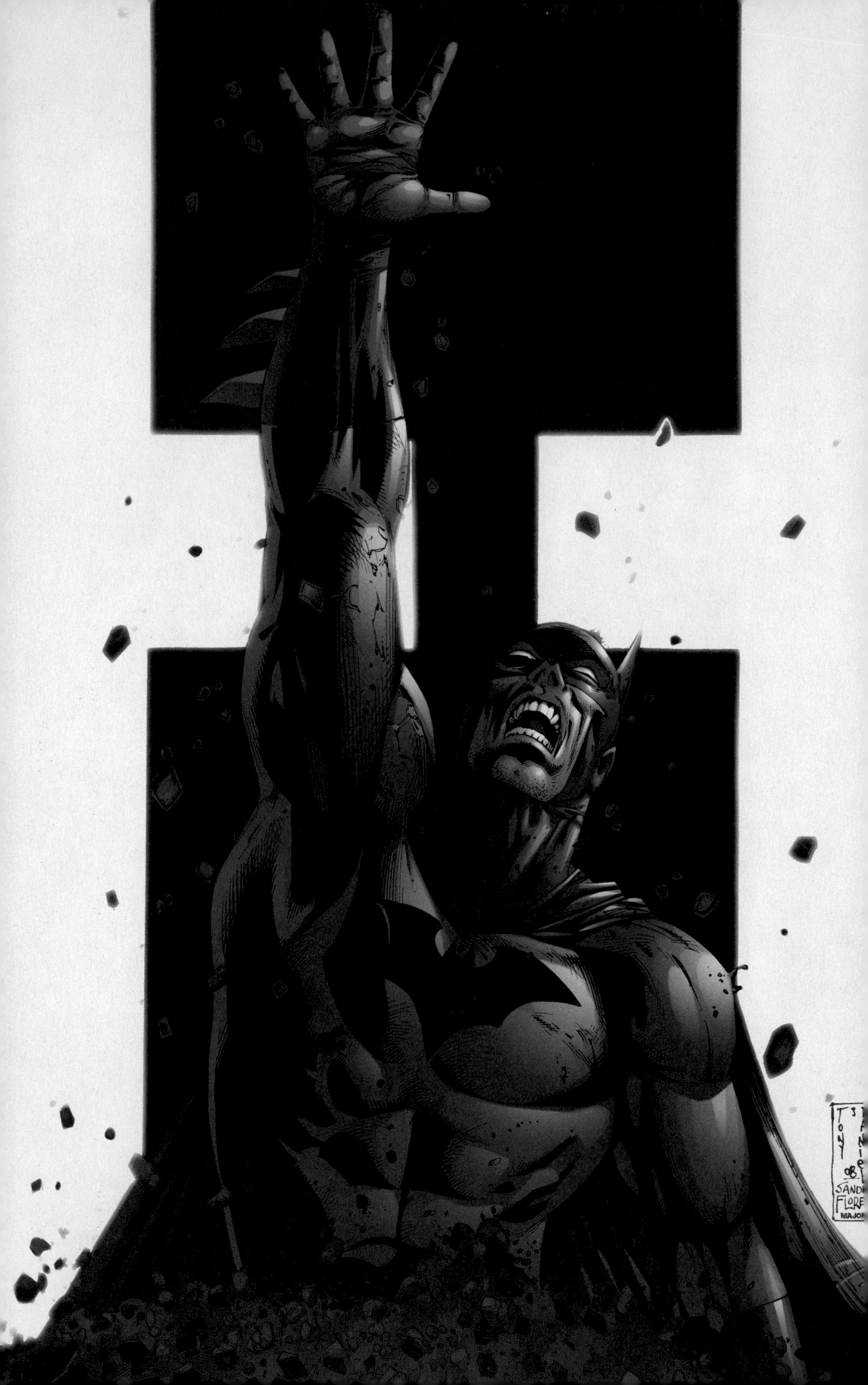

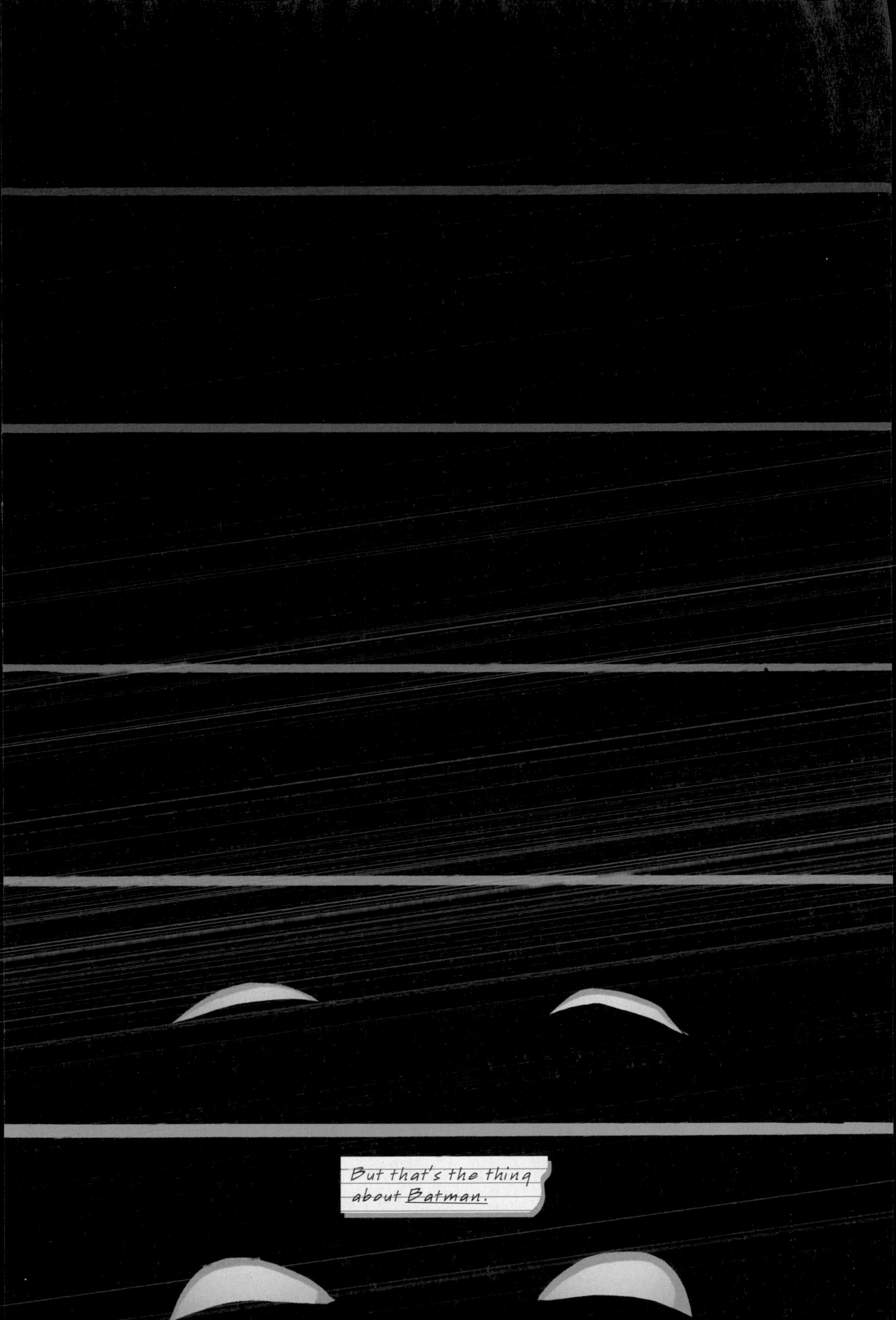
But that's the thing about Batman.

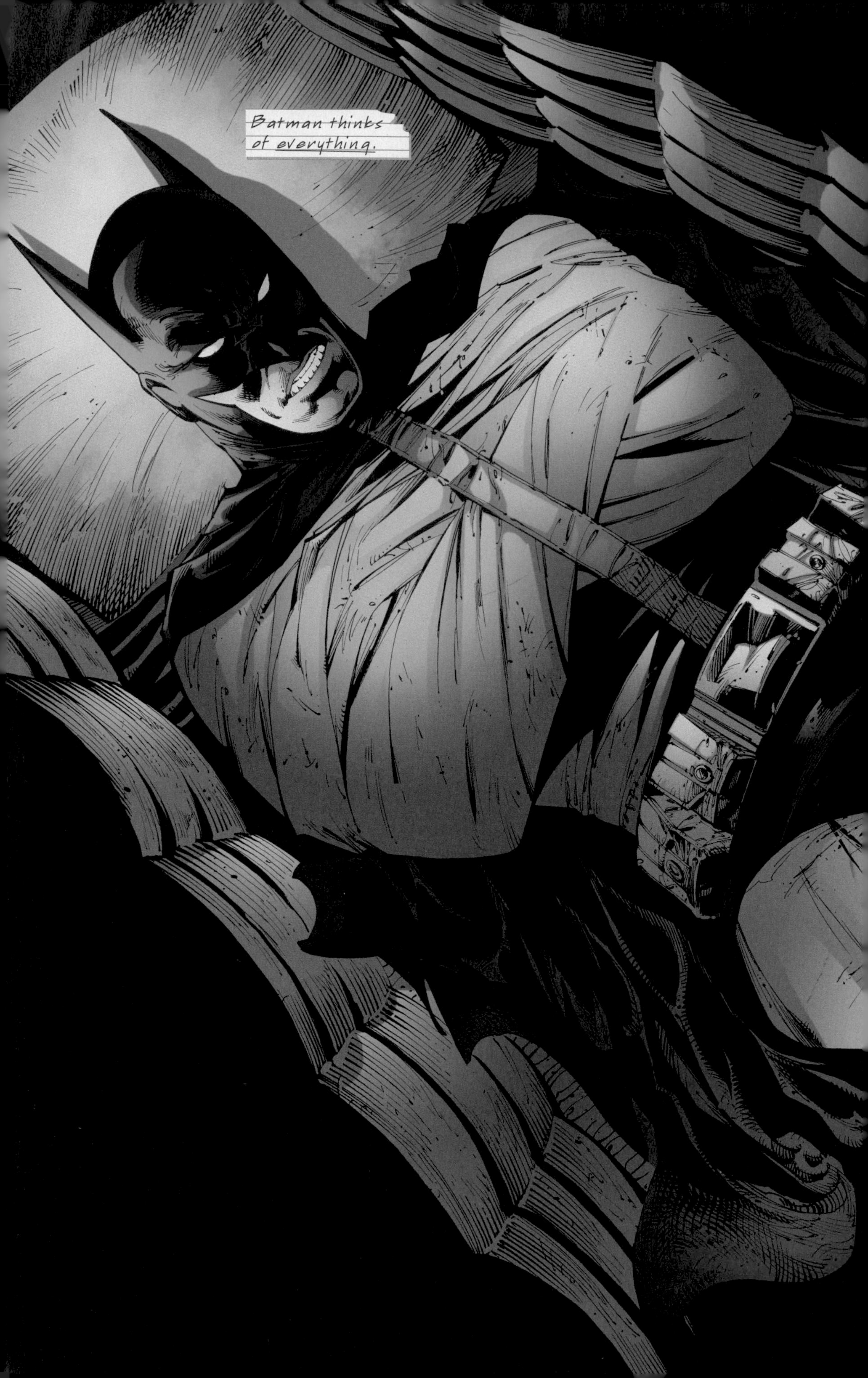
Batman thinks of everything.

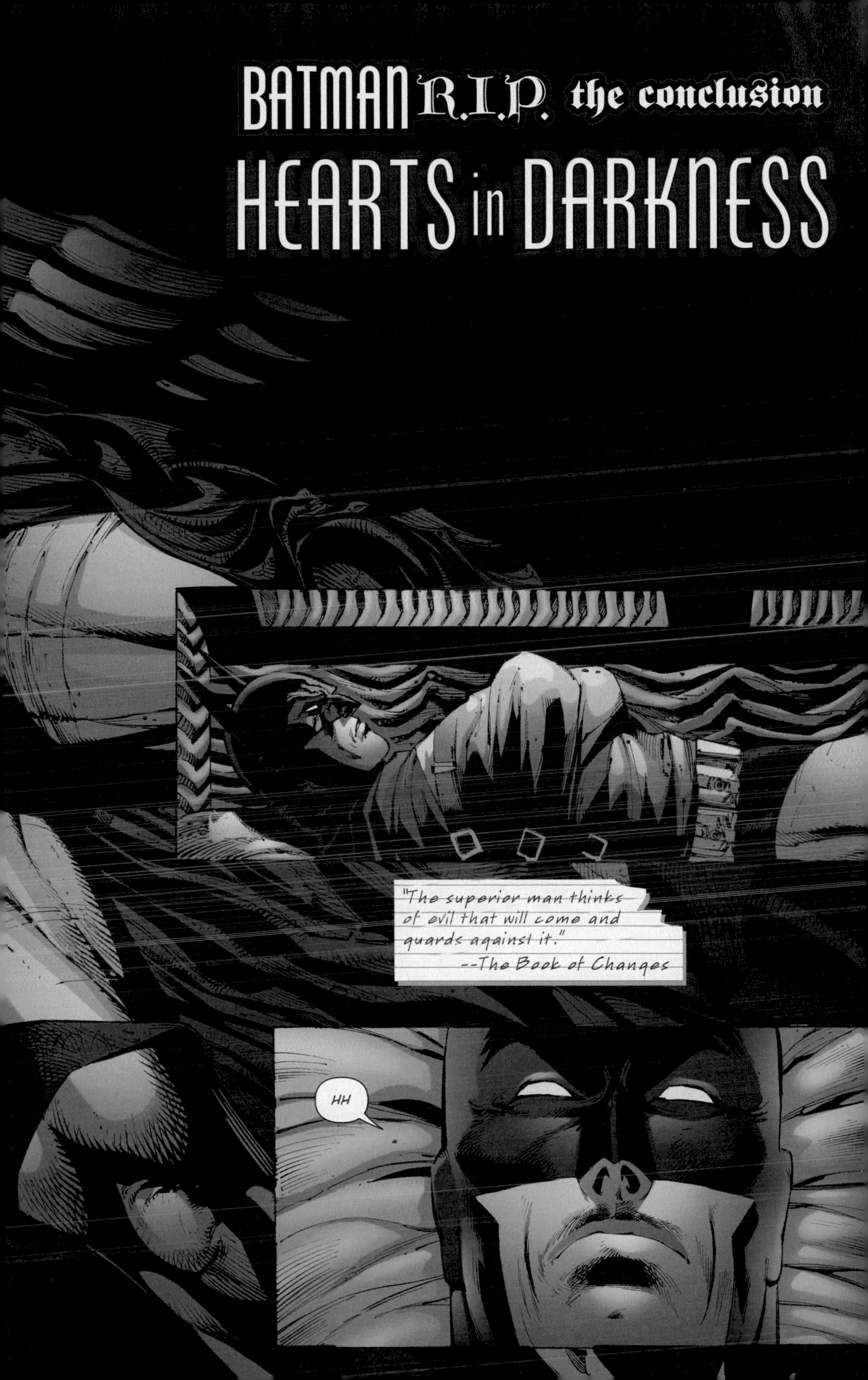
BATMAN R.I.P. the conclusion
HEARTS in DARKNESS
"The superior man thinks of evil that will come and guards against it." --The Book of Changes
HH

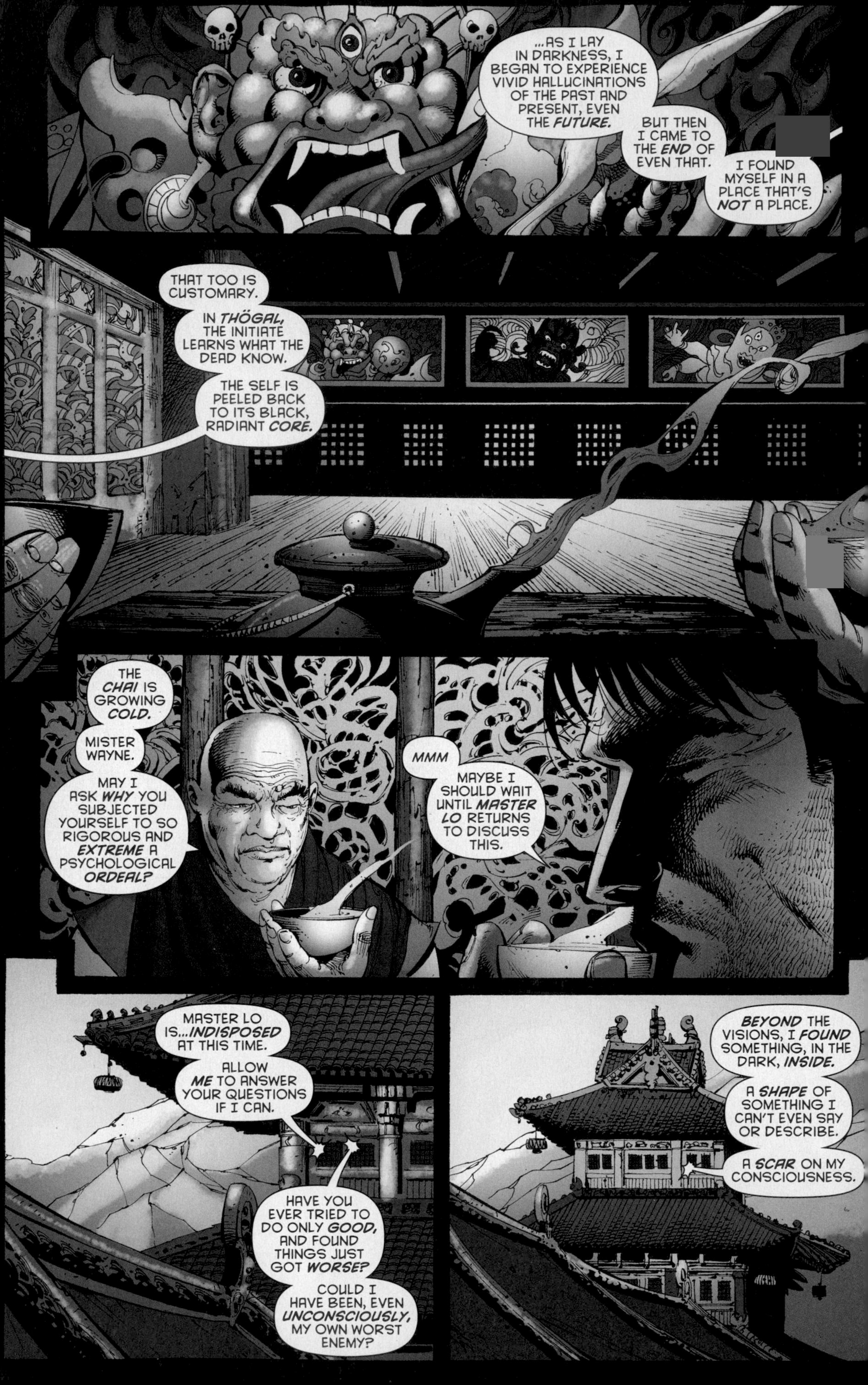

...AS I LAY IN DARKNESS, I BEGAN TO EXPERIENCE VIVID HALLUCINATIONS OF THE PAST AND PRESENT, EVEN THE FUTURE.
BUT THEN I CAME TO THE END OF EVEN THAT.
I FOUND MYSELF IN A PLACE THAT'S NOT A PLACE.
THAT TOO IS CUSTOMARY.
IN THÖGAL, THE INITIATE LEARNS WHAT THE DEAD KNOW.
THE SELF IS PEELED BACK TO ITS BLACK, RADIANT CORE.
THE CHAI IS GROWING COLD.
MISTER WAYNE.
MAY I ASK WHY YOU SUBJECTED YOURSELF TO SO RIGOROUS AND EXTREME A PSYCHOLOGICAL ORDEAL?
MMM
MAYBE I SHOULD WAIT UNTIL MASTER LO RETURNS TO DISCUSS THIS.
MASTER LO IS...INDISPOSED AT THIS TIME.
ALLOW ME TO ANSWER YOUR QUESTIONS IF I CAN.
HAVE YOU EVER TRIED TO DO ONLY GOOD, AND FOUND THINGS JUST GOT WORSE?
COULD I HAVE BEEN, EVEN UNCONSCIOUSLY, MY OWN WORST ENEMY?
BEYOND THE VISIONS, I FOUND SOMETHING, IN THE DARK, INSIDE.
A SHAPE OF SOMETHING I CAN'T EVEN SAY OR DESCRIBE.
A SCAR ON MY CONSCIOUSNESS.

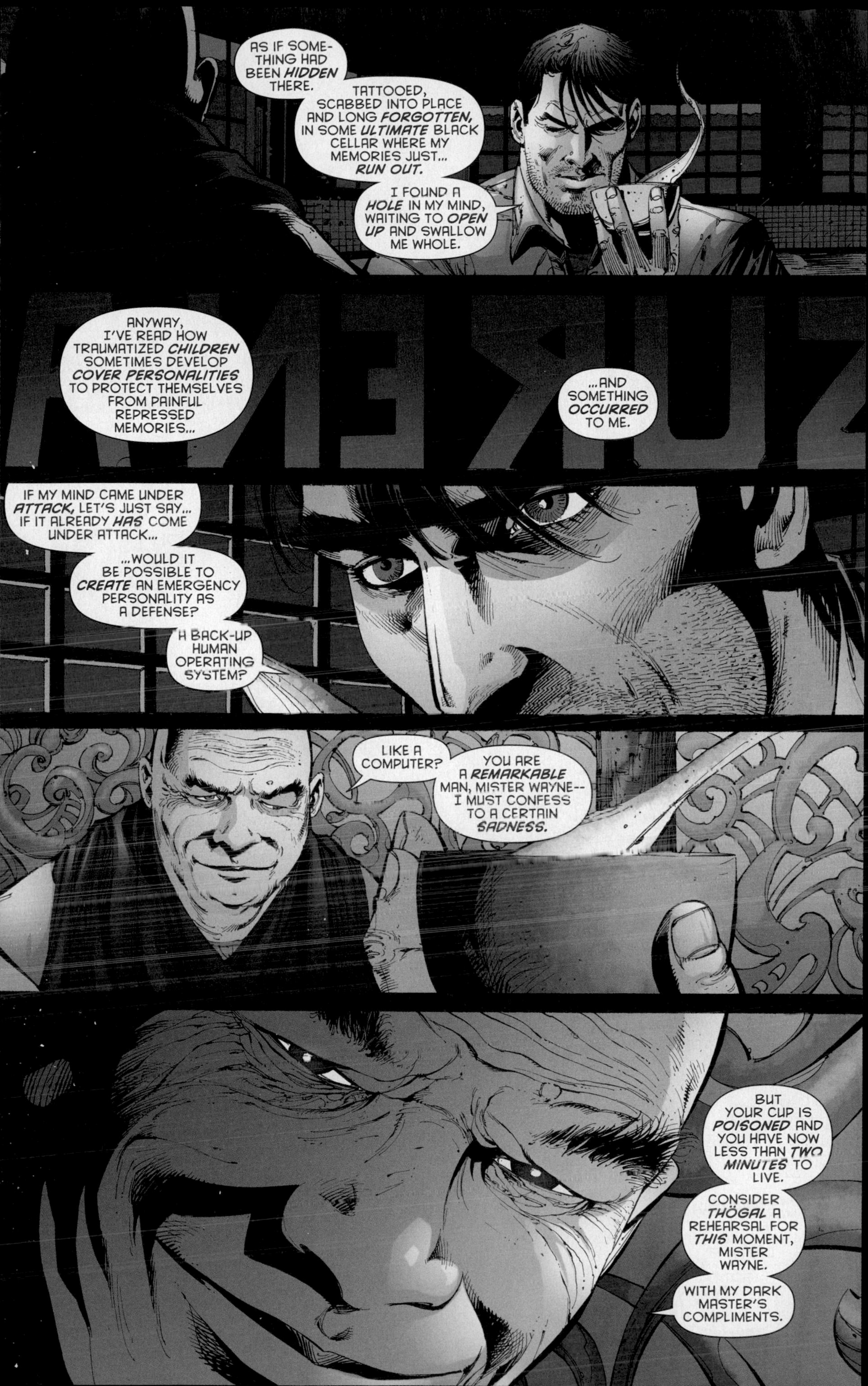
AS IF SOMETHING HAD BEEN HIDDEN THERE.
TATTOOED, SCABBED INTO PLACE AND LONG FORGOTTEN, IN SOME ULTIMATE BLACK CELLAR WHERE MY MEMORIES JUST... RUN OUT.
I FOUND A HOLE IN MY MIND, WAITING TO OPEN UP AND SWALLOW ME WHOLE.
ANYWAY, I'VE READ HOW TRAUMATIZED CHILDREN SOMETIMES DEVELOP COVER PERSONALITIES TO PROTECT THEMSELVES FROM PAINFUL REPRESSED MEMORIES...
...AND SOMETHING OCCURRED TO ME.
IF MY MIND CAME UNDER ATTACK, LET'S JUST SAY... IF IT ALREADY HAS COME UNDER ATTACK...
...WOULD IT BE POSSIBLE TO CREATE AN EMERGENCY PERSONALITY AS A DEFENSE?
A BACK-UP HUMAN OPERATING SYSTEM?
LIKE A COMPUTER?
YOU ARE A REMARKABLE MAN, MISTER WAYNE-- I MUST CONFESS TO A CERTAIN SADNESS.
BUT YOUR CUP IS POISONED AND YOU HAVE NOW LESS THAN TWO MINUTES TO LIVE.
CONSIDER THÖGAL A REHEARSAL FOR THIS MOMENT, MISTER WAYNE.
WITH MY DARK MASTER'S COMPLIMENTS.

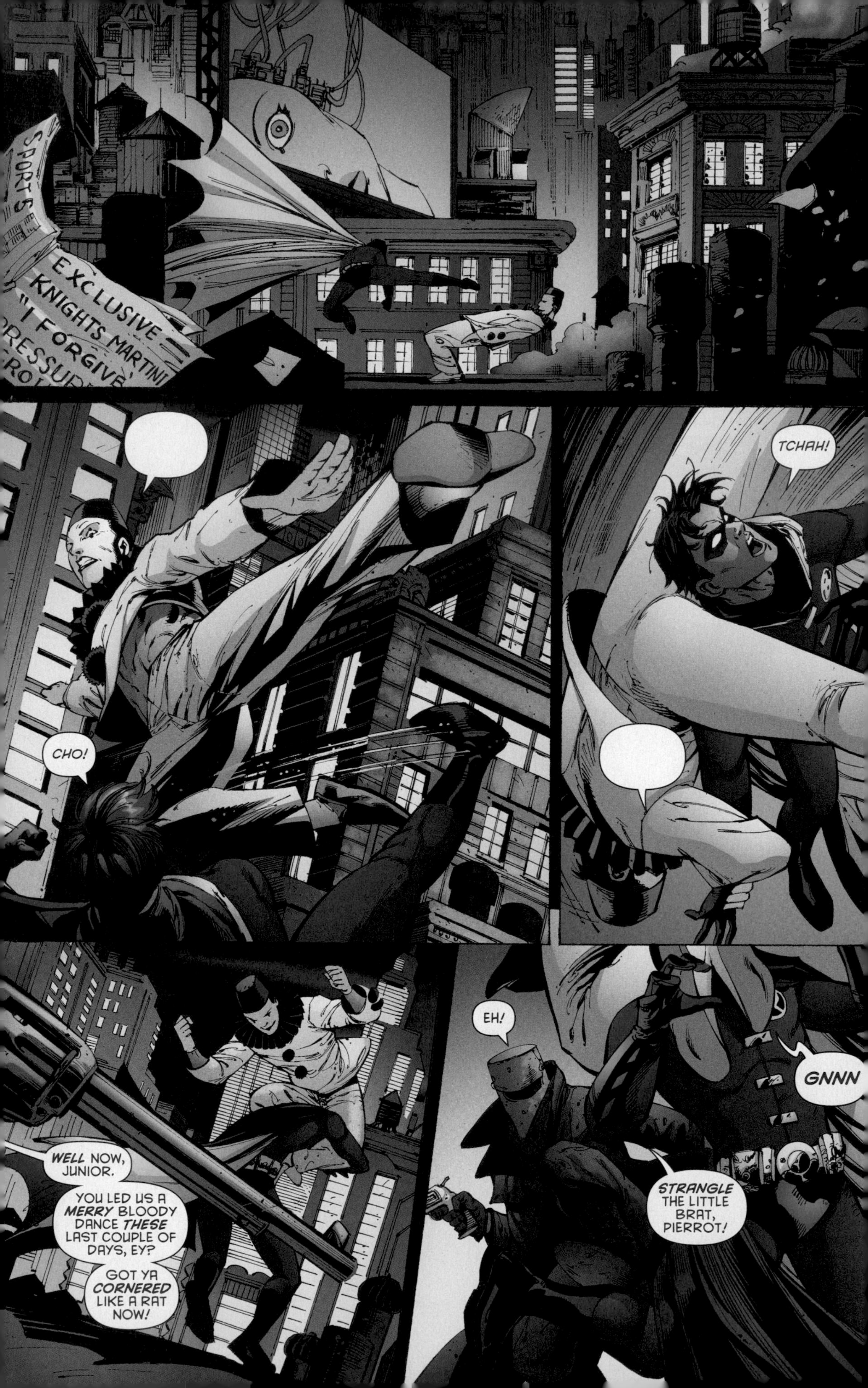
SPORTS
EXCLUSIVE
KNIGHTS MARTINI
"I FORGIVE
CHO!
TCHAH!
WELL NOW, JUNIOR.
YOU LED US A MERRY BLOODY DANCE THESE LAST COUPLE OF DAYS, EY?
GOT YA CORNERED LIKE A RAT NOW!
EH!
GNNN
STRANGLE THE LITTLE BRAT, PIERROT!

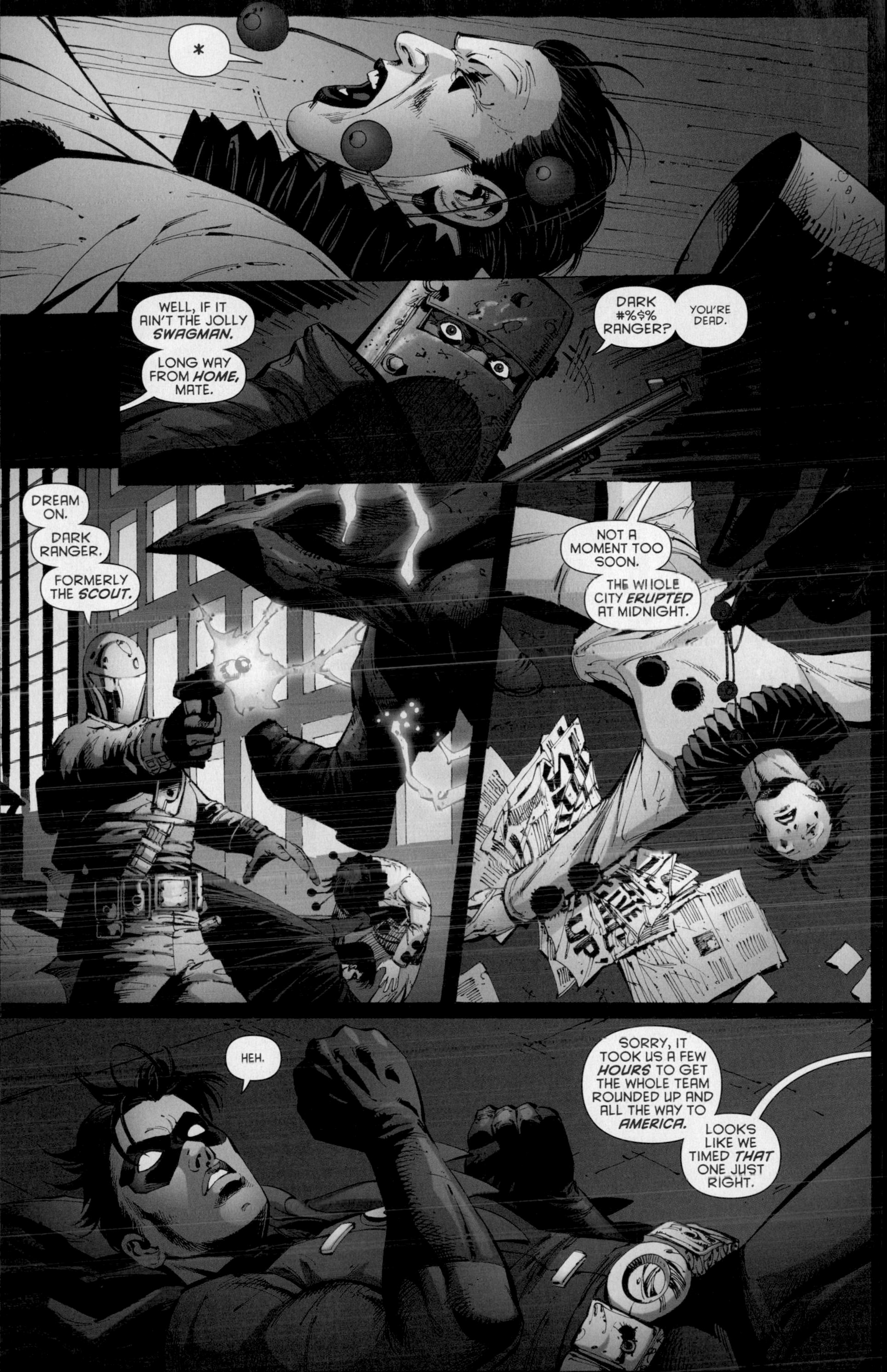
*
WELL, IF IT AIN'T THE JOLLY SWAGMAN.
LONG WAY FROM HOME, MATE.
DARK #%$% RANGER?
YOU'RE DEAD.
DREAM ON.
DARK RANGER.
FORMERLY THE SCOUT.
NOT A MOMENT TOO SOON.
THE WHOLE CITY ERUPTED AT MIDNIGHT.
HEH.
SORRY, IT TOOK US A FEW HOURS TO GET THE WHOLE TEAM ROUNDED UP AND ALL THE WAY TO AMERICA.
LOOKS LIKE WE TIMED THAT ONE JUST RIGHT.

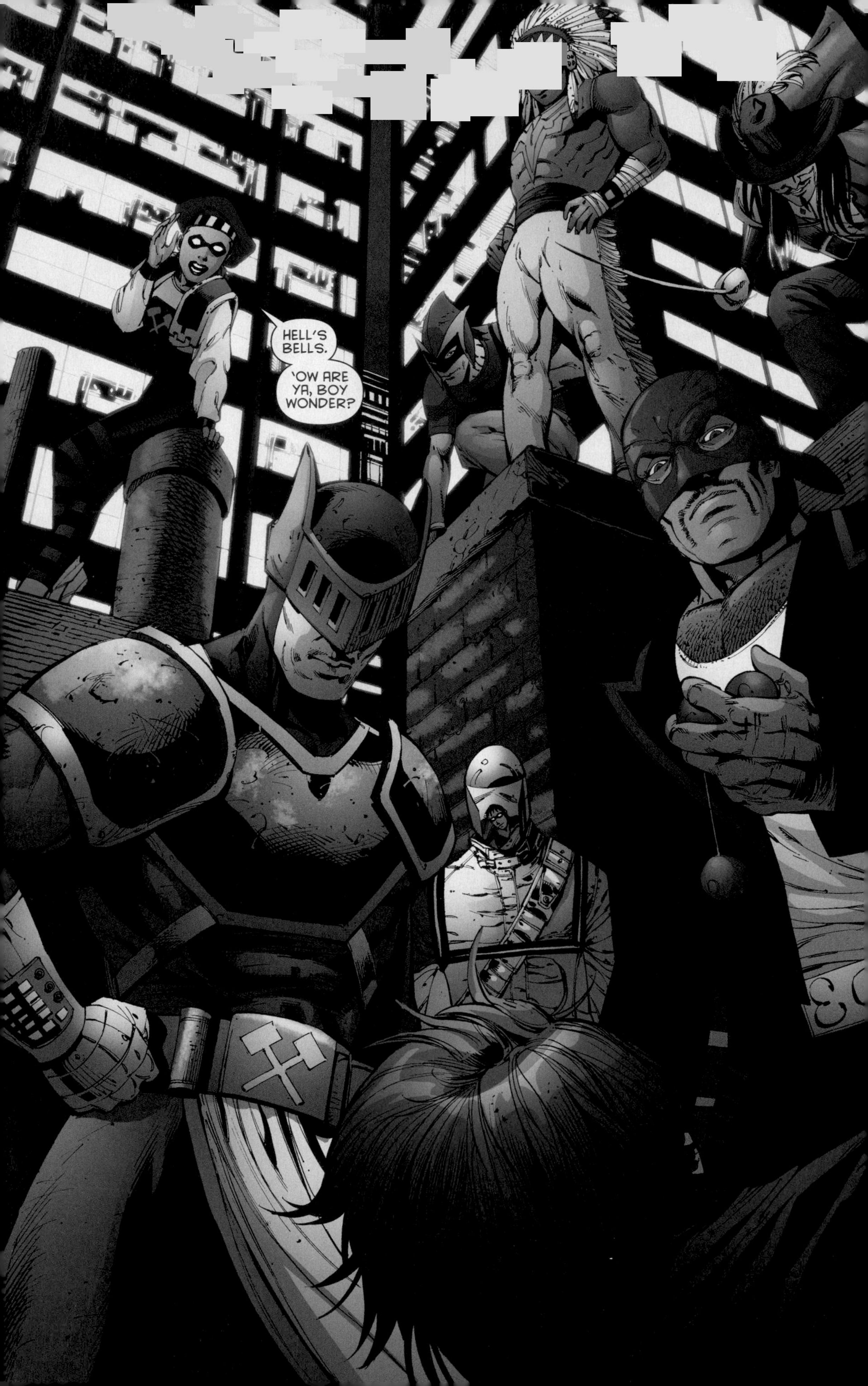
HELL'S BELLS.
'OW ARE YA, BOY WONDER?

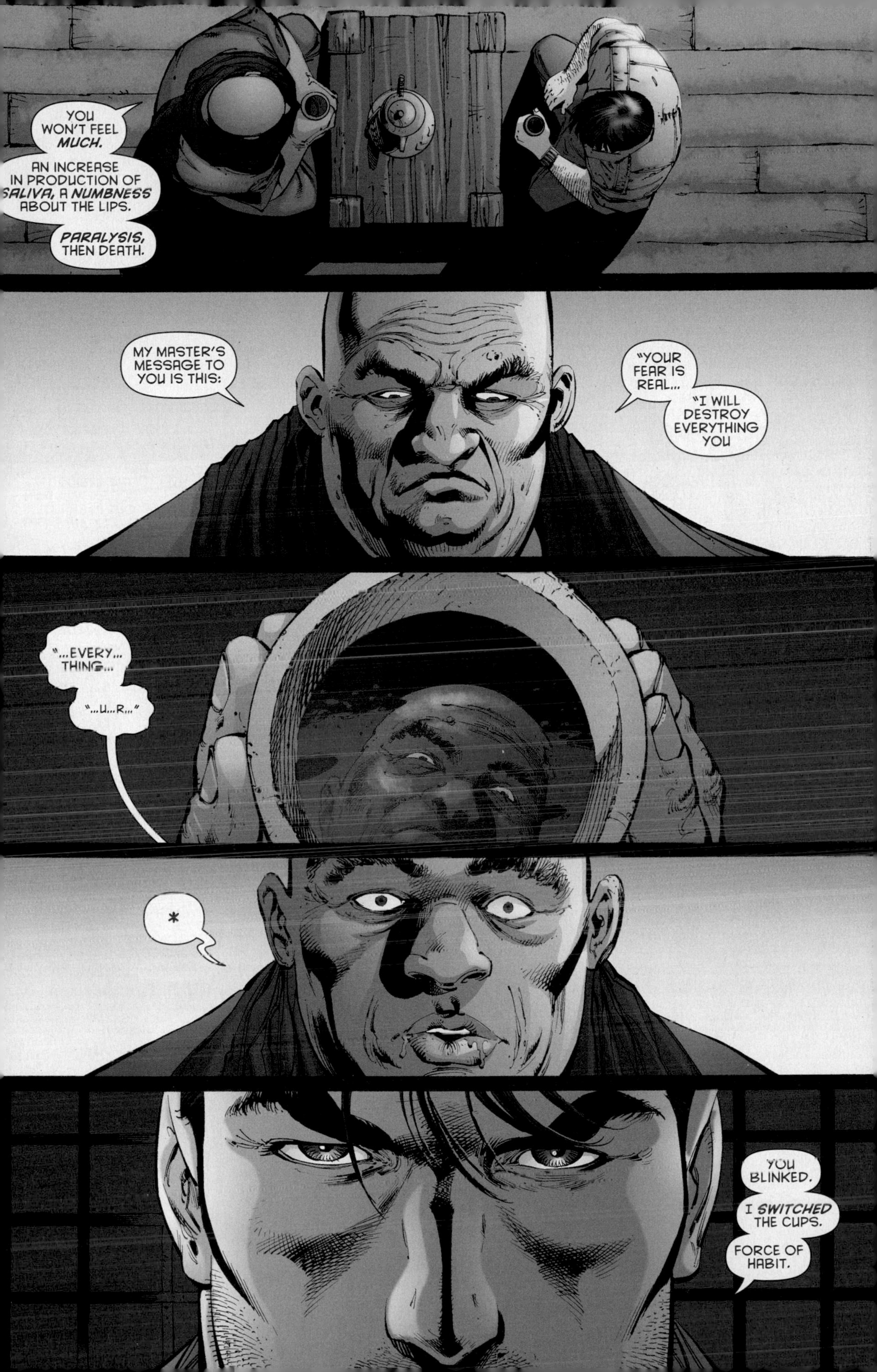
YOU WON'T FEEL *MUCH.*
AN INCREASE IN PRODUCTION OF *SALIVA,* A *NUMBNESS* ABOUT THE LIPS.
PARALYSIS, THEN DEATH.
MY MASTER'S MESSAGE TO YOU IS THIS:
"YOUR FEAR IS REAL...
"I WILL DESTROY EVERYTHING YOU
"...EVERY... THING...
"...U...R..."
*
YOU BLINKED.
I *SWITCHED* THE CUPS.
FORCE OF HABIT.

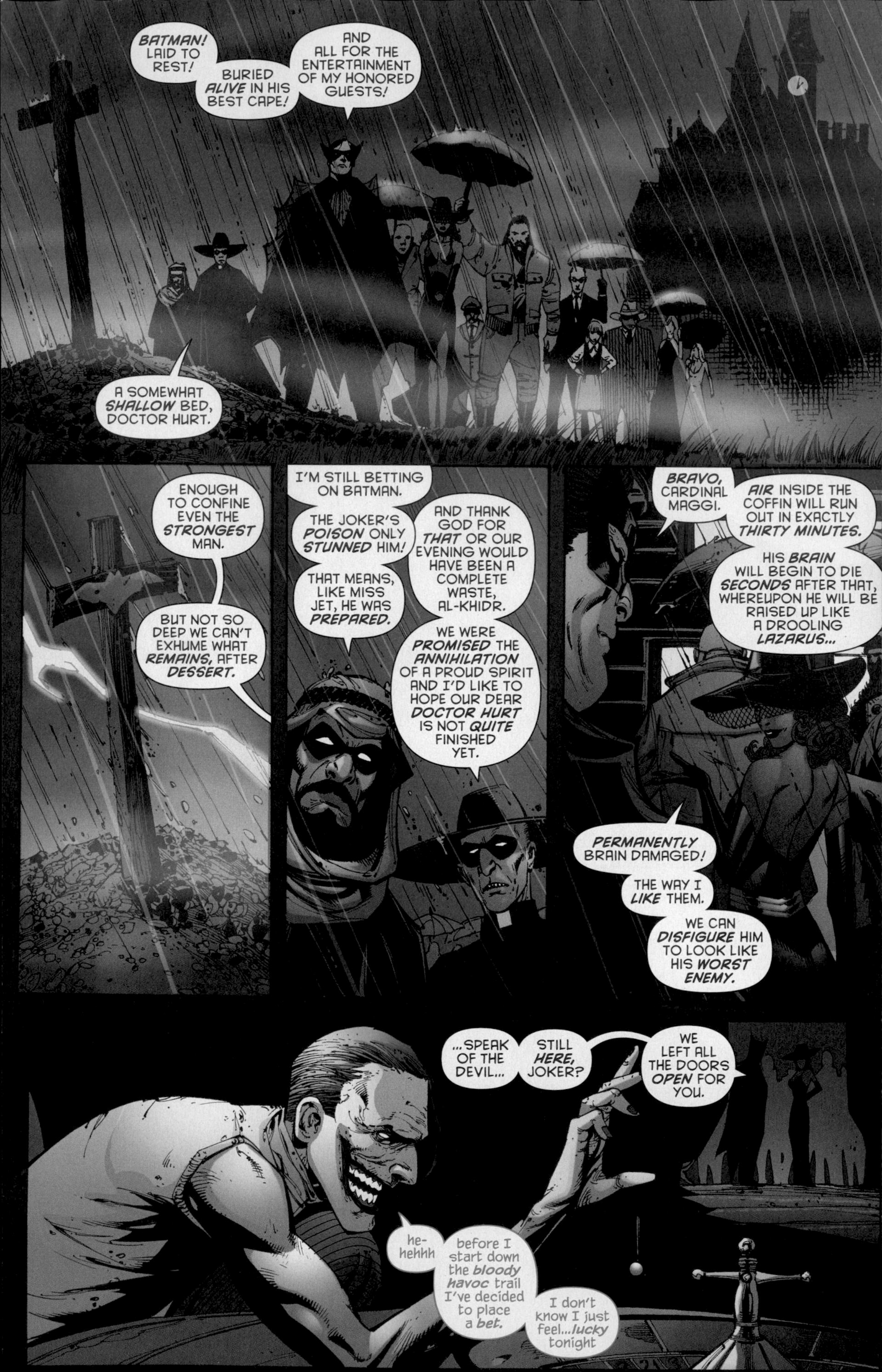
BATMAN! LAID TO REST!
BURIED ALIVE IN HIS BEST CAPE!
AND ALL FOR THE ENTERTAINMENT OF MY HONORED GUESTS!
A SOMEWHAT SHALLOW BED, DOCTOR HURT.
ENOUGH TO CONFINE EVEN THE STRONGEST MAN.
BUT NOT SO DEEP WE CAN'T EXHUME WHAT REMAINS, AFTER DESSERT.
I'M STILL BETTING ON BATMAN.
THE JOKER'S POISON ONLY STUNNED HIM!
THAT MEANS, LIKE MISS JET, HE WAS PREPARED.
AND THANK GOD FOR THAT OR OUR EVENING WOULD HAVE BEEN A COMPLETE WASTE, AL-KHIDR.
WE WERE PROMISED THE ANNIHILATION OF A PROUD SPIRIT AND I'D LIKE TO HOPE OUR DEAR DOCTOR HURT IS NOT QUITE FINISHED YET.
BRAVO, CARDINAL MAGGI.
AIR INSIDE THE COFFIN WILL RUN OUT IN EXACTLY THIRTY MINUTES.
HIS BRAIN WILL BEGIN TO DIE SECONDS AFTER THAT, WHEREUPON HE WILL BE RAISED UP LIKE A DROOLING LAZARUS...
PERMANENTLY BRAIN DAMAGED!
THE WAY I LIKE THEM.
WE CAN DISFIGURE HIM TO LOOK LIKE HIS WORST ENEMY.
...SPEAK OF THE DEVIL...
STILL HERE, JOKER?
WE LEFT ALL THE DOORS OPEN FOR YOU.
he-hehhh
before I start down the bloody havoc trail I've decided to place a bet.
I don't know I just feel...lucky tonight

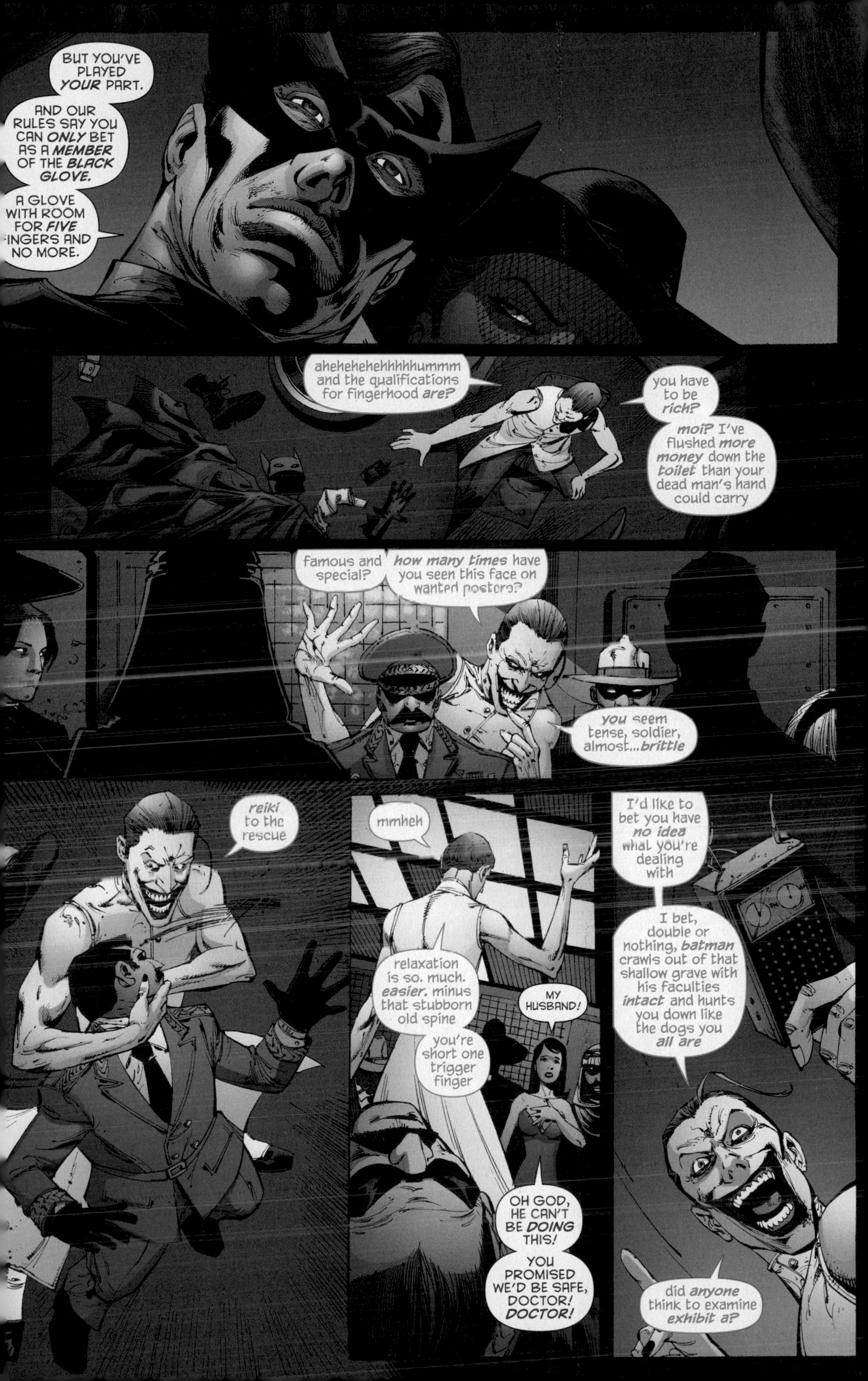
BUT YOU'VE PLAYED YOUR PART.
AND OUR RULES SAY YOU CAN ONLY BET AS A MEMBER OF THE BLACK GLOVE.
A GLOVE WITH ROOM FOR FIVE FINGERS AND NO MORE.
ahehehehehhhhhummm and the qualifications for fingerhood are?
you have to be rich?
moi? I've flushed more money down the toilet than your dead man's hand could carry
famous and special?
how many times have you seen this face on wanted posters?
you seem tense, soldier, almost...brittle
reiki to the rescue
mmheh
relaxation is so. much. easier. minus that stubborn old spine
you're short one trigger finger
MY HUSBAND!
OH GOD, HE CAN'T BE DOING THIS!
YOU PROMISED WE'D BE SAFE, DOCTOR! DOCTOR!
I'd like to bet you have no idea what you're dealing with
I bet, double or nothing, batman crawls out of that shallow grave with his faculties intact and hunts you down like the dogs you all are
did anyone think to examine exhibit a?

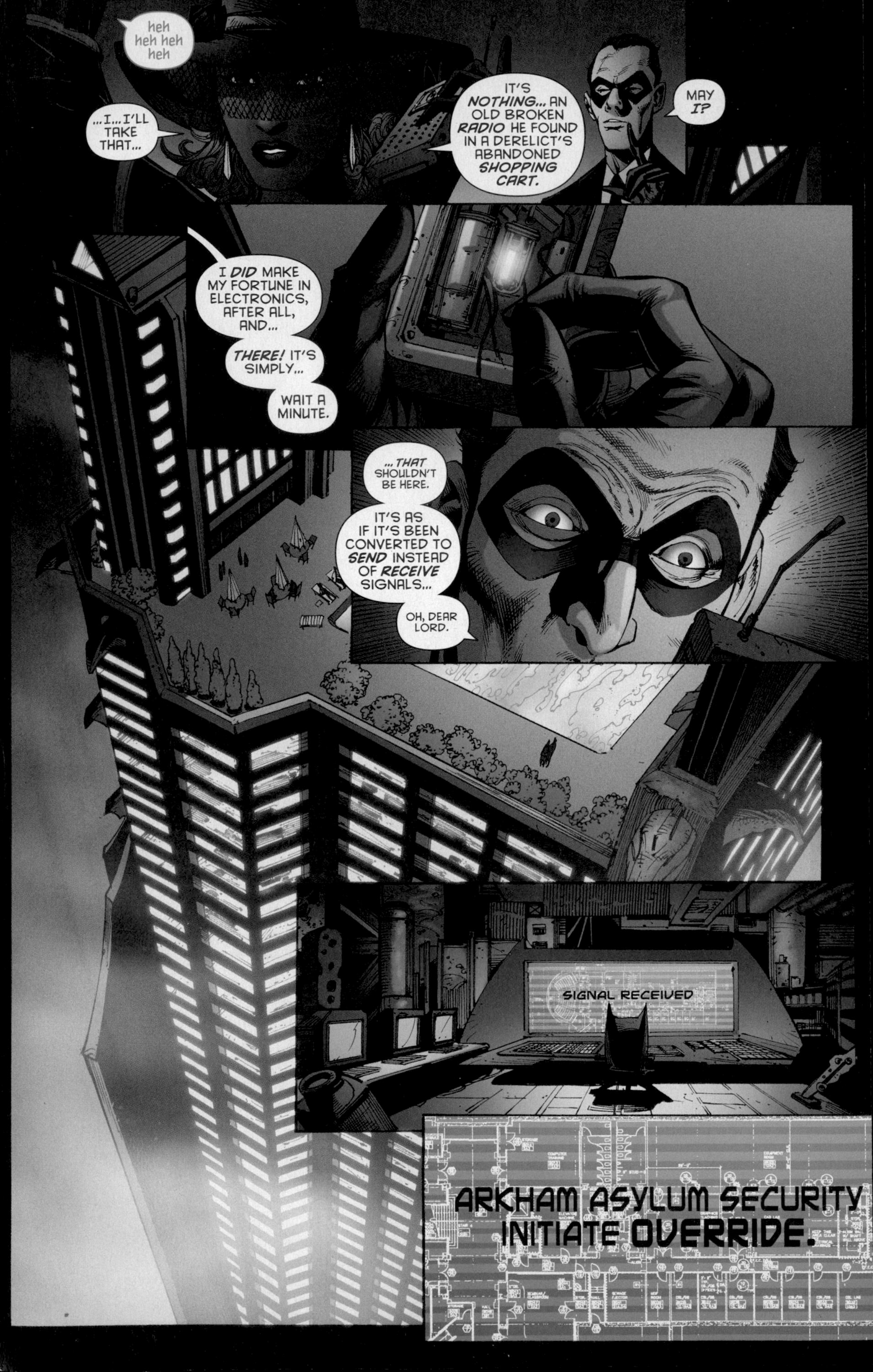
heh heh heh heh
...I...I'LL TAKE THAT...
IT'S NOTHING... AN OLD BROKEN RADIO HE FOUND IN A DERELICT'S ABANDONED SHOPPING CART.
MAY I?
I DID MAKE MY FORTUNE IN ELECTRONICS, AFTER ALL, AND...
THERE! IT'S SIMPLY...
WAIT A MINUTE.
...THAT SHOULDN'T BE HERE.
IT'S AS IF IT'S BEEN CONVERTED TO SEND INSTEAD OF RECEIVE SIGNALS...
OH, DEAR LORD.
SIGNAL RECEIVED
ARKHAM ASYLUM SECURITY
INITIATE OVERRIDE.

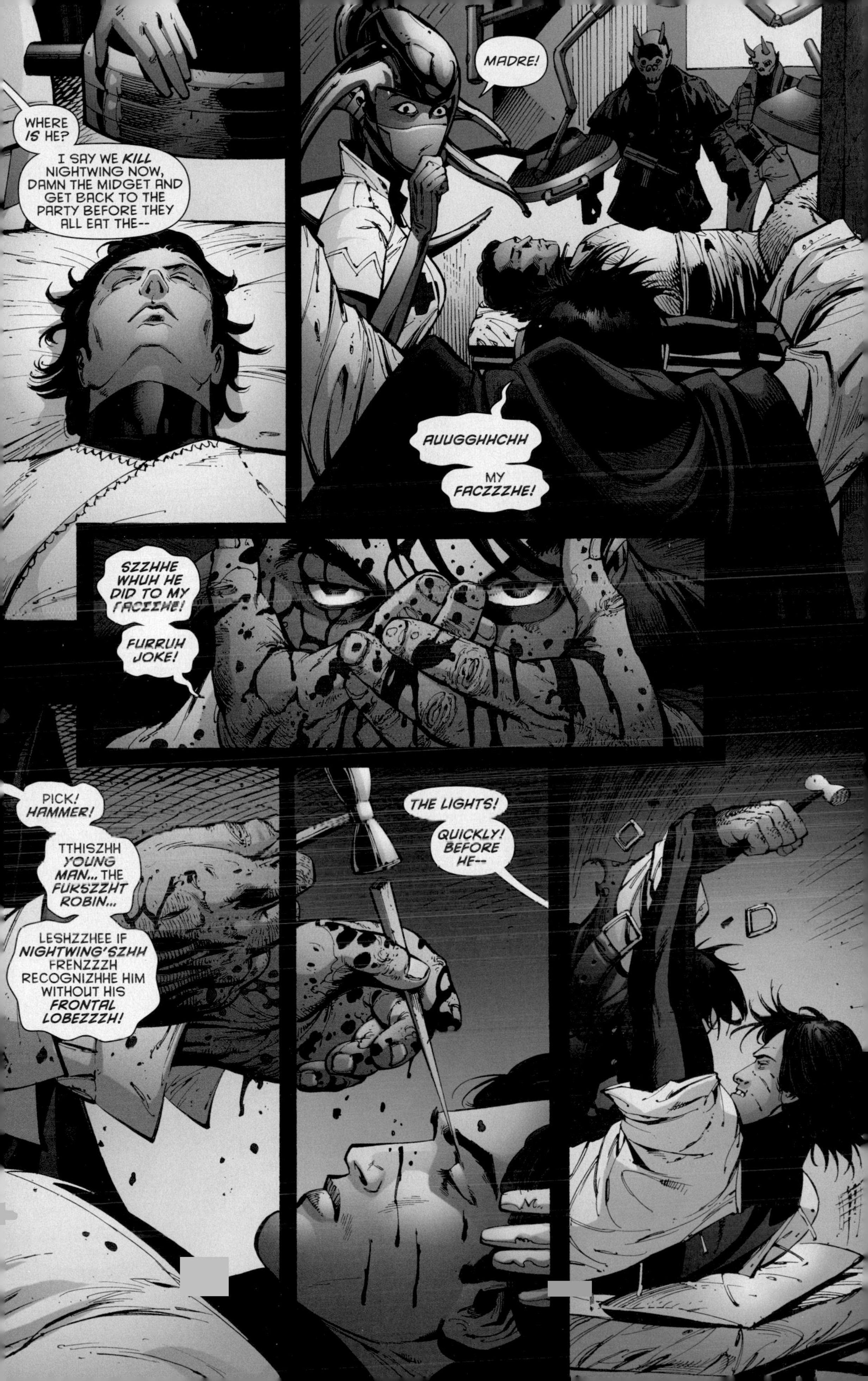

WHERE IS HE?
I SAY WE KILL NIGHTWING NOW, DAMN THE MIDGET AND GET BACK TO THE PARTY BEFORE THEY ALL EAT THE--
MADRE!
AUUGGHHCHH
MY FACZZZHE!
SZZHHE WHUH HE DID TO MY FACZZHE!
FURRUH JOKE!
PICK! HAMMER!
TTHISZHH YOUNG MAN... THE FUKSZZHT ROBIN...
LESHZZHEE IF NIGHTWING'SZHH FRENZZZH RECOGNIZHHE HIM WITHOUT HIS FRONTAL LOBEZZZH!
THE LIGHTS!
QUICKLY! BEFORE HE--

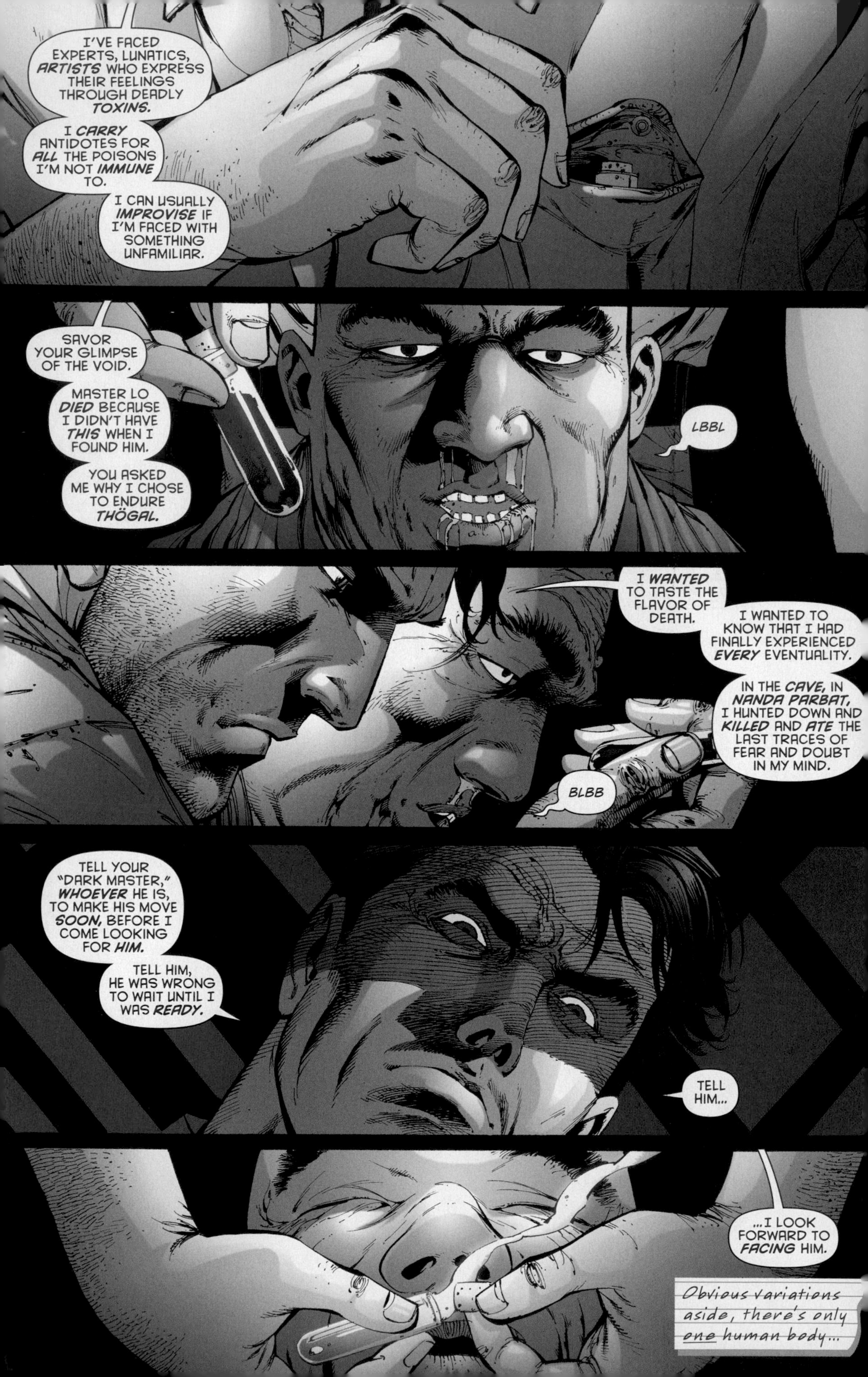
I'VE FACED EXPERTS, LUNATICS, ARTISTS WHO EXPRESS THEIR FEELINGS THROUGH DEADLY TOXINS.
I CARRY ANTIDOTES FOR ALL THE POISONS I'M NOT IMMUNE TO.
I CAN USUALLY IMPROVISE IF I'M FACED WITH SOMETHING UNFAMILIAR.
SAVOR YOUR GLIMPSE OF THE VOID.
MASTER LO DIED BECAUSE I DIDN'T HAVE THIS WHEN I FOUND HIM.
YOU ASKED ME WHY I CHOSE TO ENDURE THÖGAL.
LBBL
I WANTED TO TASTE THE FLAVOR OF DEATH.
I WANTED TO KNOW THAT I HAD FINALLY EXPERIENCED EVERY EVENTUALITY.
IN THE CAVE, IN NANDA PARBAT, I HUNTED DOWN AND KILLED AND ATE THE LAST TRACES OF FEAR AND DOUBT IN MY MIND.
BLBB
TELL YOUR "DARK MASTER," WHOEVER HE IS, TO MAKE HIS MOVE SOON, BEFORE I COME LOOKING FOR HIM.
TELL HIM, HE WAS WRONG TO WAIT UNTIL I WAS READY.
TELL HIM...
...I LOOK FORWARD TO FACING HIM.
Obvious variations aside, there's only one human body...

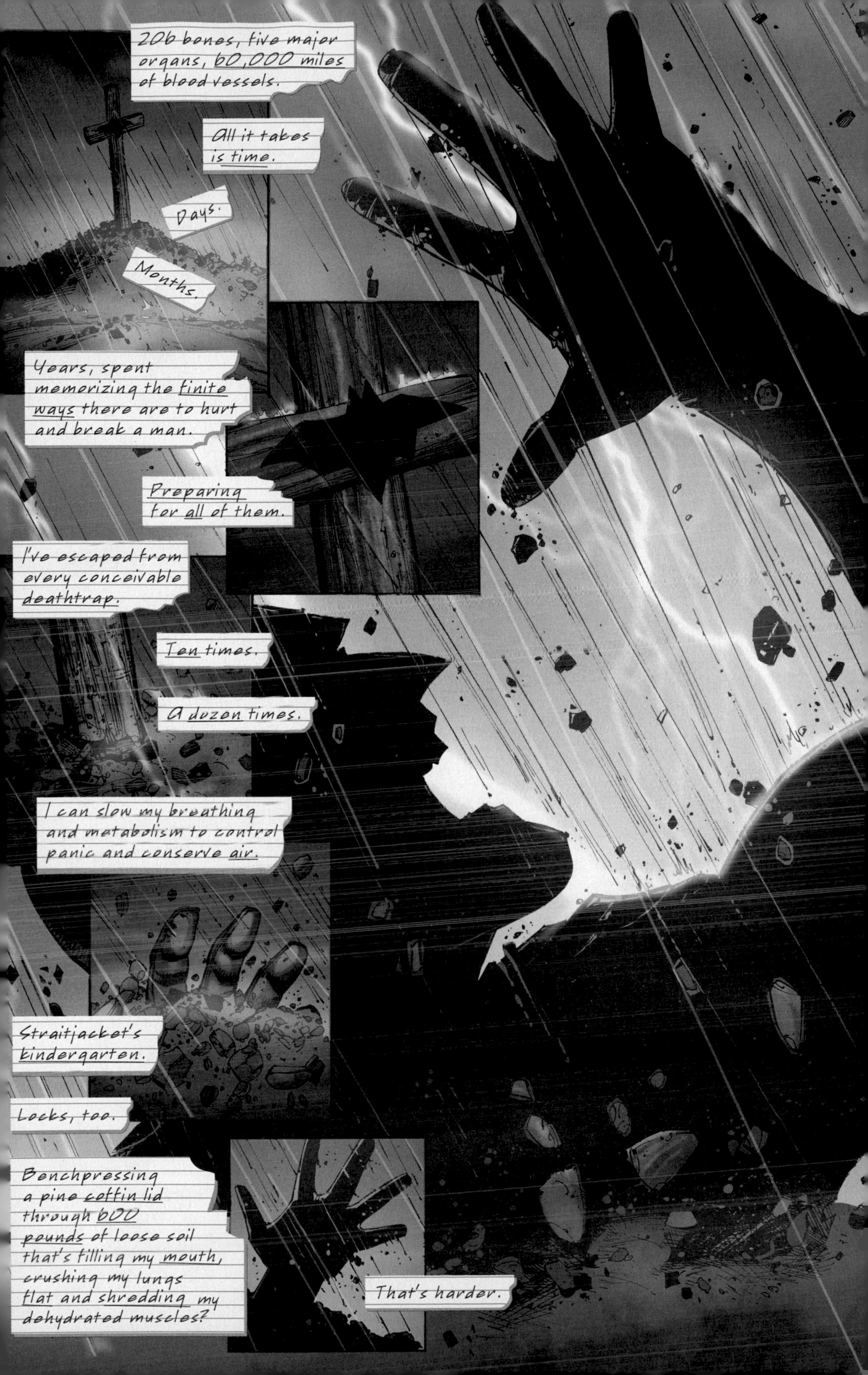
206 bones, five major organs, 60,000 miles of blood vessels.
All it takes is time.
Days.
Months.
Years, spent memorizing the finite ways there are to hurt and break a man.
Preparing for all of them.
I've escaped from every conceivable deathtrap.
Ten times.
A dozen times.
I can slow my breathing and metabolism to control panic and conserve air.
Straitjacket's kindergarten.
Locks, too.
Benchpressing a pine coffin lid through 600 pounds of loose soil that's filling my mouth, crushing my lungs flat and shredding my dehydrated muscles?
That's harder.

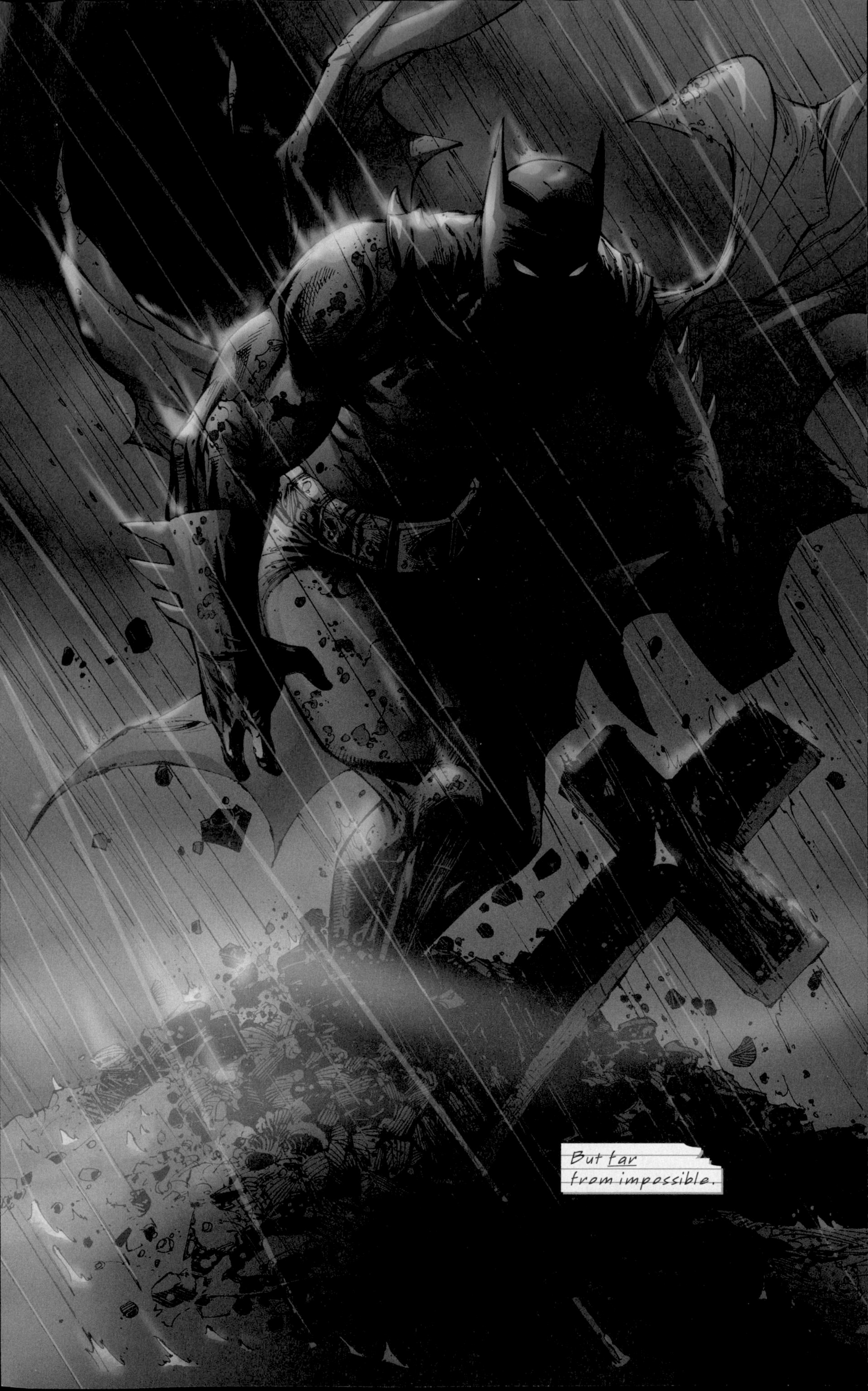
But far from impossible.

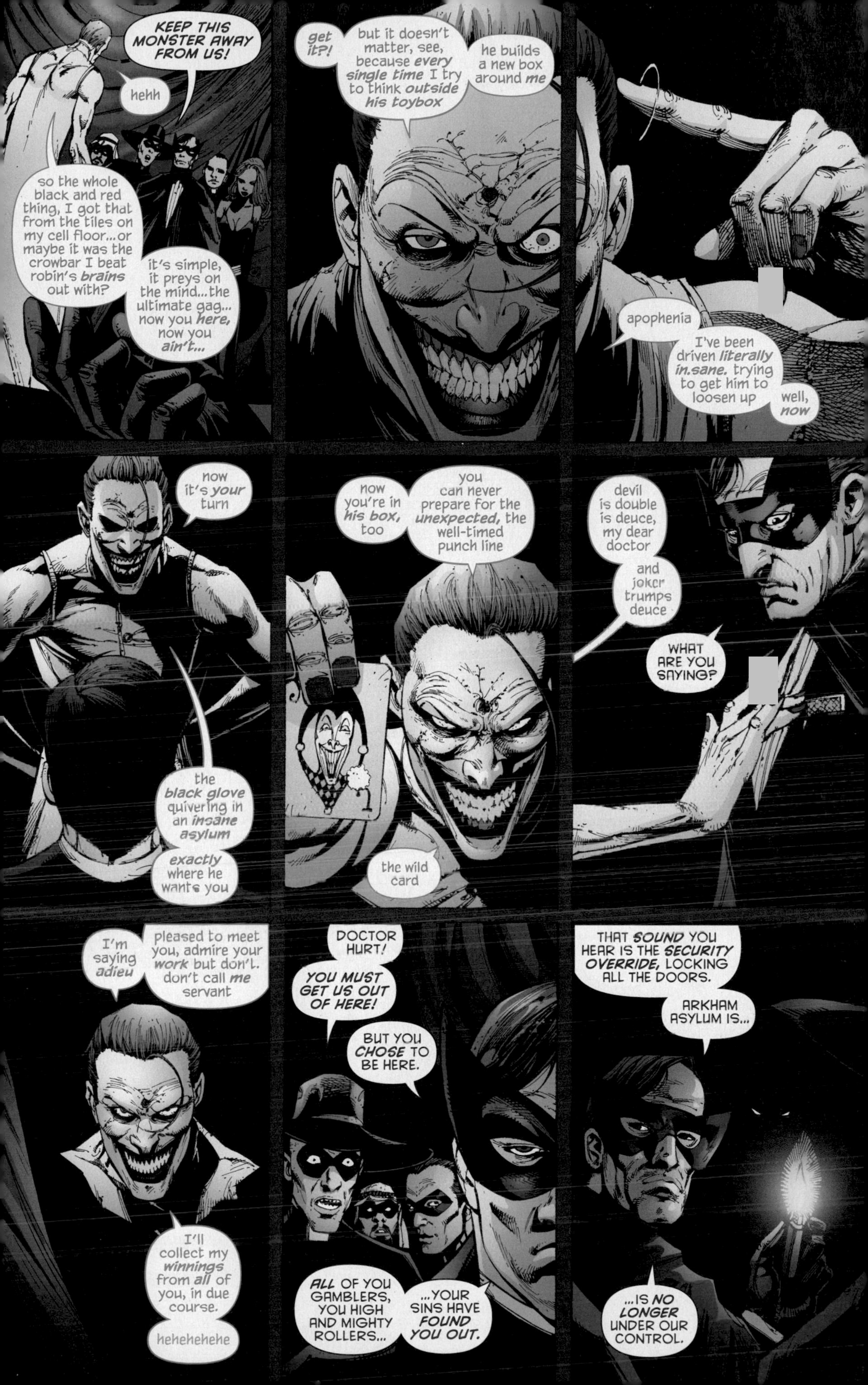
KEEP THIS MONSTER AWAY FROM US!
hehh
so the whole black and red thing, I got that from the tiles on my cell floor...or maybe it was the crowbar I beat robin's brains out with?
it's simple, it preys on the mind...the ultimate gag... now you here, now you ain't...
get it?!
but it doesn't matter, see, because every single time I try to think outside his toybox
he builds a new box around me
apophenia
I've been driven literally in.sane. trying to get him to loosen up
well, now
now it's your turn
the black glove quivering in an insane asylum
exactly where he wants you
now you're in his box, too
you can never prepare for the unexpected, the well-timed punch line
the wild card
devil is double is deuce, my dear doctor
and joker trumps deuce
WHAT ARE YOU SAYING?
I'm saying adieu
pleased to meet you, admire your work but don't. don't call me servant
I'll collect my winnings from all of you, in due course.
hehehehehe
DOCTOR HURT!
YOU MUST GET US OUT OF HERE!
BUT YOU CHOSE TO BE HERE.
ALL OF YOU GAMBLERS, YOU HIGH AND MIGHTY ROLLERS...
...YOUR SINS HAVE FOUND YOU OUT.
THAT SOUND YOU HEAR IS THE SECURITY OVERRIDE, LOCKING ALL THE DOORS.
ARKHAM ASYLUM IS...
...IS NO LONGER UNDER OUR CONTROL.

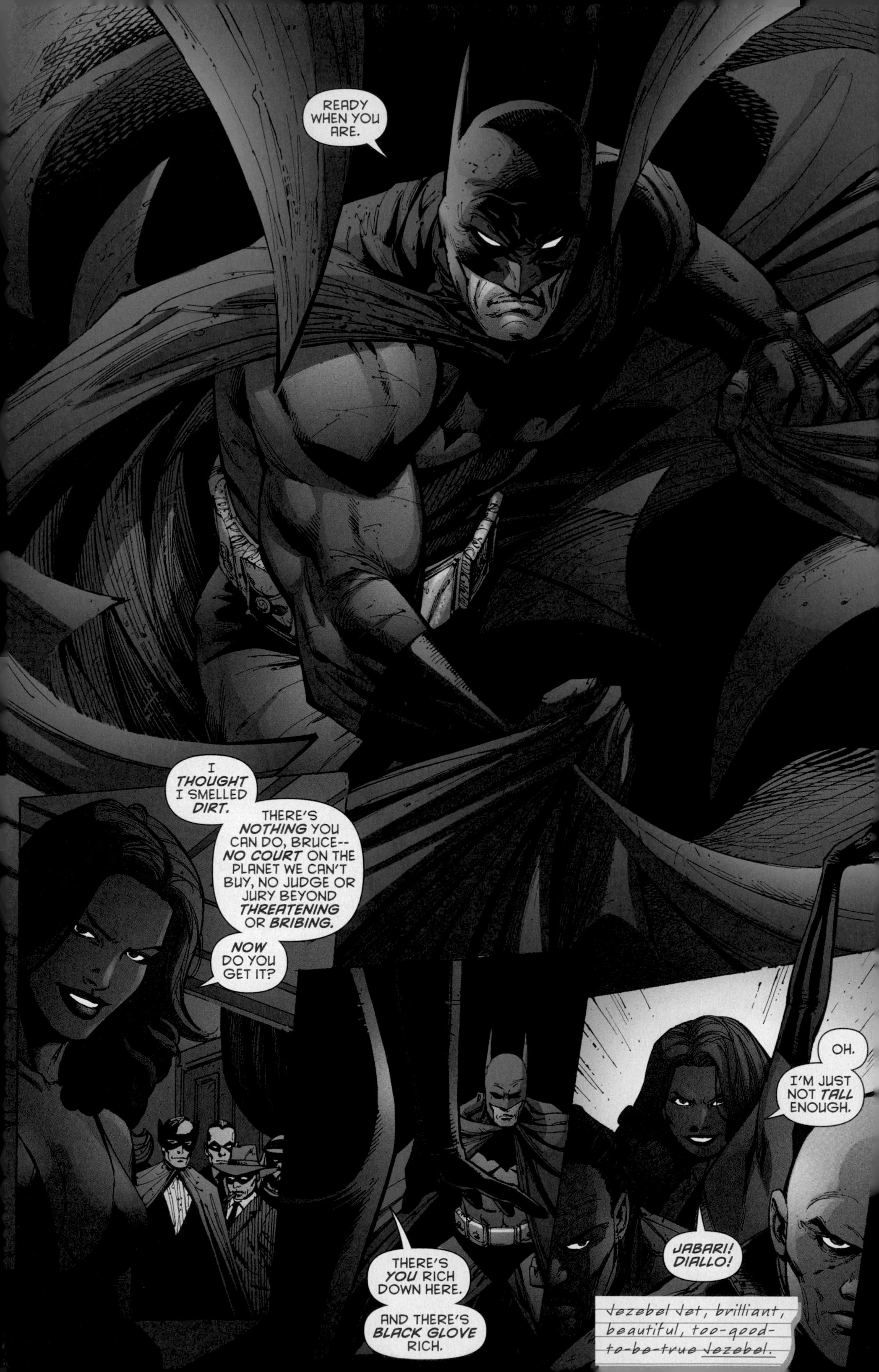
READY WHEN YOU ARE.
I THOUGHT I SMELLED DIRT.
THERE'S NOTHING YOU CAN DO, BRUCE-- NO COURT ON THE PLANET WE CAN'T BUY, NO JUDGE OR JURY BEYOND THREATENING OR BRIBING.
NOW DO YOU GET IT?
THERE'S YOU RICH DOWN HERE.
AND THERE'S BLACK GLOVE RICH.
OH.
I'M JUST NOT TALL ENOUGH.
JABARI! DIALLO!
Jezebel Jet, brilliant, beautiful, too-good-to-be-true Jezebel.

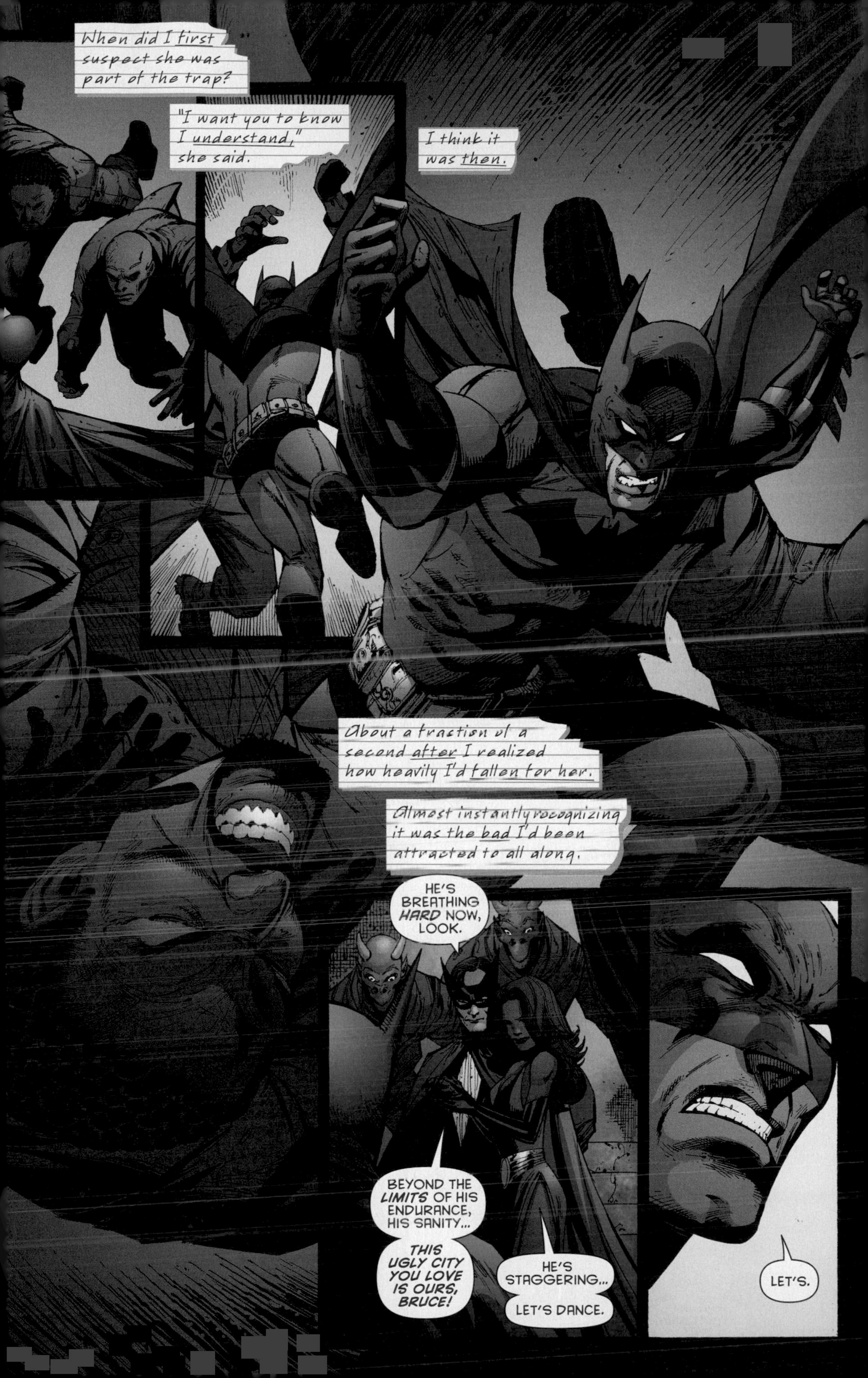

When did I first suspect she was part of the trap?
"I want you to know I understand," she said.
I think it was then.
About a fraction of a second after I realized how heavily I'd fallen for her.
Almost instantly recognizing it was the bad I'd been attracted to all along.
HE'S BREATHING HARD NOW, LOOK.
BEYOND THE LIMITS OF HIS ENDURANCE, HIS SANITY...
THIS UGLY CITY YOU LOVE IS OURS, BRUCE!
HE'S STAGGERING...
LET'S DANCE.
LET'S.

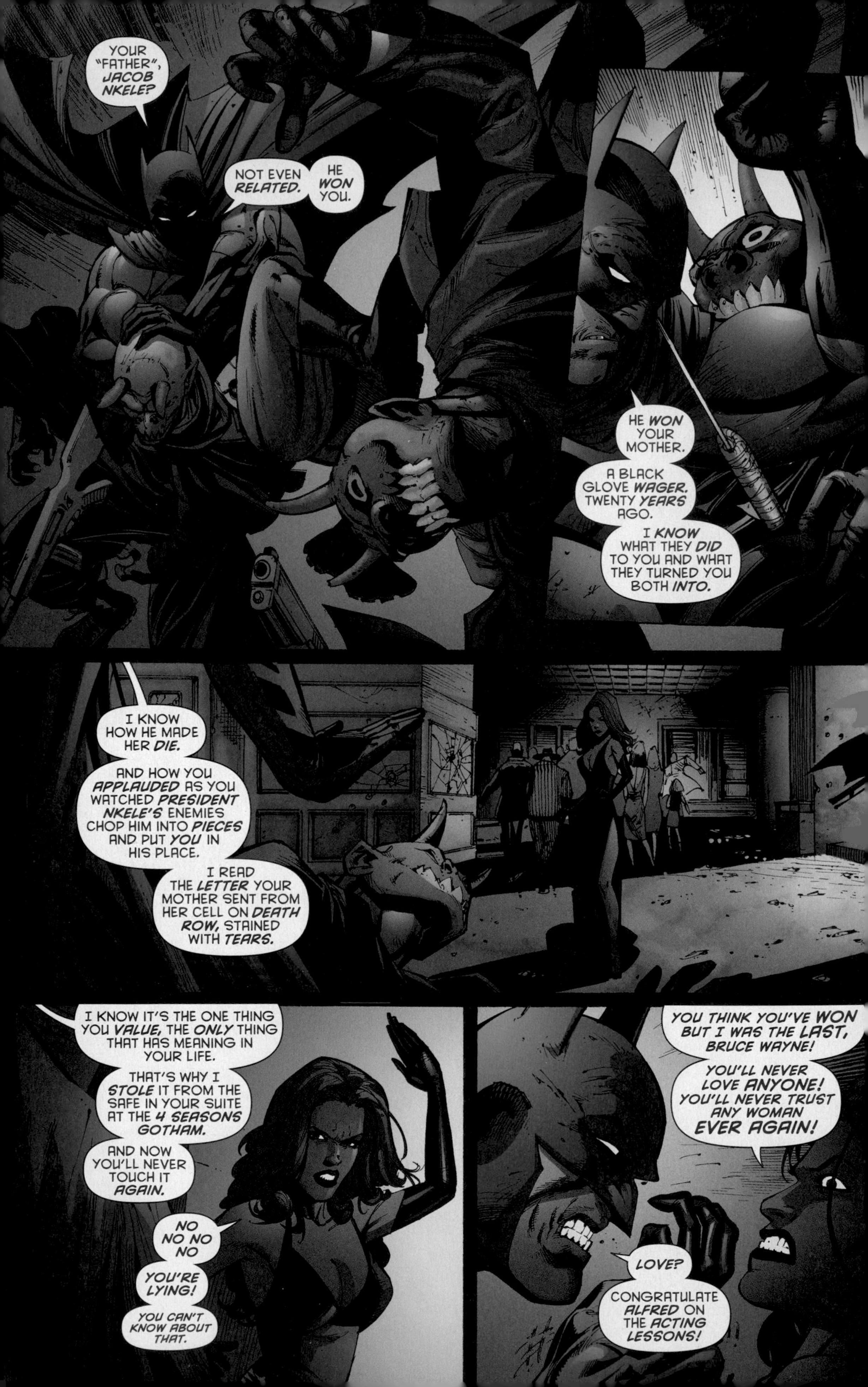
YOUR "FATHER", JACOB NKELE?
NOT EVEN RELATED.
HE WON YOU.
HE WON YOUR MOTHER.
A BLACK GLOVE WAGER. TWENTY YEARS AGO.
I KNOW WHAT THEY DID TO YOU AND WHAT THEY TURNED YOU BOTH INTO.
I KNOW HOW HE MADE HER DIE.
AND HOW YOU APPLAUDED AS YOU WATCHED PRESIDENT NKELE'S ENEMIES CHOP HIM INTO PIECES AND PUT YOU IN HIS PLACE.
I READ THE LETTER YOUR MOTHER SENT FROM HER CELL ON DEATH ROW, STAINED WITH TEARS.
I KNOW IT'S THE ONE THING YOU VALUE, THE ONLY THING THAT HAS MEANING IN YOUR LIFE.
THAT'S WHY I STOLE IT FROM THE SAFE IN YOUR SUITE AT THE 4 SEASONS GOTHAM.
AND NOW YOU'LL NEVER TOUCH IT AGAIN.
NO NO NO NO
YOU'RE LYING!
YOU CAN'T KNOW ABOUT THAT.
YOU THINK YOU'VE WON BUT I WAS THE LAST, BRUCE WAYNE!
YOU'LL NEVER LOVE ANYONE! YOU'LL NEVER TRUST ANY WOMAN EVER AGAIN!
LOVE?
CONGRATULATE ALFRED ON THE ACTING LESSONS!

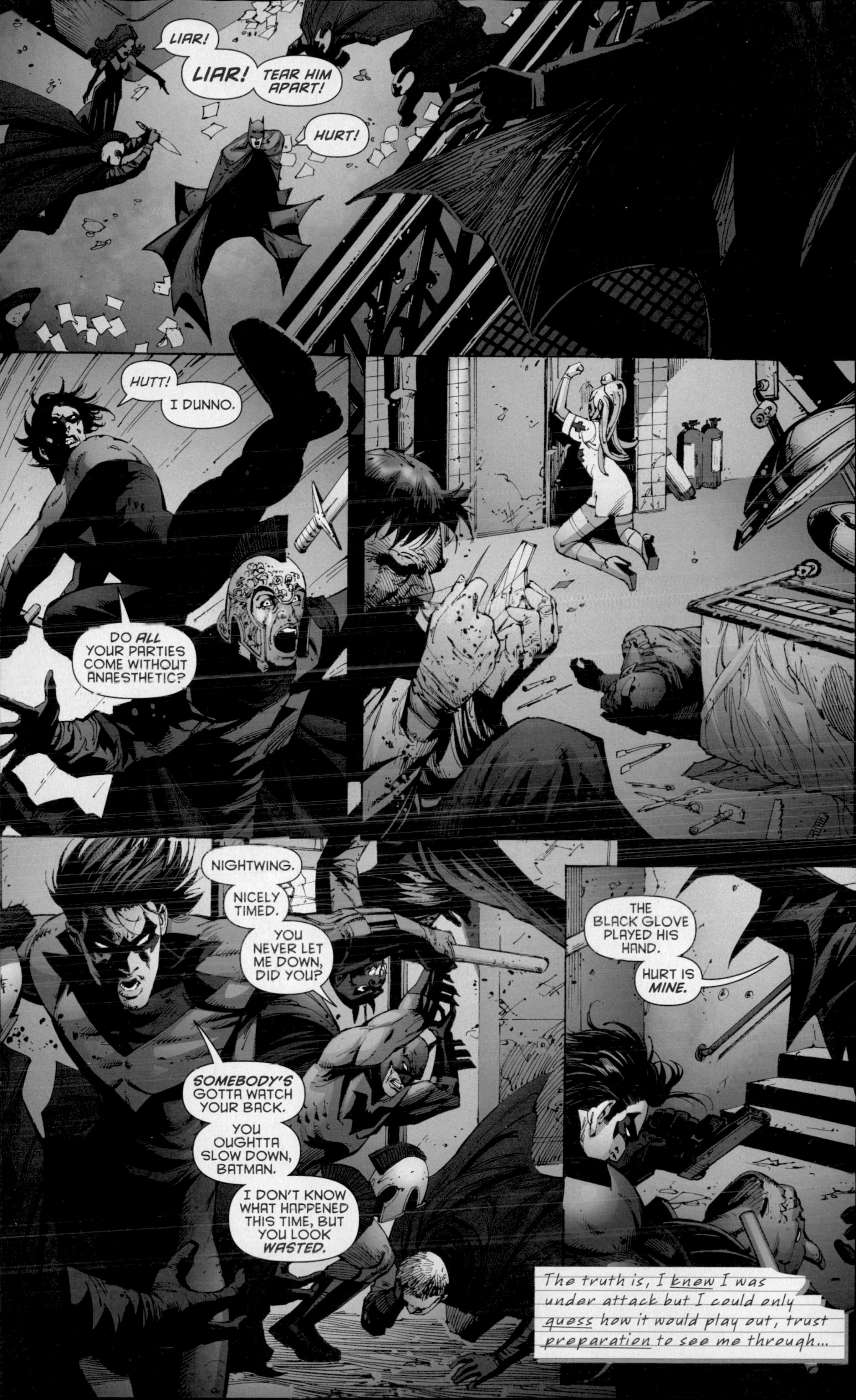
LIAR!
LIAR!
TEAR HIM APART!
HURT!
HUTT!
I DUNNO.
DO ALL YOUR PARTIES COME WITHOUT ANAESTHETIC?
NIGHTWING.
NICELY TIMED.
YOU NEVER LET ME DOWN, DID YOU?
SOMEBODY'S GOTTA WATCH YOUR BACK.
YOU OUGHTTA SLOW DOWN, BATMAN.
I DON'T KNOW WHAT HAPPENED THIS TIME, BUT YOU LOOK WASTED.
THE BLACK GLOVE PLAYED HIS HAND.
HURT IS MINE.
The truth is, I knew I was under attack but I could only guess how it would play out, trust preparation to see me through...

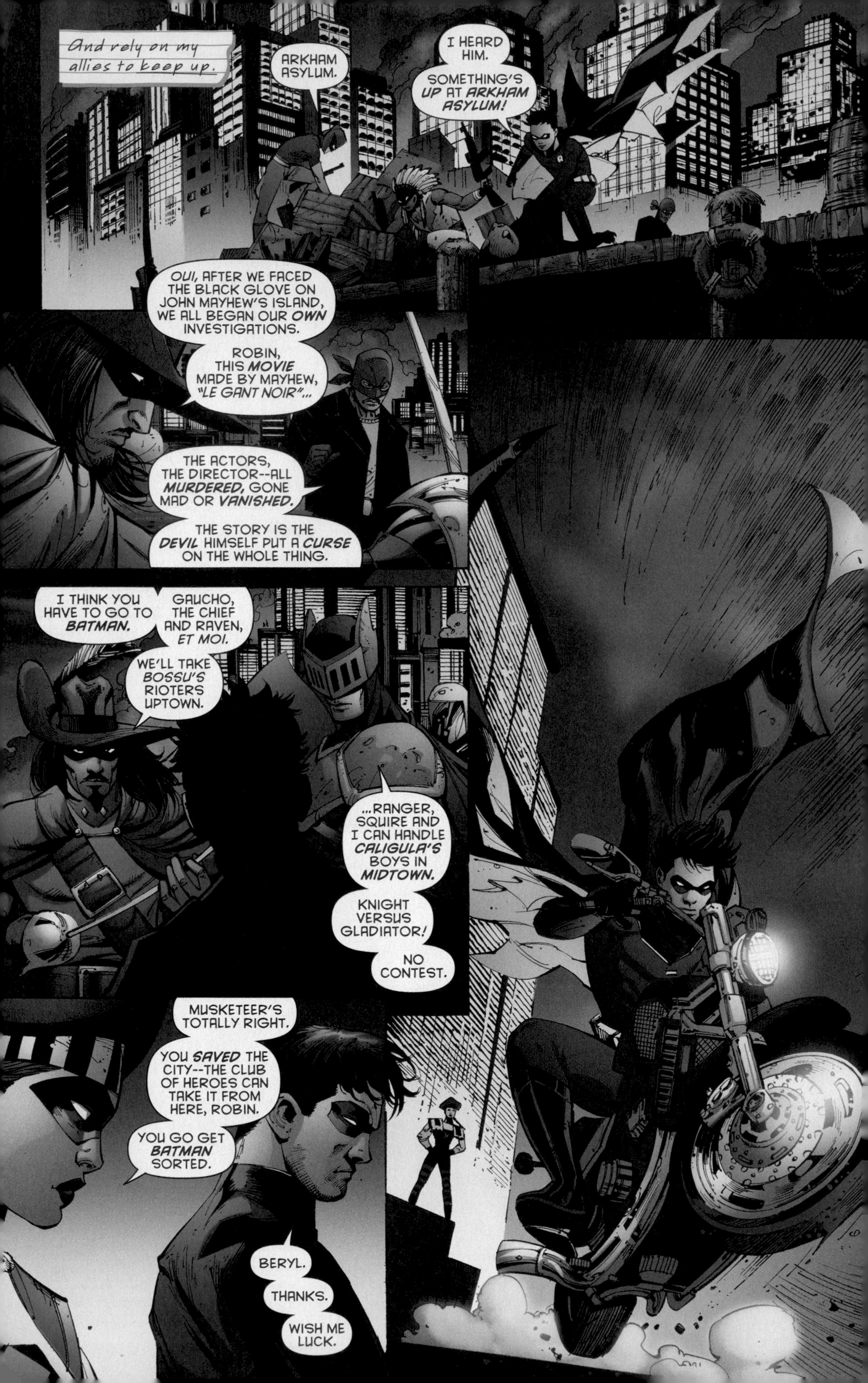
And rely on my allies to keep up.
ARKHAM ASYLUM.
I HEARD HIM.
SOMETHING'S UP AT ARKHAM ASYLUM!
OUI, AFTER WE FACED THE BLACK GLOVE ON JOHN MAYHEW'S ISLAND, WE ALL BEGAN OUR OWN INVESTIGATIONS.
ROBIN, THIS MOVIE MADE BY MAYHEW, "LE GANT NOIR"...
THE ACTORS, THE DIRECTOR--ALL MURDERED, GONE MAD OR VANISHED.
THE STORY IS THE DEVIL HIMSELF PUT A CURSE ON THE WHOLE THING.
I THINK YOU HAVE TO GO TO BATMAN.
GAUCHO, THE CHIEF AND RAVEN, ET MOI.
WE'LL TAKE BOSSU'S RIOTERS UPTOWN.
...RANGER, SQUIRE AND I CAN HANDLE CALIGULA'S BOYS IN MIDTOWN.
KNIGHT VERSUS GLADIATOR!
NO CONTEST.
MUSKETEER'S TOTALLY RIGHT.
YOU SAVED THE CITY--THE CLUB OF HEROES CAN TAKE IT FROM HERE, ROBIN.
YOU GO GET BATMAN SORTED.
BERYL.
THANKS.
WISH ME LUCK.

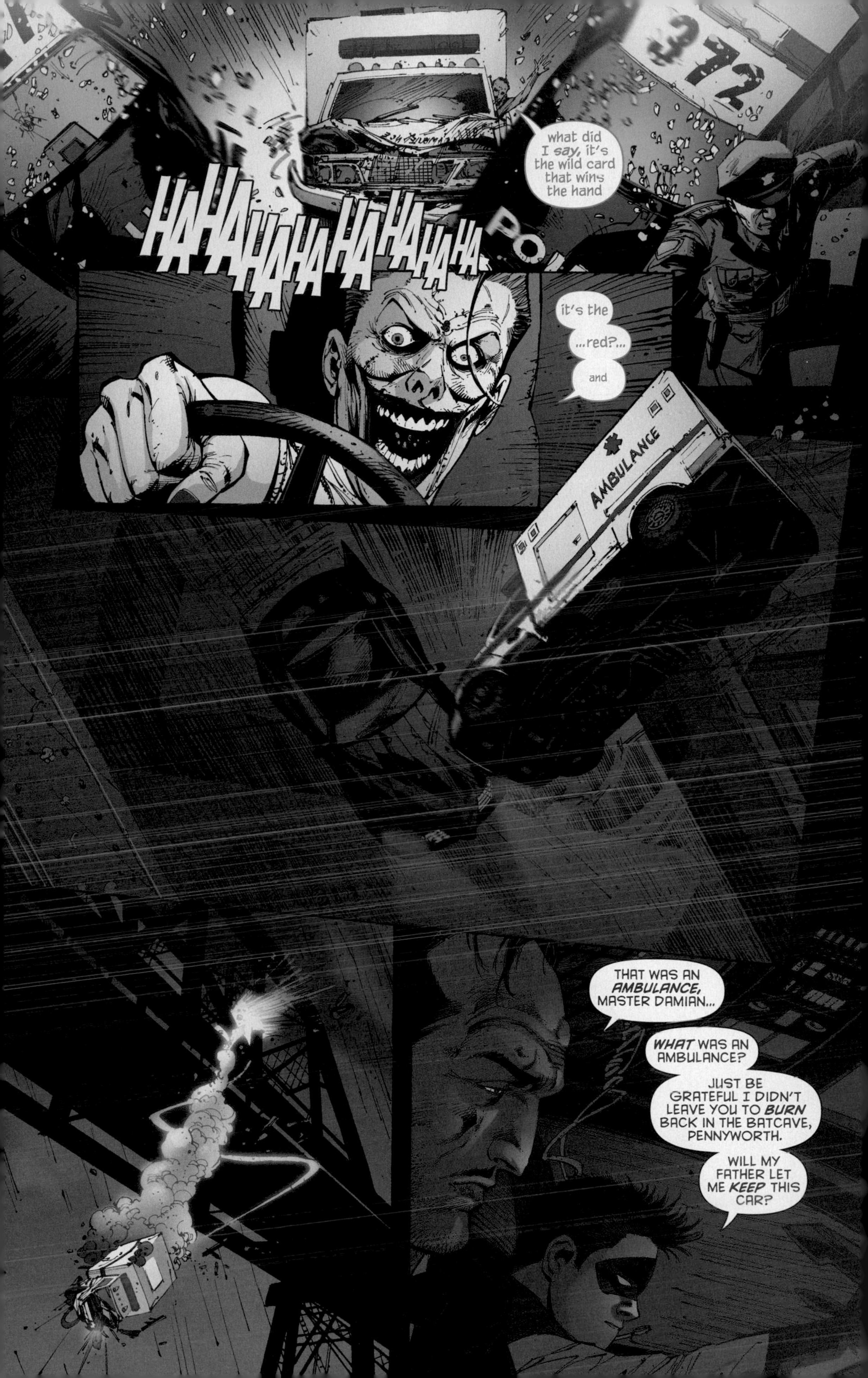

372
what did I *say,* it's the wild card that wins the hand
HAHAHAHAHAHAHAHAHAHA
PO
it's the
...red?...
and
AMBULANCE
AMBULANCE
THAT WAS AN *AMBULANCE,* MASTER DAMIAN...
WHAT WAS AN AMBULANCE?
JUST BE GRATEFUL I DIDN'T LEAVE YOU TO *BURN* BACK IN THE BATCAVE, PENNYWORTH.
WILL MY FATHER LET ME *KEEP* THIS CAR?

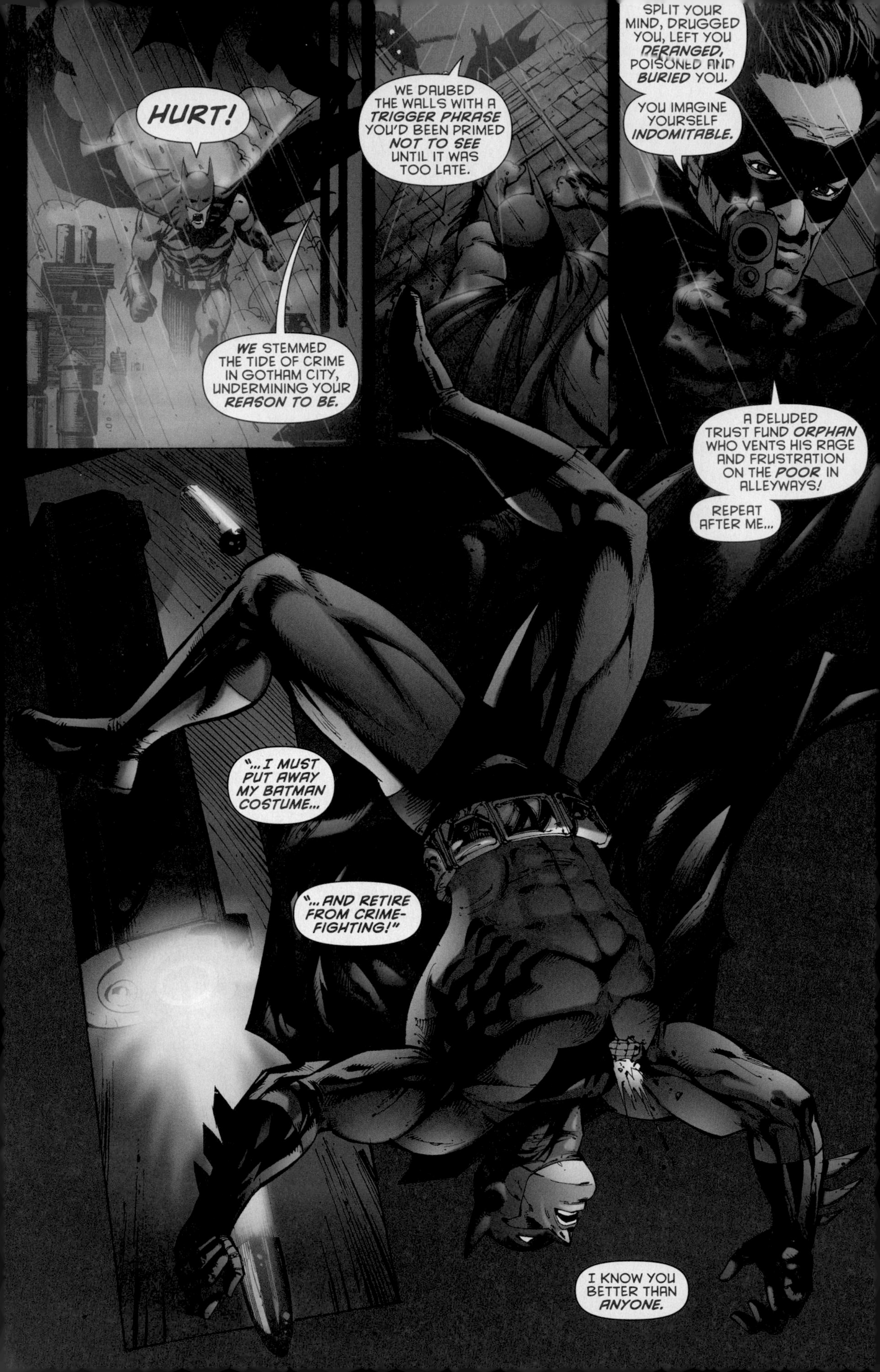
HURT!
WE STEMMED THE TIDE OF CRIME IN GOTHAM CITY, UNDERMINING YOUR REASON TO BE.
WE DAUBED THE WALLS WITH A TRIGGER PHRASE YOU'D BEEN PRIMED NOT TO SEE UNTIL IT WAS TOO LATE.
SPLIT YOUR MIND, DRUGGED YOU, LEFT YOU DERANGED, POISONED AND BURIED YOU.
YOU IMAGINE YOURSELF INDOMITABLE.
A DELUDED TRUST FUND ORPHAN WHO VENTS HIS RAGE AND FRUSTRATION ON THE POOR IN ALLEYWAYS!
REPEAT AFTER ME...
"...I MUST PUT AWAY MY BATMAN COSTUME...
"...AND RETIRE FROM CRIME-FIGHTING!"
I KNOW YOU BETTER THAN ANYONE.

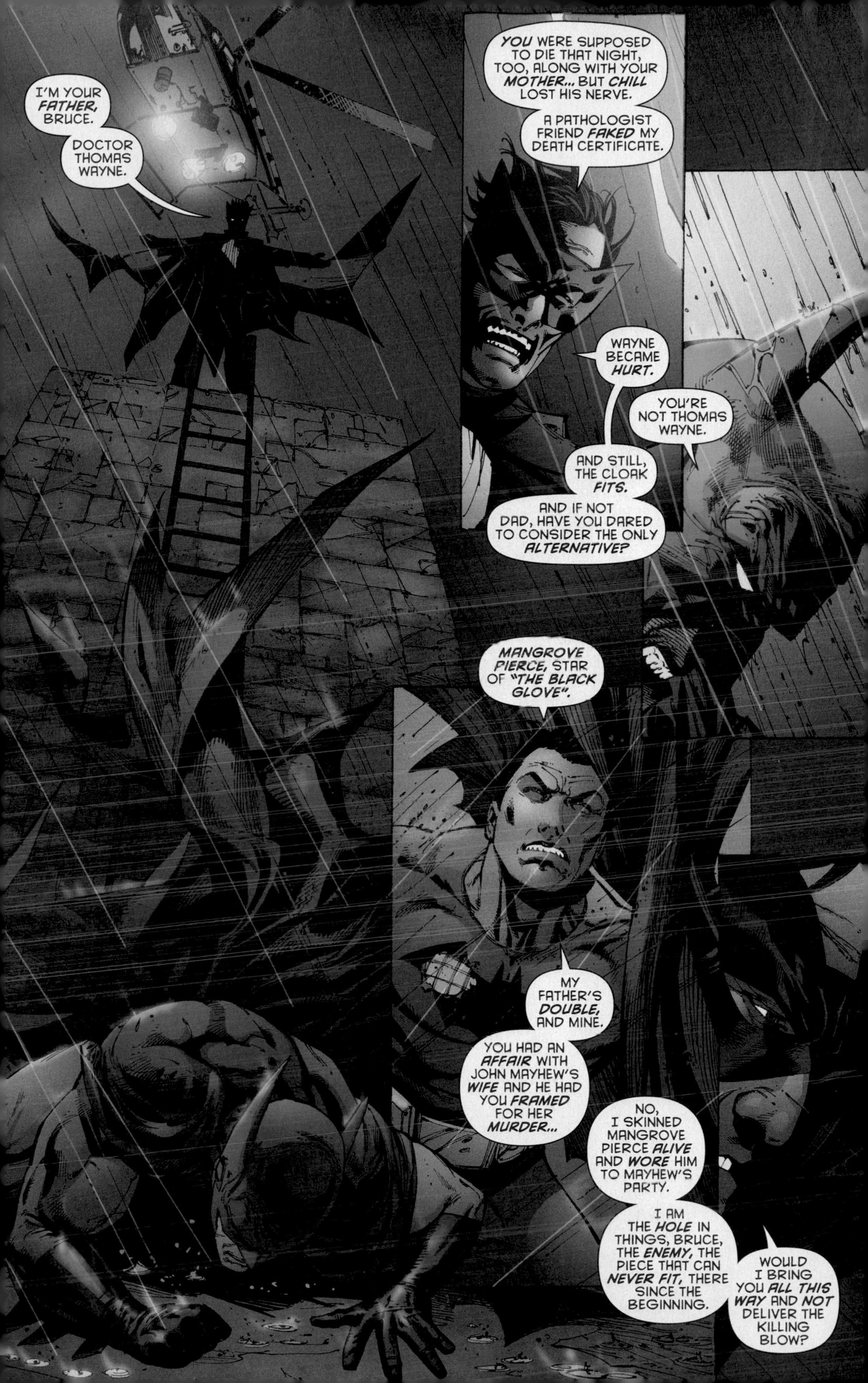
I'M YOUR FATHER, BRUCE.
DOCTOR THOMAS WAYNE.
YOU WERE SUPPOSED TO DIE THAT NIGHT, TOO, ALONG WITH YOUR MOTHER... BUT CHILL LOST HIS NERVE.
A PATHOLOGIST FRIEND FAKED MY DEATH CERTIFICATE.
WAYNE BECAME HURT.
YOU'RE NOT THOMAS WAYNE.
AND STILL, THE CLOAK FITS.
AND IF NOT DAD, HAVE YOU DARED TO CONSIDER THE ONLY ALTERNATIVE?
MANGROVE PIERCE, STAR OF "THE BLACK GLOVE".
MY FATHER'S DOUBLE, AND MINE.
YOU HAD AN AFFAIR WITH JOHN MAYHEW'S WIFE AND HE HAD YOU FRAMED FOR HER MURDER...
NO, I SKINNED MANGROVE PIERCE ALIVE AND WORE HIM TO MAYHEW'S PARTY.
I AM THE HOLE IN THINGS, BRUCE, THE ENEMY, THE PIECE THAT CAN NEVER FIT, THERE SINCE THE BEGINNING.
WOULD I BRING YOU ALL THIS WAY AND NOT DELIVER THE KILLING BLOW?

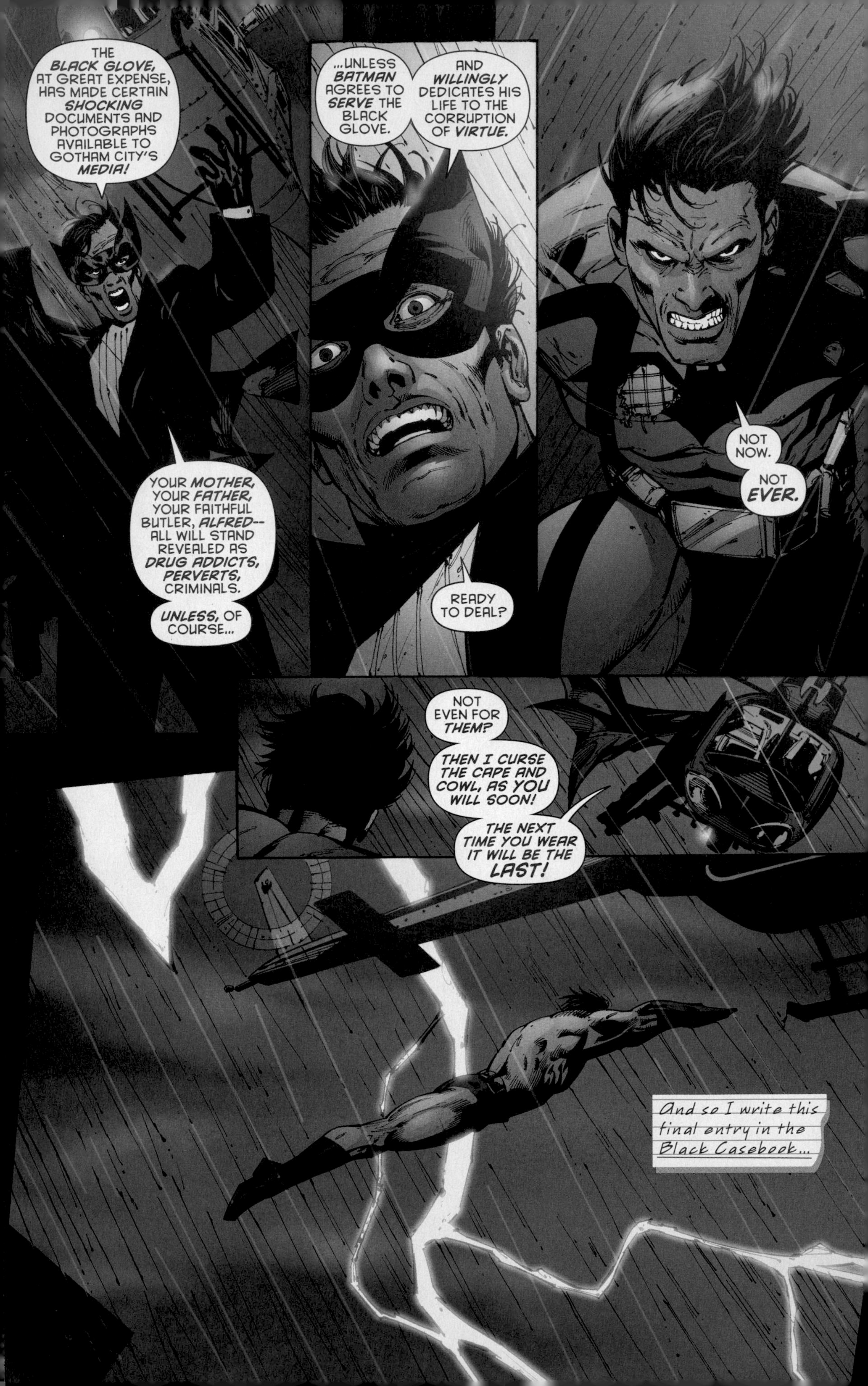
THE BLACK GLOVE, AT GREAT EXPENSE, HAS MADE CERTAIN SHOCKING DOCUMENTS AND PHOTOGRAPHS AVAILABLE TO GOTHAM CITY'S MEDIA!
YOUR MOTHER, YOUR FATHER, YOUR FAITHFUL BUTLER, ALFRED--ALL WILL STAND REVEALED AS DRUG ADDICTS, PERVERTS, CRIMINALS.
UNLESS, OF COURSE...
...UNLESS BATMAN AGREES TO SERVE THE BLACK GLOVE.
AND WILLINGLY DEDICATES HIS LIFE TO THE CORRUPTION OF VIRTUE.
READY TO DEAL?
NOT NOW.
NOT EVER.
NOT EVEN FOR THEM?
THEN I CURSE THE CAPE AND COWL, AS YOU WILL SOON!
THE NEXT TIME YOU WEAR IT WILL BE THE LAST!
And so I write this final entry in the Black Casebook...

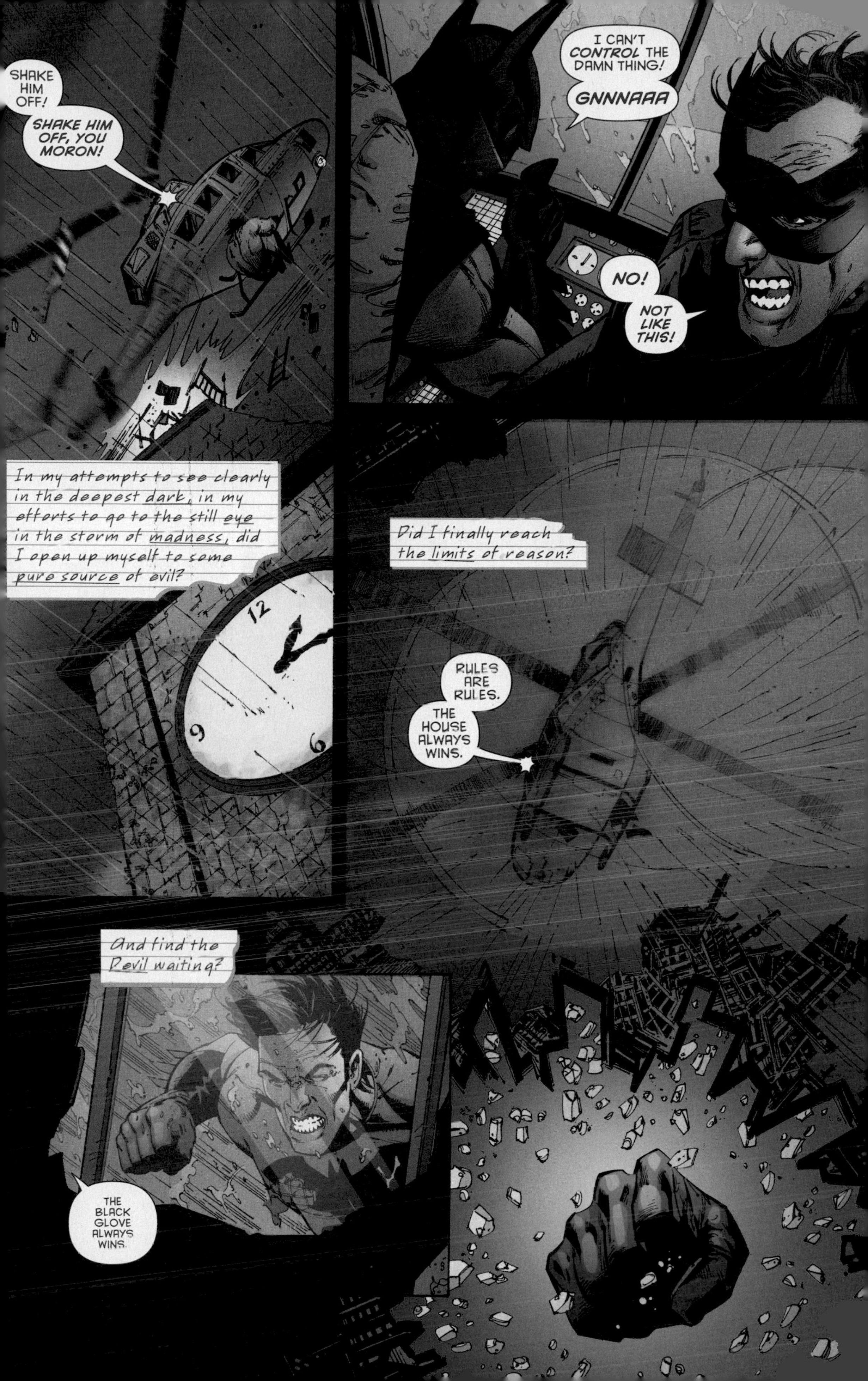
SHAKE HIM OFF!
SHAKE HIM OFF, YOU MORON!
I CAN'T CONTROL THE DAMN THING!
GNNNAAA
NO!
NOT LIKE THIS!
In my attempts to see clearly in the deepest dark, in my efforts to go to the still eye in the storm of madness, did I open up myself to some pure source of evil?
Did I finally reach the limits of reason?
RULES ARE RULES.
THE HOUSE ALWAYS WINS.
And find the Devil waiting?
THE BLACK GLOVE ALWAYS WINS.

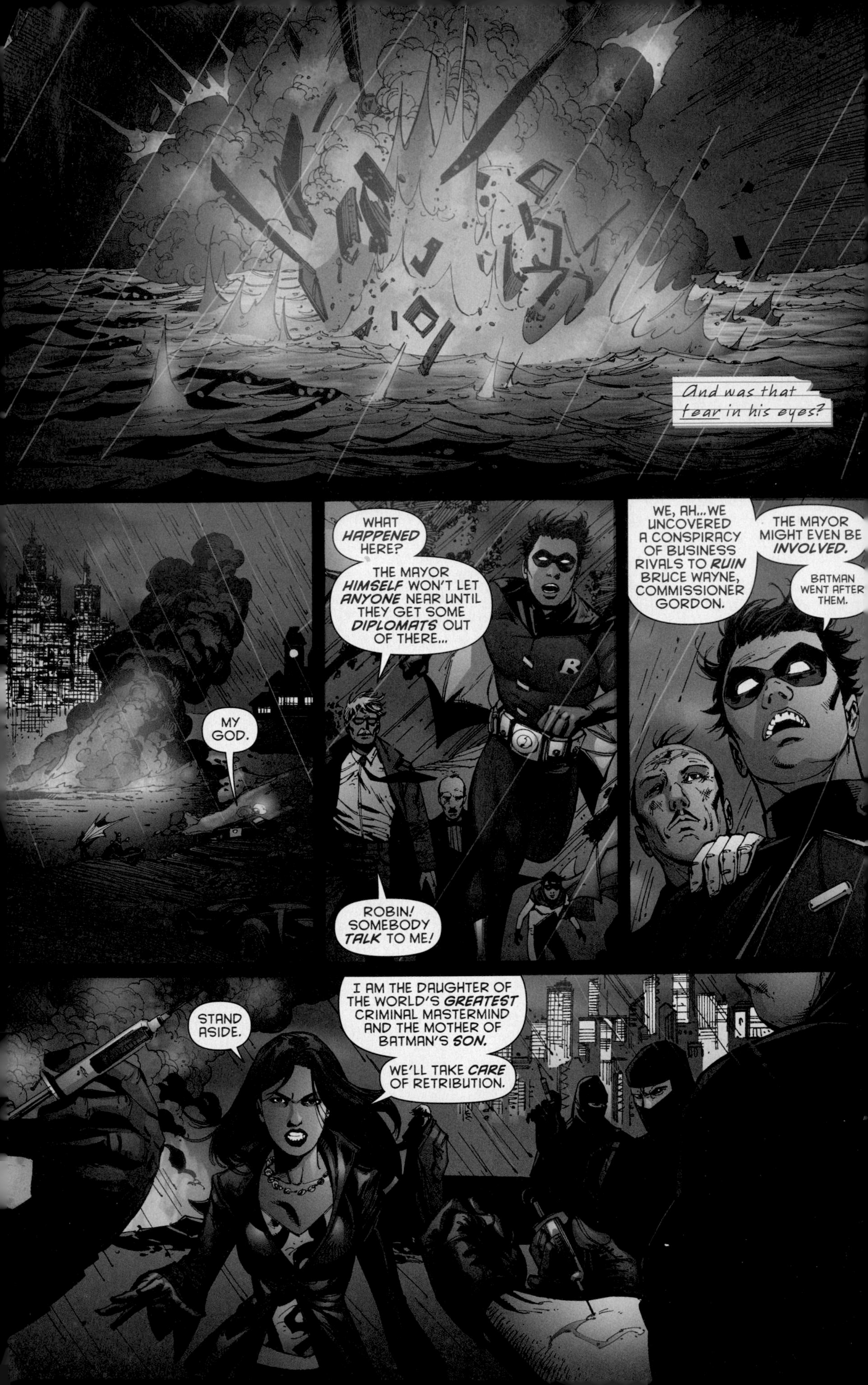
And was that fear in his eyes?
MY GOD.
WHAT HAPPENED HERE?
THE MAYOR HIMSELF WON'T LET ANYONE NEAR UNTIL THEY GET SOME DIPLOMATS OUT OF THERE...
ROBIN! SOMEBODY TALK TO ME!
WE, AH...WE UNCOVERED A CONSPIRACY OF BUSINESS RIVALS TO RUIN BRUCE WAYNE, COMMISSIONER GORDON.
THE MAYOR MIGHT EVEN BE INVOLVED.
BATMAN WENT AFTER THEM.
STAND ASIDE.
I AM THE DAUGHTER OF THE WORLD'S GREATEST CRIMINAL MASTERMIND AND THE MOTHER OF BATMAN'S SON.
WE'LL TAKE CARE OF RETRIBUTION.

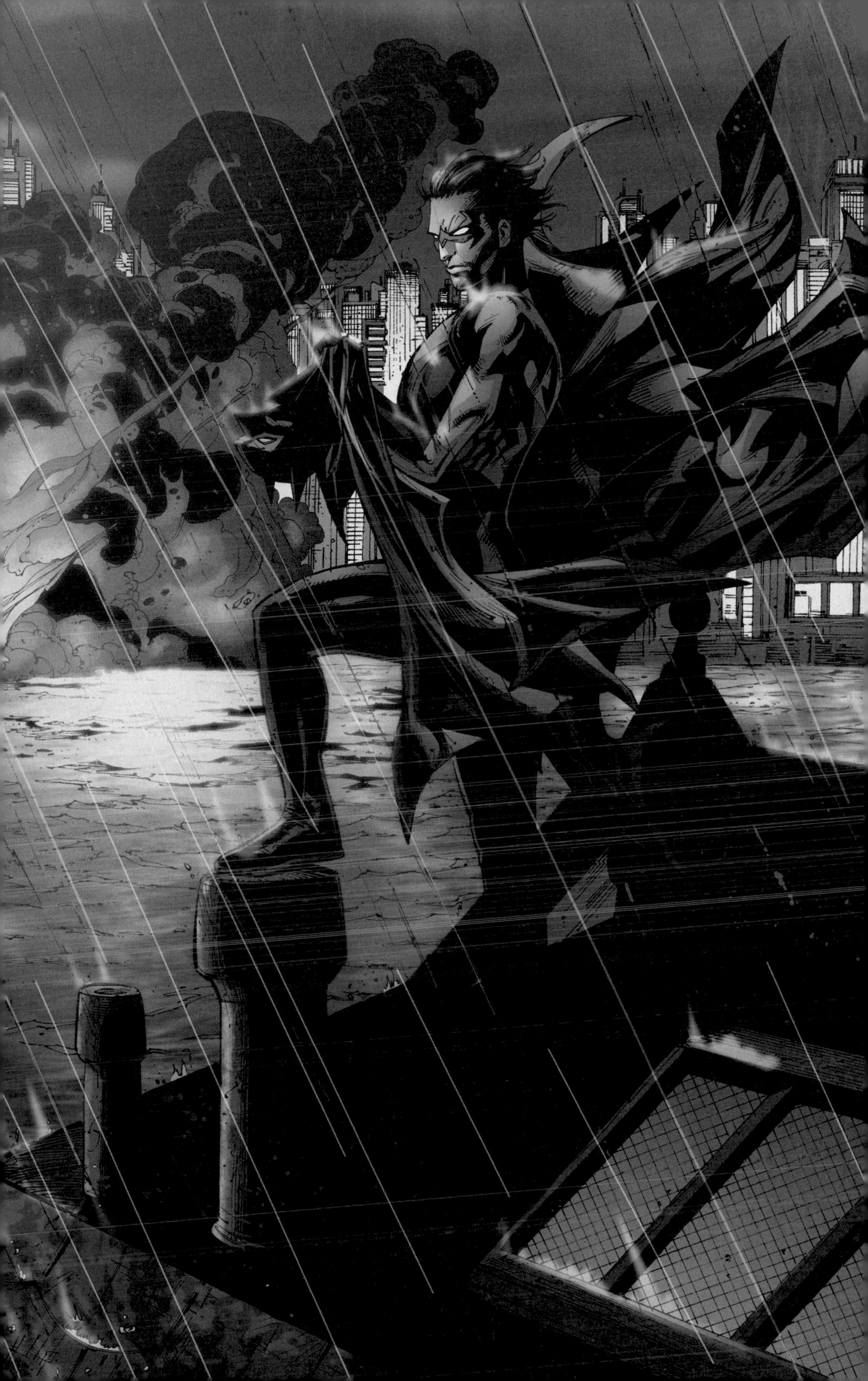

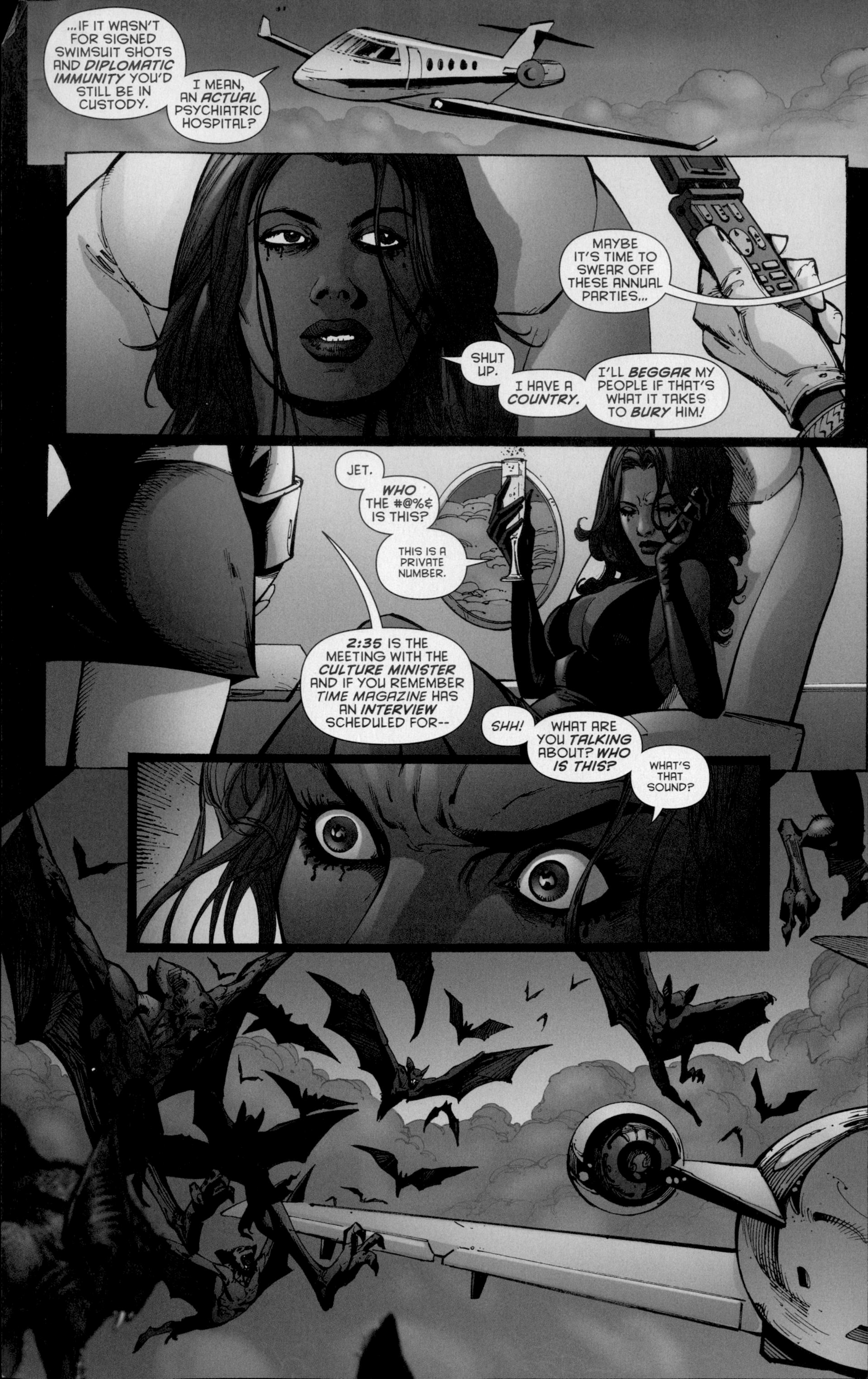
...IF IT WASN'T FOR SIGNED SWIMSUIT SHOTS AND DIPLOMATIC IMMUNITY YOU'D STILL BE IN CUSTODY.
I MEAN, AN ACTUAL PSYCHIATRIC HOSPITAL?
MAYBE IT'S TIME TO SWEAR OFF THESE ANNUAL PARTIES...
SHUT UP.
I HAVE A COUNTRY.
I'LL BEGGAR MY PEOPLE IF THAT'S WHAT IT TAKES TO BURY HIM!
JET.
WHO THE #@%& IS THIS?
THIS IS A PRIVATE NUMBER.
2:35 IS THE MEETING WITH THE CULTURE MINISTER AND IF YOU REMEMBER TIME MAGAZINE HAS AN INTERVIEW SCHEDULED FOR--
SHH!
WHAT ARE YOU TALKING ABOUT? WHO IS THIS?
WHAT'S THAT SOUND?

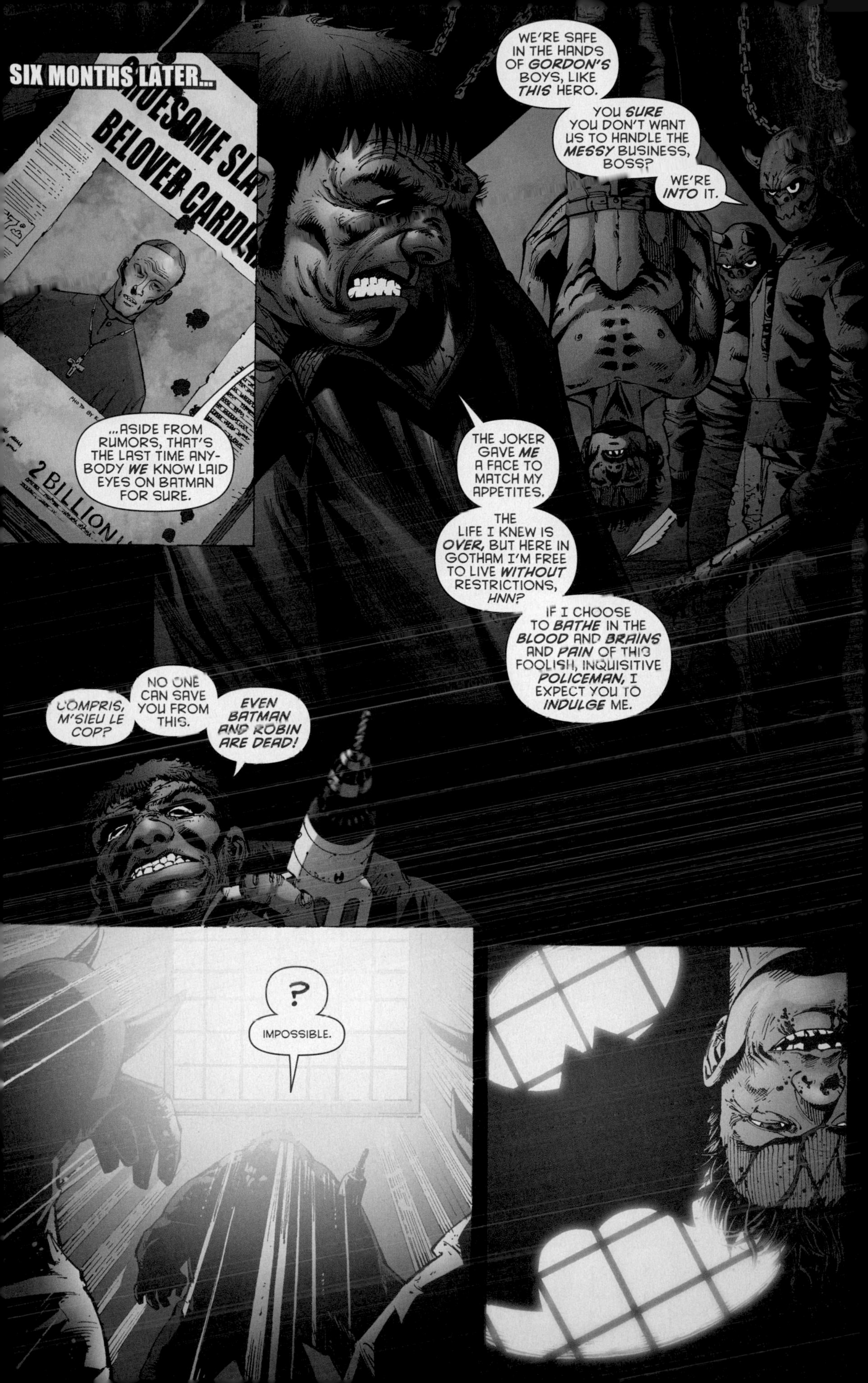
SIX MONTHS LATER...
GRUESOME SLA
BELOVED CARDI
...ASIDE FROM RUMORS, THAT'S THE LAST TIME ANY-BODY WE KNOW LAID EYES ON BATMAN FOR SURE.
2 BILLION
WE'RE SAFE IN THE HANDS OF GORDON'S BOYS, LIKE THIS HERO.
YOU SURE YOU DON'T WANT US TO HANDLE THE MESSY BUSINESS, BOSS?
WE'RE INTO IT.
THE JOKER GAVE ME A FACE TO MATCH MY APPETITES.
THE LIFE I KNEW IS OVER, BUT HERE IN GOTHAM I'M FREE TO LIVE WITHOUT RESTRICTIONS, HNN?
IF I CHOOSE TO BATHE IN THE BLOOD AND BRAINS AND PAIN OF THIS FOOLISH, INQUISITIVE POLICEMAN, I EXPECT YOU TO INDULGE ME.
COMPRIS, M'SIEU LE COP?
NO ONE CAN SAVE YOU FROM THIS.
EVEN BATMAN AND ROBIN ARE DEAD!
?
IMPOSSIBLE.

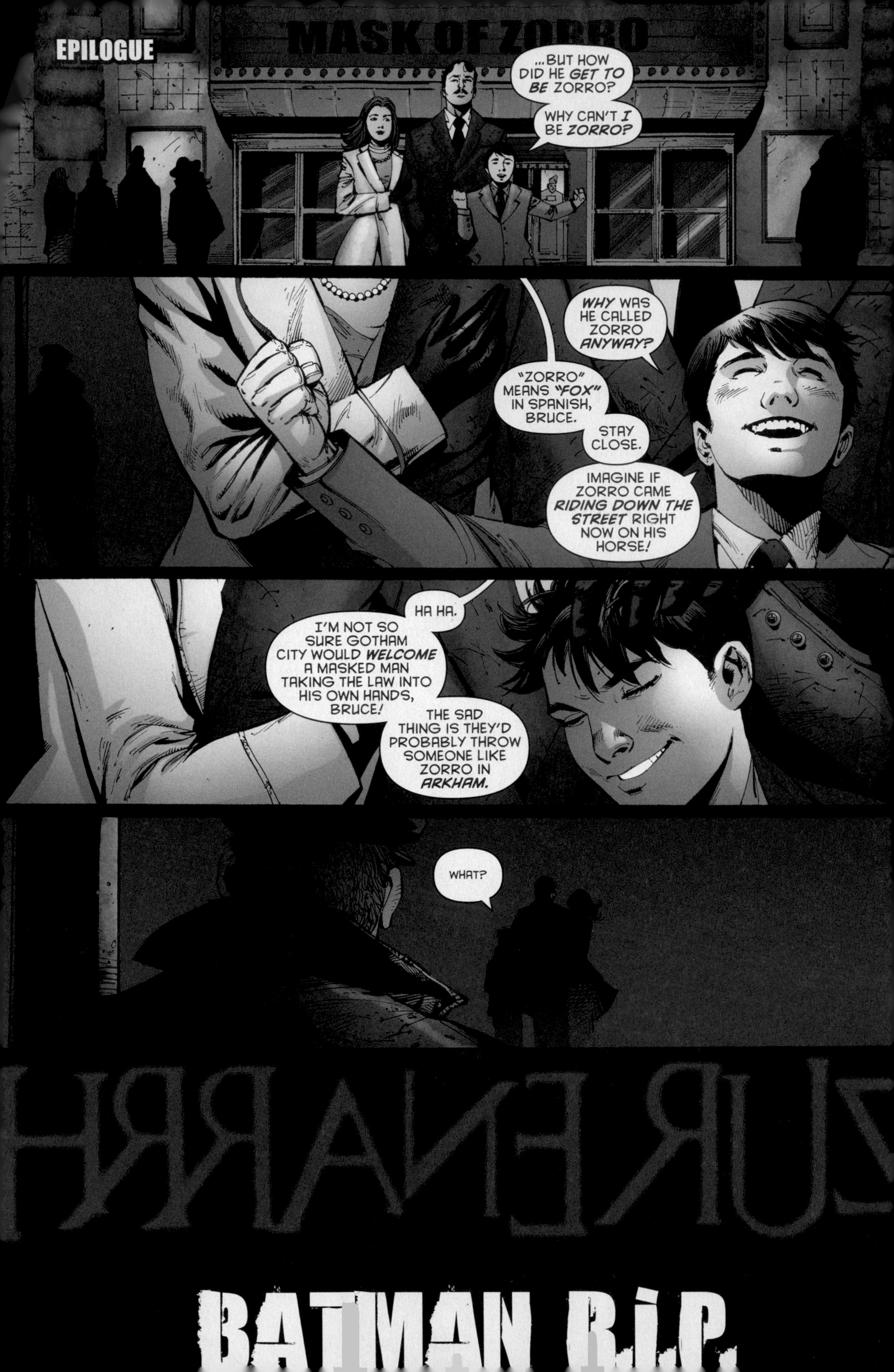
EPILOGUE
MASK OF ZORRO
...BUT HOW DID HE GET TO BE ZORRO?
WHY CAN'T I BE ZORRO?
WHY WAS HE CALLED ZORRO ANYWAY?
"ZORRO" MEANS "FOX" IN SPANISH, BRUCE.
STAY CLOSE.
IMAGINE IF ZORRO CAME RIDING DOWN THE STREET RIGHT NOW ON HIS HORSE!
HA HA.
I'M NOT SO SURE GOTHAM CITY WOULD WELCOME A MASKED MAN TAKING THE LAW INTO HIS OWN HANDS, BRUCE!
THE SAD THING IS THEY'D PROBABLY THROW SOMEONE LIKE ZORRO IN ARKHAM.
WHAT?
BATMAN R.I.P.

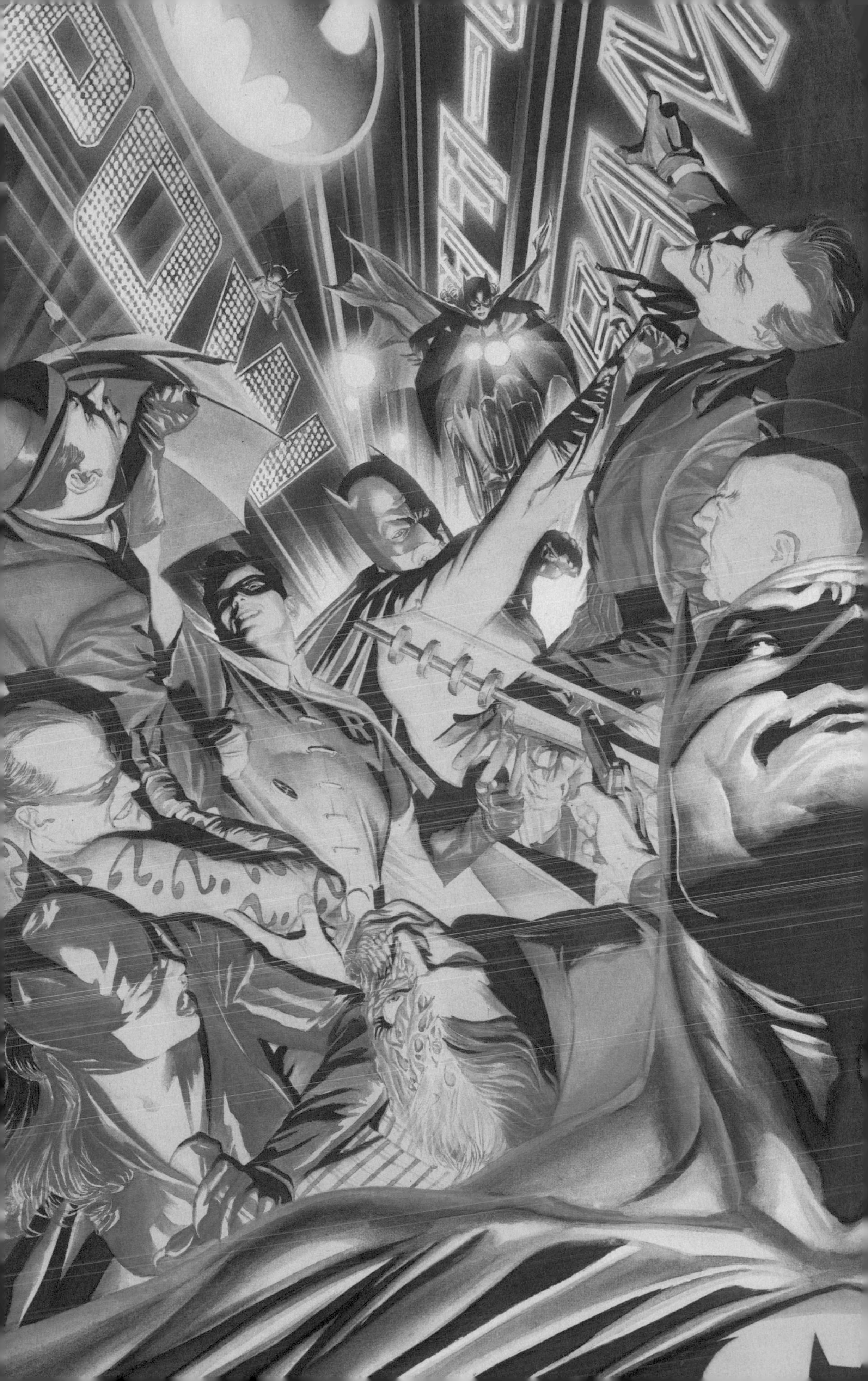

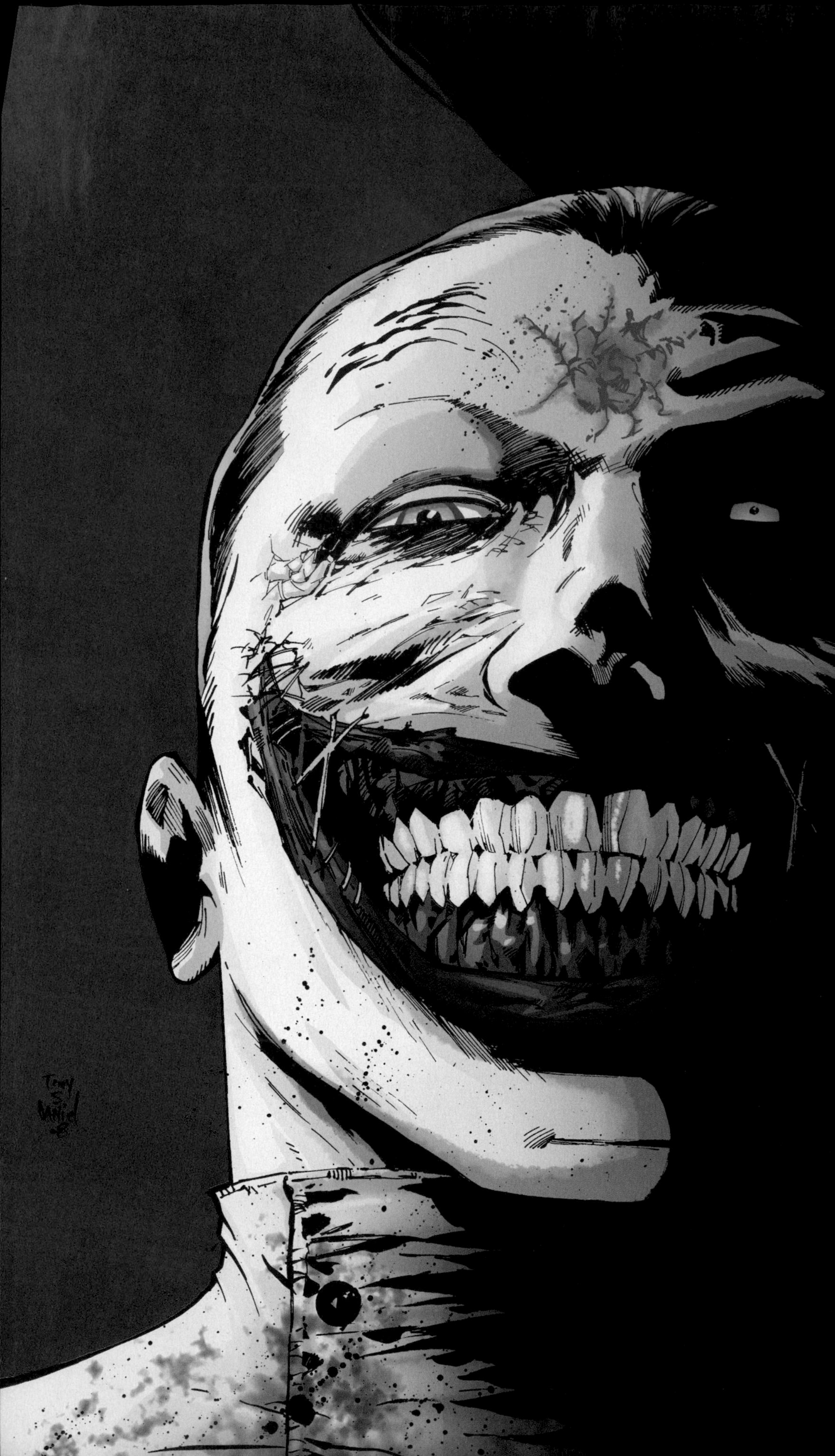

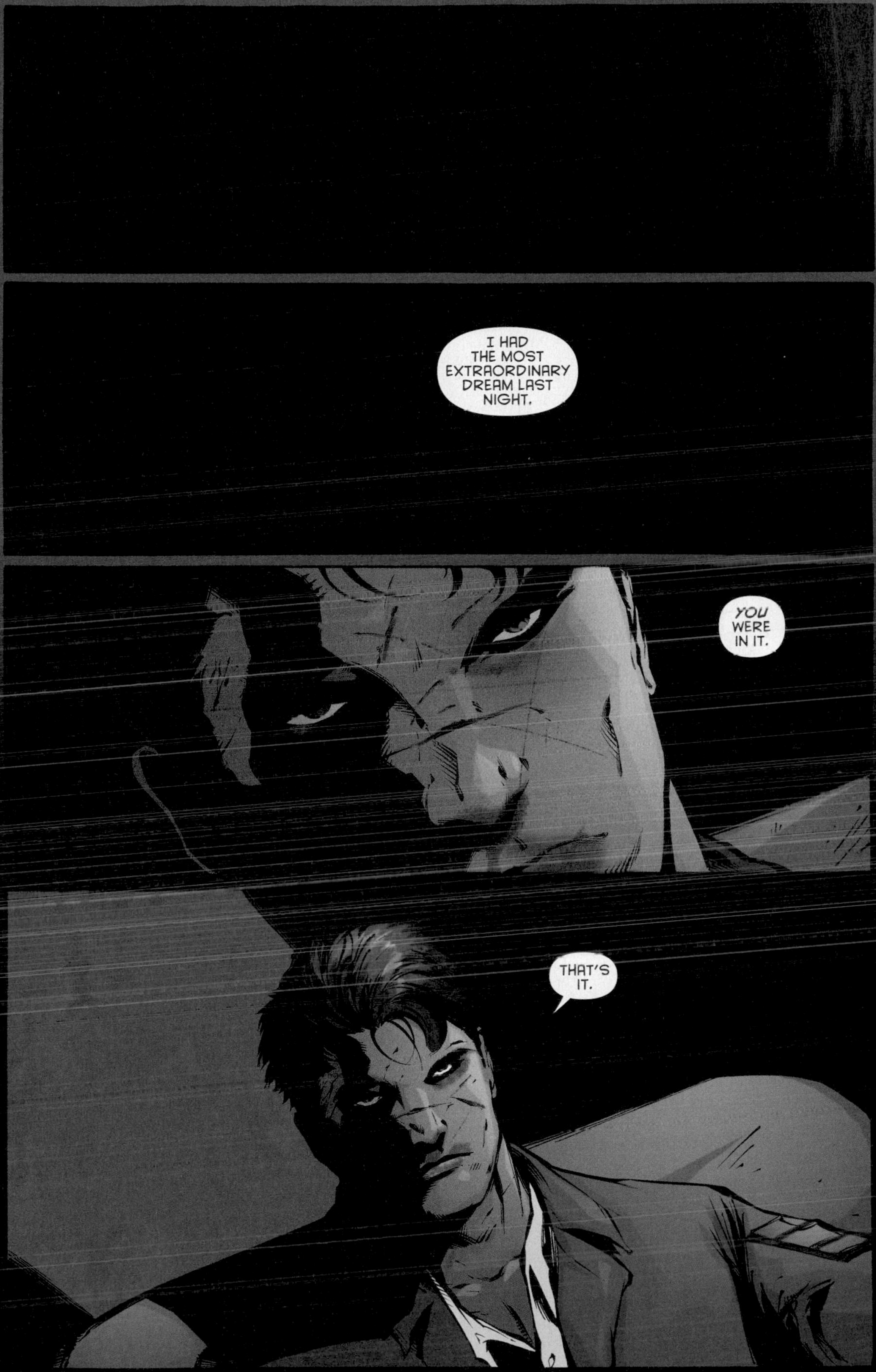
I HAD THE MOST EXTRAORDINARY DREAM LAST NIGHT.
YOU WERE IN IT.
THAT'S IT.

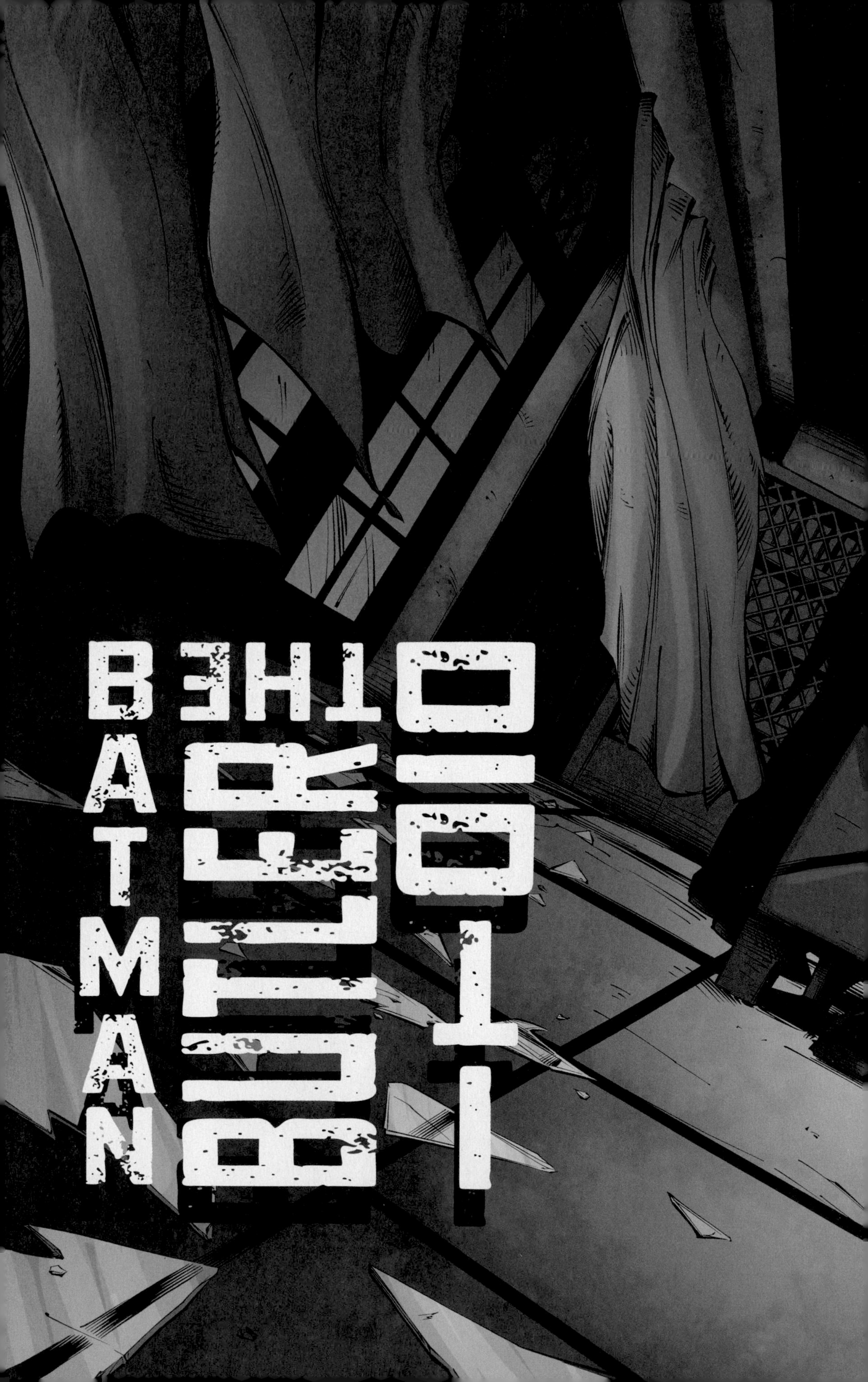
BATMAN
THE BUTLER DID IT

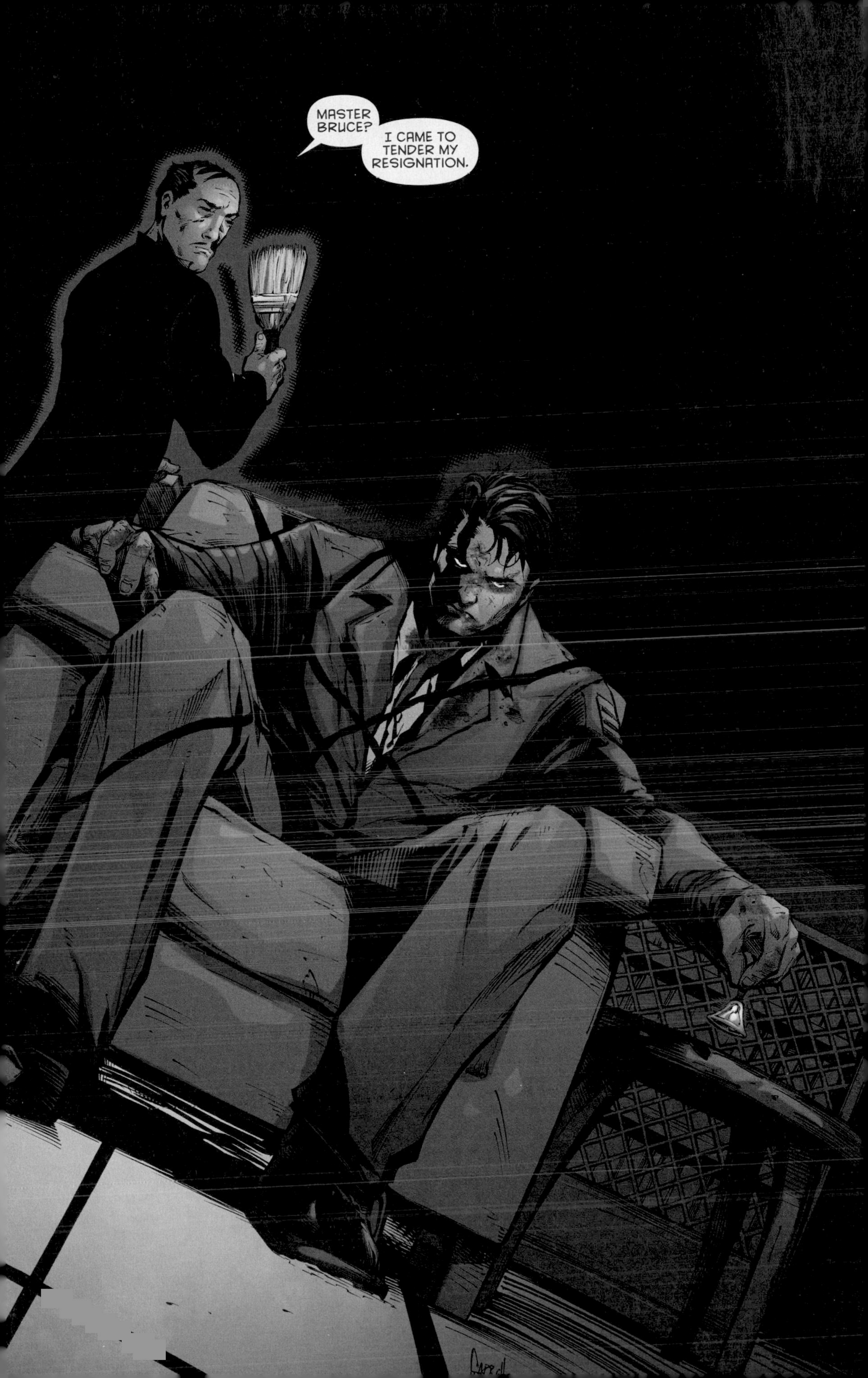
MASTER BRUCE?
I CAME TO TENDER MY RESIGNATION.

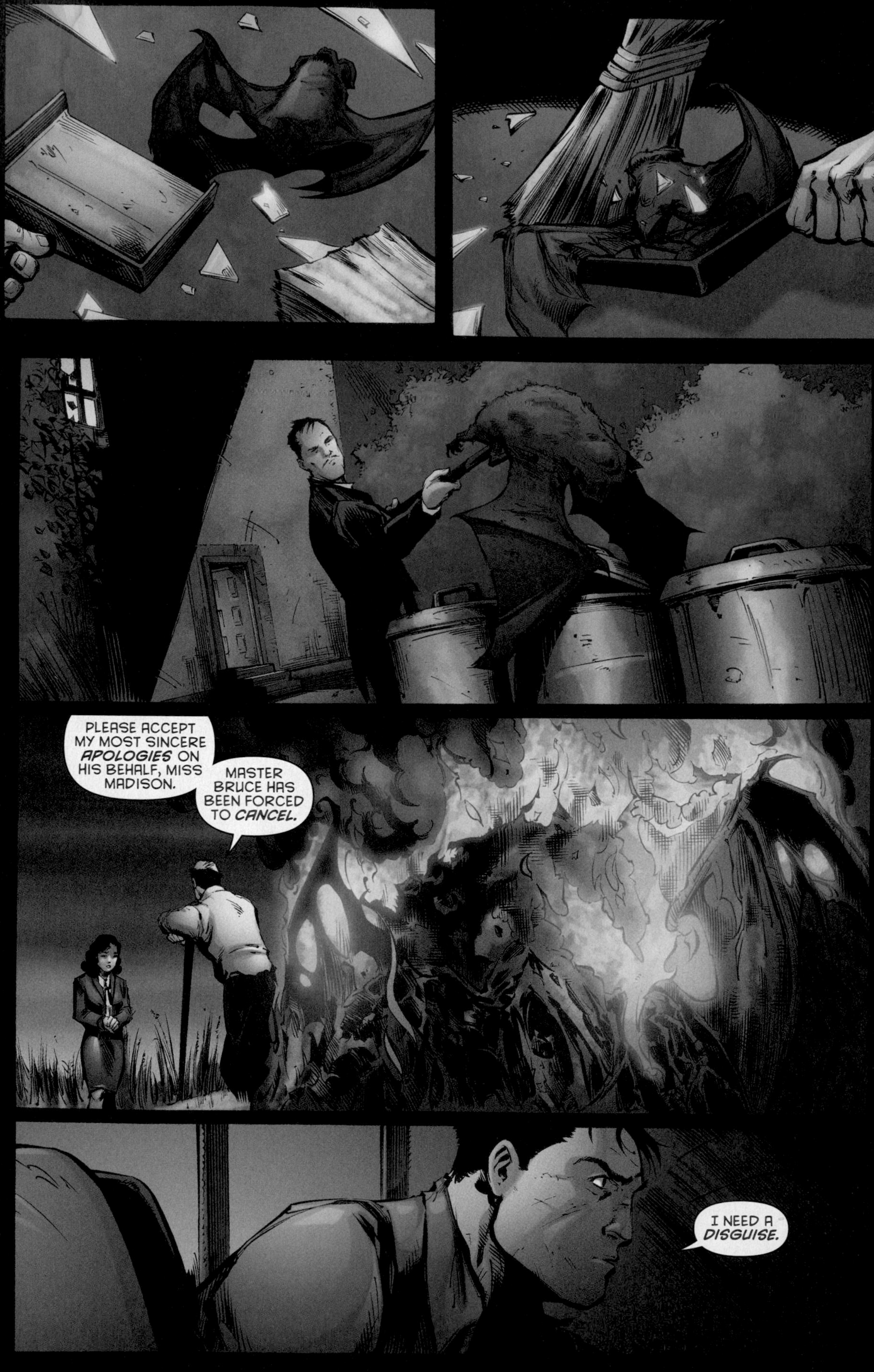

PLEASE ACCEPT MY MOST SINCERE *APOLOGIES* ON HIS BEHALF, MISS MADISON.
MASTER BRUCE HAS BEEN FORCED TO *CANCEL*.
I NEED A *DISGUISE*.

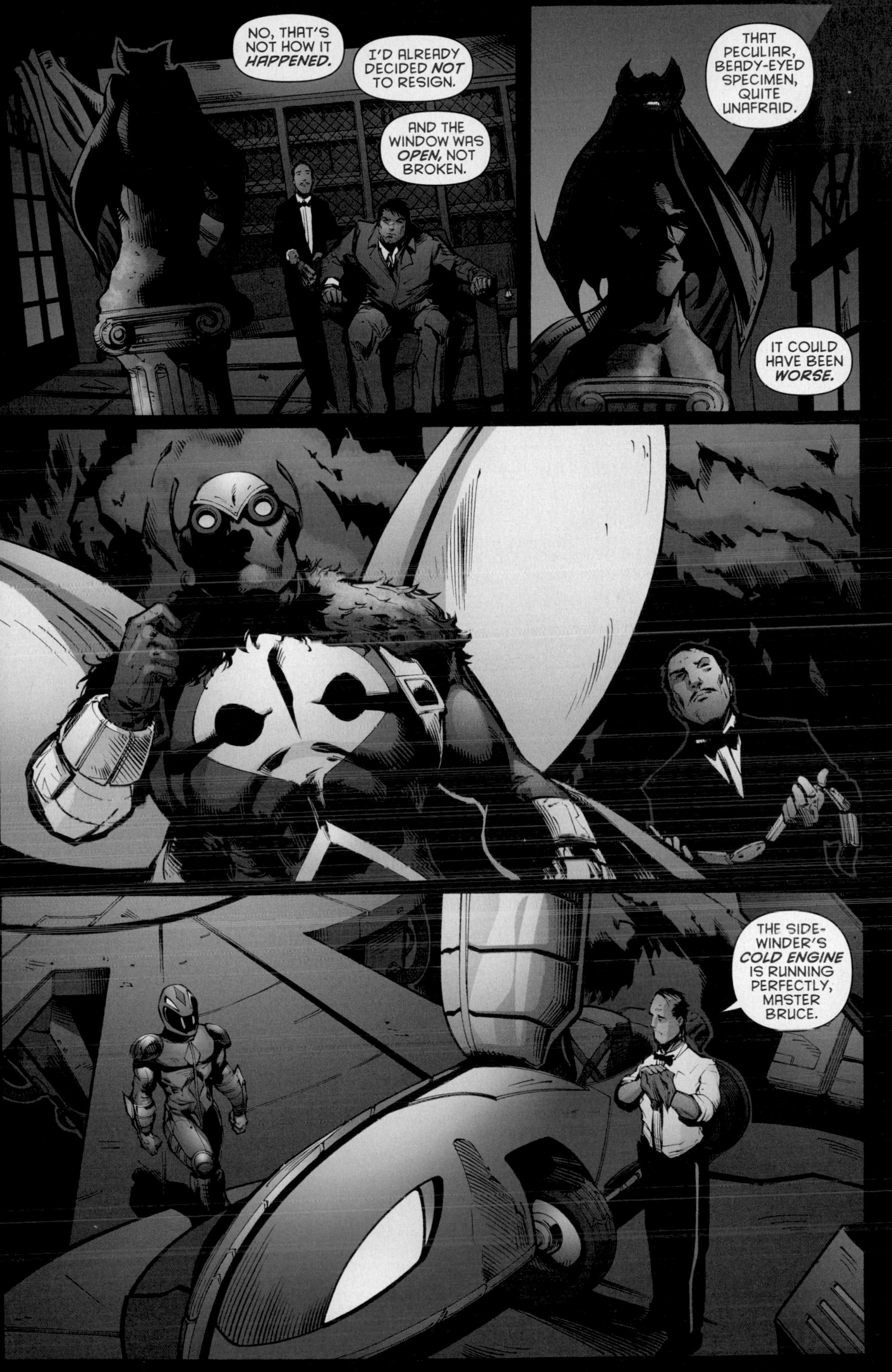
NO, THAT'S NOT HOW IT HAPPENED.
I'D ALREADY DECIDED NOT TO RESIGN.
AND THE WINDOW WAS OPEN, NOT BROKEN.
THAT PECULIAR, BEADY-EYED SPECIMEN, QUITE UNAFRAID.
IT COULD HAVE BEEN WORSE.
THE SIDE-WINDER'S COLD ENGINE IS RUNNING PERFECTLY, MASTER BRUCE.

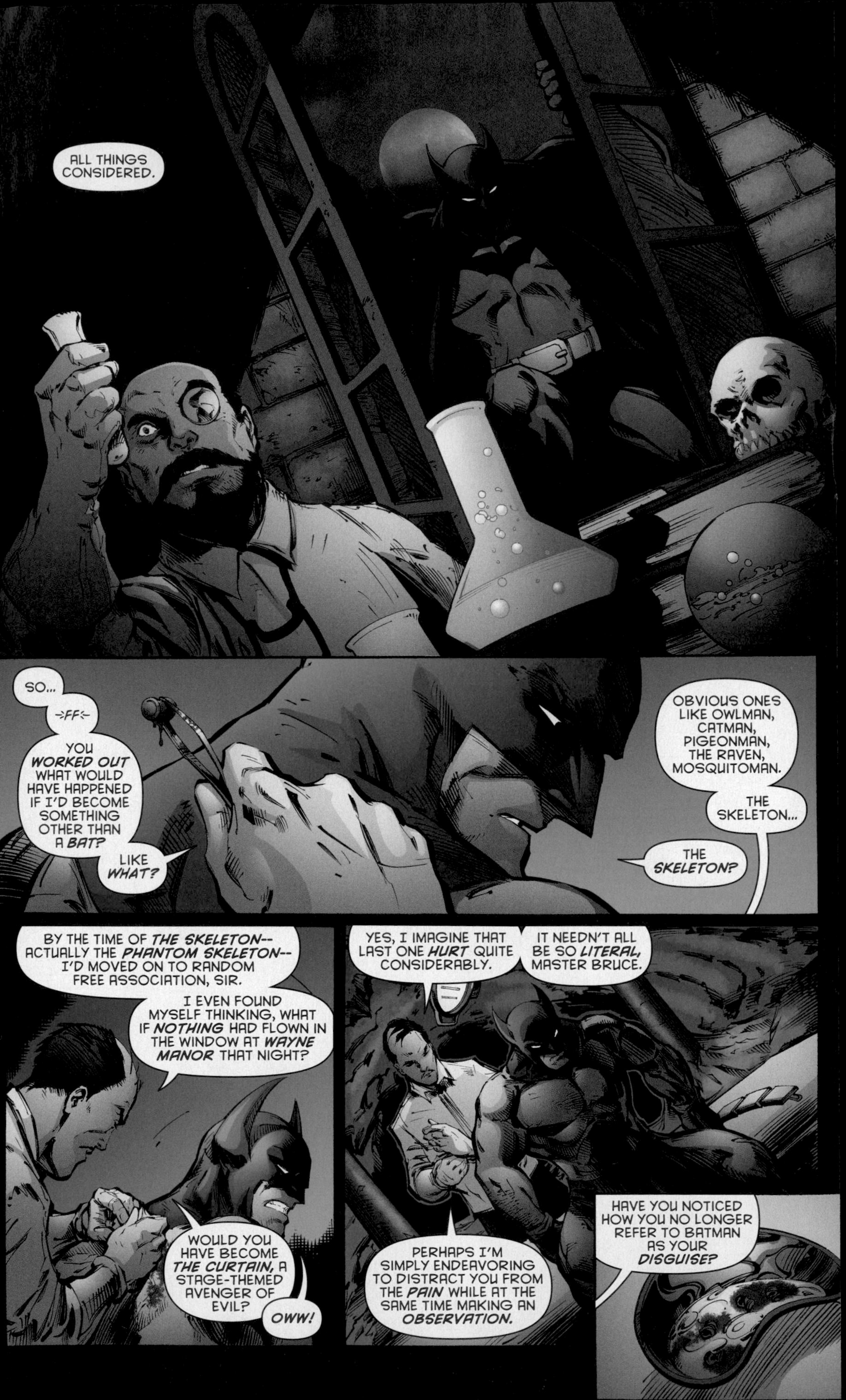
ALL THINGS CONSIDERED.
SO...
-FF-
YOU WORKED OUT WHAT WOULD HAVE HAPPENED IF I'D BECOME SOMETHING OTHER THAN A BAT?
LIKE WHAT?
OBVIOUS ONES LIKE OWLMAN, CATMAN, PIGEONMAN, THE RAVEN, MOSQUITOMAN.
THE SKELETON...
THE SKELETON?
BY THE TIME OF THE SKELETON-- ACTUALLY THE PHANTOM SKELETON-- I'D MOVED ON TO RANDOM FREE ASSOCIATION, SIR.
I EVEN FOUND MYSELF THINKING, WHAT IF NOTHING HAD FLOWN IN THE WINDOW AT WAYNE MANOR THAT NIGHT?
WOULD YOU HAVE BECOME THE CURTAIN, A STAGE-THEMED AVENGER OF EVIL?
OWW!
YES, I IMAGINE THAT LAST ONE HURT QUITE CONSIDERABLY.
IT NEEDN'T ALL BE SO LITERAL, MASTER BRUCE.
PERHAPS I'M SIMPLY ENDEAVORING TO DISTRACT YOU FROM THE PAIN WHILE AT THE SAME TIME MAKING AN OBSERVATION.
HAVE YOU NOTICED HOW YOU NO LONGER REFER TO BATMAN AS YOUR DISGUISE?

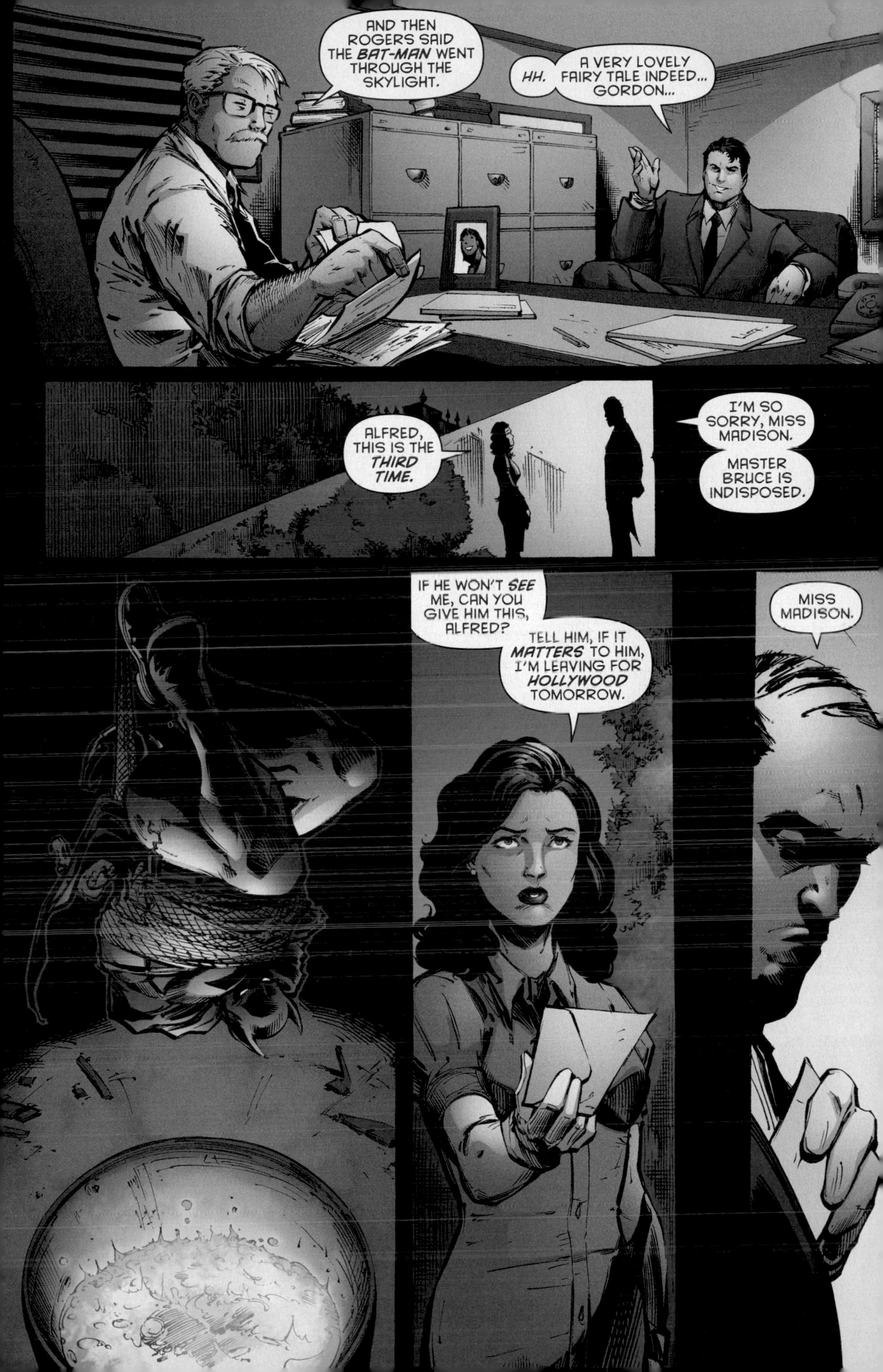
AND THEN ROGERS SAID THE BAT-MAN WENT THROUGH THE SKYLIGHT.
HH.
A VERY LOVELY FAIRY TALE INDEED... GORDON...
ALFRED, THIS IS THE THIRD TIME.
I'M SO SORRY, MISS MADISON.
MASTER BRUCE IS INDISPOSED.
IF HE WON'T SEE ME, CAN YOU GIVE HIM THIS, ALFRED?
TELL HIM, IF IT MATTERS TO HIM, I'M LEAVING FOR HOLLYWOOD TOMORROW.
MISS MADISON.

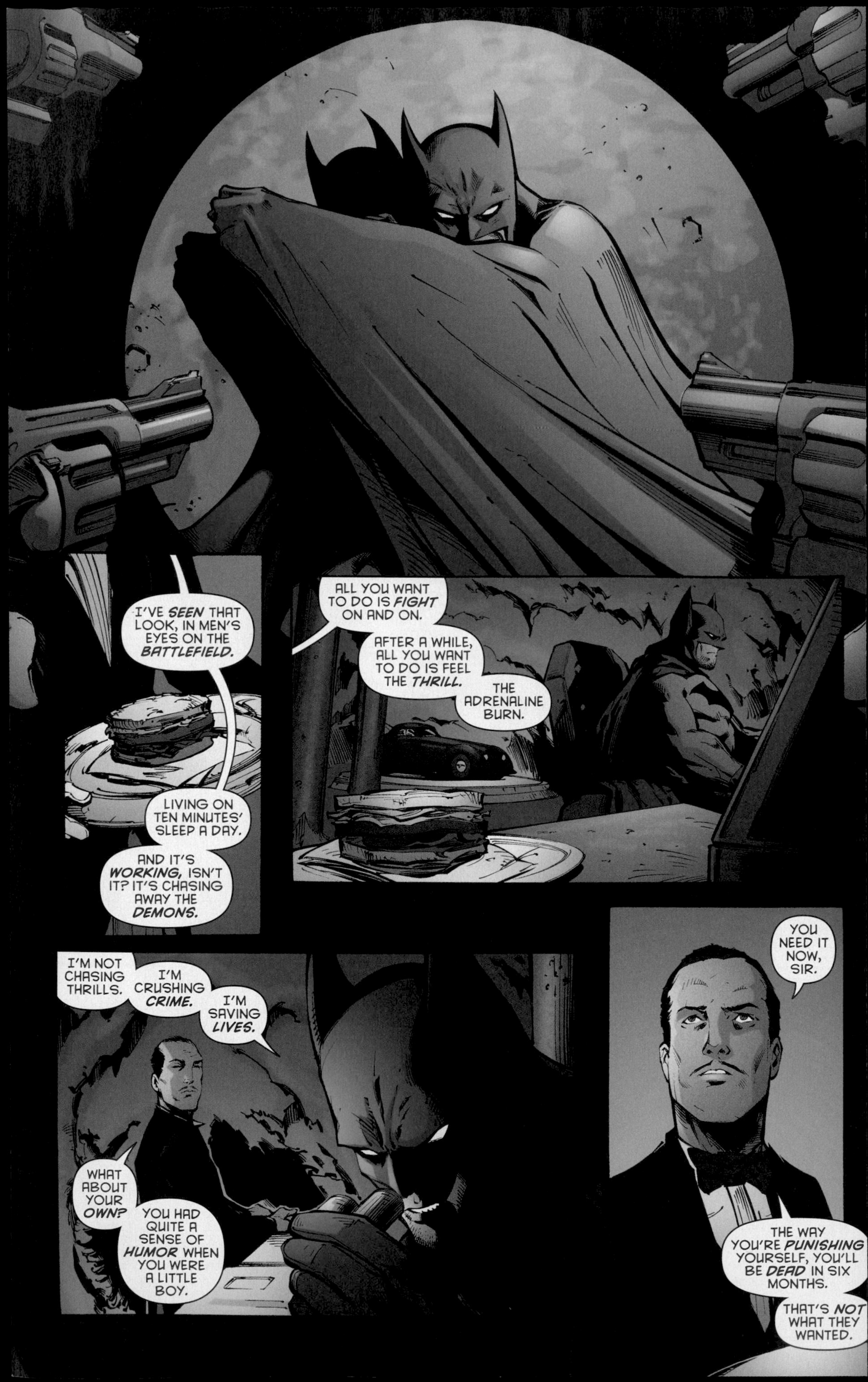
I'VE SEEN THAT LOOK, IN MEN'S EYES ON THE BATTLEFIELD.
LIVING ON TEN MINUTES' SLEEP A DAY.
AND IT'S WORKING, ISN'T IT? IT'S CHASING AWAY THE DEMONS.
ALL YOU WANT TO DO IS FIGHT ON AND ON.
AFTER A WHILE, ALL YOU WANT TO DO IS FEEL THE THRILL.
THE ADRENALINE BURN.
I'M NOT CHASING THRILLS.
I'M CRUSHING CRIME.
I'M SAVING LIVES.
WHAT ABOUT YOUR OWN?
YOU HAD QUITE A SENSE OF HUMOR WHEN YOU WERE A LITTLE BOY.
YOU NEED IT NOW, SIR.
THE WAY YOU'RE PUNISHING YOURSELF, YOU'LL BE DEAD IN SIX MONTHS.
THAT'S NOT WHAT THEY WANTED.

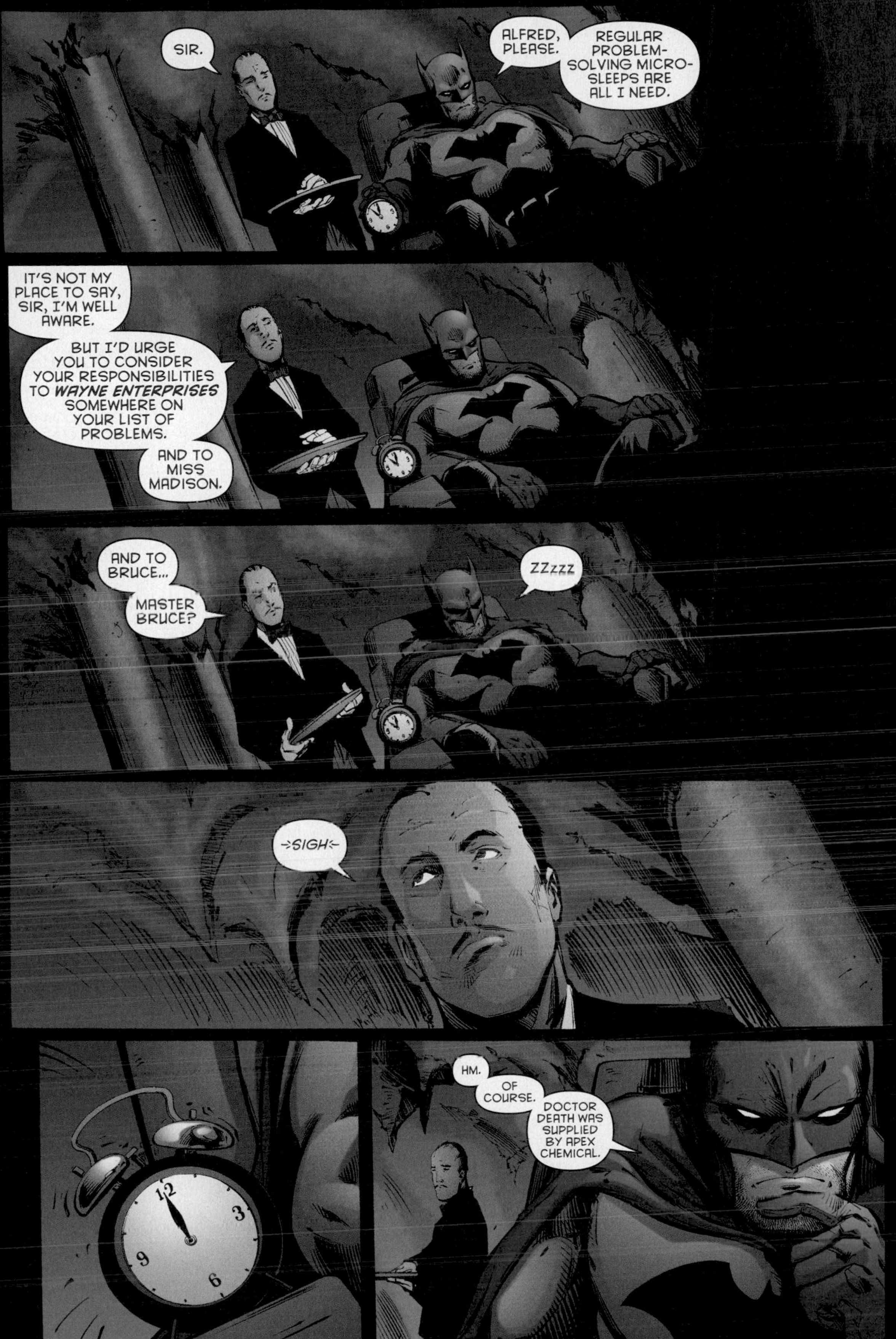
SIR.
ALFRED, PLEASE.
REGULAR PROBLEM-SOLVING MICRO-SLEEPS ARE ALL I NEED.
IT'S NOT MY PLACE TO SAY, SIR, I'M WELL AWARE.
BUT I'D URGE YOU TO CONSIDER YOUR RESPONSIBILITIES TO WAYNE ENTERPRISES SOMEWHERE ON YOUR LIST OF PROBLEMS.
AND TO MISS MADISON.
AND TO BRUCE...
MASTER BRUCE?
ZZzzz
SIGH
HM.
OF COURSE.
DOCTOR DEATH WAS SUPPLIED BY APEX CHEMICAL.

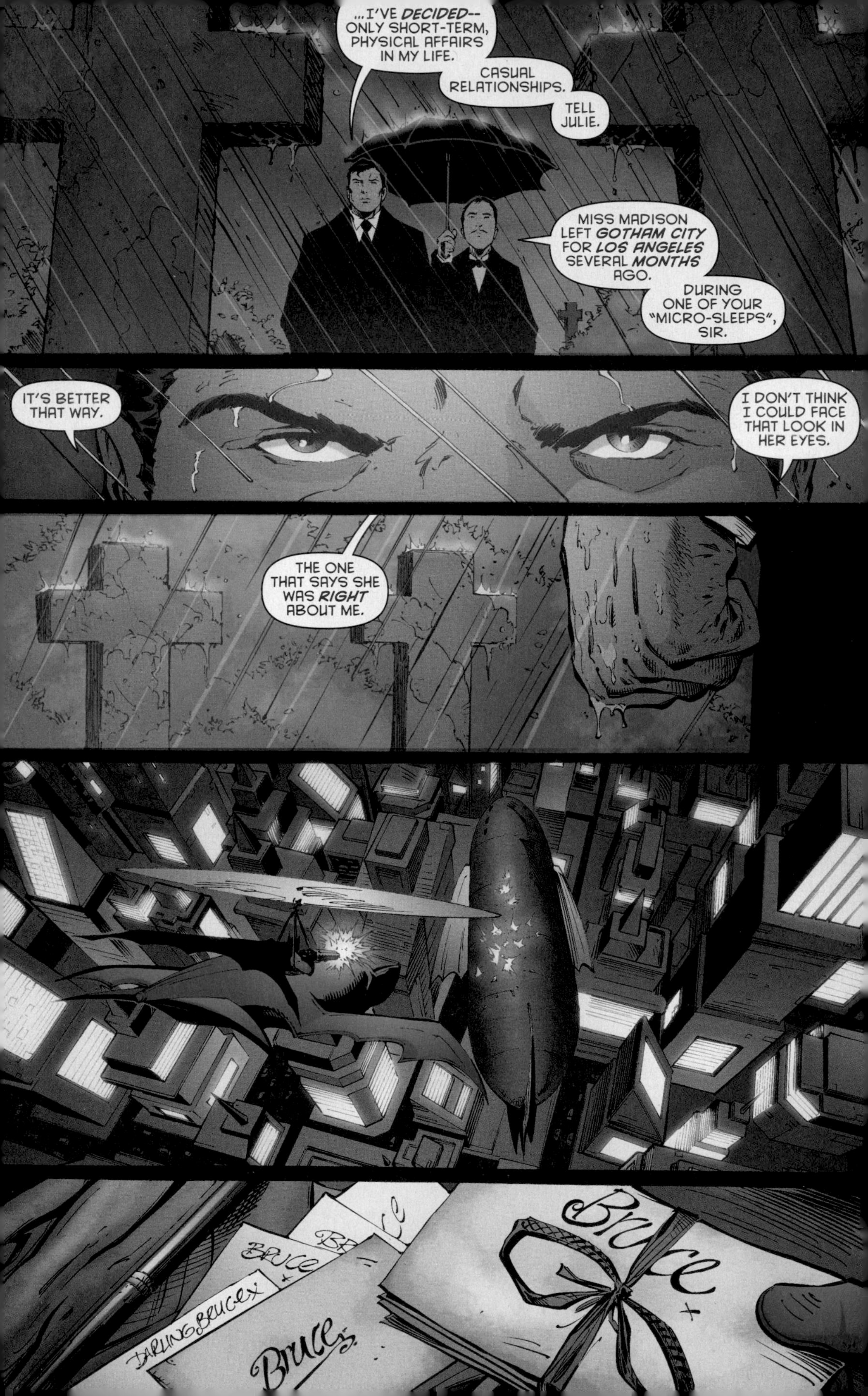
...I'VE DECIDED-- ONLY SHORT-TERM, PHYSICAL AFFAIRS IN MY LIFE.
CASUAL RELATIONSHIPS.
TELL JULIE.
MISS MADISON LEFT GOTHAM CITY FOR LOS ANGELES SEVERAL MONTHS AGO.
DURING ONE OF YOUR "MICRO-SLEEPS", SIR.
IT'S BETTER THAT WAY.
I DON'T THINK I COULD FACE THAT LOOK IN HER EYES.
THE ONE THAT SAYS SHE WAS RIGHT ABOUT ME.
Bruce
DARLING BRUCE x
Bruce

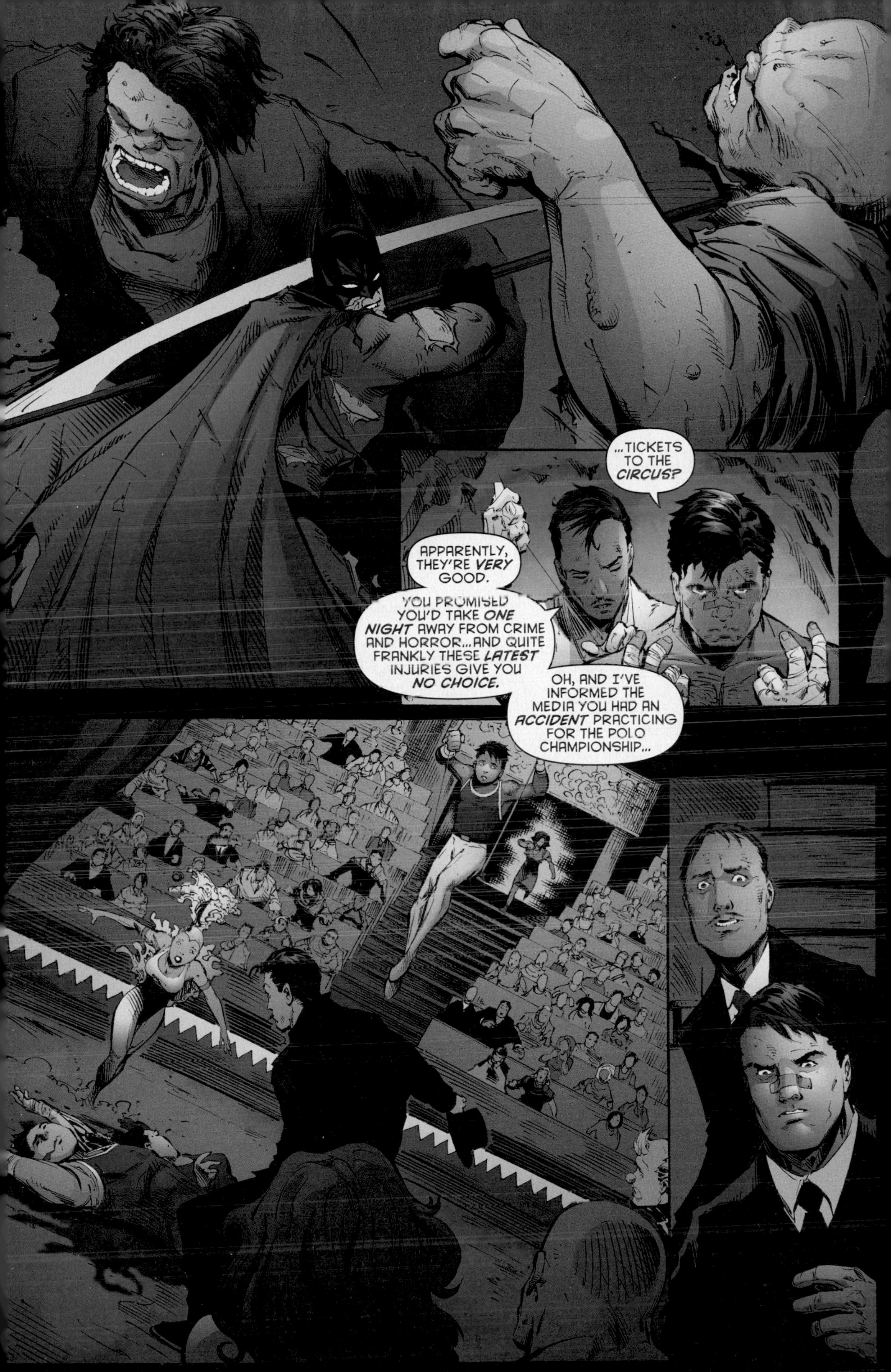
...TICKETS TO THE CIRCUS?
APPARENTLY, THEY'RE VERY GOOD.
YOU PROMISED YOU'D TAKE ONE NIGHT AWAY FROM CRIME AND HORROR...AND QUITE FRANKLY THESE LATEST INJURIES GIVE YOU NO CHOICE.
OH, AND I'VE INFORMED THE MEDIA YOU HAD AN ACCIDENT PRACTICING FOR THE POLO CHAMPIONSHIP...

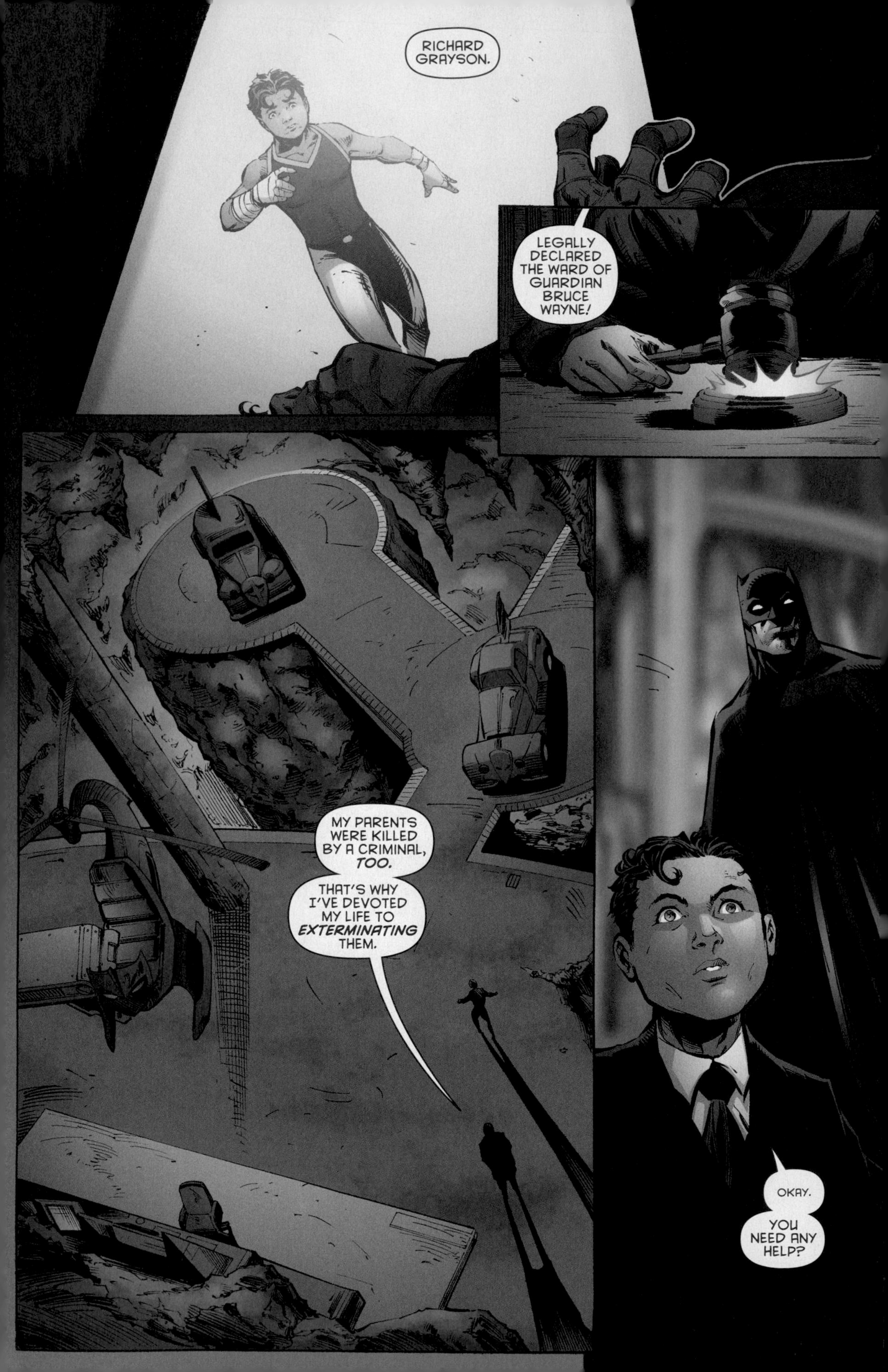
RICHARD GRAYSON.
LEGALLY DECLARED THE WARD OF GUARDIAN BRUCE WAYNE!
MY PARENTS WERE KILLED BY A CRIMINAL, TOO.
THAT'S WHY I'VE DEVOTED MY LIFE TO EXTERMINATING THEM.
OKAY.
YOU NEED ANY HELP?

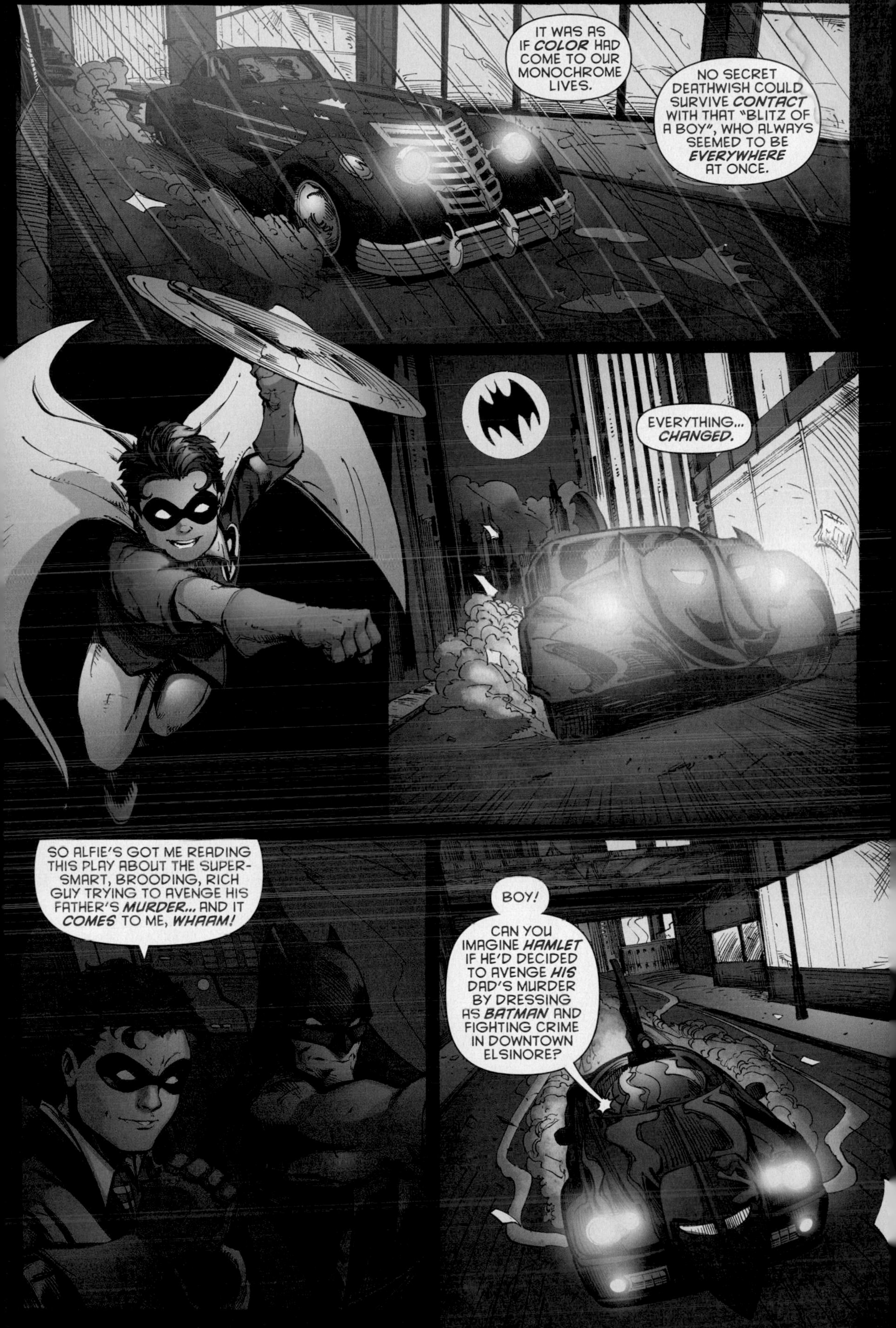
IT WAS AS IF COLOR HAD COME TO OUR MONOCHROME LIVES.
NO SECRET DEATHWISH COULD SURVIVE CONTACT WITH THAT "BLITZ OF A BOY", WHO ALWAYS SEEMED TO BE EVERYWHERE AT ONCE.
EVERYTHING... CHANGED.
SO ALFIE'S GOT ME READING THIS PLAY ABOUT THE SUPER-SMART, BROODING, RICH GUY TRYING TO AVENGE HIS FATHER'S MURDER... AND IT COMES TO ME, WHAAM!
BOY!
CAN YOU IMAGINE HAMLET IF HE'D DECIDED TO AVENGE HIS DAD'S MURDER BY DRESSING AS BATMAN AND FIGHTING CRIME IN DOWNTOWN ELSINORE?

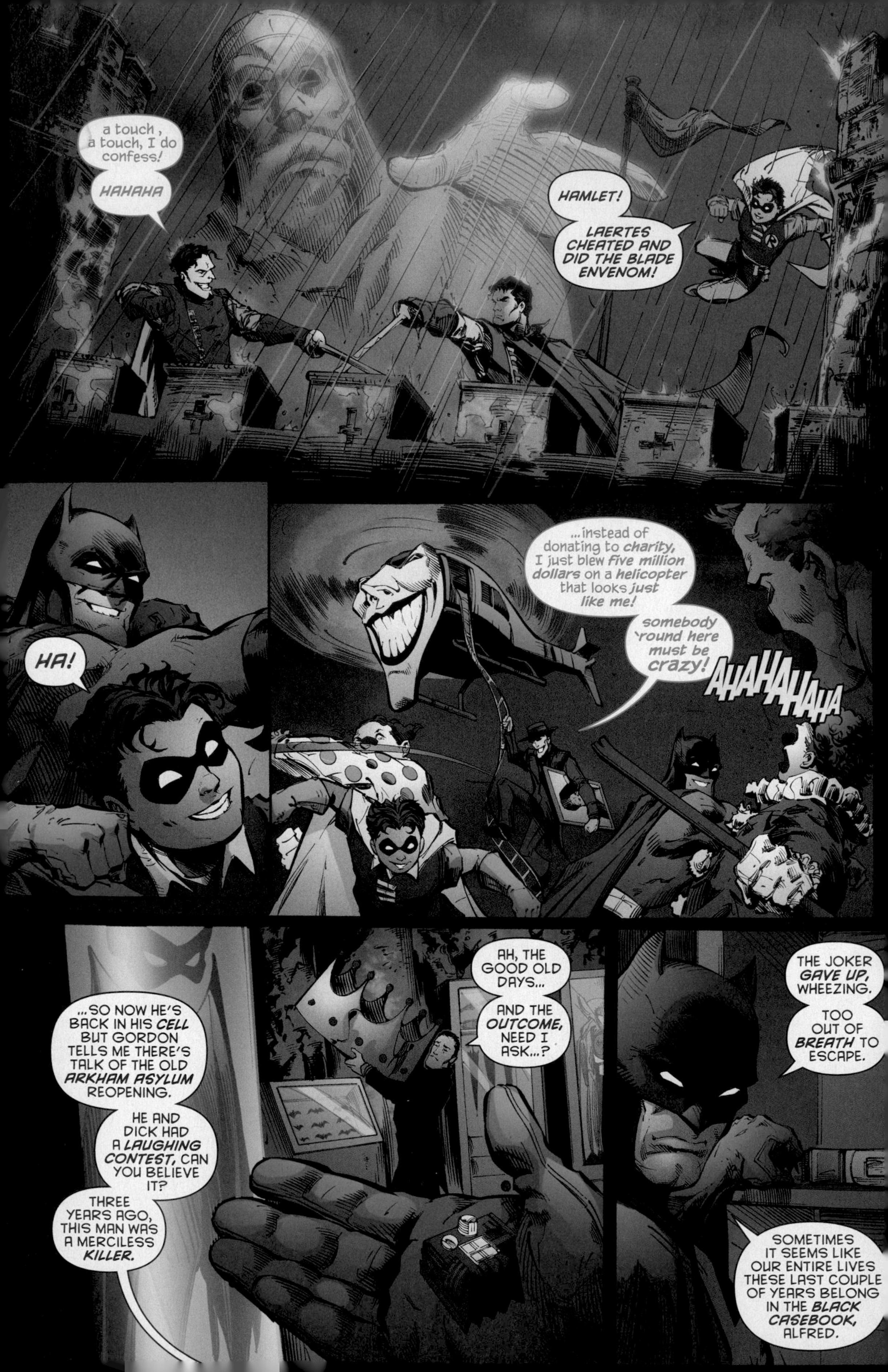

a touch, a touch, I do confess!
HAHAHA
HAMLET!
LAERTES CHEATED AND DID THE BLADE ENVENOM!
HA!
...instead of donating to charity, I just blew five million dollars on a helicopter that looks just like me!
somebody 'round here must be crazy!
AHAHAHAHA
...SO NOW HE'S BACK IN HIS CELL BUT GORDON TELLS ME THERE'S TALK OF THE OLD ARKHAM ASYLUM REOPENING.
HE AND DICK HAD A LAUGHING CONTEST, CAN YOU BELIEVE IT?
THREE YEARS AGO, THIS MAN WAS A MERCILESS KILLER.
AH, THE GOOD OLD DAYS...
AND THE OUTCOME, NEED I ASK...?
THE JOKER GAVE UP, WHEEZING.
TOO OUT OF BREATH TO ESCAPE.
SOMETIMES IT SEEMS LIKE OUR ENTIRE LIVES THESE LAST COUPLE OF YEARS BELONG IN THE BLACK CASEBOOK, ALFRED.

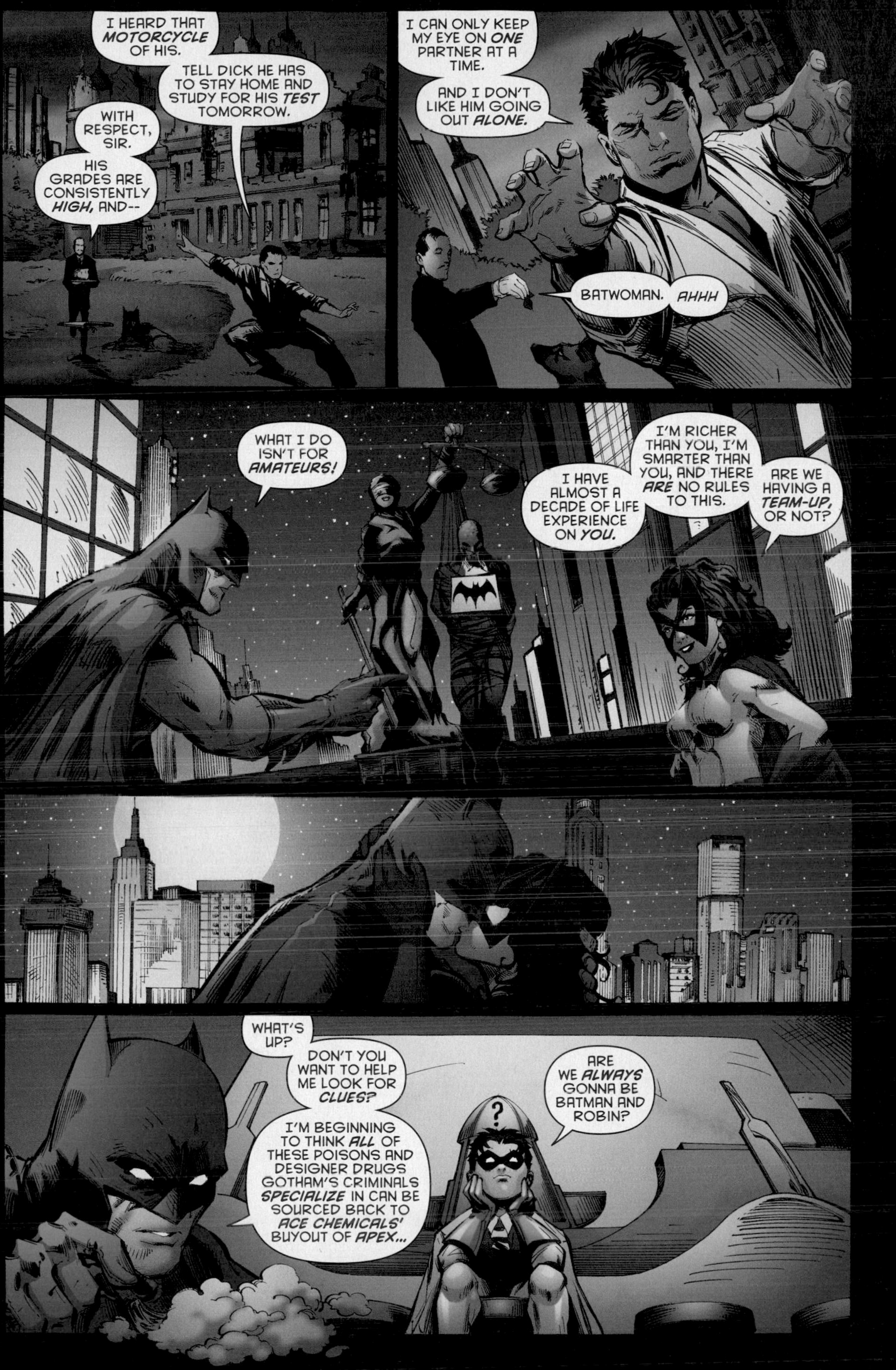

I HEARD THAT *MOTORCYCLE* OF HIS.
TELL DICK HE HAS TO STAY HOME AND STUDY FOR HIS *TEST* TOMORROW.
WITH RESPECT, SIR.
HIS GRADES ARE CONSISTENTLY *HIGH,* AND--
I CAN ONLY KEEP MY EYE ON *ONE* PARTNER AT A TIME.
AND I DON'T LIKE HIM GOING OUT *ALONE.*
BATWOMAN.
AHHH
WHAT I DO ISN'T FOR *AMATEURS!*
I HAVE ALMOST A DECADE OF LIFE EXPERIENCE ON *YOU.*
I'M RICHER THAN YOU, I'M SMARTER THAN YOU, AND THERE *ARE* NO RULES TO THIS.
ARE WE HAVING A *TEAM-UP,* OR NOT?
WHAT'S UP?
DON'T YOU WANT TO HELP ME LOOK FOR *CLUES?*
I'M BEGINNING TO THINK *ALL* OF THESE POISONS AND DESIGNER DRUGS GOTHAM'S CRIMINALS *SPECIALIZE* IN CAN BE SOURCED BACK TO *ACE CHEMICALS'* BUYOUT OF *APEX...*
ARE WE *ALWAYS* GONNA BE BATMAN AND ROBIN?

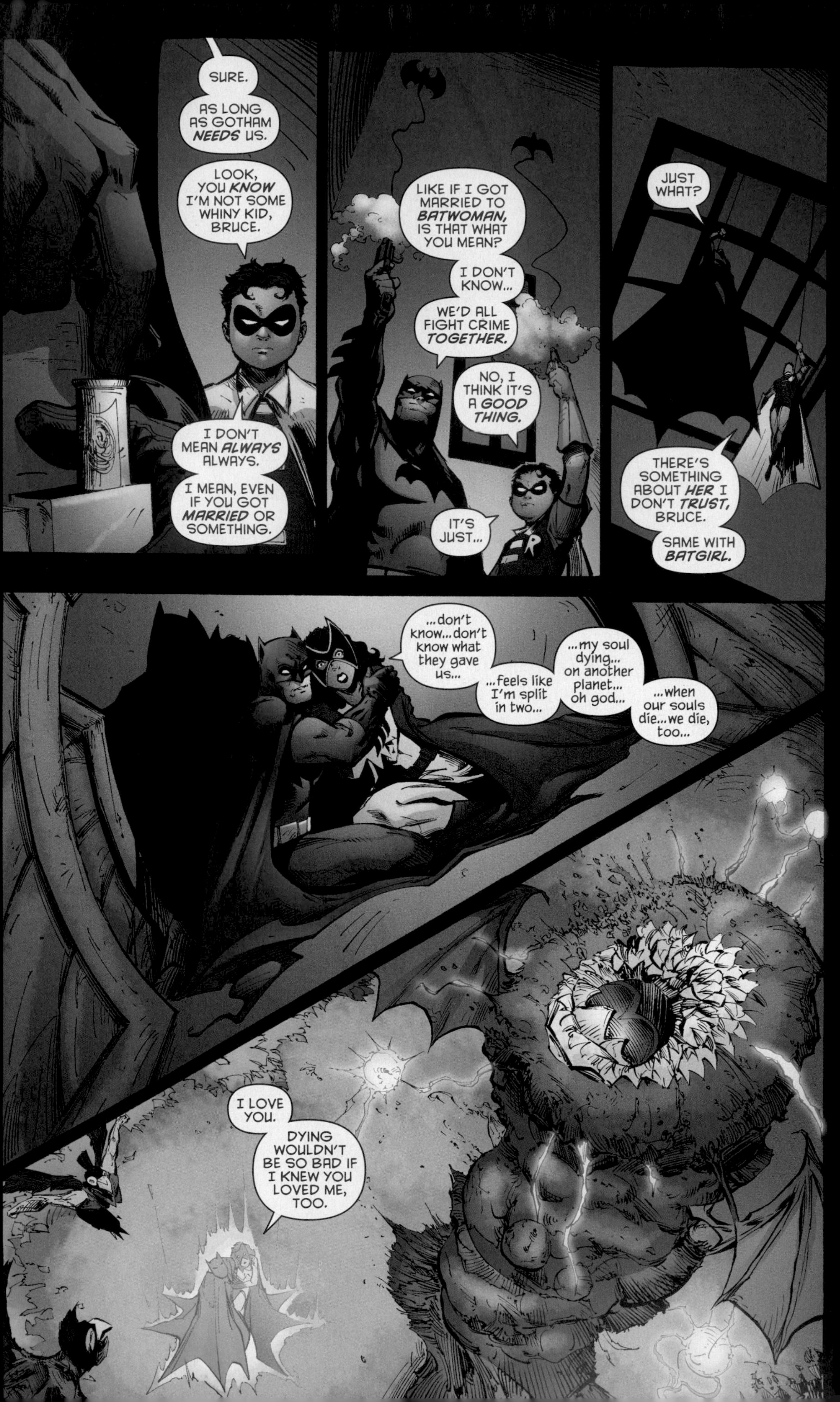
SURE.
AS LONG AS GOTHAM NEEDS US.
LOOK, YOU KNOW I'M NOT SOME WHINY KID, BRUCE.
I DON'T MEAN ALWAYS ALWAYS.
I MEAN, EVEN IF YOU GOT MARRIED OR SOMETHING.
LIKE IF I GOT MARRIED TO BATWOMAN, IS THAT WHAT YOU MEAN?
I DON'T KNOW...
WE'D ALL FIGHT CRIME TOGETHER.
NO, I THINK IT'S A GOOD THING.
IT'S JUST...
JUST WHAT?
THERE'S SOMETHING ABOUT HER I DON'T TRUST, BRUCE.
SAME WITH BATGIRL.
...don't know...don't know what they gave us...
...feels like I'm split in two...
...my soul dying... on another planet... oh god...
...when our souls die...we die, too...
I LOVE YOU.
DYING WOULDN'T BE SO BAD IF I KNEW YOU LOVED ME, TOO.

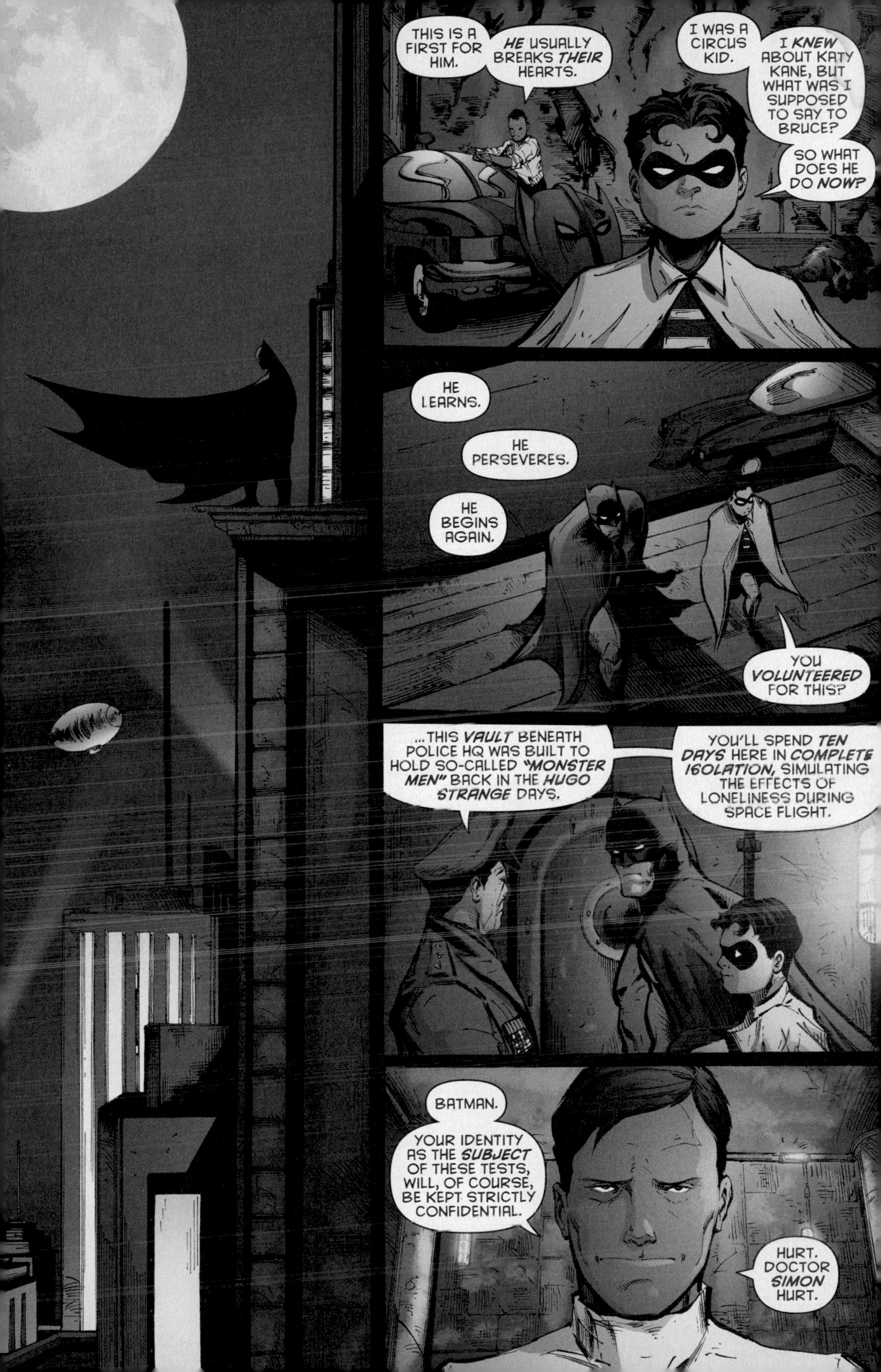
THIS IS A FIRST FOR HIM.
HE USUALLY BREAKS *THEIR* HEARTS.
I WAS A CIRCUS KID.
I *KNEW* ABOUT KATY KANE, BUT WHAT WAS I SUPPOSED TO SAY TO BRUCE?
SO WHAT DOES HE DO *NOW?*
HE LEARNS.
HE PERSEVERES.
HE BEGINS AGAIN.
YOU *VOLUNTEERED* FOR THIS?
...THIS *VAULT* BENEATH POLICE HQ WAS BUILT TO HOLD SO-CALLED *"MONSTER MEN"* BACK IN THE *HUGO STRANGE* DAYS.
YOU'LL SPEND *TEN DAYS* HERE IN *COMPLETE ISOLATION,* SIMULATING THE EFFECTS OF LONELINESS DURING SPACE FLIGHT.
BATMAN.
YOUR IDENTITY AS THE *SUBJECT* OF THESE TESTS, WILL, OF COURSE, BE KEPT STRICTLY CONFIDENTIAL.
HURT. DOCTOR *SIMON* HURT.

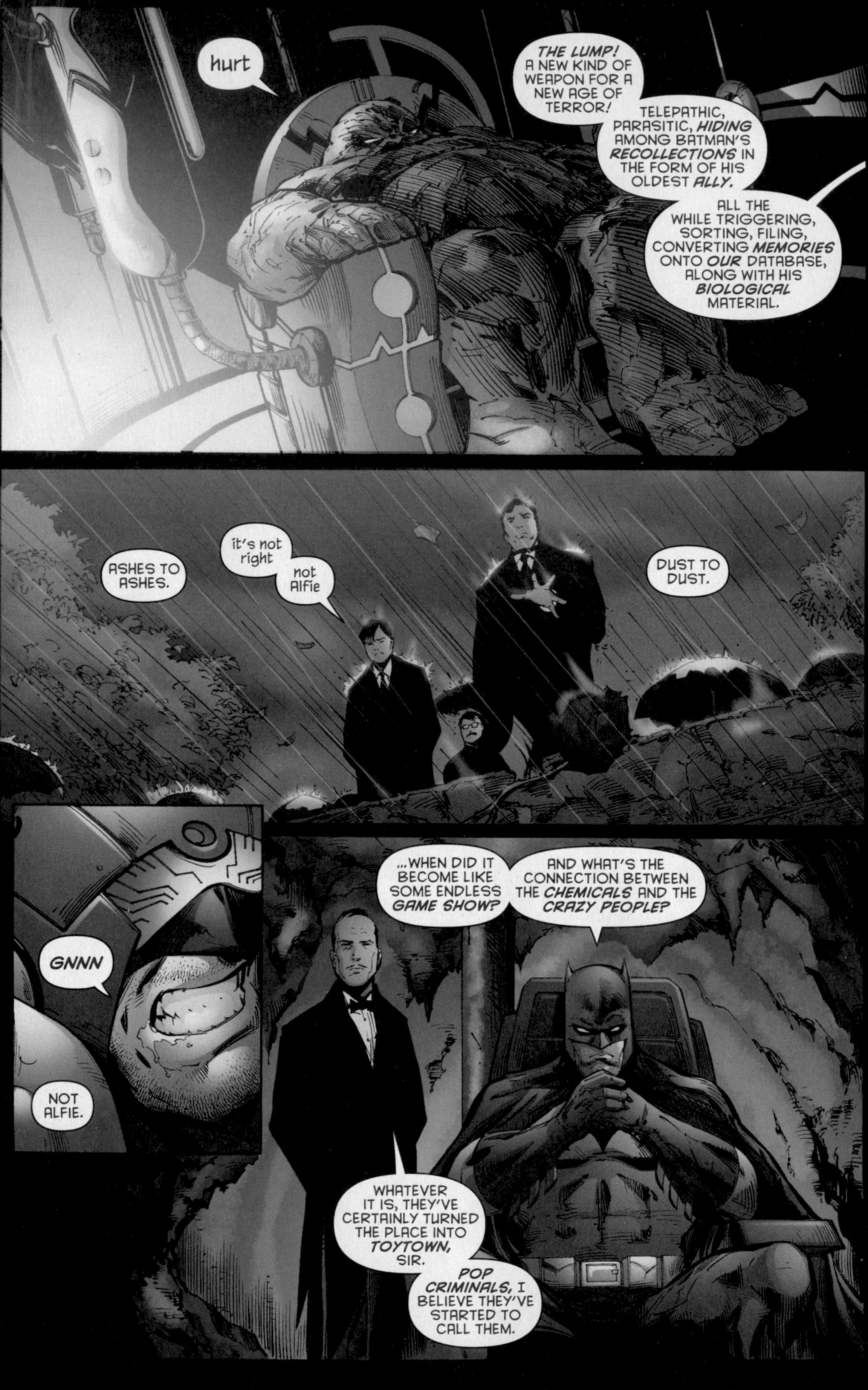
hurt
THE LUMP! A NEW KIND OF WEAPON FOR A NEW AGE OF TERROR!
TELEPATHIC, PARASITIC, HIDING AMONG BATMAN'S RECOLLECTIONS IN THE FORM OF HIS OLDEST ALLY.
ALL THE WHILE TRIGGERING, SORTING, FILING, CONVERTING MEMORIES ONTO OUR DATABASE, ALONG WITH HIS BIOLOGICAL MATERIAL.
ASHES TO ASHES.
it's not right
not Alfie
DUST TO DUST.
GNNN
NOT ALFIE.
...WHEN DID IT BECOME LIKE SOME ENDLESS GAME SHOW?
AND WHAT'S THE CONNECTION BETWEEN THE CHEMICALS AND THE CRAZY PEOPLE?
WHATEVER IT IS, THEY'VE CERTAINLY TURNED THE PLACE INTO TOYTOWN, SIR.
POP CRIMINALS, I BELIEVE THEY'VE STARTED TO CALL THEM.

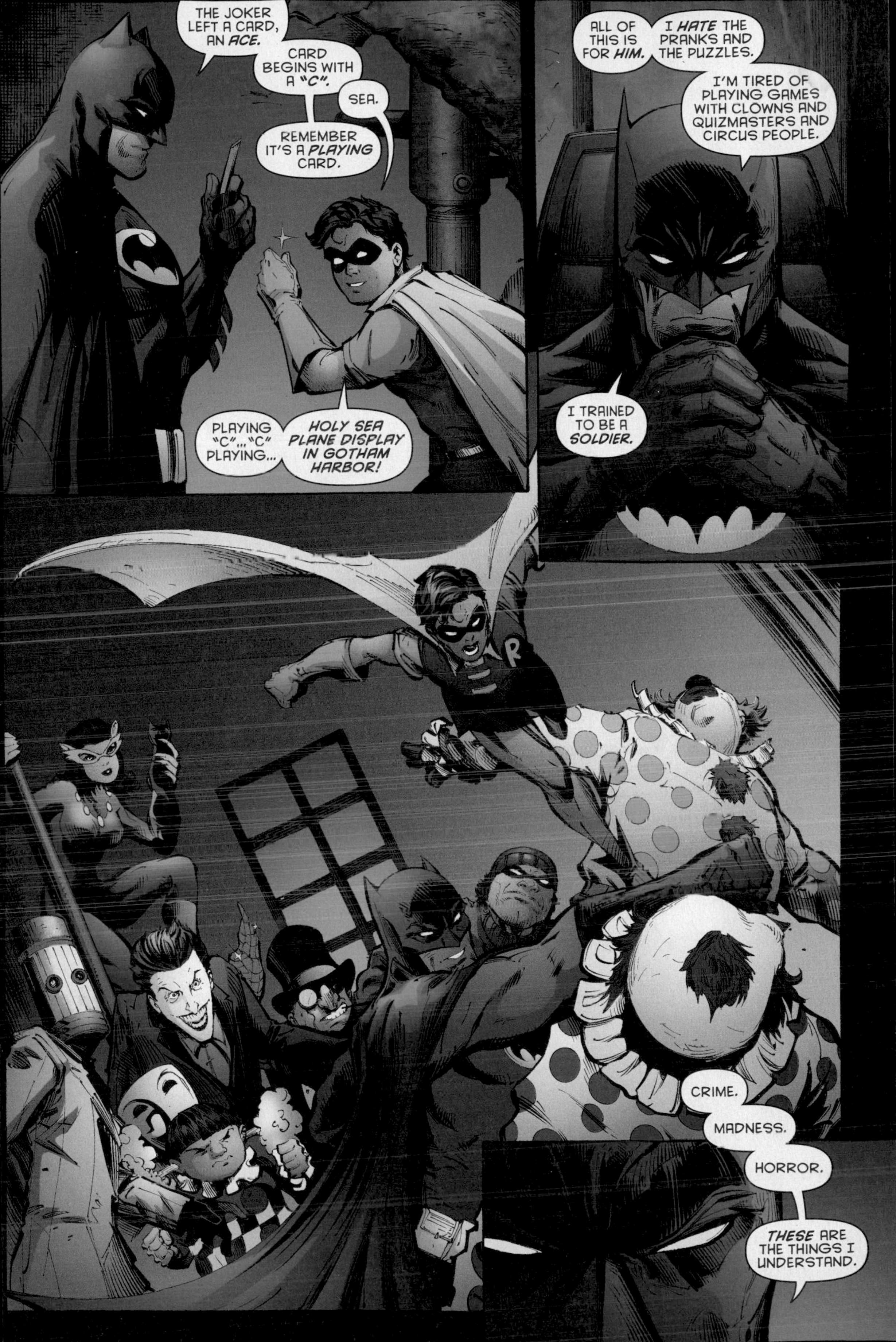
THE JOKER LEFT A CARD, AN ACE.
CARD BEGINS WITH A "C".
SEA.
REMEMBER IT'S A PLAYING CARD.
PLAYING "C"..."C" PLAYING...
HOLY SEA PLANE DISPLAY IN GOTHAM HARBOR!
ALL OF THIS IS FOR HIM.
I HATE THE PRANKS AND THE PUZZLES.
I'M TIRED OF PLAYING GAMES WITH CLOWNS AND QUIZMASTERS AND CIRCUS PEOPLE.
I TRAINED TO BE A SOLDIER.
CRIME.
MADNESS.
HORROR.
THESE ARE THE THINGS I UNDERSTAND.

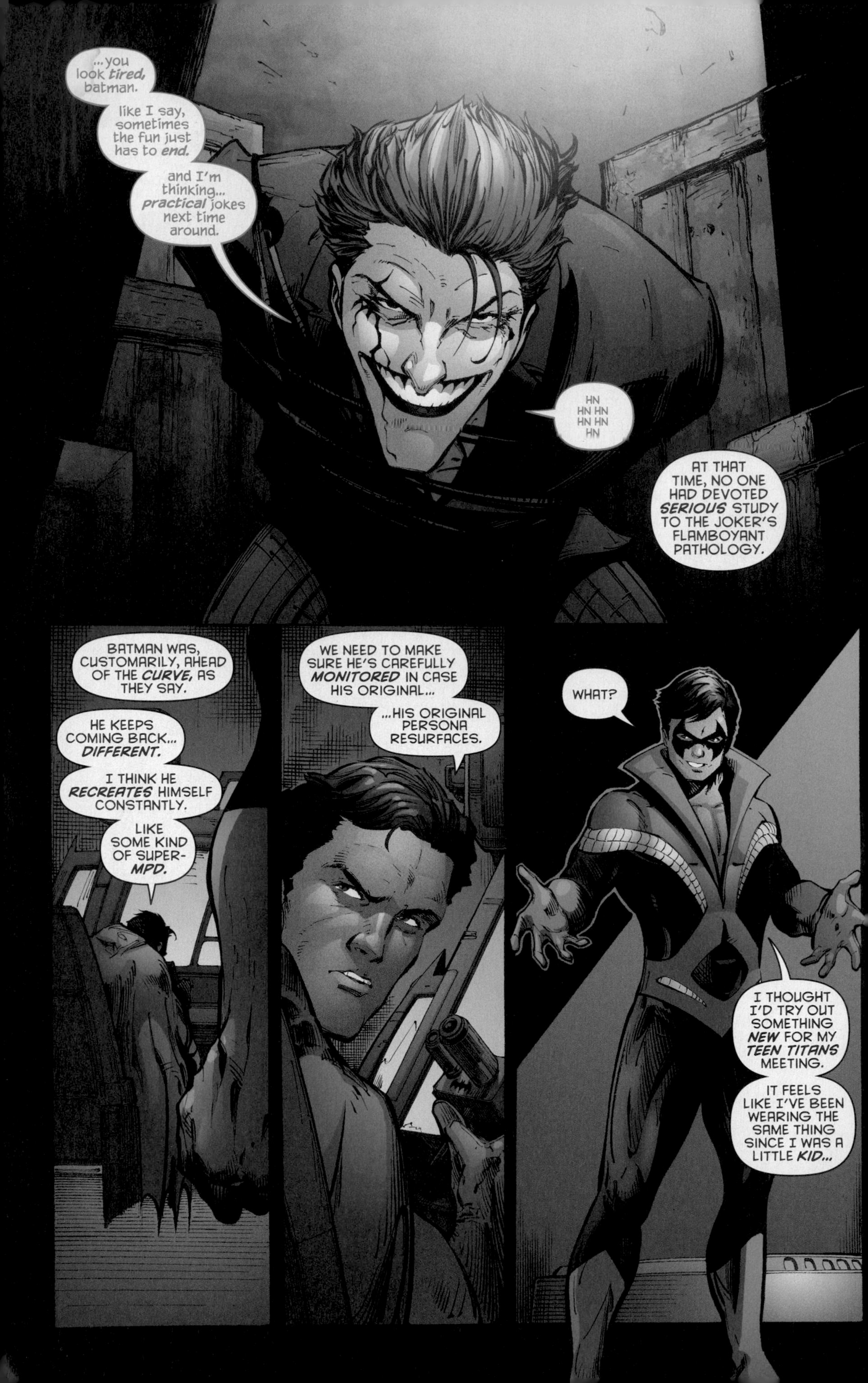
...you look *tired,* batman.
like I say, sometimes the fun just has to *end.*
and I'm thinking... *practical* jokes next time around.
HN HN HN HN HN HN
AT THAT TIME, NO ONE HAD DEVOTED *SERIOUS* STUDY TO THE JOKER'S FLAMBOYANT PATHOLOGY.
BATMAN WAS, CUSTOMARILY, AHEAD OF THE *CURVE,* AS THEY SAY.
HE KEEPS COMING BACK... *DIFFERENT.*
I THINK HE *RECREATES* HIMSELF CONSTANTLY.
LIKE SOME KIND OF SUPER-*MPD.*
WE NEED TO MAKE SURE HE'S CAREFULLY *MONITORED* IN CASE HIS ORIGINAL...
...HIS ORIGINAL PERSONA RESURFACES.
WHAT?
I THOUGHT I'D TRY OUT SOMETHING *NEW* FOR MY *TEEN TITANS* MEETING.
IT FEELS LIKE I'VE BEEN WEARING THE SAME THING SINCE I WAS A LITTLE *KID...*

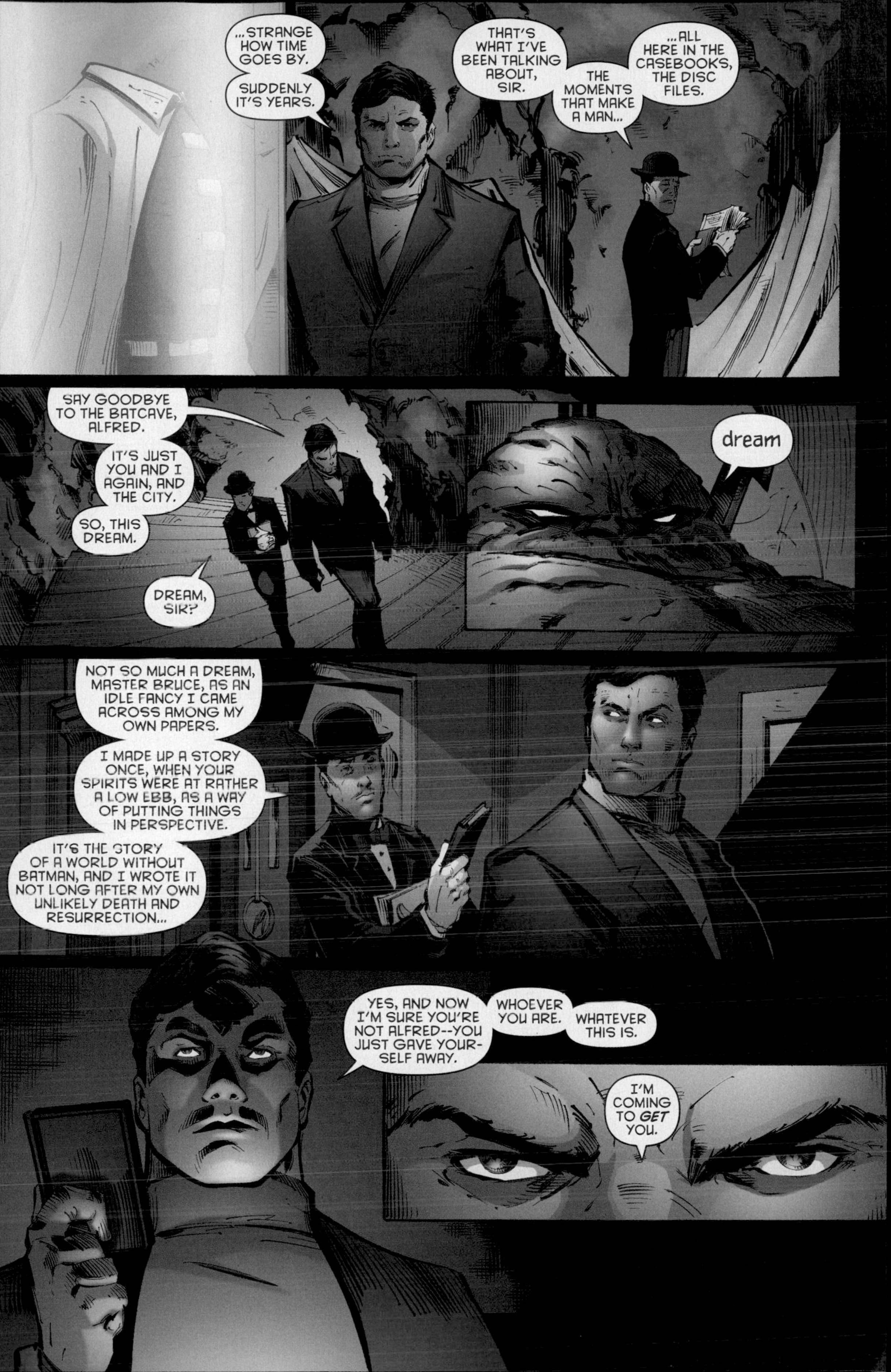
...STRANGE HOW TIME GOES BY.
SUDDENLY IT'S YEARS.
THAT'S WHAT I'VE BEEN TALKING ABOUT, SIR.
THE MOMENTS THAT MAKE A MAN...
...ALL HERE IN THE CASEBOOKS, THE DISC FILES.
SAY GOODBYE TO THE BATCAVE, ALFRED.
IT'S JUST YOU AND I AGAIN, AND THE CITY.
SO, THIS DREAM.
DREAM, SIR?
dream
NOT SO MUCH A DREAM, MASTER BRUCE, AS AN IDLE FANCY I CAME ACROSS AMONG MY OWN PAPERS.
I MADE UP A STORY ONCE, WHEN YOUR SPIRITS WERE AT RATHER A LOW EBB, AS A WAY OF PUTTING THINGS IN PERSPECTIVE.
IT'S THE STORY OF A WORLD WITHOUT BATMAN, AND I WROTE IT NOT LONG AFTER MY OWN UNLIKELY DEATH AND RESURRECTION...
YES, AND NOW I'M SURE YOU'RE NOT ALFRED--YOU JUST GAVE YOURSELF AWAY.
WHOEVER YOU ARE.
WHATEVER THIS IS.
I'M COMING TO GET YOU.

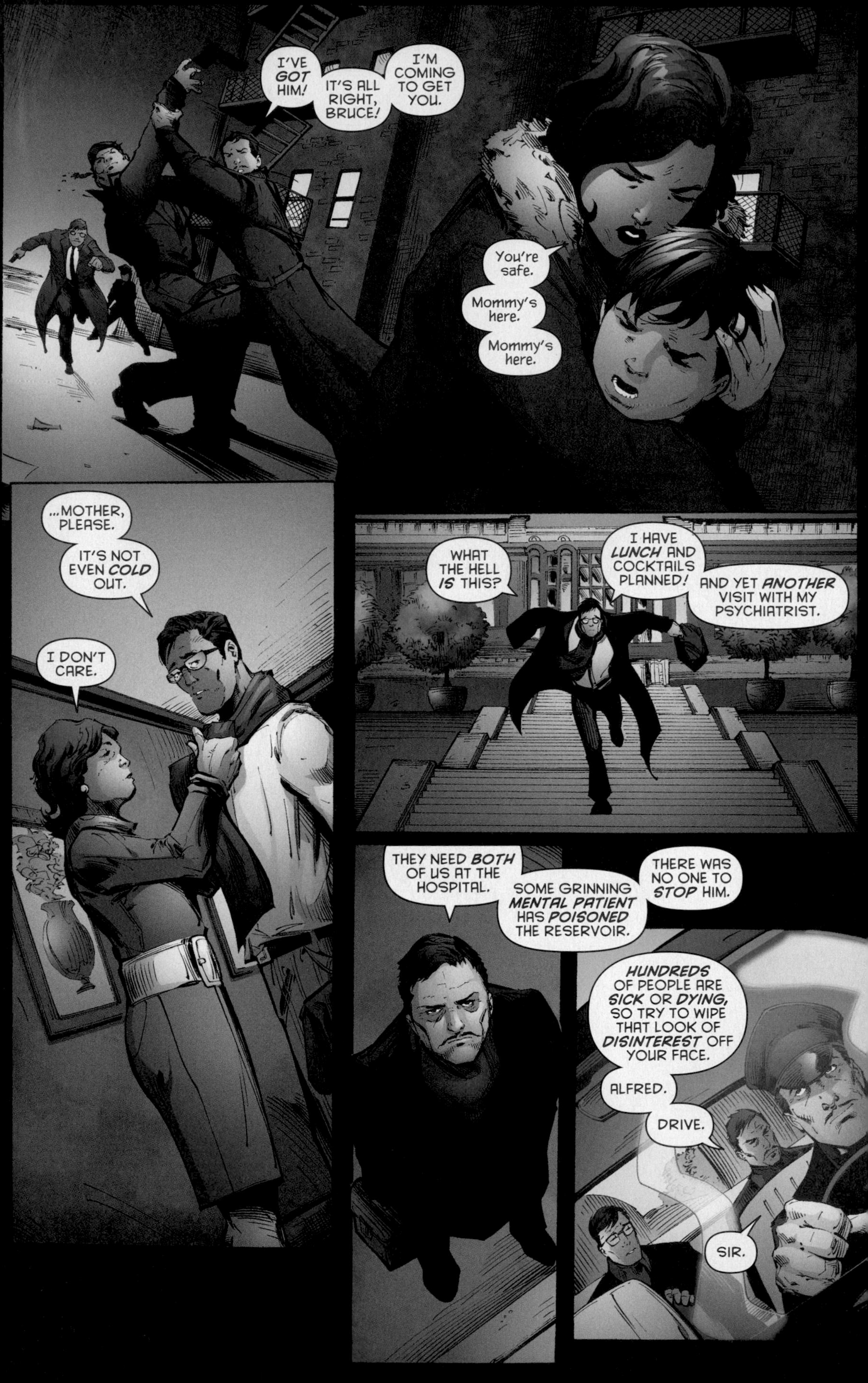
I'VE GOT HIM!
IT'S ALL RIGHT, BRUCE!
I'M COMING TO GET YOU.
You're safe.
Mommy's here.
Mommy's here.
...MOTHER, PLEASE.
IT'S NOT EVEN COLD OUT.
I DON'T CARE.
WHAT THE HELL IS THIS?
I HAVE LUNCH AND COCKTAILS PLANNED!
AND YET ANOTHER VISIT WITH MY PSYCHIATRIST.
THEY NEED BOTH OF US AT THE HOSPITAL.
SOME GRINNING MENTAL PATIENT HAS POISONED THE RESERVOIR.
THERE WAS NO ONE TO STOP HIM.
HUNDREDS OF PEOPLE ARE SICK OR DYING, SO TRY TO WIPE THAT LOOK OF DISINTEREST OFF YOUR FACE.
ALFRED.
DRIVE.
SIR.

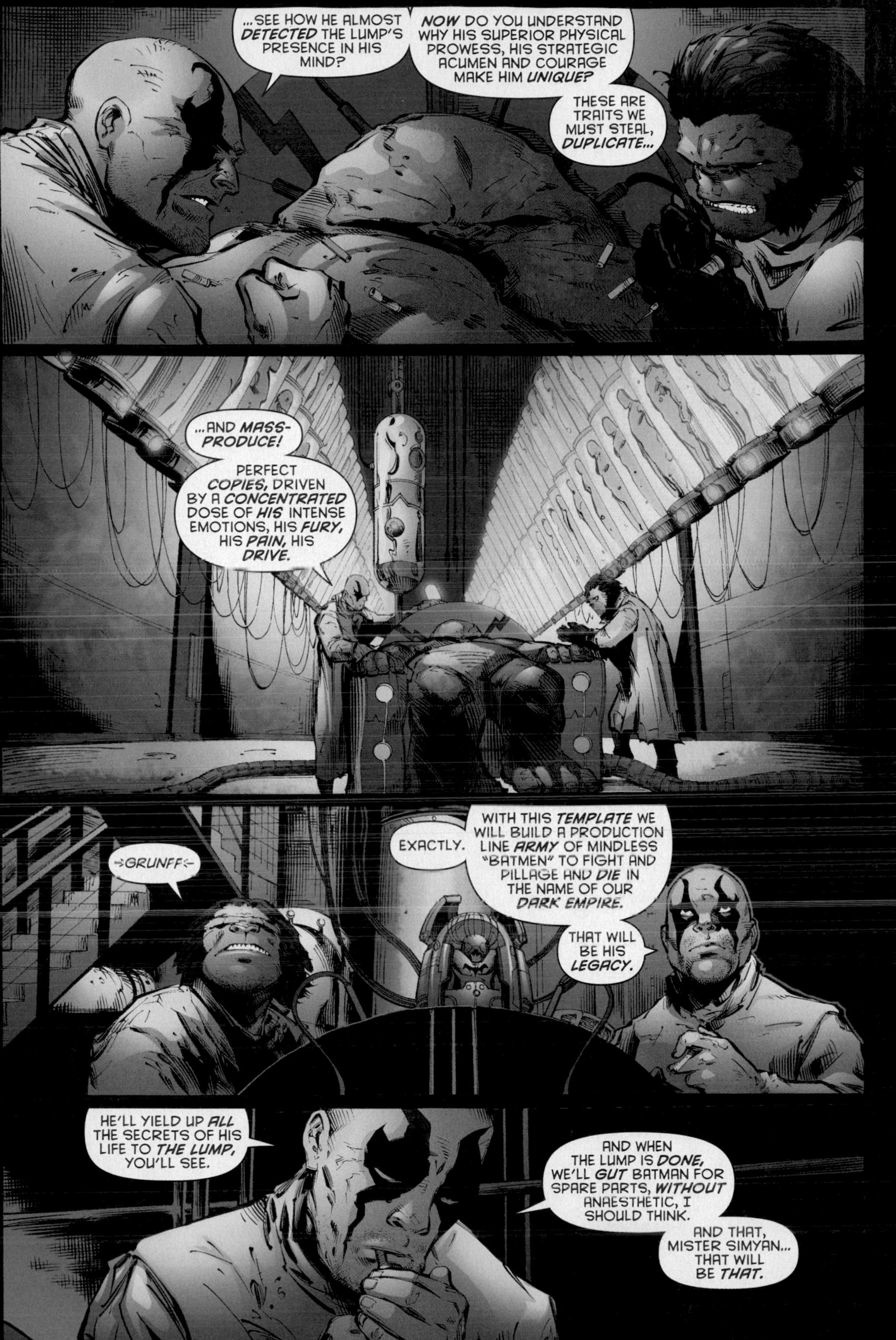
...SEE HOW HE ALMOST DETECTED THE LUMP'S PRESENCE IN HIS MIND?
NOW DO YOU UNDERSTAND WHY HIS SUPERIOR PHYSICAL PROWESS, HIS STRATEGIC ACUMEN AND COURAGE MAKE HIM UNIQUE?
THESE ARE TRAITS WE MUST STEAL, DUPLICATE...
...AND MASS-PRODUCE!
PERFECT COPIES, DRIVEN BY A CONCENTRATED DOSE OF HIS INTENSE EMOTIONS, HIS FURY, HIS PAIN, HIS DRIVE.
-GRUNFF-
EXACTLY.
WITH THIS TEMPLATE WE WILL BUILD A PRODUCTION LINE ARMY OF MINDLESS "BATMEN" TO FIGHT AND PILLAGE AND DIE IN THE NAME OF OUR DARK EMPIRE.
THAT WILL BE HIS LEGACY.
HE'LL YIELD UP ALL THE SECRETS OF HIS LIFE TO THE LUMP, YOU'LL SEE.
AND WHEN THE LUMP IS DONE, WE'LL GUT BATMAN FOR SPARE PARTS, WITHOUT ANAESTHETIC, I SHOULD THINK.
AND THAT, MISTER SIMYAN... THAT WILL BE THAT.

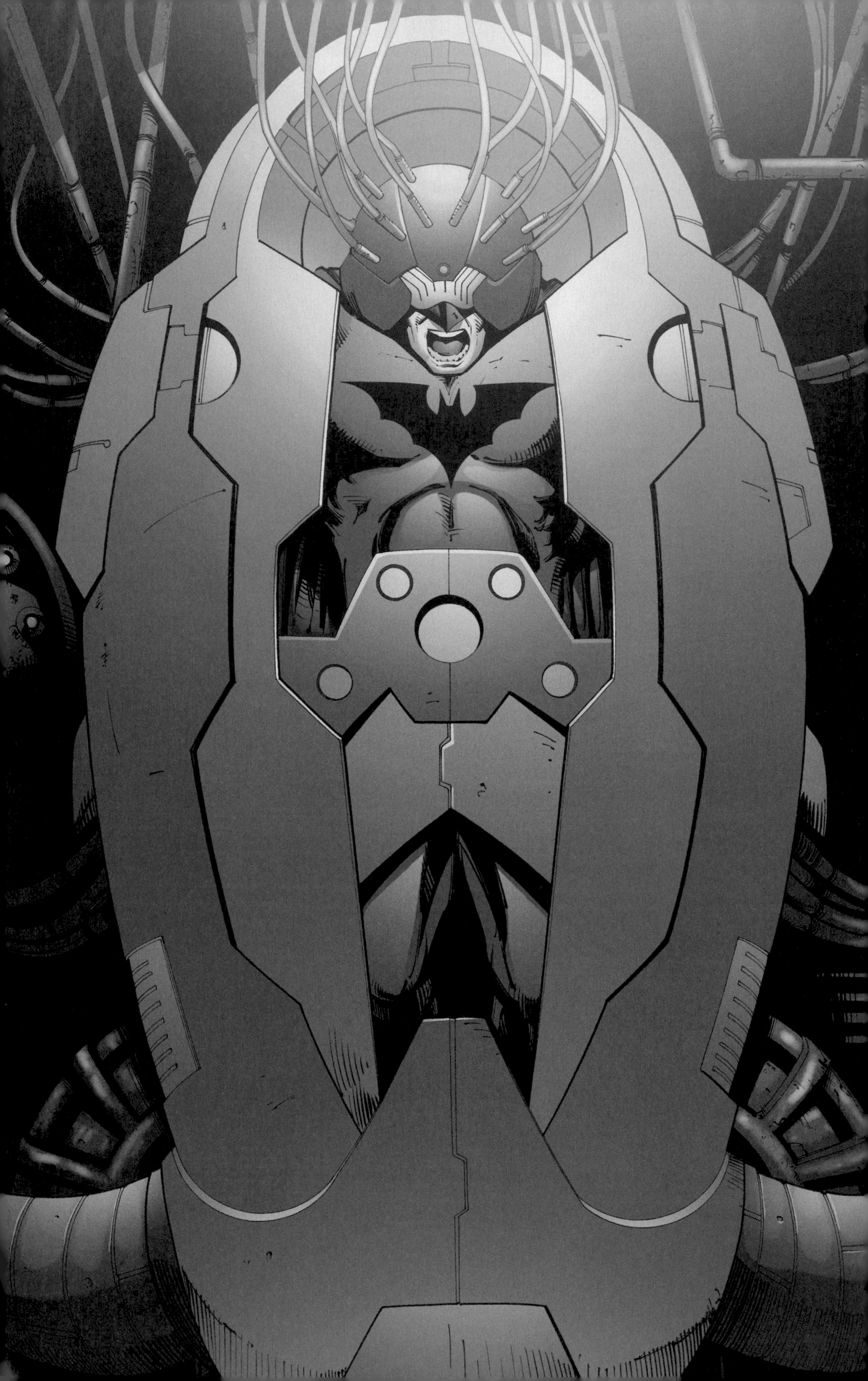

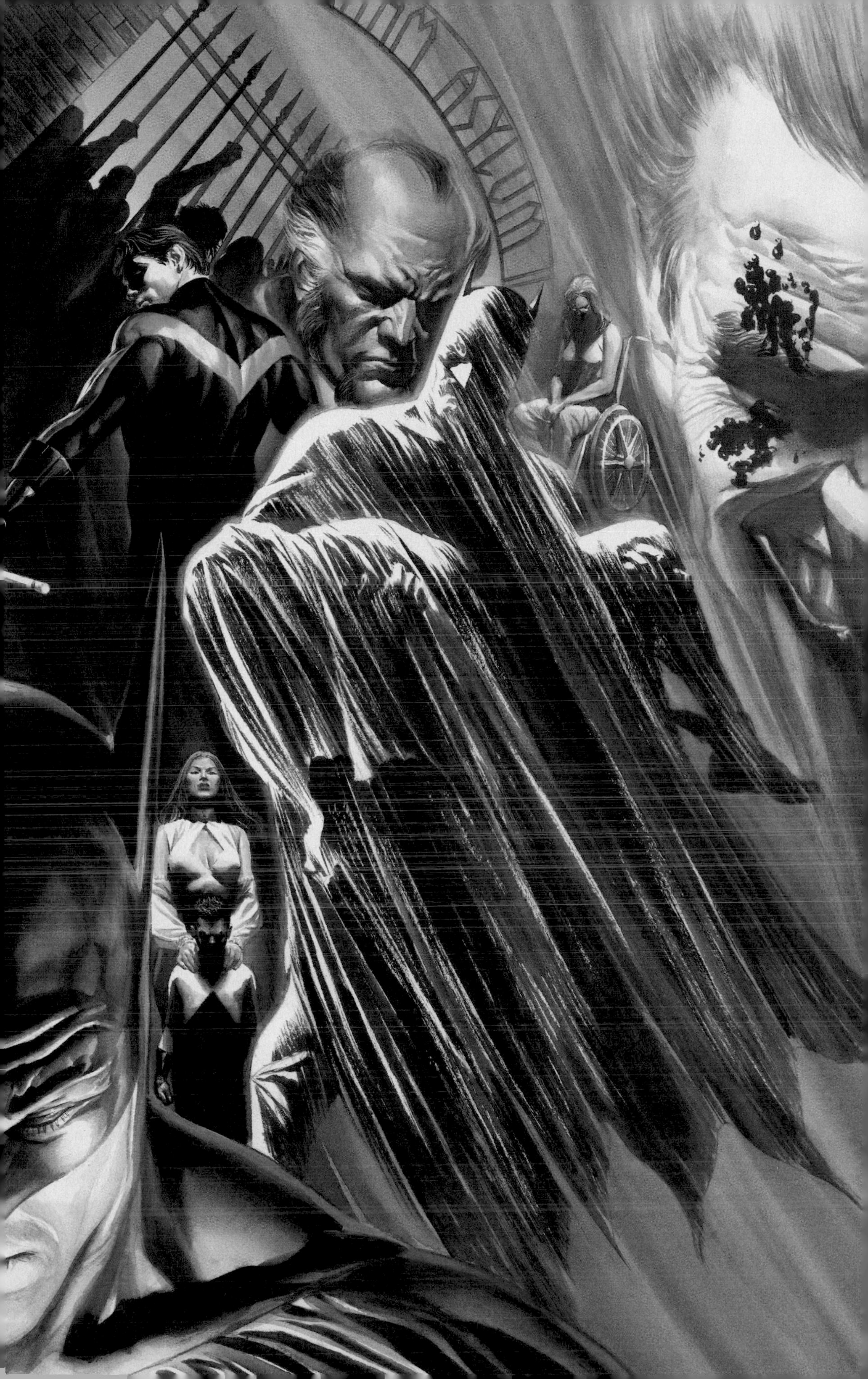
ASYLUM

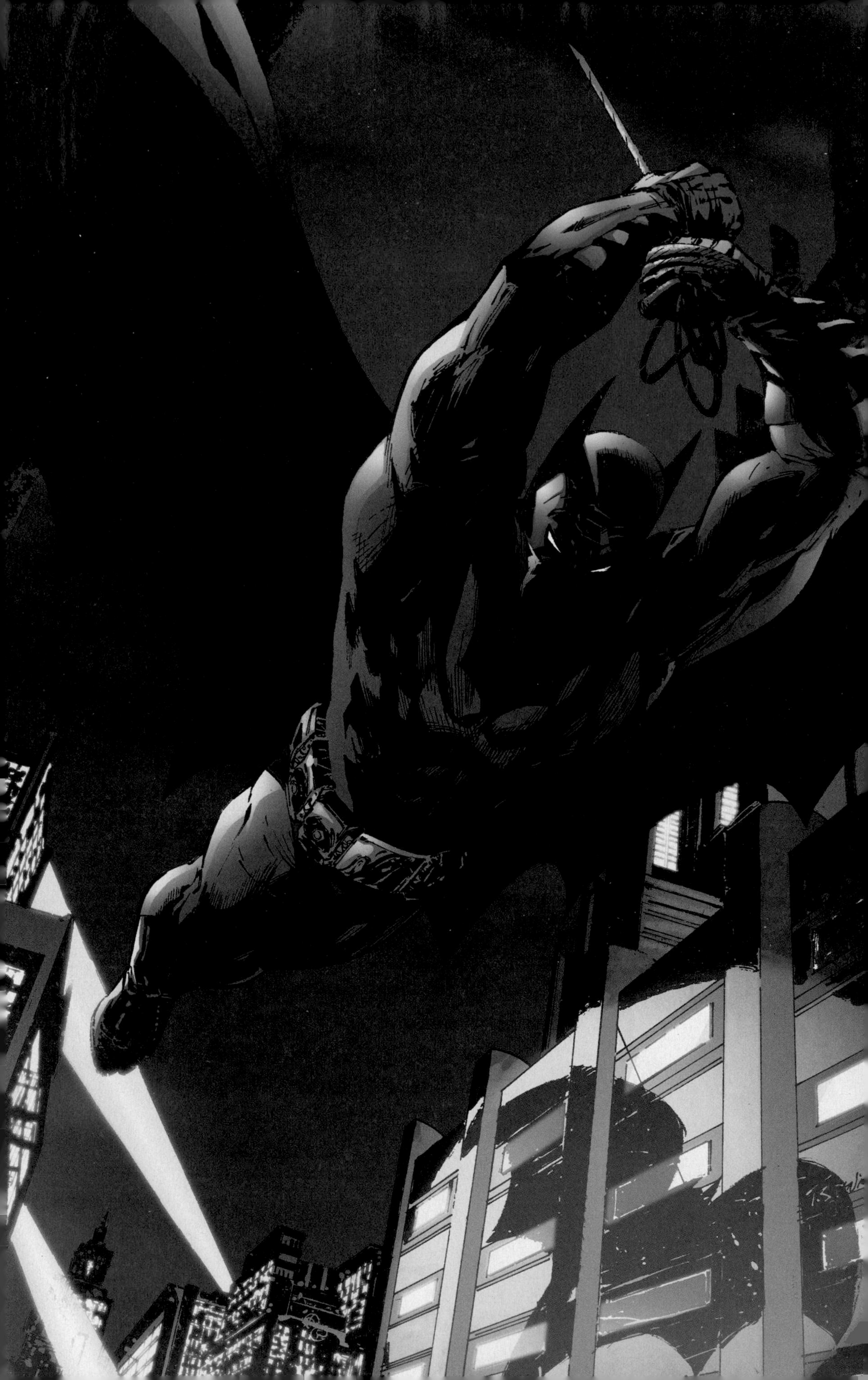

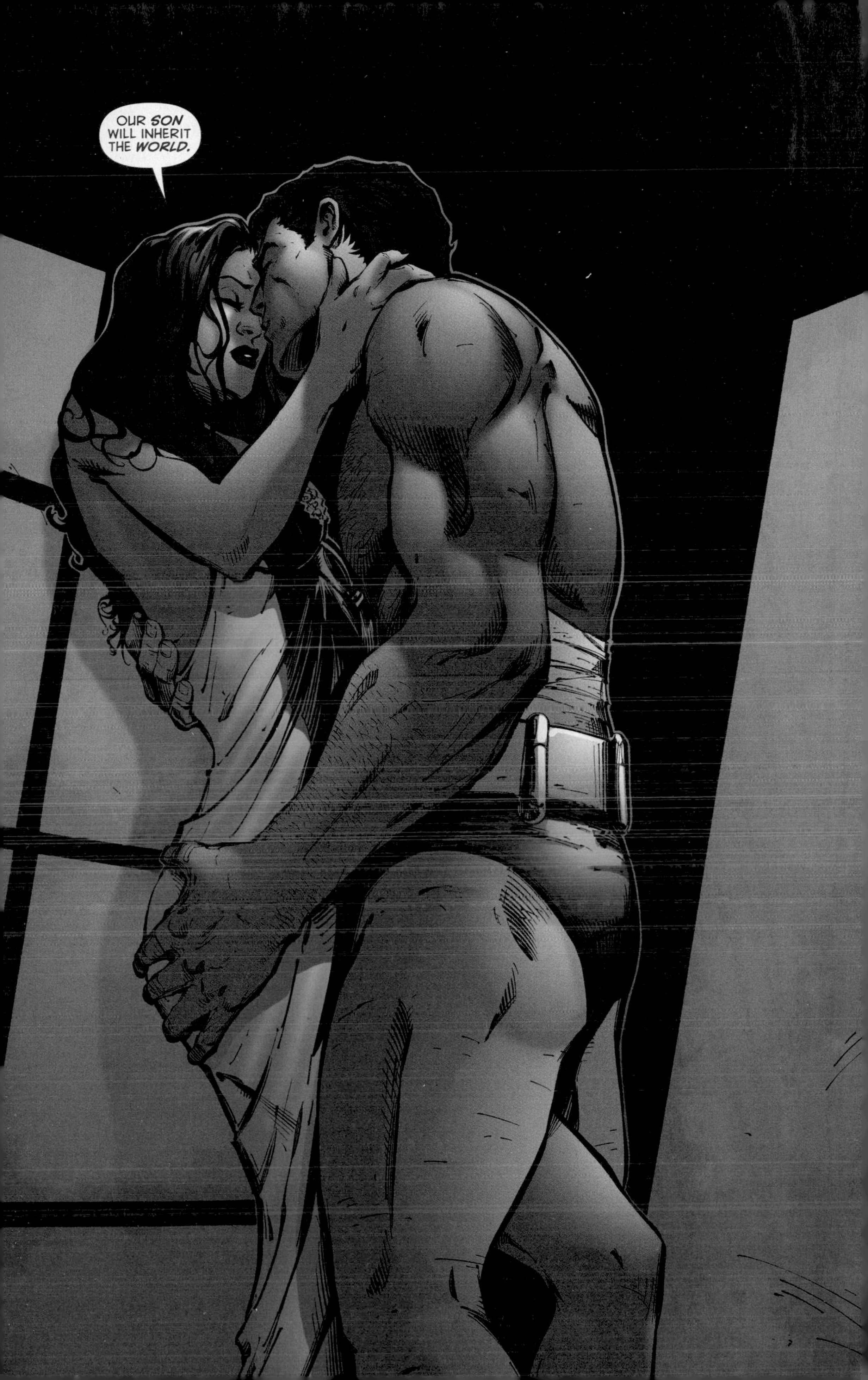
OUR *SON* WILL INHERIT THE *WORLD.*

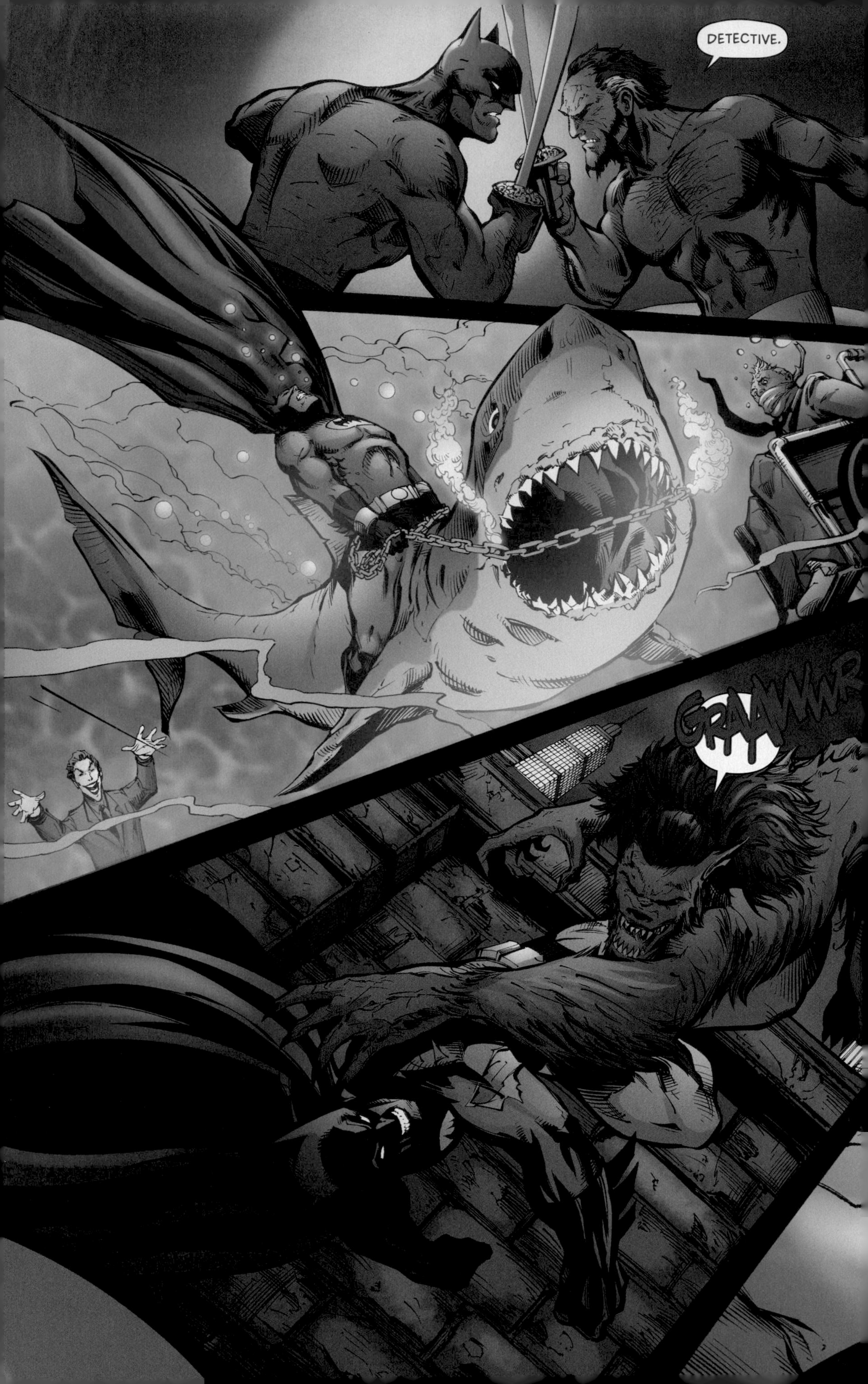
DETECTIVE.
GRAAWWR

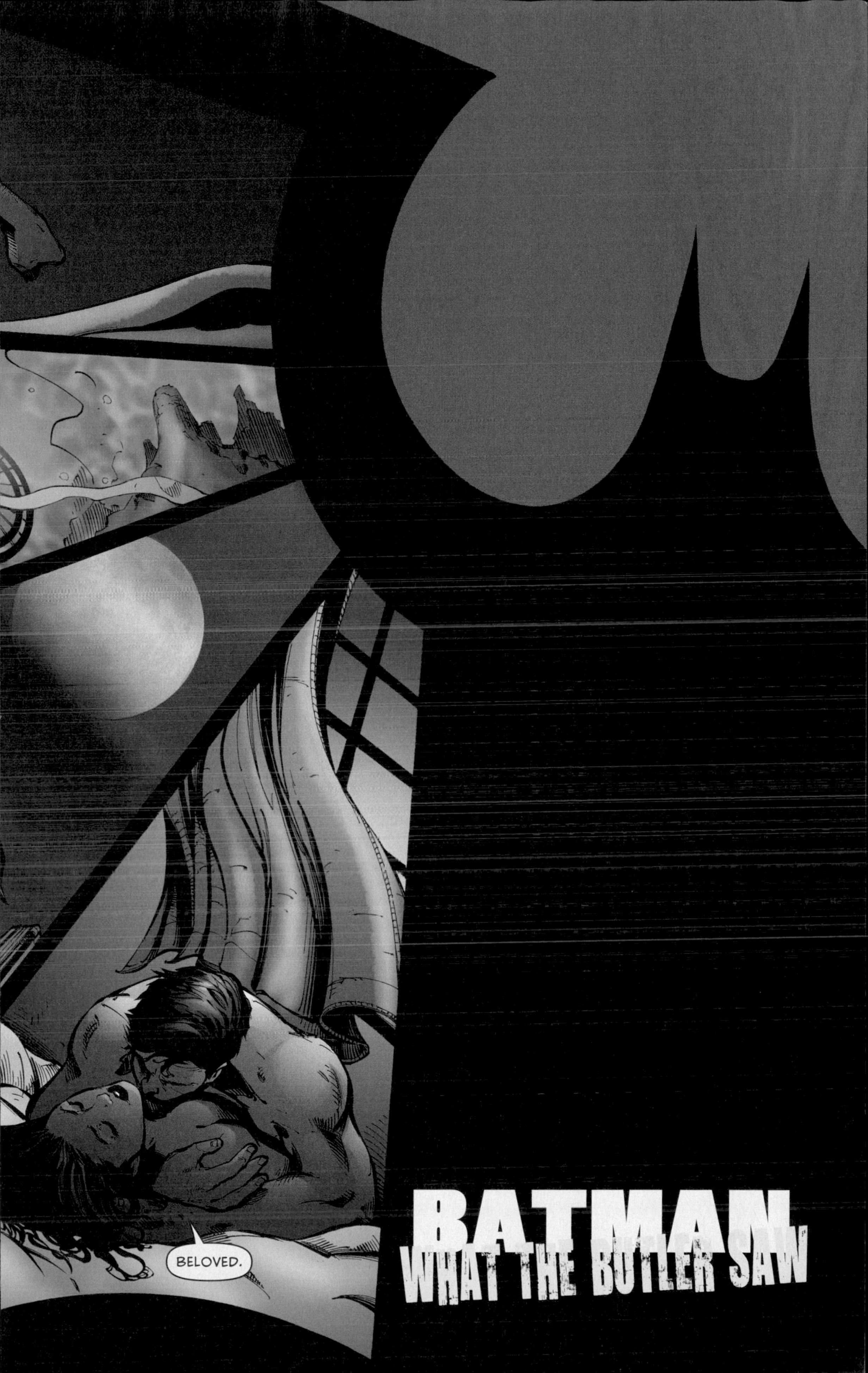
BELOVED.
BATMAN
WHAT THE BUTLER SAW

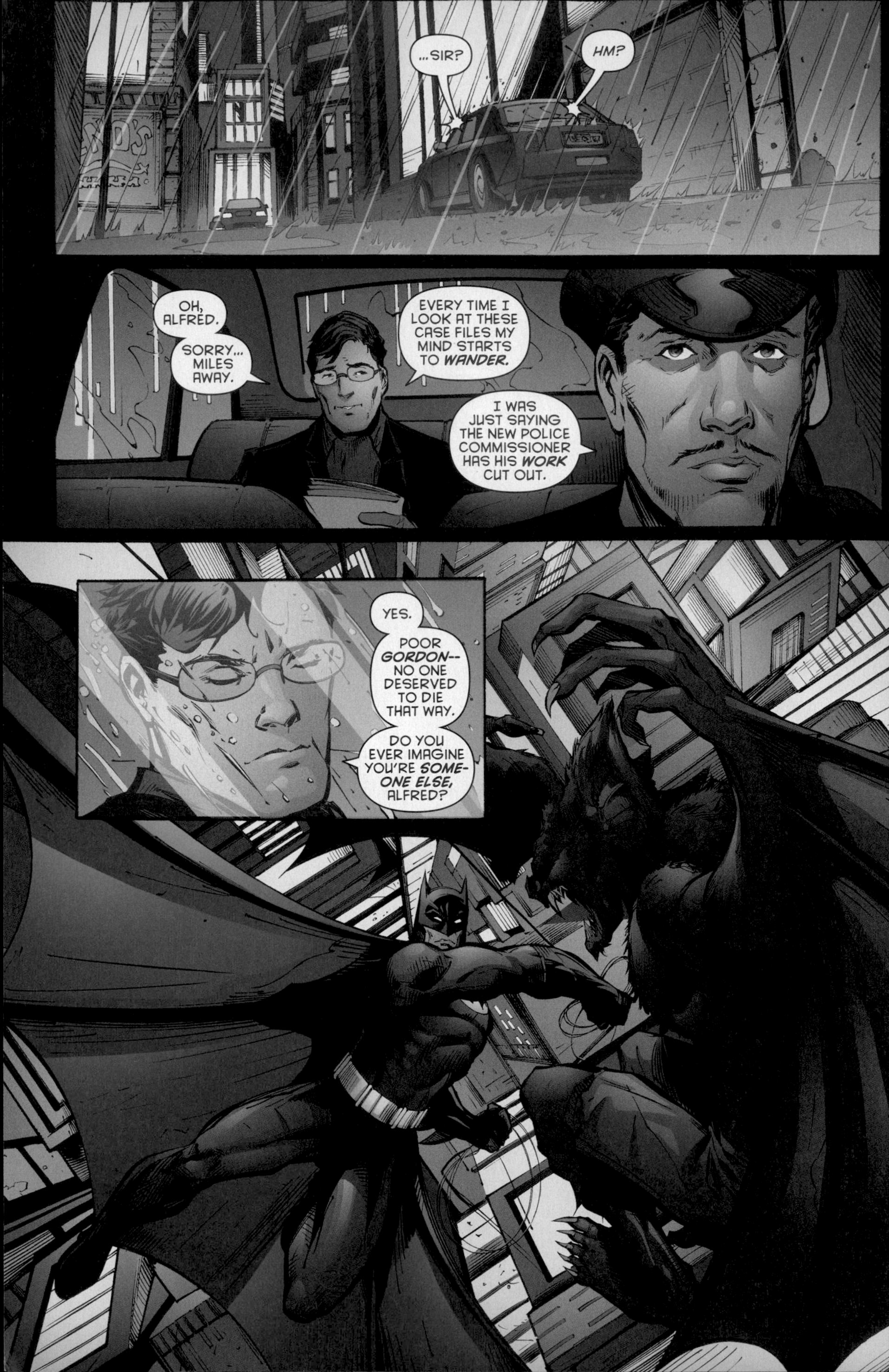
...SIR?
HM?
OH, ALFRED.
SORRY... MILES AWAY.
EVERY TIME I LOOK AT THESE CASE FILES MY MIND STARTS TO *WANDER.*
I WAS JUST SAYING THE NEW POLICE COMMISSIONER HAS HIS *WORK* CUT OUT.
YES.
POOR *GORDON--* NO ONE DESERVED TO DIE THAT WAY.
DO YOU EVER IMAGINE YOU'RE *SOMEONE ELSE,* ALFRED?

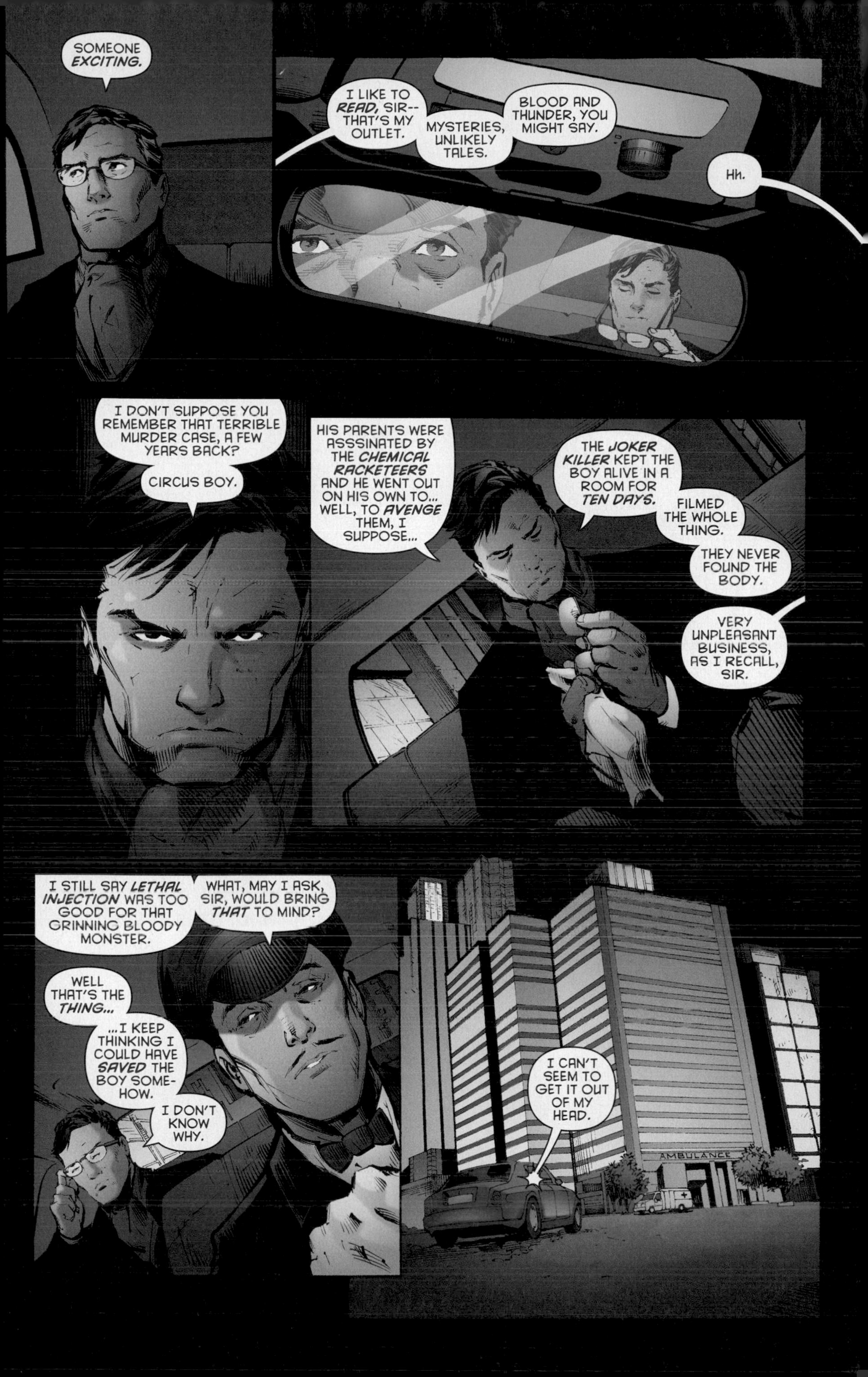
SOMEONE EXCITING.
I LIKE TO READ, SIR-- THAT'S MY OUTLET.
MYSTERIES, UNLIKELY TALES.
BLOOD AND THUNDER, YOU MIGHT SAY.
Hh.
I DON'T SUPPOSE YOU REMEMBER THAT TERRIBLE MURDER CASE, A FEW YEARS BACK?
CIRCUS BOY.
HIS PARENTS WERE ASSSINATED BY THE CHEMICAL RACKETEERS AND HE WENT OUT ON HIS OWN TO... WELL, TO AVENGE THEM, I SUPPOSE...
THE JOKER KILLER KEPT THE BOY ALIVE IN A ROOM FOR TEN DAYS.
FILMED THE WHOLE THING.
THEY NEVER FOUND THE BODY.
VERY UNPLEASANT BUSINESS, AS I RECALL, SIR.
I STILL SAY LETHAL INJECTION WAS TOO GOOD FOR THAT GRINNING BLOODY MONSTER.
WHAT, MAY I ASK, SIR, WOULD BRING THAT TO MIND?
WELL THAT'S THE THING...
...I KEEP THINKING I COULD HAVE SAVED THE BOY SOMEHOW.
I DON'T KNOW WHY.
I CAN'T SEEM TO GET IT OUT OF MY HEAD.
AMBULANCE

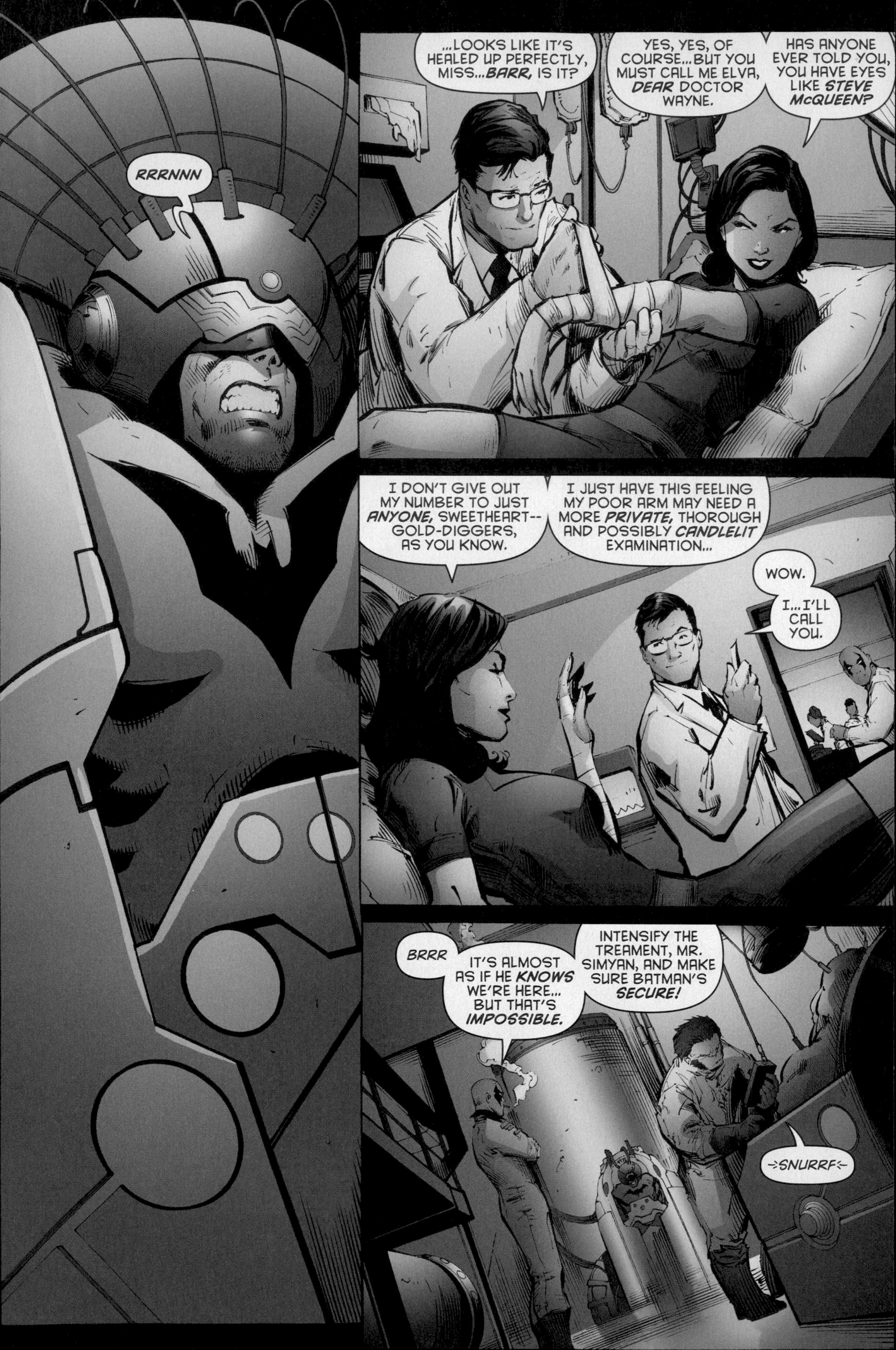
RRRNNN
...LOOKS LIKE IT'S HEALED UP PERFECTLY, MISS...BARR, IS IT?
YES, YES, OF COURSE...BUT YOU MUST CALL ME ELVA, DEAR DOCTOR WAYNE.
HAS ANYONE EVER TOLD YOU, YOU HAVE EYES LIKE STEVE McQUEEN?
I DON'T GIVE OUT MY NUMBER TO JUST ANYONE, SWEETHEART--GOLD-DIGGERS, AS YOU KNOW.
I JUST HAVE THIS FEELING MY POOR ARM MAY NEED A MORE PRIVATE, THOROUGH AND POSSIBLY CANDLELIT EXAMINATION...
WOW.
I...I'LL CALL YOU.
BRRR
IT'S ALMOST AS IF HE KNOWS WE'RE HERE... BUT THAT'S IMPOSSIBLE.
INTENSIFY THE TREAMENT, MR. SIMYAN, AND MAKE SURE BATMAN'S SECURE!
SNURRF

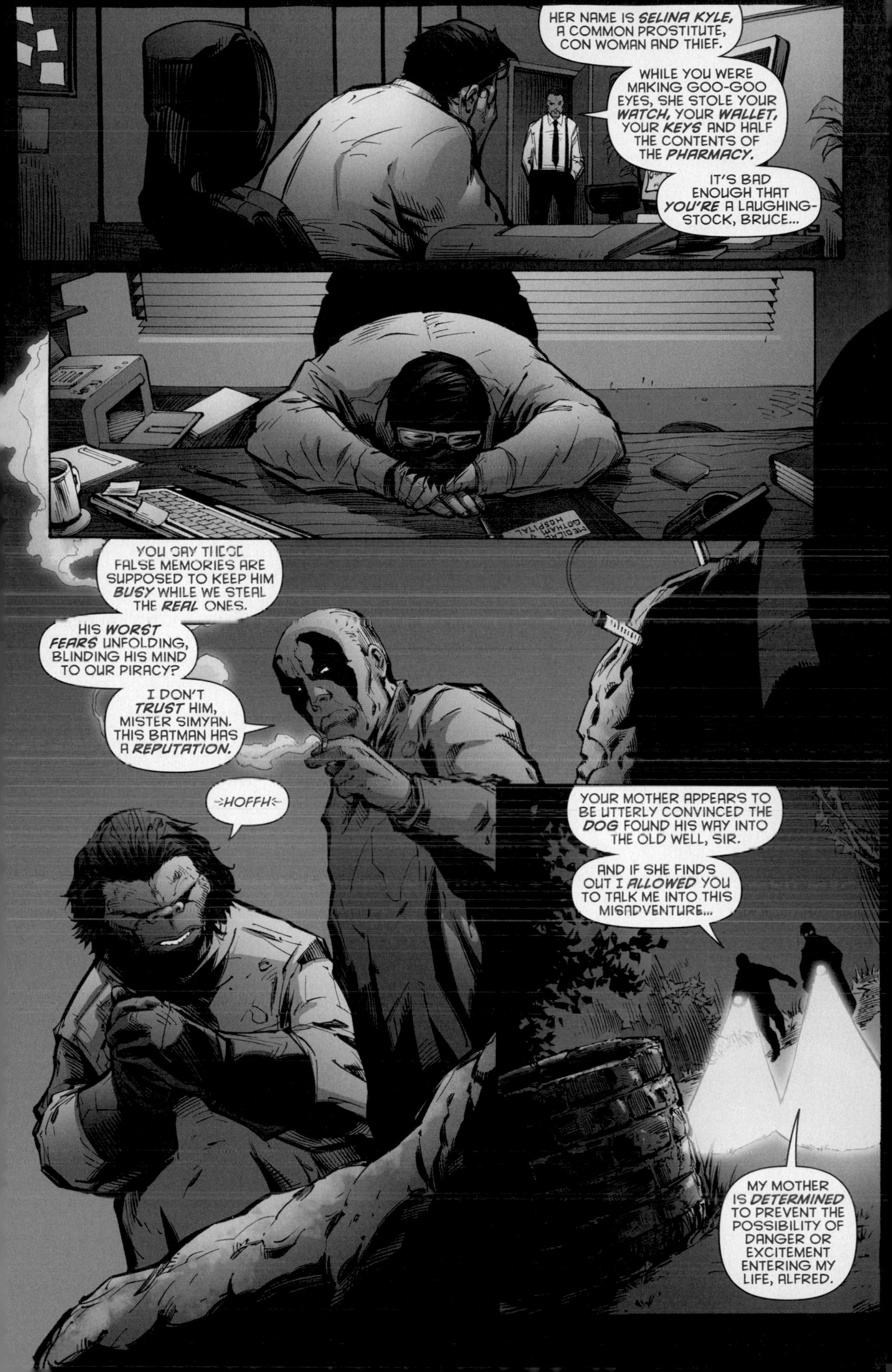
HER NAME IS SELINA KYLE, A COMMON PROSTITUTE, CON WOMAN AND THIEF.
WHILE YOU WERE MAKING GOO-GOO EYES, SHE STOLE YOUR WATCH, YOUR WALLET, YOUR KEYS AND HALF THE CONTENTS OF THE PHARMACY.
IT'S BAD ENOUGH THAT YOU'RE A LAUGHING-STOCK, BRUCE...
YOU SAY THESE FALSE MEMORIES ARE SUPPOSED TO KEEP HIM BUSY WHILE WE STEAL THE REAL ONES.
HIS WORST FEARS UNFOLDING, BLINDING HIS MIND TO OUR PIRACY?
I DON'T TRUST HIM, MISTER SIMYAN. THIS BATMAN HAS A REPUTATION.
HOFFH
YOUR MOTHER APPEARS TO BE UTTERLY CONVINCED THE DOG FOUND HIS WAY INTO THE OLD WELL, SIR.
AND IF SHE FINDS OUT I ALLOWED YOU TO TALK ME INTO THIS MISADVENTURE...
MY MOTHER IS DETERMINED TO PREVENT THE POSSIBILITY OF DANGER OR EXCITEMENT ENTERING MY LIFE, ALFRED.

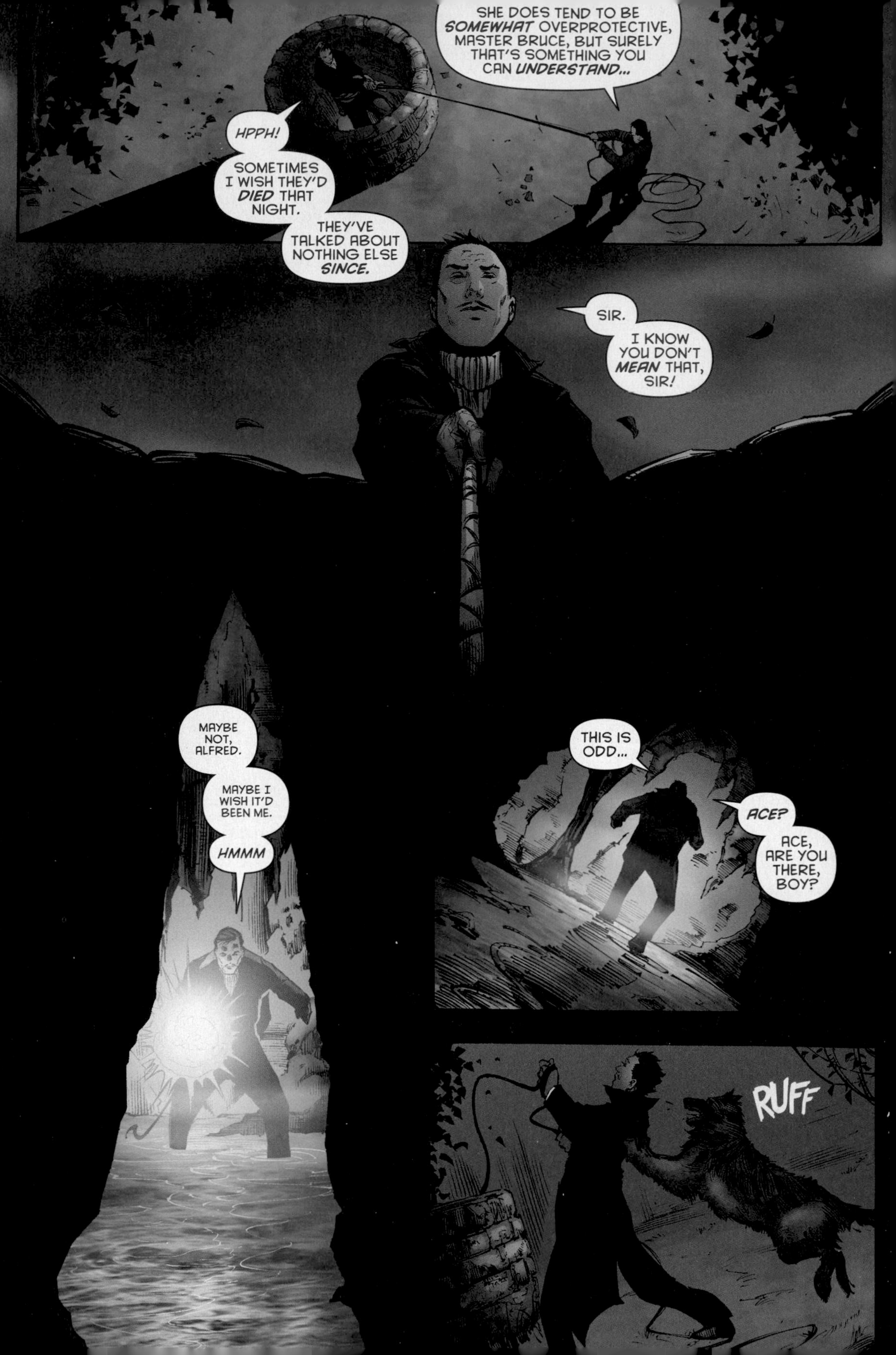
SHE DOES TEND TO BE SOMEWHAT OVERPROTECTIVE, MASTER BRUCE, BUT SURELY THAT'S SOMETHING YOU CAN UNDERSTAND...
HPPH!
SOMETIMES I WISH THEY'D DIED THAT NIGHT.
THEY'VE TALKED ABOUT NOTHING ELSE SINCE.
SIR.
I KNOW YOU DON'T MEAN THAT, SIR!
MAYBE NOT, ALFRED.
MAYBE I WISH IT'D BEEN ME.
HMMM
THIS IS ODD...
ACE?
ACE, ARE YOU THERE, BOY?
RUFF

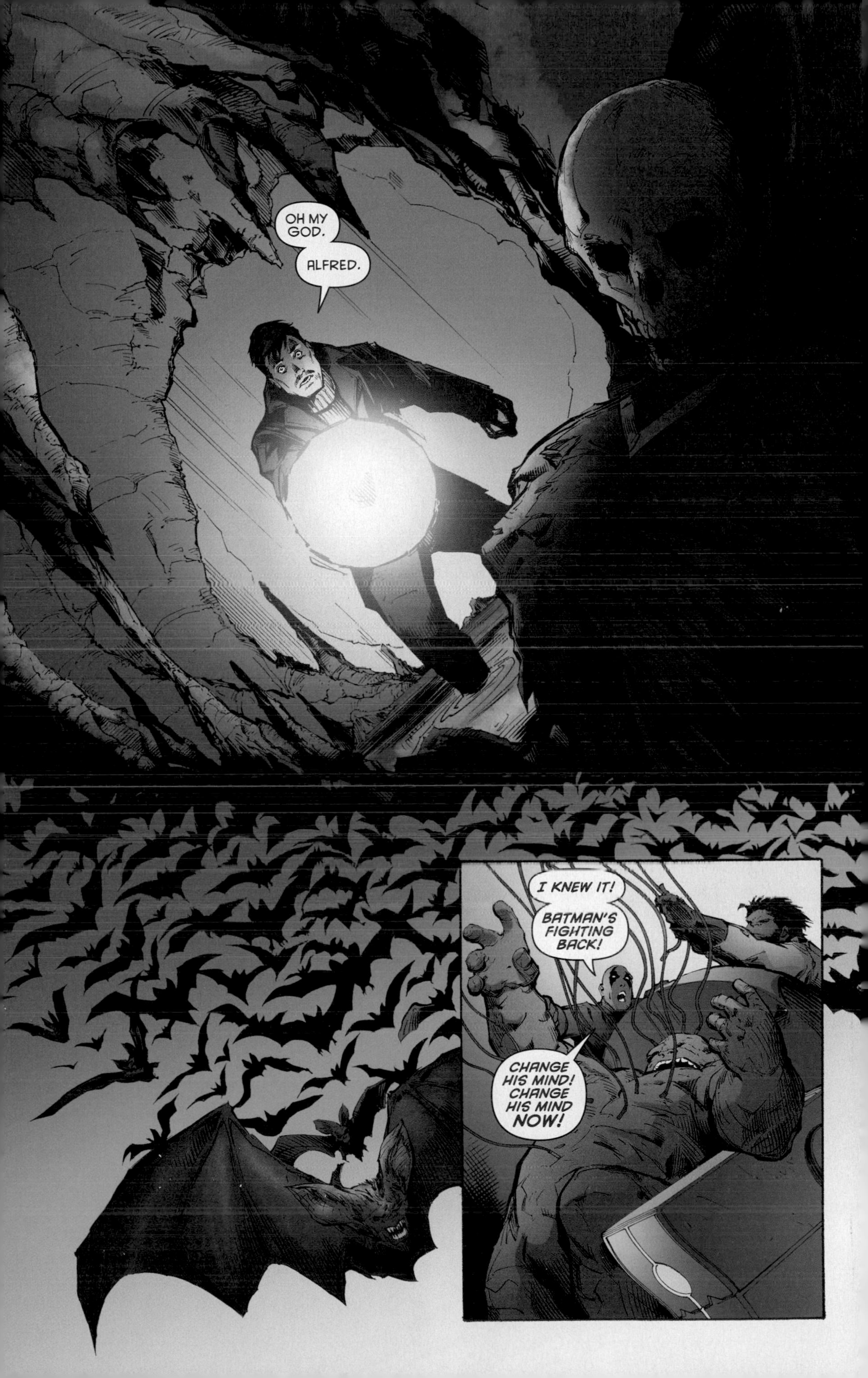
OH MY GOD.
ALFRED.
I KNEW IT!
BATMAN'S FIGHTING BACK!
CHANGE HIS MIND! CHANGE HIS MIND NOW!

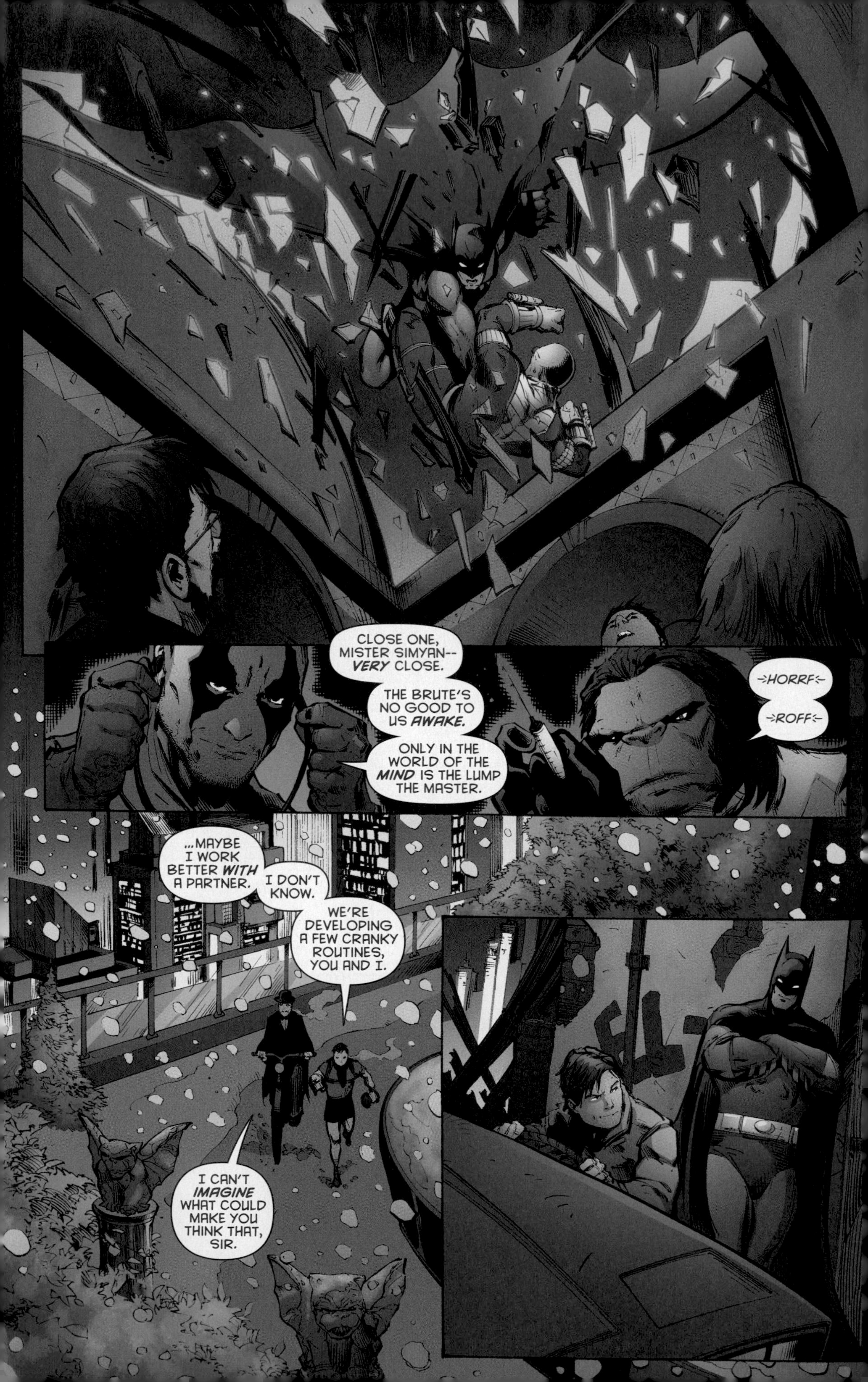
CLOSE ONE, MISTER SIMYAN-- VERY CLOSE.
THE BRUTE'S NO GOOD TO US AWAKE.
ONLY IN THE WORLD OF THE MIND IS THE LUMP THE MASTER.
-HORRF-
-ROFF-
...MAYBE I WORK BETTER WITH A PARTNER.
I DON'T KNOW.
WE'RE DEVELOPING A FEW CRANKY ROUTINES, YOU AND I.
I CAN'T IMAGINE WHAT COULD MAKE YOU THINK THAT, SIR.

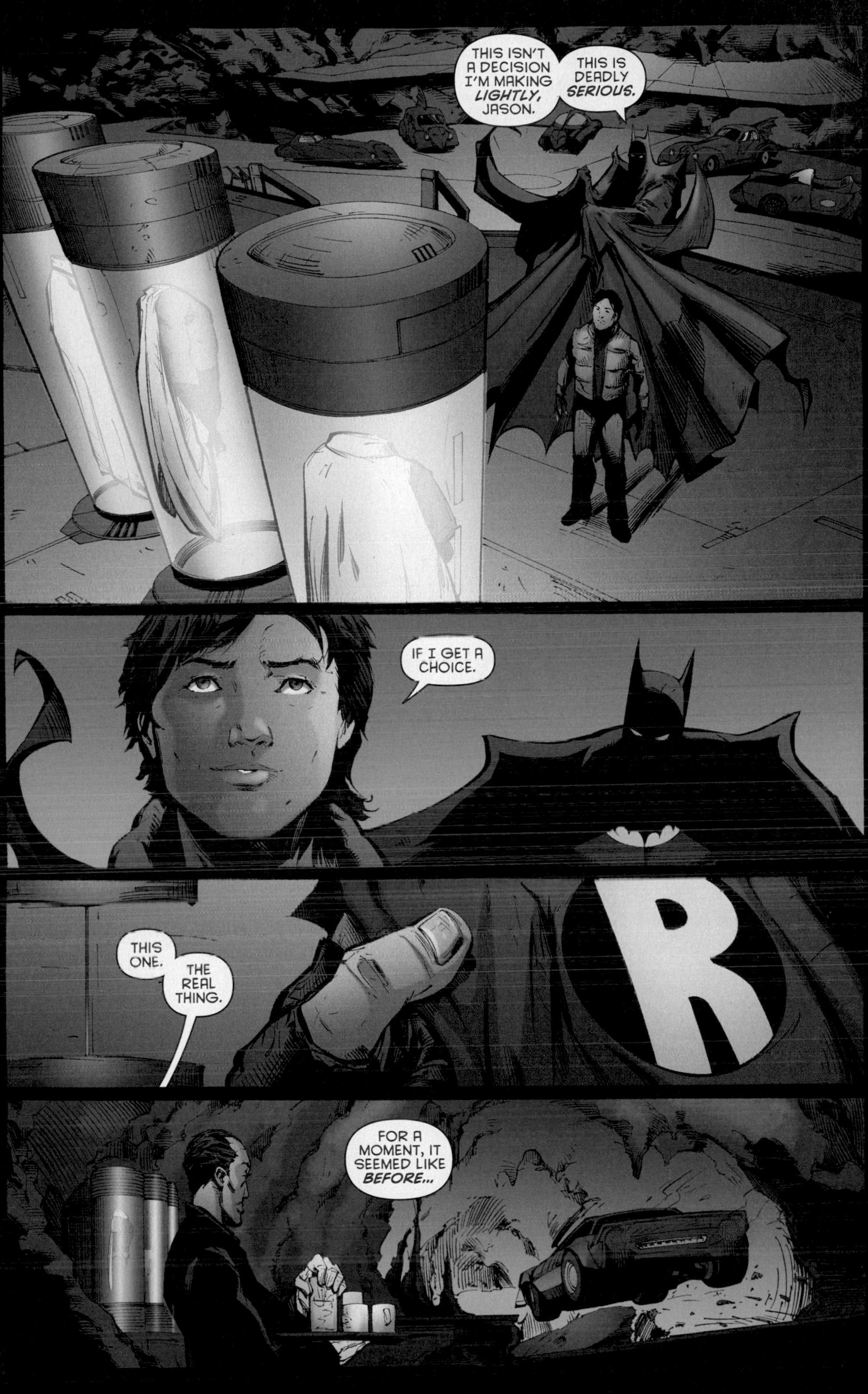
THIS ISN'T A DECISION I'M MAKING *LIGHTLY,* JASON.
THIS IS DEADLY *SERIOUS.*
IF I GET A CHOICE.
THIS ONE.
THE REAL THING.
FOR A MOMENT, IT SEEMED LIKE *BEFORE...*

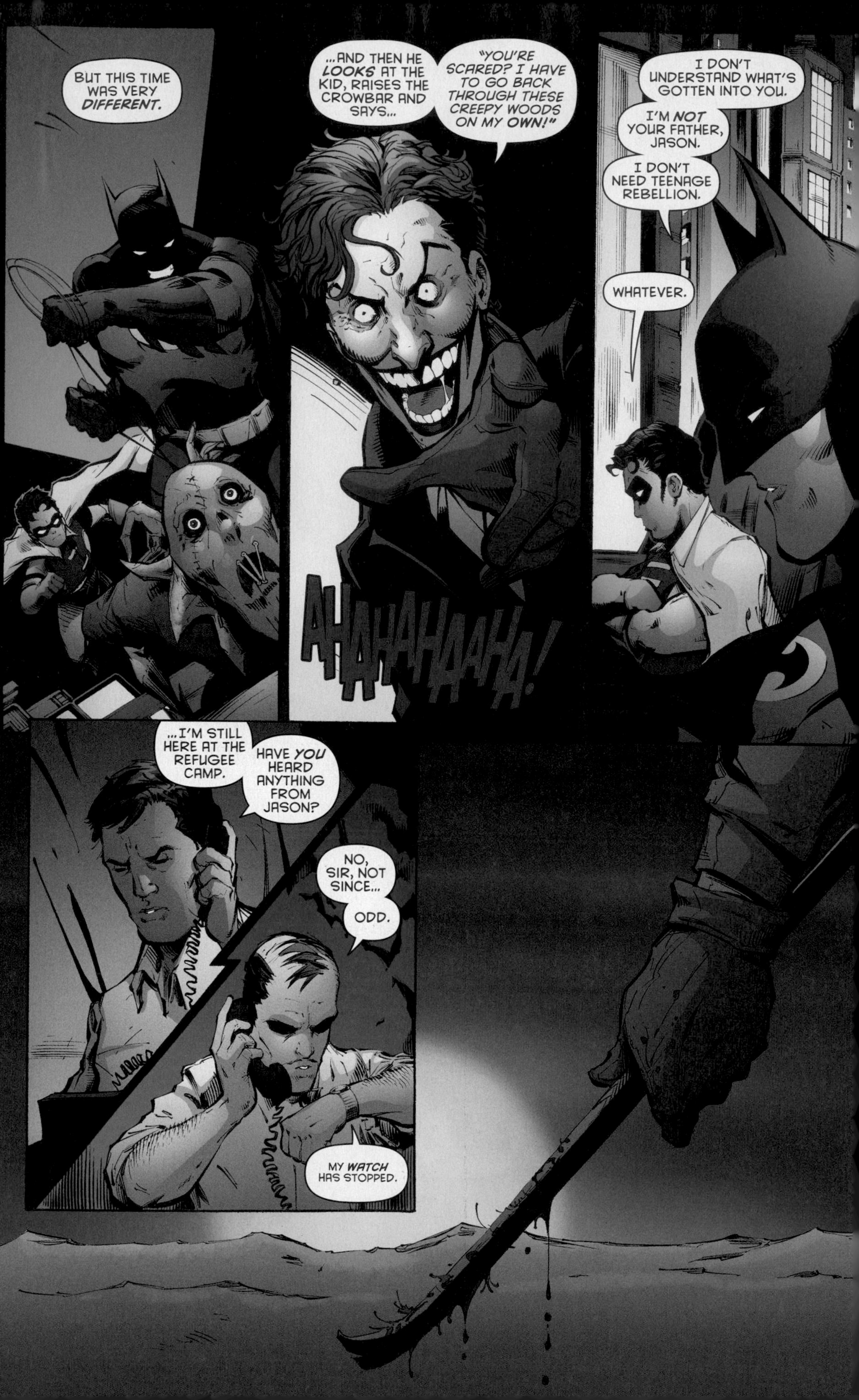
BUT THIS TIME WAS VERY *DIFFERENT.*
...AND THEN HE ***LOOKS*** AT THE KID, RAISES THE CROWBAR AND SAYS...
*"YOU'RE SCARED? I HAVE TO GO BACK THROUGH THESE CREEPY WOODS ON MY **OWN!**"*
AHAHAHAAAHA!
I DON'T UNDERSTAND WHAT'S GOTTEN INTO YOU.
I'M ***NOT*** YOUR FATHER, JASON.
I DON'T NEED TEENAGE REBELLION.
WHATEVER.
...I'M STILL HERE AT THE REFUGEE CAMP.
HAVE ***YOU*** HEARD ANYTHING FROM JASON?
NO, SIR, NOT SINCE...
ODD.
MY ***WATCH*** HAS STOPPED.

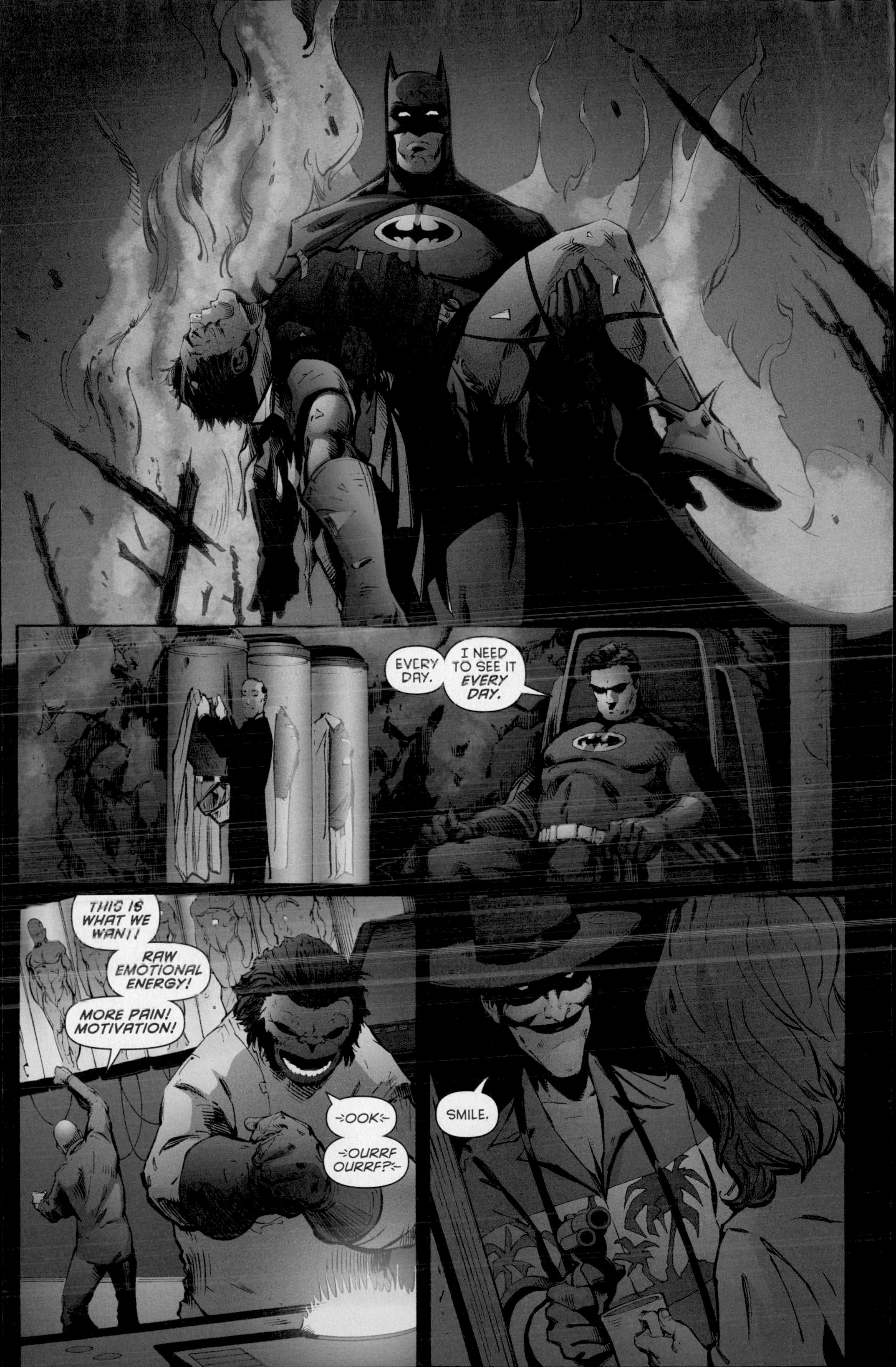
EVERY DAY.
I NEED TO SEE IT EVERY DAY.
THIS IS WHAT WE WANT!
RAW EMOTIONAL ENERGY!
MORE PAIN! MOTIVATION!
OOK
OURRF OURRF?
SMILE.

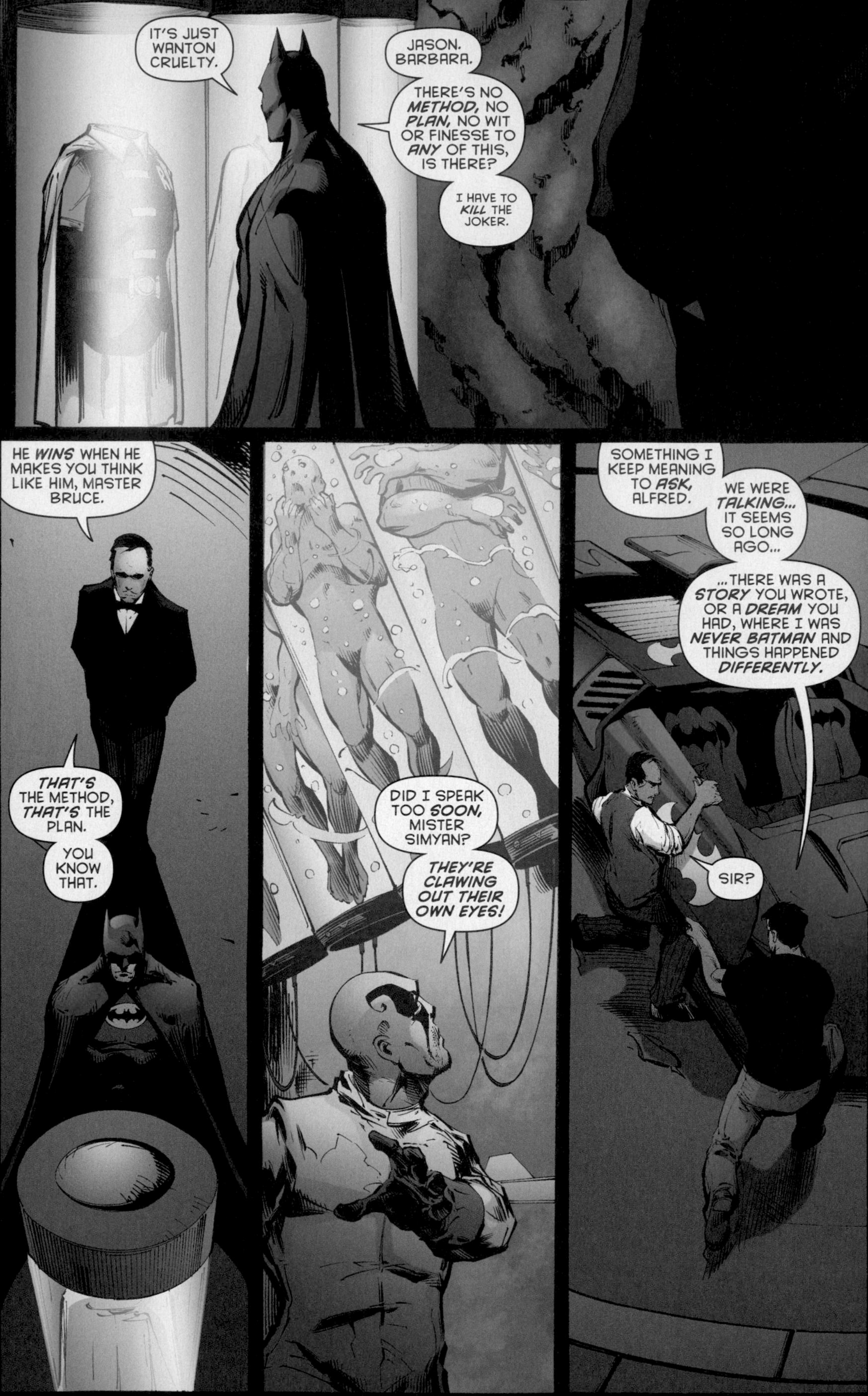
IT'S JUST WANTON CRUELTY.
JASON. BARBARA.
THERE'S NO METHOD, NO PLAN, NO WIT OR FINESSE TO ANY OF THIS, IS THERE?
I HAVE TO KILL THE JOKER.
HE WINS WHEN HE MAKES YOU THINK LIKE HIM, MASTER BRUCE.
THAT'S THE METHOD, THAT'S THE PLAN.
YOU KNOW THAT.
DID I SPEAK TOO SOON, MISTER SIMYAN?
THEY'RE CLAWING OUT THEIR OWN EYES!
SOMETHING I KEEP MEANING TO ASK, ALFRED.
WE WERE TALKING... IT SEEMS SO LONG AGO...
...THERE WAS A STORY YOU WROTE, OR A DREAM YOU HAD, WHERE I WAS NEVER BATMAN AND THINGS HAPPENED DIFFERENTLY.
SIR?

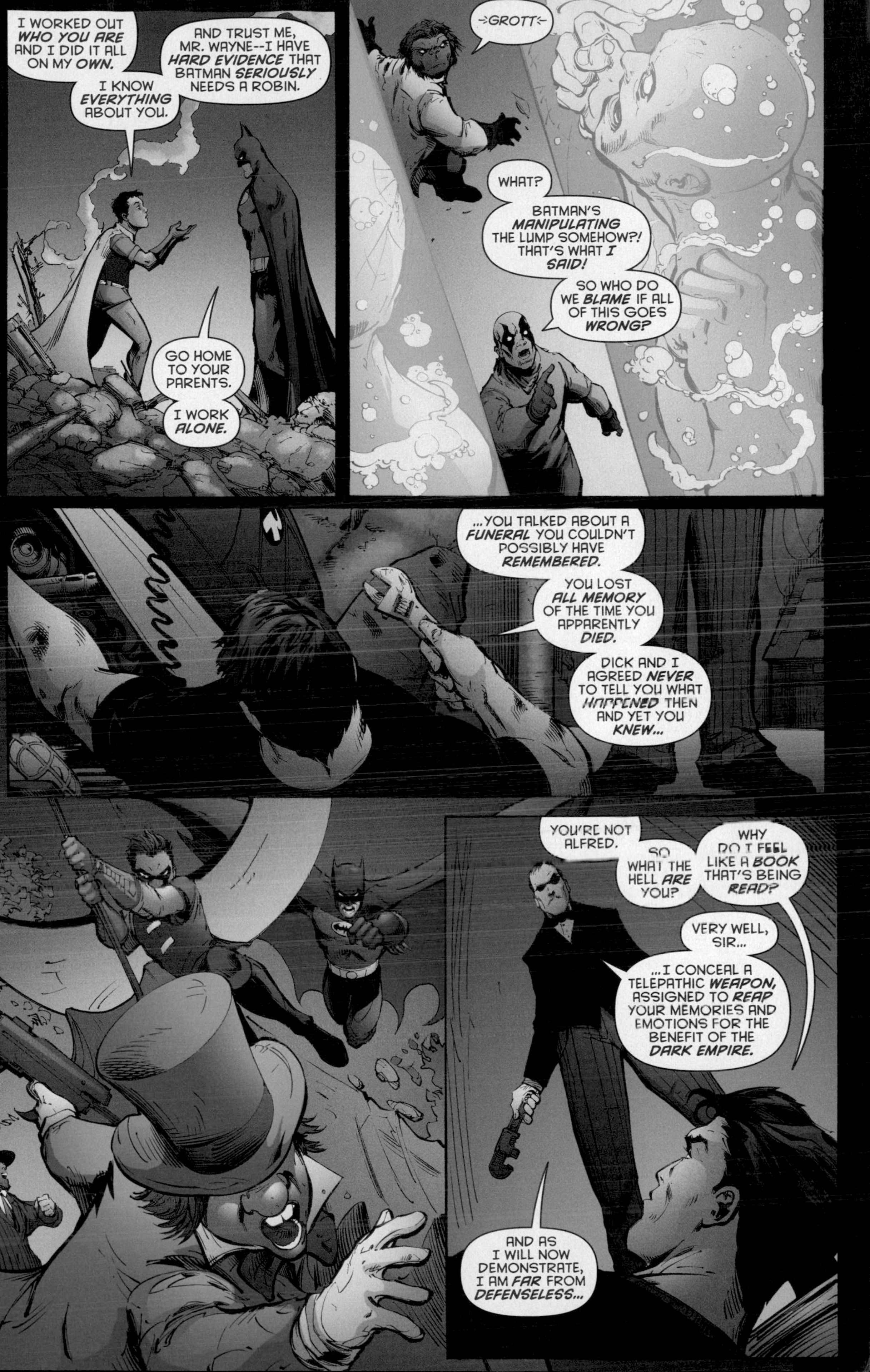

I WORKED OUT WHO YOU ARE AND I DID IT ALL ON MY OWN.
I KNOW EVERYTHING ABOUT YOU.
AND TRUST ME, MR. WAYNE--I HAVE HARD EVIDENCE THAT BATMAN SERIOUSLY NEEDS A ROBIN.
GO HOME TO YOUR PARENTS.
I WORK ALONE.
GROTT
WHAT?
BATMAN'S MANIPULATING THE LUMP SOMEHOW?! THAT'S WHAT I SAID!
SO WHO DO WE BLAME IF ALL OF THIS GOES WRONG?
...YOU TALKED ABOUT A FUNERAL YOU COULDN'T POSSIBLY HAVE REMEMBERED.
YOU LOST ALL MEMORY OF THE TIME YOU APPARENTLY DIED.
DICK AND I AGREED NEVER TO TELL YOU WHAT HAPPENED THEN AND YET YOU KNEW...
YOU'RE NOT ALFRED.
SO WHAT THE HELL ARE YOU?
WHY DO I FEEL LIKE A BOOK THAT'S BEING READ?
VERY WELL, SIR...
...I CONCEAL A TELEPATHIC WEAPON, ASSIGNED TO REAP YOUR MEMORIES AND EMOTIONS FOR THE BENEFIT OF THE DARK EMPIRE.
AND AS I WILL NOW DEMONSTRATE, I AM FAR FROM DEFENSELESS...

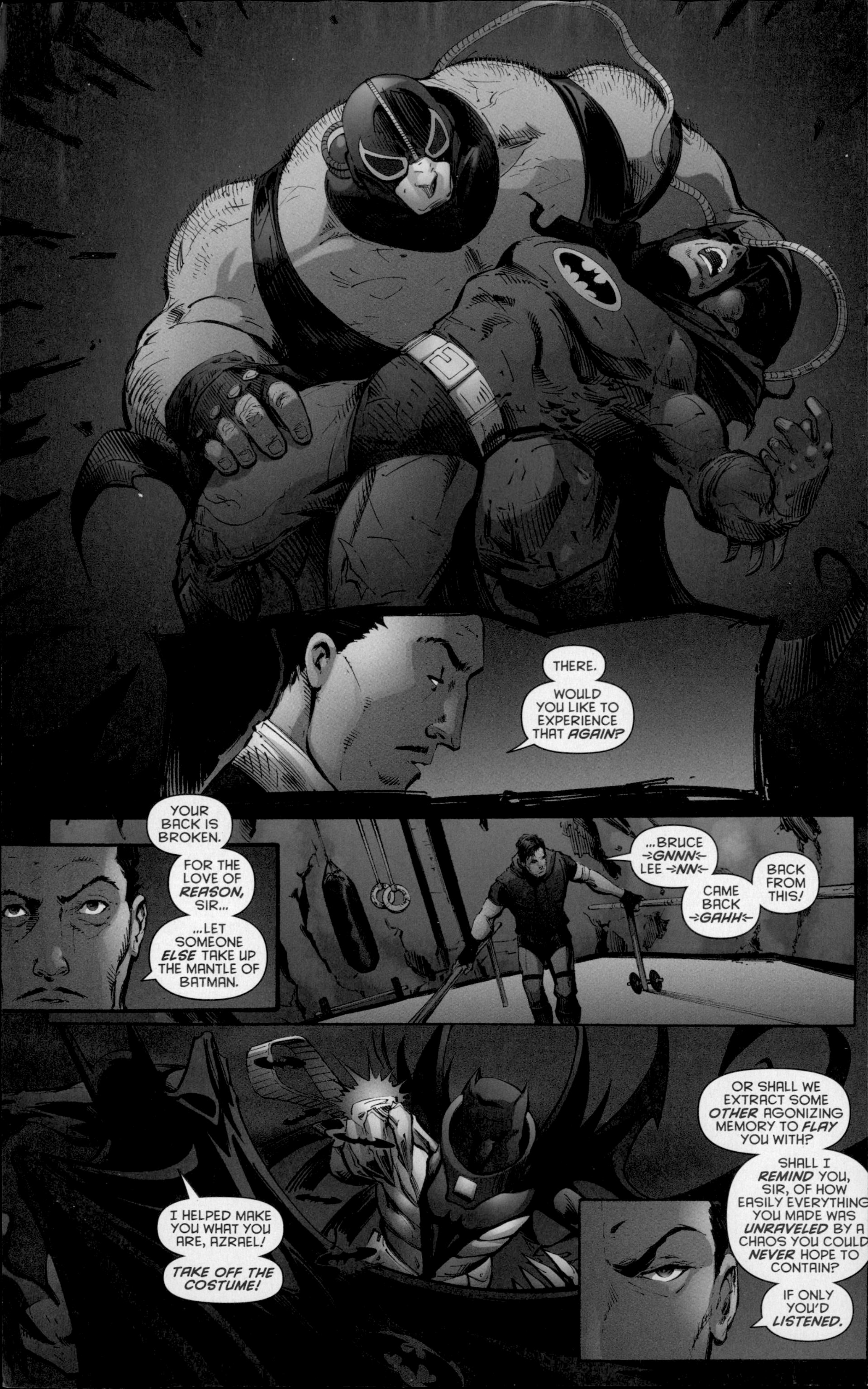
THERE.
WOULD YOU LIKE TO EXPERIENCE THAT AGAIN?
YOUR BACK IS BROKEN.
FOR THE LOVE OF REASON, SIR...
...LET SOMEONE ELSE TAKE UP THE MANTLE OF BATMAN.
...BRUCE ~GNNN~ LEE ~NN~
CAME BACK ~GAHH~
BACK FROM THIS!
OR SHALL WE EXTRACT SOME OTHER AGONIZING MEMORY TO FLAY YOU WITH?
SHALL I REMIND YOU, SIR, OF HOW EASILY EVERYTHING YOU MADE WAS UNRAVELED BY A CHAOS YOU COULD NEVER HOPE TO CONTAIN?
IF ONLY YOU'D LISTENED.
I HELPED MAKE YOU WHAT YOU ARE, AZRAEL!
TAKE OFF THE COSTUME!

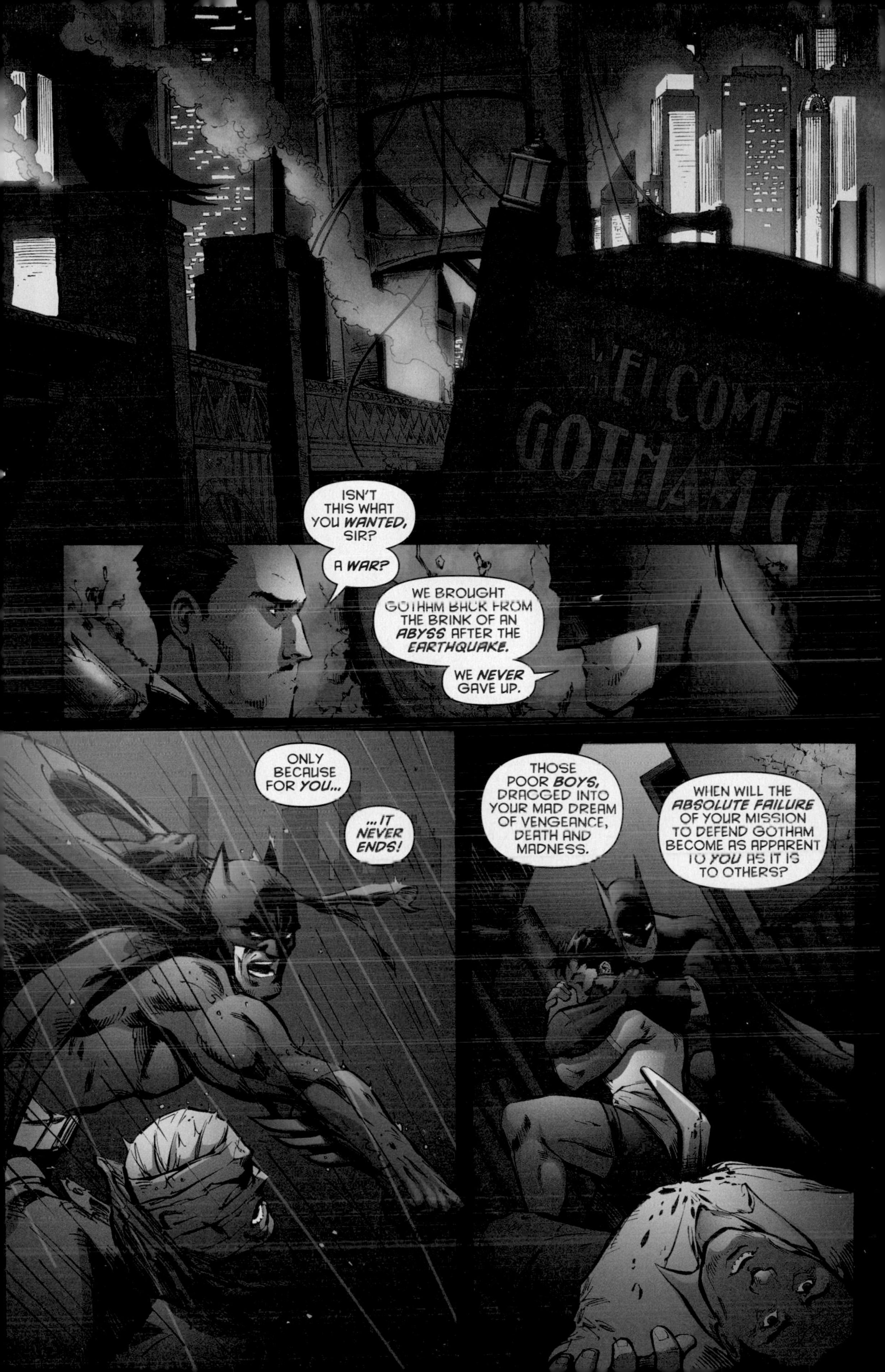
WELCOME
GOTHAM
ISN'T THIS WHAT YOU *WANTED*, SIR?
A *WAR?*
WE BROUGHT GOTHAM BACK FROM THE BRINK OF AN *ABYSS* AFTER THE *EARTHQUAKE.*
WE *NEVER* GAVE UP.
ONLY BECAUSE FOR *YOU*...
...*IT NEVER ENDS!*
THOSE POOR *BOYS,* DRAGGED INTO YOUR MAD DREAM OF VENGEANCE, DEATH AND MADNESS.
WHEN WILL THE *ABSOLUTE FAILURE* OF YOUR MISSION TO DEFEND GOTHAM BECOME AS APPARENT TO *YOU* AS IT IS TO OTHERS?

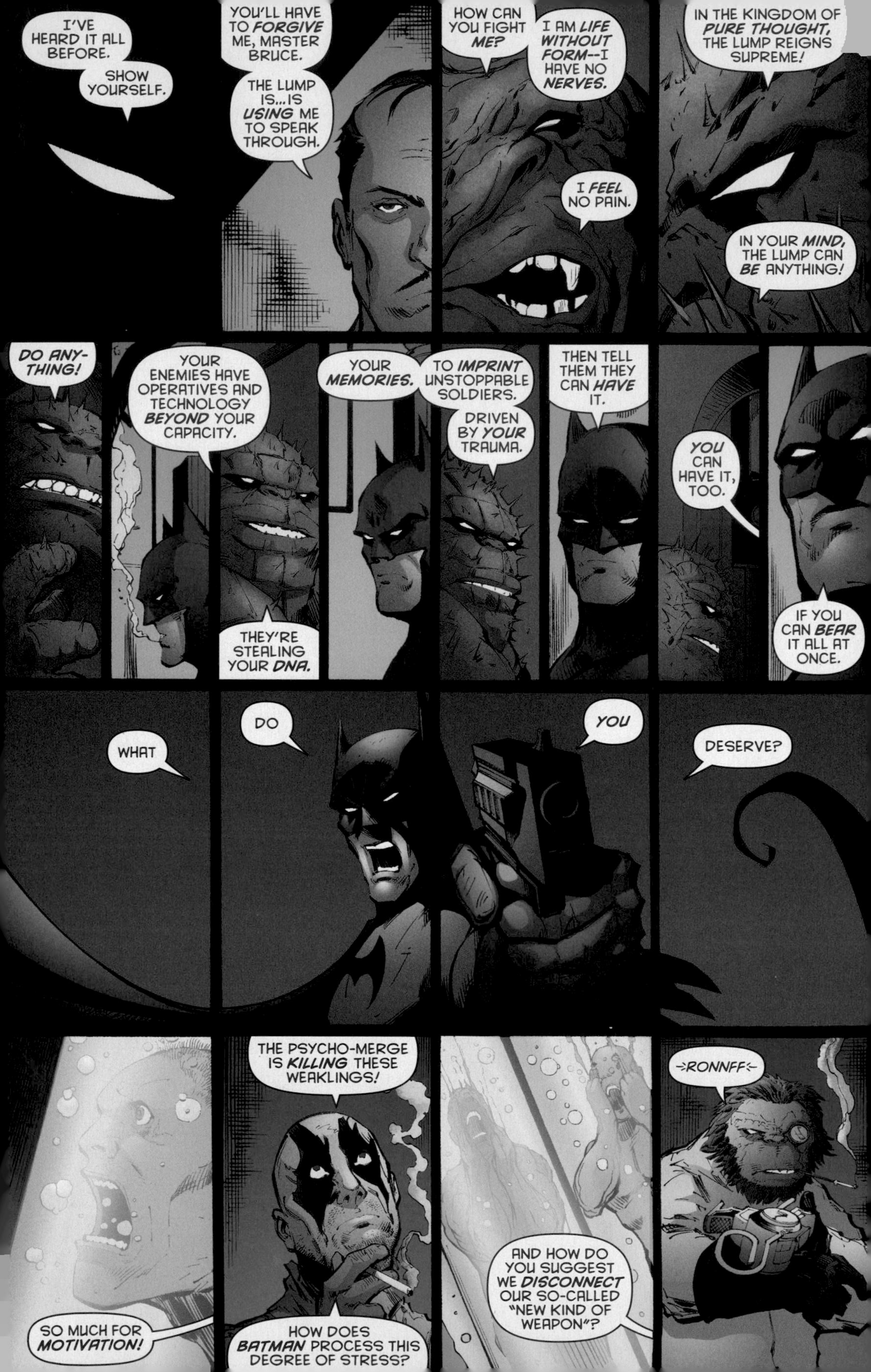

I'VE HEARD IT ALL BEFORE.
SHOW YOURSELF.
YOU'LL HAVE TO FORGIVE ME, MASTER BRUCE.
THE LUMP IS...IS USING ME TO SPEAK THROUGH.
HOW CAN YOU FIGHT ME?
I AM LIFE WITHOUT FORM--I HAVE NO NERVES.
I FEEL NO PAIN.
IN THE KINGDOM OF PURE THOUGHT, THE LUMP REIGNS SUPREME!
IN YOUR MIND, THE LUMP CAN BE ANYTHING!
DO ANY-THING!
YOUR ENEMIES HAVE OPERATIVES AND TECHNOLOGY BEYOND YOUR CAPACITY.
THEY'RE STEALING YOUR DNA.
YOUR MEMORIES.
TO IMPRINT UNSTOPPABLE SOLDIERS.
DRIVEN BY YOUR TRAUMA.
THEN TELL THEM THEY CAN HAVE IT.
YOU CAN HAVE IT, TOO.
IF YOU CAN BEAR IT ALL AT ONCE.
WHAT
DO
YOU
DESERVE?
SO MUCH FOR MOTIVATION!
THE PSYCHO-MERGE IS KILLING THESE WEAKLINGS!
HOW DOES BATMAN PROCESS THIS DEGREE OF STRESS?
AND HOW DO YOU SUGGEST WE DISCONNECT OUR SO-CALLED "NEW KIND OF WEAPON"?
-RONNFF-

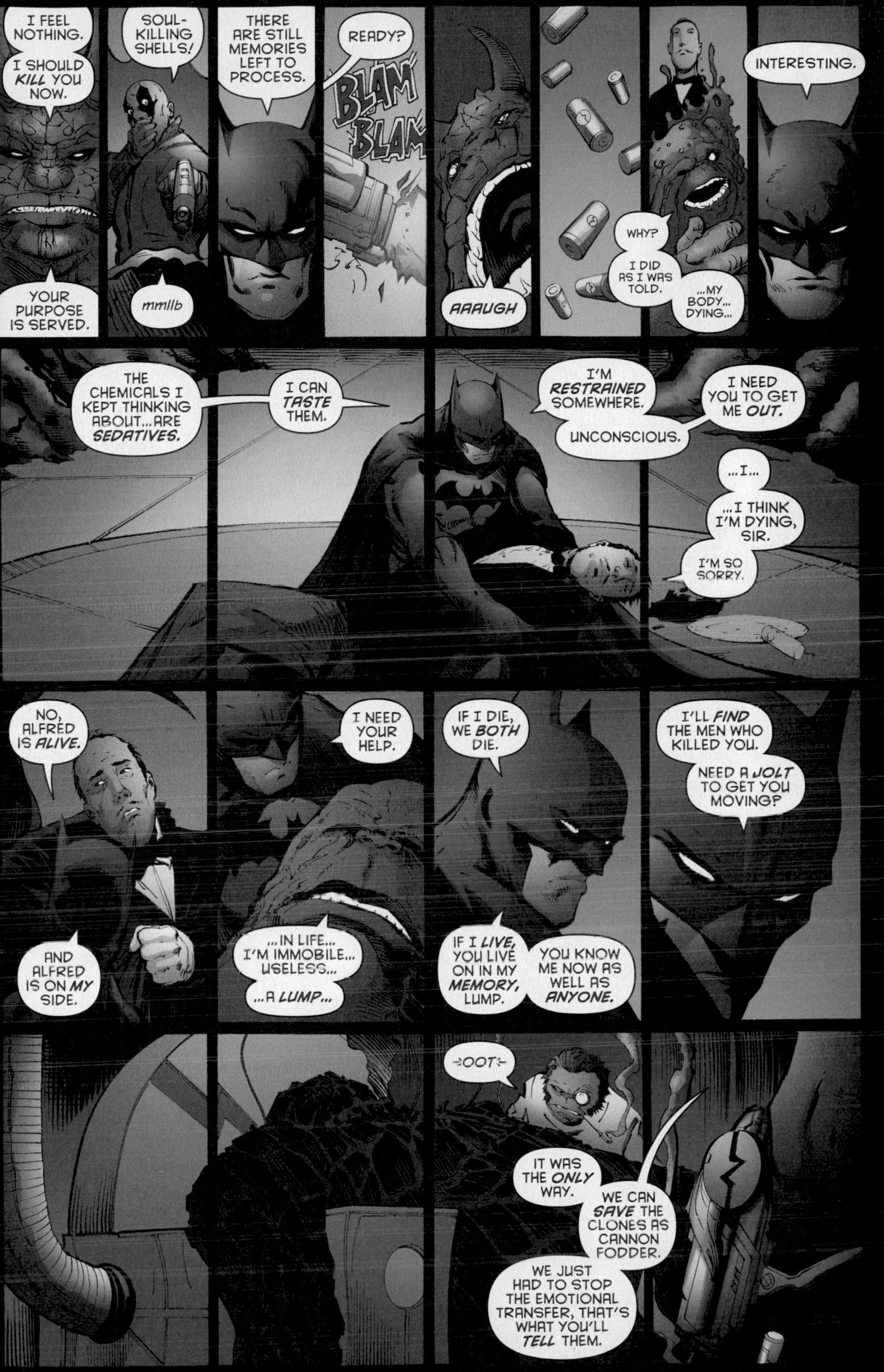
I FEEL NOTHING.
I SHOULD KILL YOU NOW.
YOUR PURPOSE IS SERVED.
SOUL-KILLING SHELLS!
mmllb
THERE ARE STILL MEMORIES LEFT TO PROCESS.
READY?
BLAM BLAM
AAAUGH
WHY?
I DID AS I WAS TOLD.
...MY BODY... DYING...
INTERESTING.
THE CHEMICALS I KEPT THINKING ABOUT...ARE SEDATIVES.
I CAN TASTE THEM.
I'M RESTRAINED SOMEWHERE.
UNCONSCIOUS.
I NEED YOU TO GET ME OUT.
...I...
...I THINK I'M DYING, SIR.
I'M SO SORRY.
NO, ALFRED IS ALIVE.
AND ALFRED IS ON MY SIDE.
I NEED YOUR HELP.
...IN LIFE... I'M IMMOBILE... USELESS...
...A LUMP...
IF I DIE, WE BOTH DIE.
IF I LIVE, YOU LIVE ON IN MY MEMORY, LUMP.
YOU KNOW ME NOW AS WELL AS ANYONE.
I'LL FIND THE MEN WHO KILLED YOU.
NEED A JOLT TO GET YOU MOVING?
-OOT-
IT WAS THE ONLY WAY.
WE CAN SAVE THE CLONES AS CANNON FODDER.
WE JUST HAD TO STOP THE EMOTIONAL TRANSFER, THAT'S WHAT YOU'LL TELL THEM.

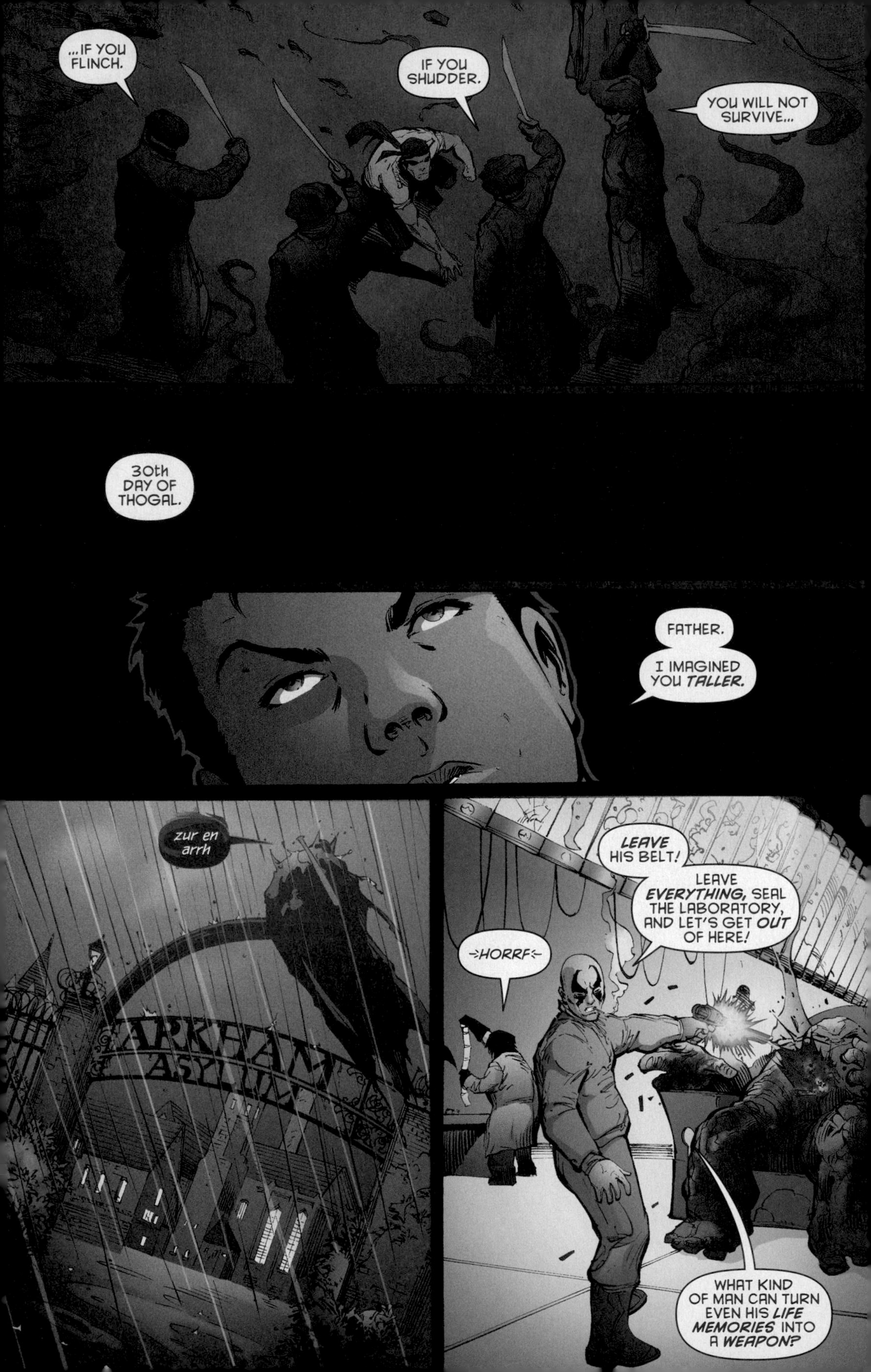

...IF YOU FLINCH.
IF YOU SHUDDER.
YOU WILL NOT SURVIVE...
30th DAY OF THOGAL.
FATHER.
I IMAGINED YOU TALLER.
zur en arrh
ARKHAM ASYLUM
LEAVE HIS BELT!
LEAVE EVERYTHING, SEAL THE LABORATORY, AND LET'S GET OUT OF HERE!
HORRF
WHAT KIND OF MAN CAN TURN EVEN HIS LIFE MEMORIES INTO A WEAPON?

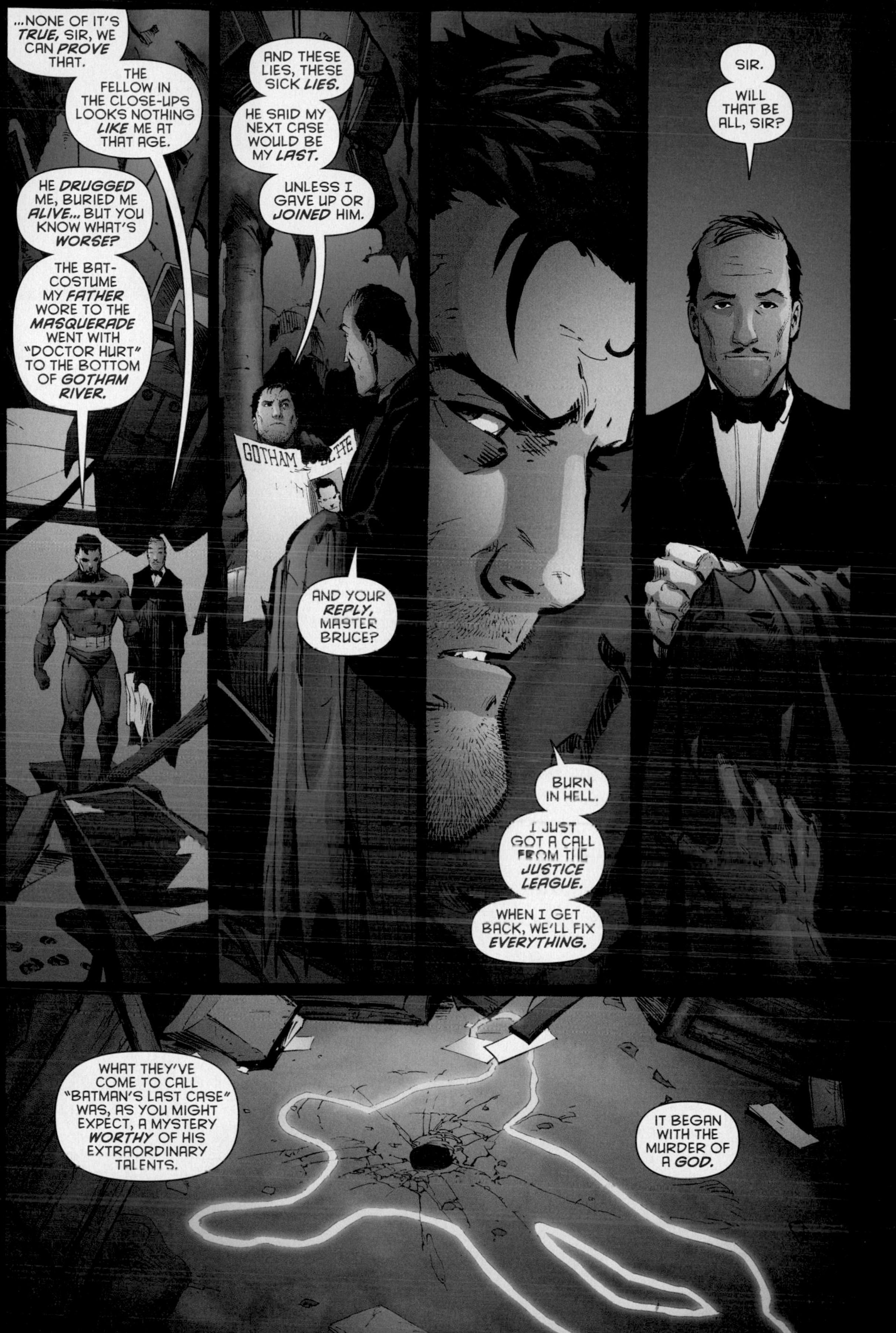
...NONE OF IT'S TRUE, SIR, WE CAN PROVE THAT.
THE FELLOW IN THE CLOSE-UPS LOOKS NOTHING LIKE ME AT THAT AGE.
HE DRUGGED ME, BURIED ME ALIVE... BUT YOU KNOW WHAT'S WORSE?
THE BAT-COSTUME MY FATHER WORE TO THE MASQUERADE WENT WITH "DOCTOR HURT" TO THE BOTTOM OF GOTHAM RIVER.
AND THESE LIES, THESE SICK LIES.
HE SAID MY NEXT CASE WOULD BE MY LAST.
UNLESS I GAVE UP OR JOINED HIM.
GOTHAM
AND YOUR REPLY, MASTER BRUCE?
BURN IN HELL.
I JUST GOT A CALL FROM THE JUSTICE LEAGUE.
WHEN I GET BACK, WE'LL FIX EVERYTHING.
SIR.
WILL THAT BE ALL, SIR?
WHAT THEY'VE COME TO CALL "BATMAN'S LAST CASE" WAS, AS YOU MIGHT EXPECT, A MYSTERY WORTHY OF HIS EXTRAORDINARY TALENTS.
IT BEGAN WITH THE MURDER OF A GOD.

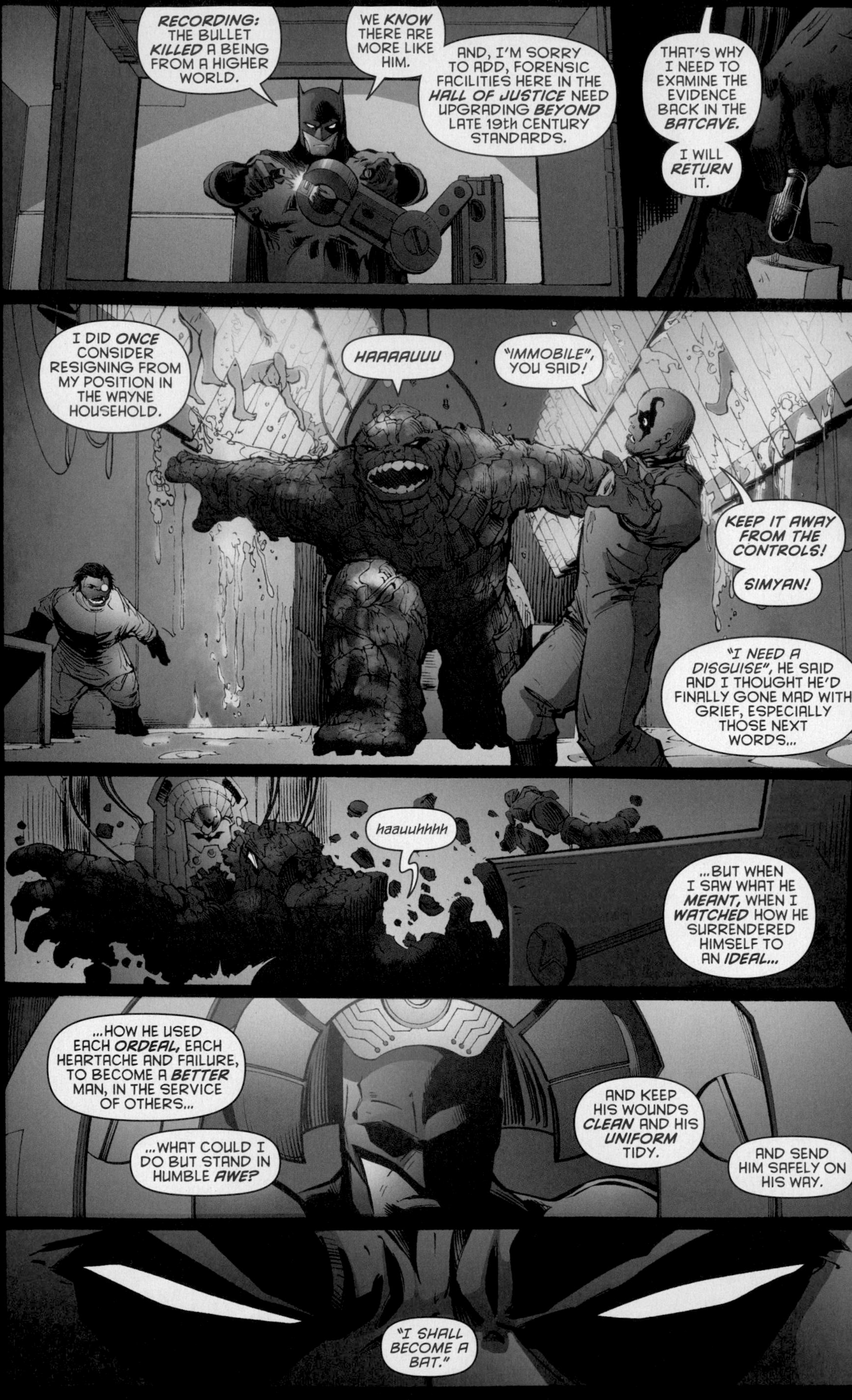
RECORDING: THE BULLET KILLED A BEING FROM A HIGHER WORLD.
WE KNOW THERE ARE MORE LIKE HIM.
AND, I'M SORRY TO ADD, FORENSIC FACILITIES HERE IN THE HALL OF JUSTICE NEED UPGRADING BEYOND LATE 19th CENTURY STANDARDS.
THAT'S WHY I NEED TO EXAMINE THE EVIDENCE BACK IN THE BATCAVE.
I WILL RETURN IT.
I DID ONCE CONSIDER RESIGNING FROM MY POSITION IN THE WAYNE HOUSEHOLD.
HAAAAUUU
"IMMOBILE", YOU SAID!
KEEP IT AWAY FROM THE CONTROLS!
SIMYAN!
"I NEED A DISGUISE", HE SAID AND I THOUGHT HE'D FINALLY GONE MAD WITH GRIEF, ESPECIALLY THOSE NEXT WORDS...
haauuhhhh
...BUT WHEN I SAW WHAT HE MEANT, WHEN I WATCHED HOW HE SURRENDERED HIMSELF TO AN IDEAL...
...HOW HE USED EACH ORDEAL, EACH HEARTACHE AND FAILURE, TO BECOME A BETTER MAN, IN THE SERVICE OF OTHERS...
...WHAT COULD I DO BUT STAND IN HUMBLE AWE?
AND KEEP HIS WOUNDS CLEAN AND HIS UNIFORM TIDY.
AND SEND HIM SAFELY ON HIS WAY.
"I SHALL BECOME A BAT."

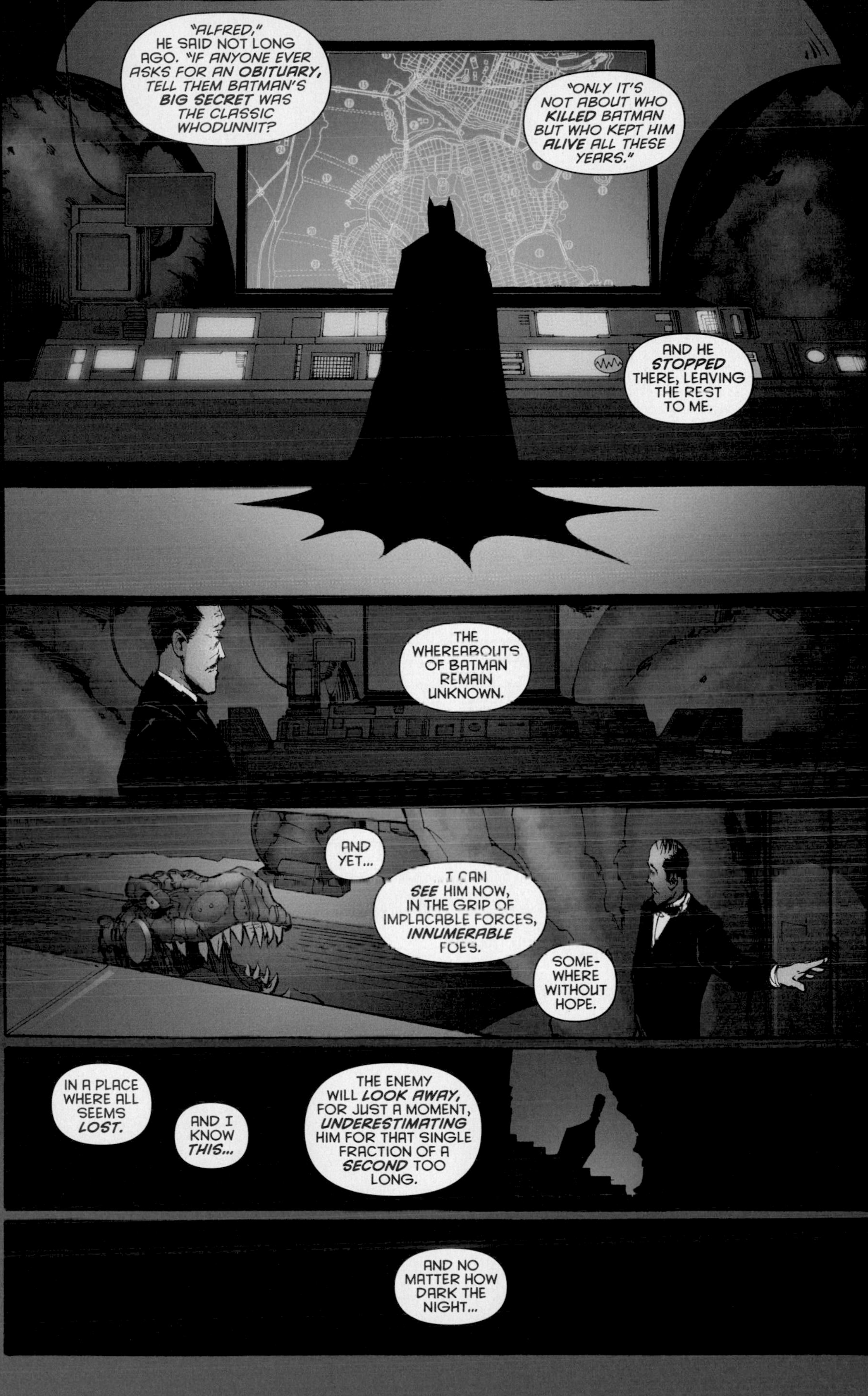
"ALFRED," HE SAID NOT LONG AGO. "IF ANYONE EVER ASKS FOR AN OBITUARY, TELL THEM BATMAN'S BIG SECRET WAS THE CLASSIC WHODUNNIT?
"ONLY IT'S NOT ABOUT WHO KILLED BATMAN BUT WHO KEPT HIM ALIVE ALL THESE YEARS."
AND HE STOPPED THERE, LEAVING THE REST TO ME.
THE WHEREABOUTS OF BATMAN REMAIN UNKNOWN.
AND YET...
...I CAN SEE HIM NOW, IN THE GRIP OF IMPLACABLE FORCES, INNUMERABLE FOES.
SOME-WHERE WITHOUT HOPE.
IN A PLACE WHERE ALL SEEMS LOST.
AND I KNOW THIS...
THE ENEMY WILL LOOK AWAY, FOR JUST A MOMENT, UNDERESTIMATING HIM FOR THAT SINGLE FRACTION OF A SECOND TOO LONG.
AND NO MATTER HOW DARK THE NIGHT...

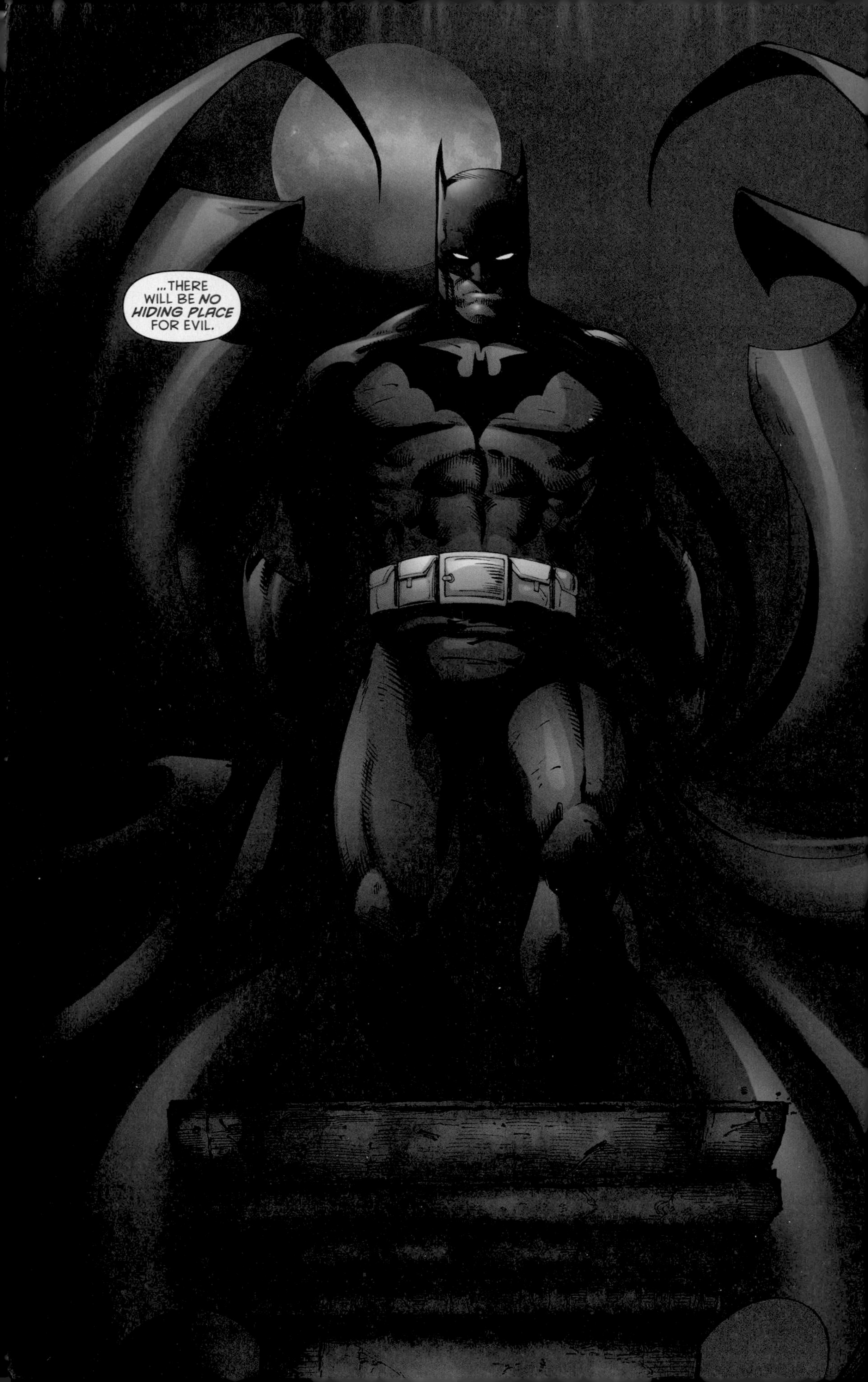
...THERE WILL BE *NO HIDING PLACE* FOR EVIL.

Breaking down
the
BAT

Preliminary artwork by
Tony S. Daniel
Thumbnails by
Grant Morrison

GRANT MORRISON DCU ZERO

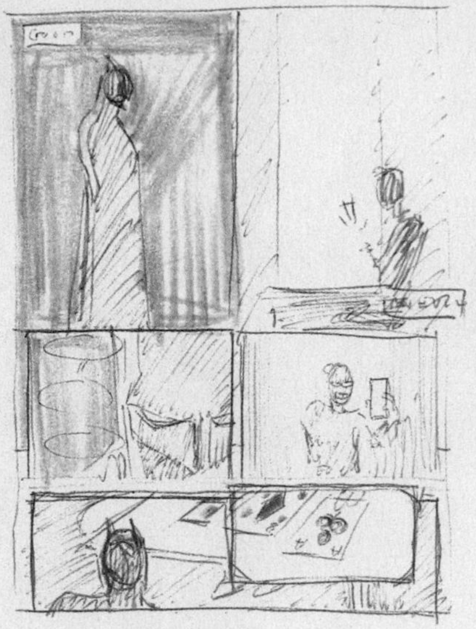

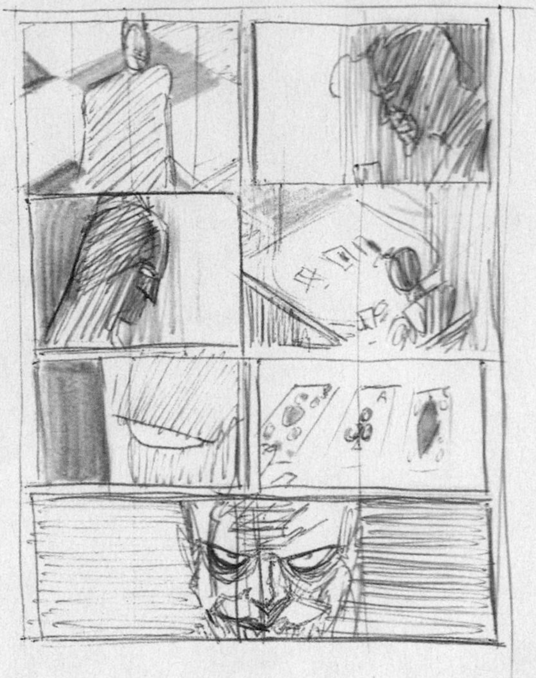

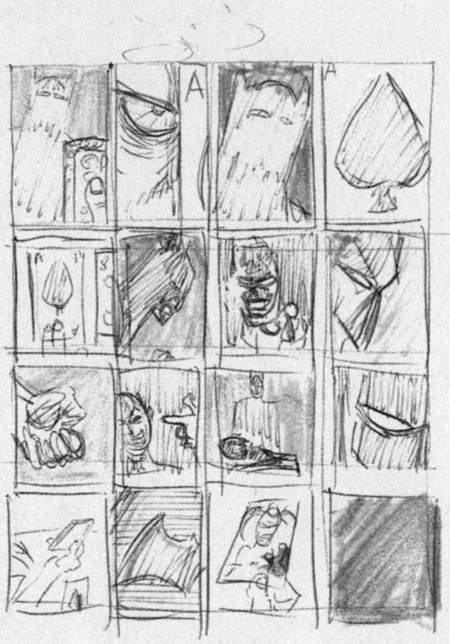

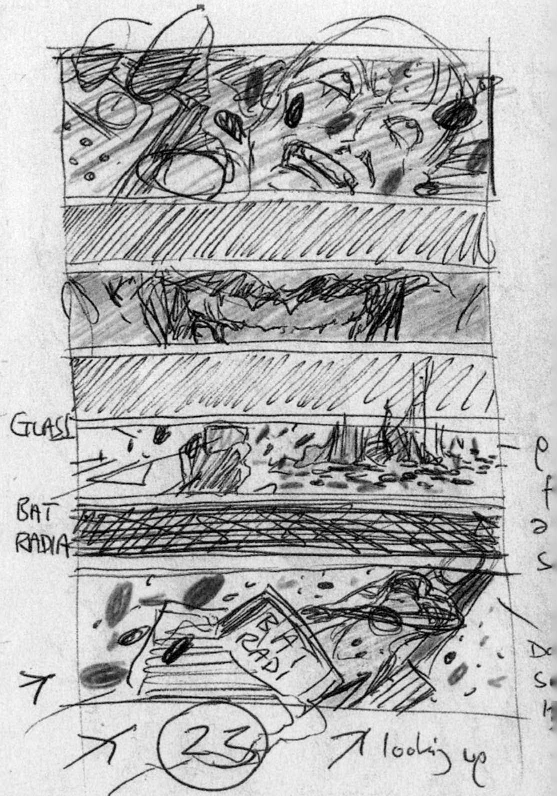
GLASS
BAT
RADIA
BAT
RADI
23
looking up

BATMAN SEQUENCE

DCU ZERO - TONY DANIEL

HI TONY - THE LAYOUT FOR THE PAGES SHOULD BE A LITTLE LIKE THIS - YOU DON'T HAVE TO FOLLOW IT SLAVISHLY AS LONG AS THE CHECKERBOARD, BACK + FORWARD EFFECT WORKS

THANKS

GRANT

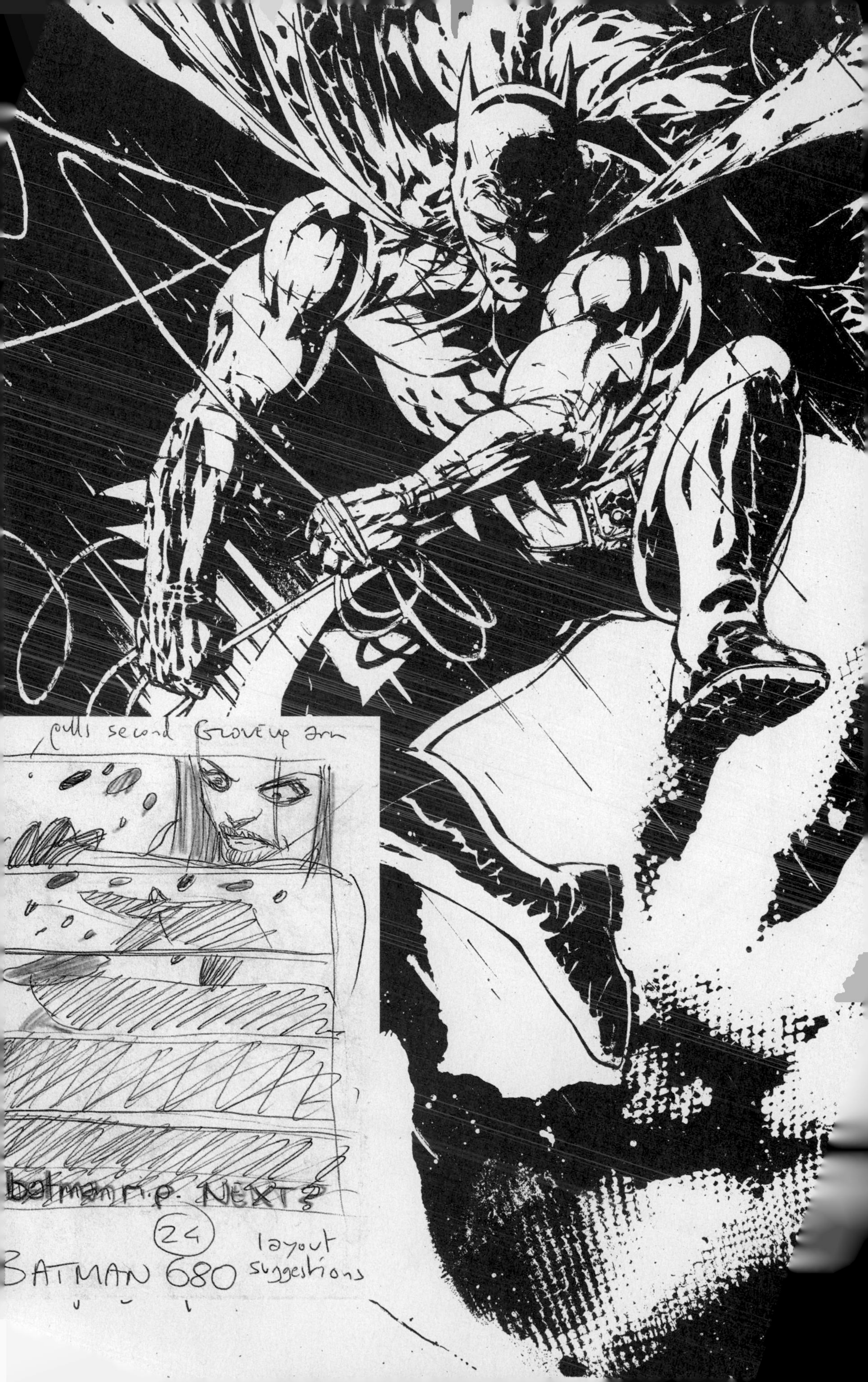
pulls second Glove up arm
batman r.i.p. NEXT?
24
BATMAN 680
layout suggestions

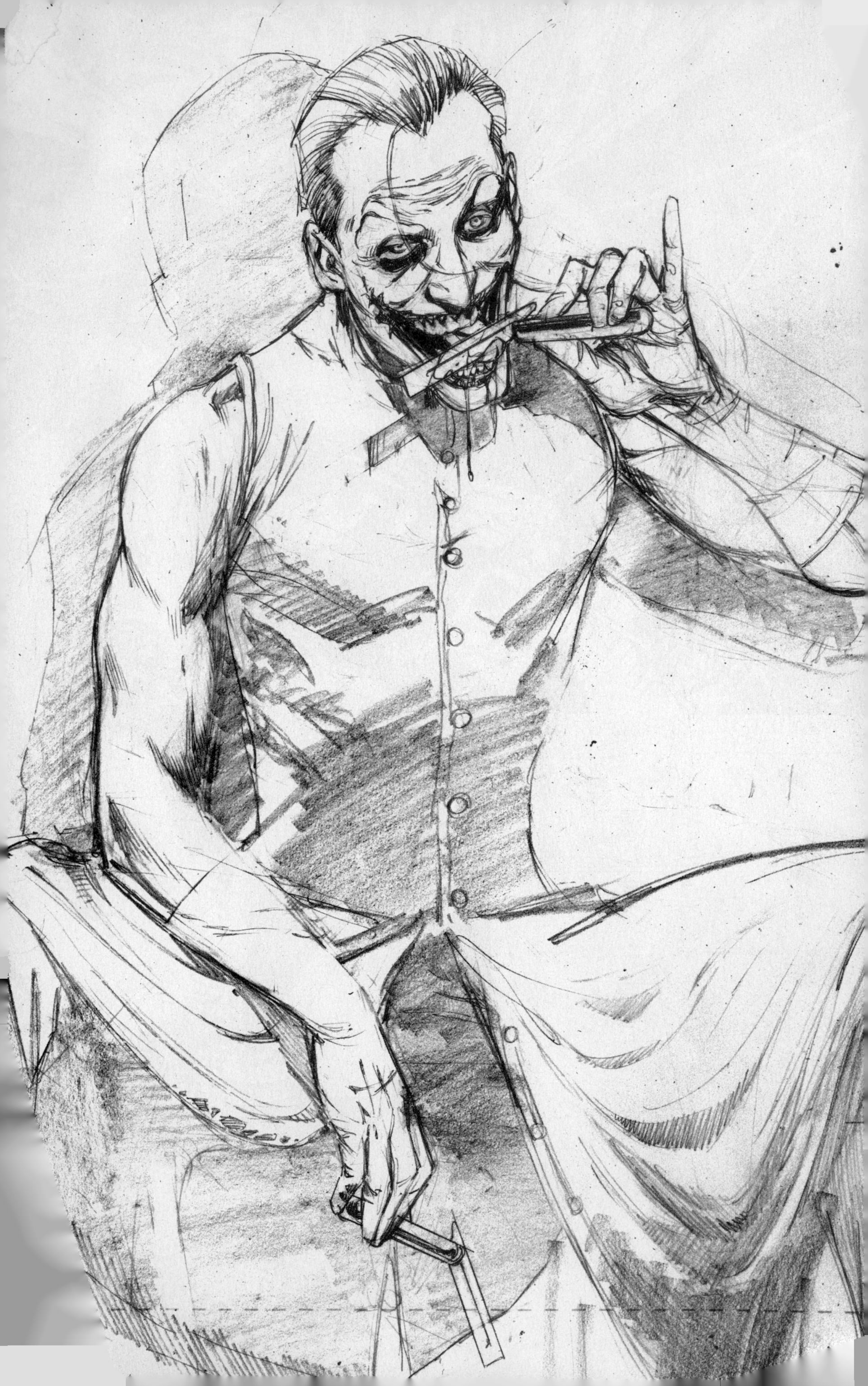

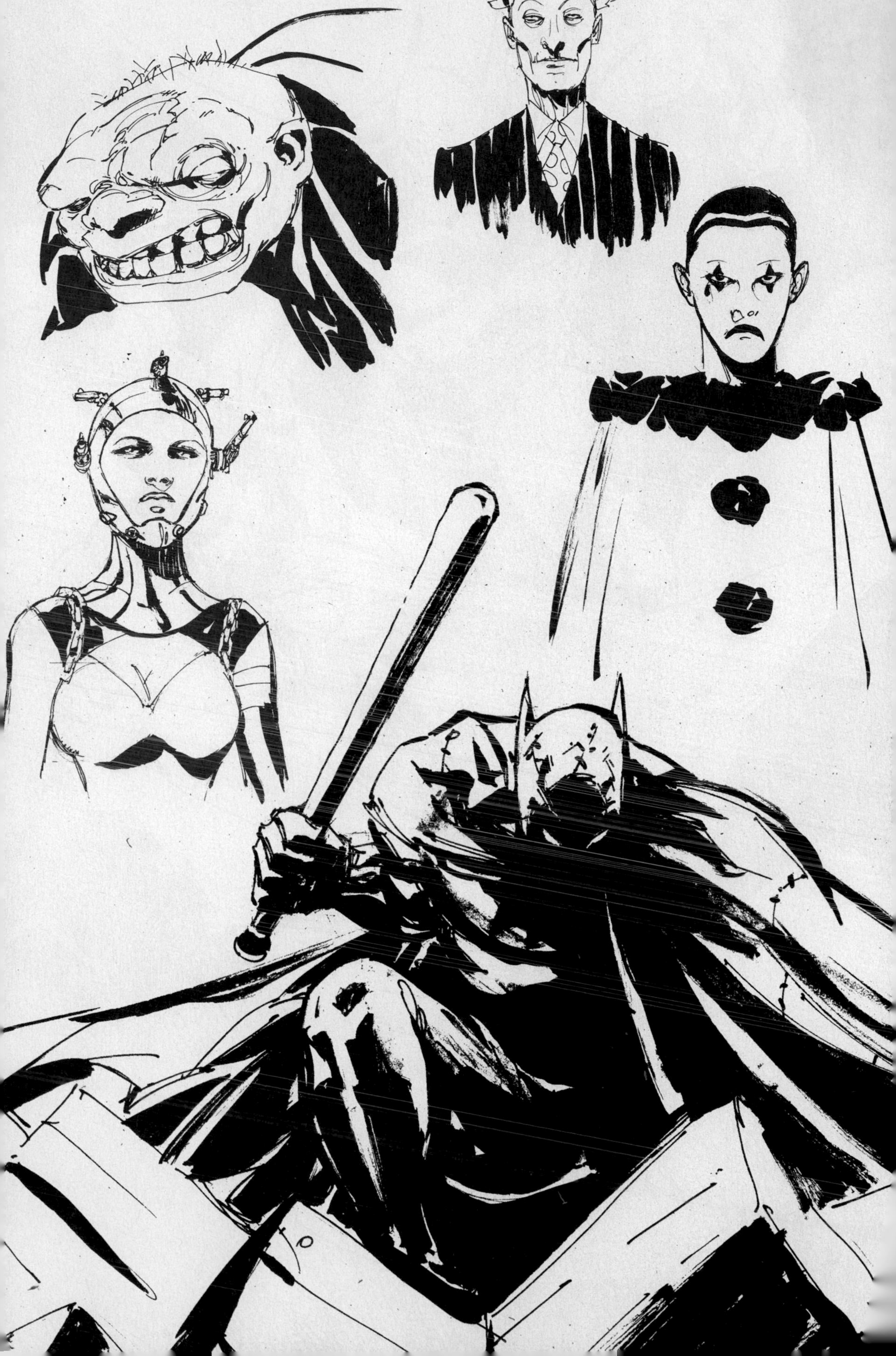

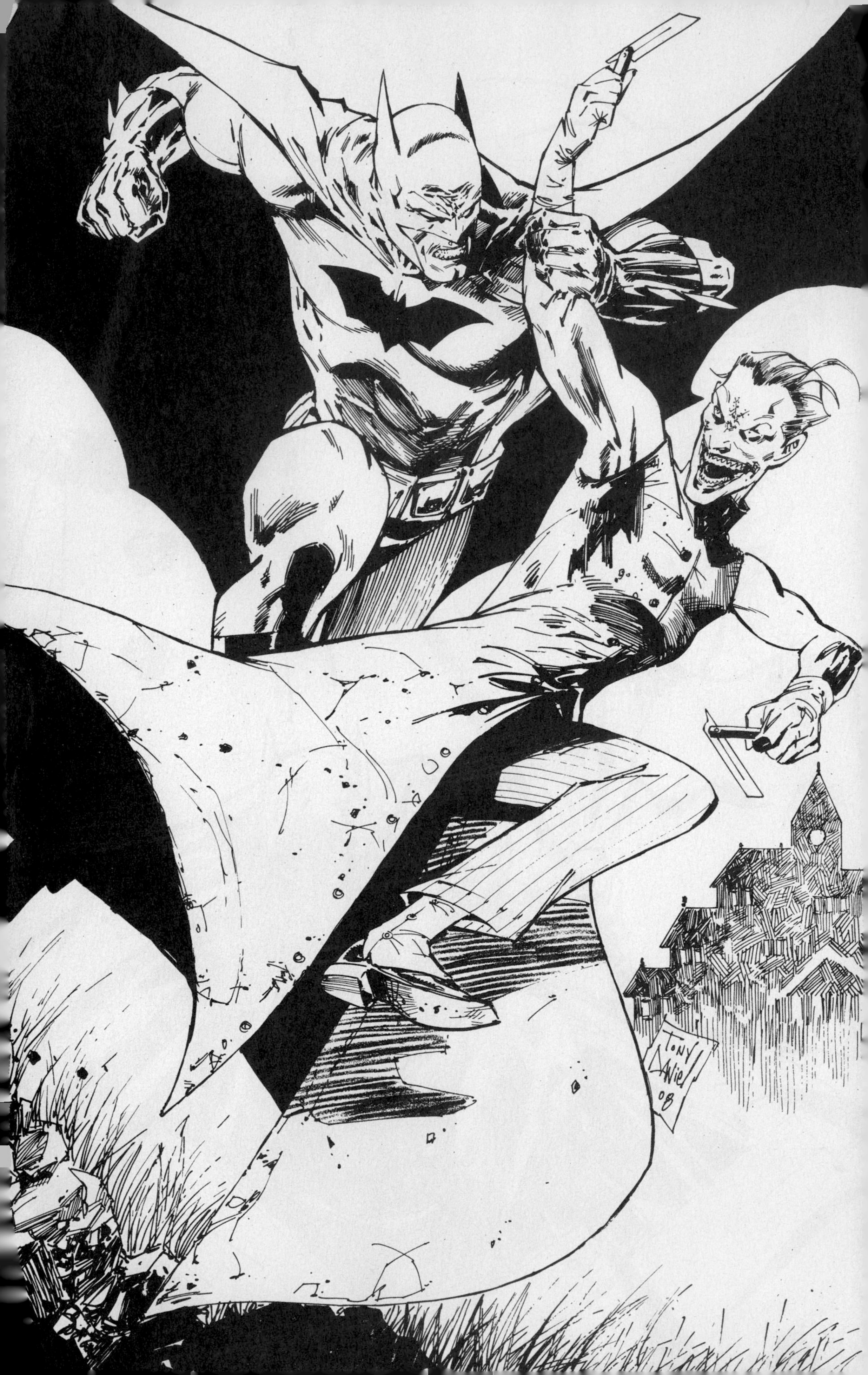
TONY DANIEL 08

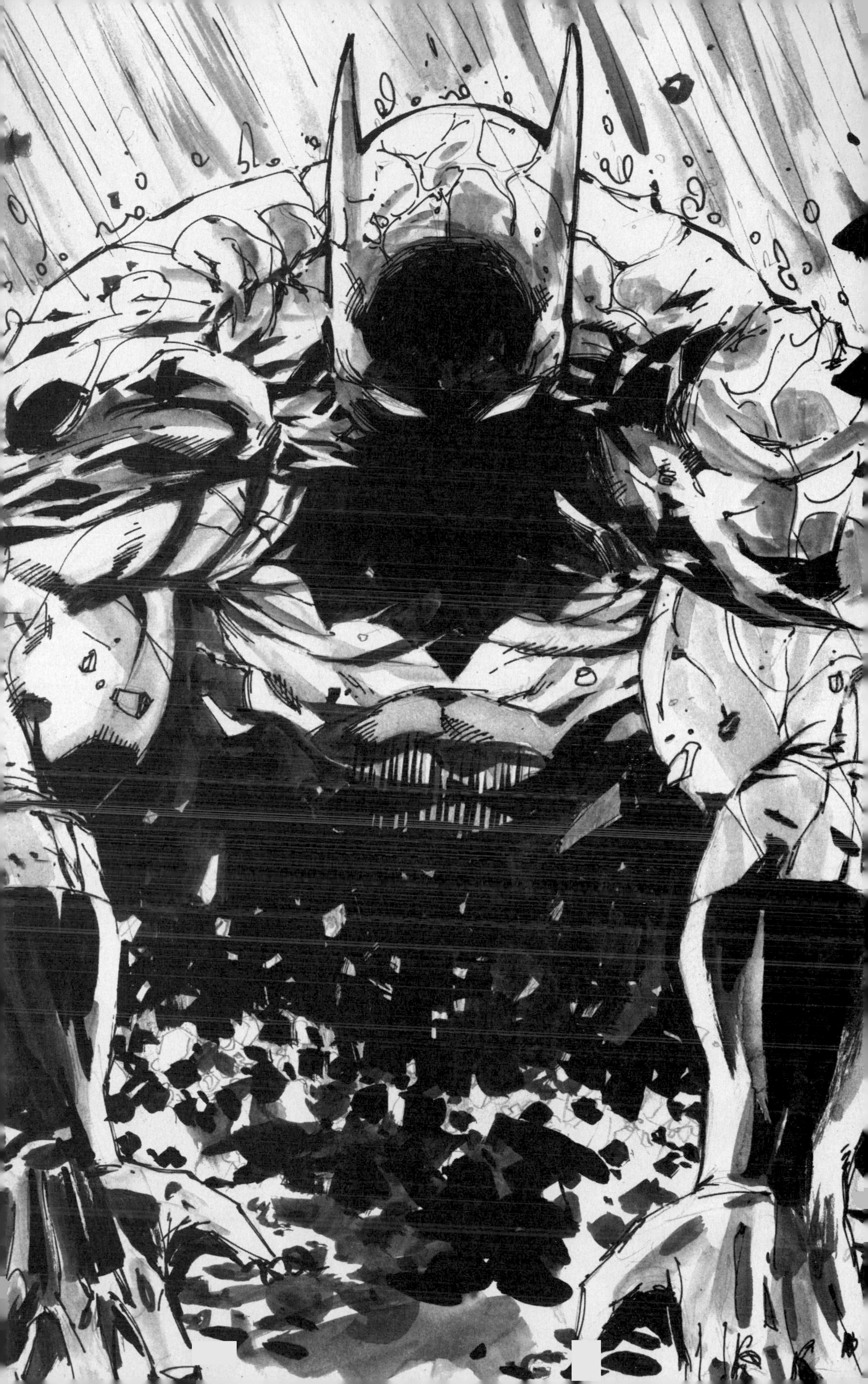

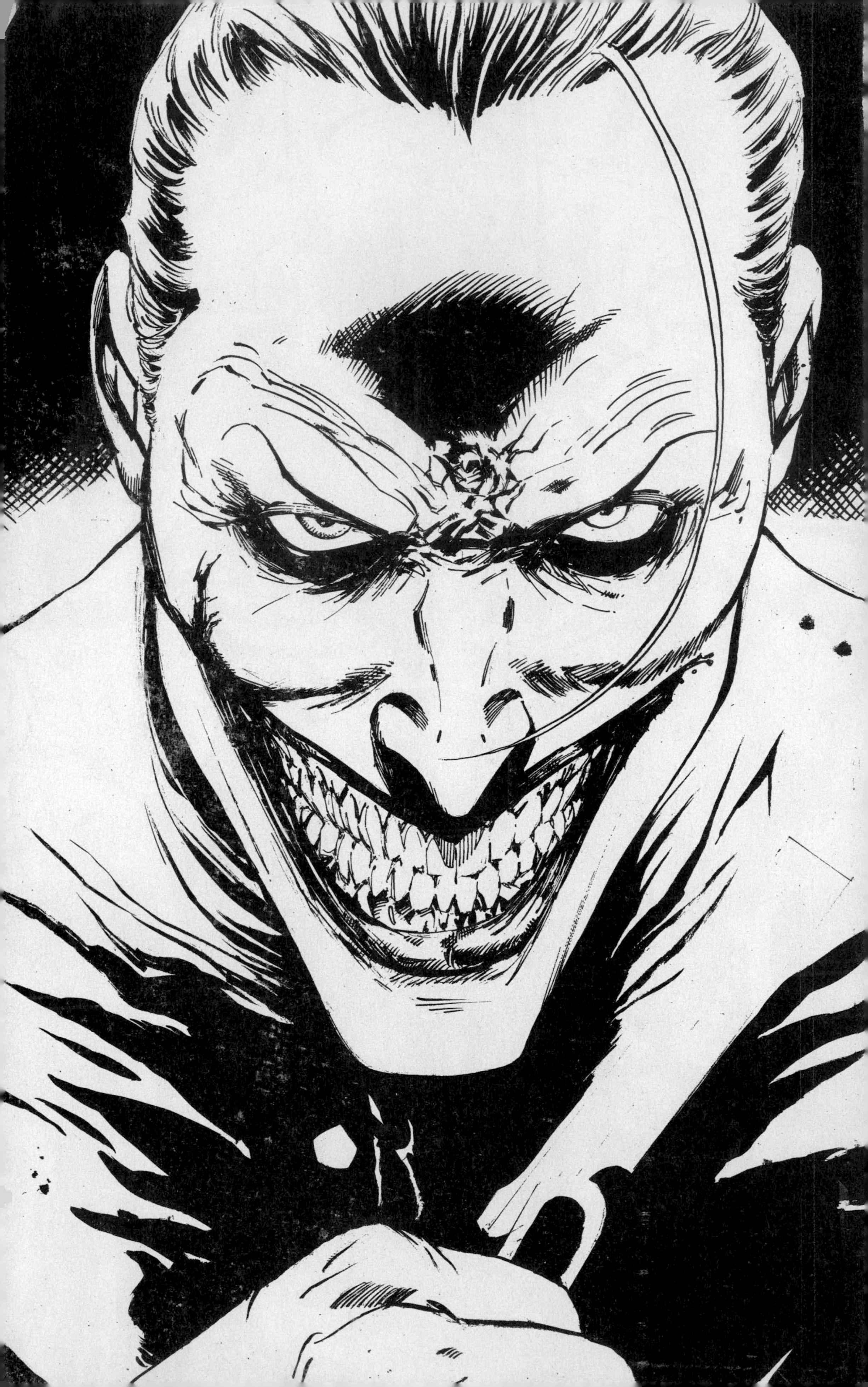